Reason and
Therapeutic Change

G000069268

The Whurr Counselling and Psychotherapy Series seeks to publish selected works of foremost experts in the field of counselling and psychotherapy. Each volume features the best of a key figure's work, bringing together papers that have been published widely in the professional literature. In this way the work of leading counsellors and psychotherapists is made accessible in single volumes.

Windy Dryden
Series Editor

Titles in the Counselling and Psychotherapy Series

Person-centred Counselling: Therapeutic and Spiritual Dimensions
Brian Thorne

Reason and Therapeutic change
Windy Dryden

The Essential Arnold Lazarus
Edited by Windy Dryden

Breakthroughs and Integrations: Collected Papers in Psychology and Psychotherapy
John Rowan

From Medicine to Psychotherapy
Mark Aveline

Reason and Therapeutic Change

Windy Dryden

Counselling and Psychotherapy Series

Seriers Editor: Windy Dryden

Whurr Publishers Ltd
London

© Windy Dryden 1991

First published 1991 by
Whurr Publishers Ltd.
19B Compton Terrace, London N1 2UN, England

Reprinted 2004

All rights reserved. No part of this publication may be reproduced, stored in a retrieval system, or transmitted in any form or by any means, electronic, mechanical, photocopying, recording or otherwise, without the prior permission of Whurr Publishers Limited.

This publication is sold subject to the conditions that it shall not, by way of trade or otherwise, be lent, resold, hired out, or otherwise circulated without the publisher's prior consent in any form of binding or cover other than that in which it is published and without a similar condition including this condition being imposed upon any subsequent purchaser.

British Library Cataloguing in Publication Data
Dryden, Windy
   Reason and therapeutic change.
   I. Title
   616.89

   ISBN 1-870332-92-X

Composition by Scribe Design, Gillingham, Kent
Printed and bound in Great Britain by Athenaeum Press Ltd, Newcastle-upon-Tyne

Preface

This volume contains virtually all of my published writings on rational–emotive therapy that appeared as journal articles and book chapters in the period 1979–1990.

The writings are grouped into six parts. Parts I and II focus on basic RET theory and practice respectively: Part I contains a long major statement on general RET theory that I wrote with Albert Ellis, followed by a chapter that outlines the rational-emotive conceptualisation of the common emotional problems that clients bring to counselling and psychotherapy. Part II opens with a long major statement on the basic practice of RET, again co-authored with Ellis. This is followed by shorter chapters on the RET treatment sequence and the process of RET, and the section concludes with a brief consideration of commonly expressed misconceptions of RET.

Part III contains three chapters on the vicissitudes of the therapeutic relationship in RET. The first considers the applicability of the concept of the therapeutic alliance to the practice of RET. The second is an interview I conducted with Albert Ellis that focuses on the issue of therapist warmth in RET, and the third discusses the advantages and disadvantages of therapist self-disclosure in RET.

Part IV contains three chapters on more advanced theoretical and practical topics. The first discusses the issues of language and meaning in RET and advocates the development of a shared vocabulary between therapist and client; the second considers the use of chaining in the assessment of clients' problems in RET and outlines four such chains; and the third discusses and exemplifies the use of vivid methods in RET and provides an effective counter to the erroneous view that RET is an overly intellectualised therapy.

Part V is centred on applications of RET to different therapeutic settings. The first two chapters consider the use of RET in couples therapy and conciliation counselling, respectively. Next, the part RET has to play in a comprehensive approach to social skills training is considered. Finally, Ellis's famous Friday night workshop is the focus of consideration. This is a workshop that Ellis runs every Friday night when he is in New York where he demonstrates RET with two volunteers and invites discussion from the rest of the audience.

Part VI includes chapters that place RET in a broader therapeutic context. The first in this section briefly compares RET with psychoanalytical therapy in the treatment of depression, whilst the second is a response to a faulty criticism of RET often made by analytically oriented therapists, namely that it does not deal with the past. The third in this section compares RET with Beck's cognitive therapy based on my experiences of being trained in both forms of therapy in the late 1970s and early 1980s. In the next chapter I consider an issue that emerges from a distinction made by Ellis between specialised and general RET: this is that RET therapists are faced with the grim reality that some clients cannot or will not work towards philosophical change – the preferred option of specialised RET. In such cases, they are called upon to make compromises in approach, thus broadening their work and practising so-called general RET. This article details these compromises. Finally, in this section, there are two chapters that consider RET as an eclectic therapy, the second showing the development of my thought on this issue 5 years after the first was published.

The book closes on a personal note in the epilogue. Here I briefly outline how I have used RET to overcome my personal problems.

This book represents just over a decade's work. During that time many people associated with RET have been enormously helpful to me and supportive of my efforts. I would like to take this opportunity to thank the following (who are listed in alphabetical order): Ray DiGiuseppe, Dom DiMattia, the late Bill Dunn (to whom this book is dedicated), Albert Ellis, Jack Gordon, Paul Hauck, Steve Palmer, Bev Pieren, Al Raitt, Debbie Steinberg, Gina Vega, Steve Weinrach, Richard Wessler and Sheenah Hankin-Wessler, Ruth Wessler, Janet Wolfe, Joe Yankura, my Dutch colleagues and all present and past employees of the Institute for RET in New York.

Windy Dryden
London, January 1991

Contents

This book is dedicated to the memory of Bill Dunn.

Part I
Basic RET Theory

Chapter 1
The General Theory of RET

The Historical Development of RET

Albert Ellis founded rational–emotive therapy (RET) in 1955 when he was a New York clinical psychologist, having begun his career in the helping professions in the early 1940s. As a result of research he was doing at that time for a massive work to be entitled *The Case of Sexual Liberty*, Ellis gained a local reputation for being an authority on sexual and marital relationships. He was consulted by his friends on their sexual and relationship problems and discovered that he could be successful in helping them with these problems in a short period of time. He decided to pursue formal training in clinical psychology, after discovering that there were no formal training possibilities then offered in sex and marital counselling. After getting a PhD degree in clinical psychology, Ellis chose to be trained in psychoanalysis, believing then that it was the deepest and most effective form of psychotherapy available. He decided on this course of action because his experiences as an informal sex–marital counsellor had taught him that disturbed relationships were really a product of disturbed persons, 'and that if people were truly to be helped to live happily with each other they first had better be shown how they could live peacefully with themselves' (Ellis, 1962, p. 3).

Ellis initially enjoyed working as a psychoanalyst, partly because it allowed him to express both his helping and problem-solving interests. However, he became increasingly dissatisfied with psychoanalysis as an effective and efficient form of treatment. In the early 1950s, Ellis began to experiment with different forms of therapy, including psychoanalytically oriented psychotherapy and eclectic–analytical therapy. But although he became more effective with his clients, he remained dissatisfied with the

Written with Albert Ellis, and first published in 1987.

3

efficiency of these methods. During this period of experimentation Ellis returned to his lifelong hobby of reading philosophy to help him with his search for an effective and efficient form of therapy. One of the major influences on his thought at that time was the work of the Greek and Roman Stoic philosophers (e.g. Epictetus and Marcus Aurelius). They emphasised the primacy of philosophical causation of psychological disturbances – a viewpoint that was not popular in America in the 1950s – and de-emphasised the part played by psychoanalytical psychodynamic factors. In essence, the Stoic viewpoint, which stated that people are disturbed not by things but by their view of things, became the foundation of RET, and this perspective (following his pioneering formulations) remains at the heart of present-day cognitive–behavioural approaches to psychotherapy.

Major philosophical influences

Apart from Stoicism, present-day RET owes a philosophical debt to a number of other sources that have influenced its development. Immanuel Kant's writings on the power (and limitations) of cognition and ideation strongly impressed Ellis (1981a), and the work of Spinoza and Schopenhauer was also important in this respect. Philosophers of science, such as Popper (1959, 1963), Reichenbach (1953), and Russell (1965), were also influential in helping Ellis see that all humans develop hypotheses about the nature of the world. Moreover, these philosophers stressed the importance of testing out the validity of such hypotheses rather than assuming that they are necessarily correct. The practice of RET is synonymous, in many respects, with the logico-empirical methods of science (Ellis, 1962, 1979a). RET also stresses the flexibility and antidogmatism of the scientific method and opposes all dogmas, just as science does, and holds that rigid absolutism is the very core of human disturbances (Ellis, 1983a).

Although the philosophy of RET is at variance with devout religiosity, in one respect Christian philosophy has been most influential. RET's theory of human value (which will be discussed later) is similar to the Christian viewpoint of condemning the sin but forgiving the sinner (Hauck, 1972; Powell, 1976; Ellis, 1983a). Due to its stand on self-acceptance and its bias against all forms of human rating, RET allies itself with the philosophy of ethical humanism (Russell, 1930, 1965), which opposes the deification and devil-ification of humans. Because RET considers that humans are at the centre of their universe (but not of *the* universe) and have the power of choice (but not of unlimited choice) with regard to their emotional realm, it has its roots in the existential philosophies of Heidegger (1949) and Tillich (1977). Indeed, RET has a pronounced humanistic–existential outlook (Ellis, 1973).

Ellis was also influenced, particularly in the 1960s, by the work of the general semanticists (e.g. Korzybski, 1933). These theorists outlined the powerful effect that language has on thought and the fact that our emotional processes are heavily dependent on the way we, as humans, structure our thought by the language we employ.

Major psychological influences

In developing RET, Ellis has similarly been influenced by the work of a number of psychologists. He received a training analysis from an analyst of the Karen Horney school, and Horney's (1950) concept of the 'tyranny of the shoulds' was certainly an early influence on his emphasis on the primacy of absolute, dogmatic, evaluative thought in the development and maintenance of much psychological disturbance.

The work of Adler was important to the development of RET in several respects. 'Adler (1927) was the first great therapist to really emphasize inferiority feelings – while RET similarly stresses self-rating and the ego anxiety to which it leads. Like Adler and his Individual Psychology, RET also emphasizes people's goals, purposes, values and meanings. RET also follows Adler in regard to the use of active–directive teaching, the stress placed on social interest, the use of holistic and humanistic outlook, and the employment of a highly cognitive–persuasive form of psychological treatment' (Ellis, 1981a).

Although RET was originally termed 'rational psychotherapy', it has always advocated the use of behavioural methods as well as cognitive and emotive techniques in the practice of therapy. Indeed, Ellis utilised some of the methods advocated by some of the earliest pioneers in behaviour therapy (Watson and Rayner, 1920; M.C. Jones, 1924; Dunlap, 1932), first in overcoming his own early fears of speaking in public and of approaching women, and second in the active–directive form of sex therapy that he practised in the early 1950s. This behavioural active–directive emphasis remains prominent in present-day RET.

In its 30 years of existence, RET has been practised in various therapeutic modalities (individual, group, marital and family), by many kinds of helping professionals (e.g. psychologists, psychiatrists, social workers), and with a variety of client populations (e.g. adults, children, the elderly) suffering from a wide range of psychological disorders. Apart from its use in counselling and psychotherapy, rational–emotive principles have been applied in educational, industrial and commercial settings. A recent development has been the application of RET to public education in the form of 9-hour intensive workshops. In this respect, it is playing a significant role in the field of preventive psychology. RET is practised throughout the world, and there are RET 'Institutes' in the USA, the Netherlands, Italy, Germany, Australia, England and Mexico. It is thus a well-established form of cognitive-behavioural therapy.

Major Theoretical Concepts

RET is based on a set of assumptions that stress the complexity and fluidity of human beings. Given this fundamental view of human nature, RET rests on the following theoretical concepts.

Goals, purposes and rationality

According to RET theory, humans are happiest when they establish important life goals and purposes, and actively strive to attain these. It is argued that, in establishing and pursuing these goals and purposes, human beings had better mind the fact that they live in a social world and that a philosophy of self-interest, where a person places him- or herself first, also implies putting others a close second. This is in contrast to a philosophy of selfishness where the desires of others are neither respected nor regarded. Given that humans will tend to be goal-directed, *rational* in RET theory means 'that which helps people to achieve their basic goals and purposes, whereas "irrational" means that which prevents them from achieving these goals and purposes' (Dryden, 1984a, p. 238). Thus, rationality is not defined in any absolute sense, but is relative in nature.

Humanistic emphasis

RET does not pretend to be 'purely' objective, scientific or technique-centred, but takes a definite humanistic–existential approach to human problems and their basic solutions. It primarily deals with disturbed human evaluations, emotions and behaviours. It is highly rational and scientific but uses rationality and science in the service of humans in an attempt to enable them to live and be happy. It is hedonistic, but it espouses long-range instead of short-range hedonism so that people may achieve the pleasure of the moment and that of the future and may arrive at maximum freedom *and* discipline. It hypothesises that nothing superhuman probably exists and that devout belief in superhuman agencies tends to foster dependency and increase emotional disturbance. It assumes that no humans, whatever their antisocial or obnoxious behaviour, are damnable or subhuman. It particularly emphasises the importance of will and choice in human affairs, even though it accepts the likelihood that some human behaviour is partially determined by biological, social and other forces (Ellis, 1973, 1984a; Bandura, 1977).

The interaction of psychological processes and the place of cognition

RET theory has from its inception stressed an interactive view of human psychological processes. Cognitions, emotions and behaviours are not experienced in isolation and often, particularly in the realm of psychological disturbance, overlap to a significant degree. Recently, RET has stressed the inferential nature of activating events and has shown how events (or, more correctly, how we perceive events) again interact with our cognitive evaluations, emotions and behaviours (Ellis, 1984a). This point will be amplified in the section entitled 'The ABCs of RET: An expanded framework'.

Given this interactional view, it is true, however, that RET is most noted for the special place it has accorded cognition in human psychological processes, particularly the role that evaluative thought plays in psychological health and disturbance. One of RET's unique contributions to the field of cognitive–behaviour therapy lies in its distinction between rational and irrational beliefs. Rational beliefs are evaluative cognitions of personal significance that are preferential (i.e. non-absolute) in nature. They are expressed in the form of 'desires', 'preferences', 'wishes', 'likes' and 'dislikes'. Positive feelings of pleasure and satisfaction are experienced when humans get what they desire, whereas negative feelings of displeasure and dissatisfaction (e.g. sadness, concern, regret, annoyance) are experienced when they do not get what they desire. These negative feelings (the strength of which is closely related to the importance of the desire) are regarded as appropriate responses to negative events and do not significantly interfere with the pursuit of established or new goals and purposes. These beliefs, then, are 'rational' in two respects. First, they are relative and, secondly, they do not impede the attainment of basic goals and purposes.

Irrational beliefs, however, differ in two respects from rational beliefs. First, they are absolute (or dogmatic) in nature and are expressed in the form of 'musts', 'shoulds', 'oughts', 'have-tos', etc. Secondly, as such they lead to negative emotions that largely interfere with goal pursuit and attainment (e.g. depression, anxiety, guilt, anger). Rational beliefs tend strongly to underlie functional behaviours, whereas irrational beliefs underpin dysfunctional behaviours such as withdrawal, procrastination, alcoholism and substance abuse (Ellis, 1982a).

Two basic biological tendencies

Unlike most other theories of therapy, which stress the impact of significant life events on the development of psychological disturbance, RET theory hypothesises that the biological tendency of humans to think irrationally has a notable impact on such disturbance. Its view that irrational thinking is heavily determined by biological factors (always interacting with influential environmental conditions) rests on the seeming ease with which humans think crookedly and the prevalence of such thinking even among people who have been rationally raised (Ellis, 1976a). Whilst Ellis has acknowledged that there are social influences operating here, he has also noted:

'even if everybody had had the most rational upbringing, virtually all humans would often irrationally escalate their individual and social preferences into absolutistic demands on (a) themselves, (b) other people, and (c) the universe around them' (Ellis, 1984a, p. 20).

The following constitutes evidence in favour of RET's hypothesis of the biological basis of human irrationality:

1. Virtually all humans, including bright and competent people, show evidence of major human irrationalities.
2. Virtually all the disturbance-creating irrationalities (absolutistic shoulds and musts) that are found in our society are also found in just about all social and cultural groups that have been studied historically and anthropologically.
3. Many of the irrational behaviours that we engage in, such as procrastination and lack of self-discipline, go counter to the teachings of parents, peers and the mass media.
4. Humans – even bright and intelligent people – often adopt other irrationalities after giving up former ones.
5. People who vigorously oppose various kinds of irrational behaviours often fall prey to these very irrationalities. Atheists and agnostics exhibit zealous and absolutistic philosophies and highly religious individuals act immorally.
6. Insight into irrational thought and behaviours helps only partially to change them. For example, people can acknowledge that drinking alcohol in large quantities is harmful, yet this knowledge does not necessarily help them abstain from heavy drinking.
7. Humans often return to irrational habits and behavioural patterns even though they have often worked hard to overcome them.
8. People often find it easier to learn self-defeating than self-enhancing behaviours. Thus, people very easily overeat but have great trouble following a sensible diet.
9. Psychotherapists who presumably should preferably be good role models of rationality often act irrationally in their personal and professional lives.
10. People frequently delude themselves into believing that certain bad experiences (e.g. divorce, stress and other misfortunes) will not happen to them (Ellis, 1976a, 1979a).

However, RET holds that humans have a second basic biological tendency, namely, to exercise the power of human choice and to work towards changing their irrational thinking. Thus, they have (1) the ability to see that they make themselves disturbed by the irrational views they bring to situations, (2) the ability to see that they can change their thinking and, most importantly, (3) the ability to work actively and continually towards changing this thinking by the application of cognitive, emotive and behavioural methods. Whilst RET theory asserts that humans have a strong biological tendency to think irrationally (as well as rationally), it holds that they are by no means slaves to this tendency and can transcend (although not fully) its effects. In the final analysis then, the RET image of the person is quite an optimistic one (Ellis, 1973; Ellis and Bernard, 1983, 1985).

Two fundamental human disturbances

According to RET, humans can make absolute demands on self, other people and the world (Ellis, 1984a). However, if these demands are more closely investigated, they can be seen to fall into two major categories of psychological disturbance: ego disturbance and discomfort disturbance (Ellis, 1979b, 1980a).

In ego disturbance a person makes a demand on self, others and the world, and if these demands are not met in the past, present or future, the person becomes disturbed by damning 'self'. As I have shown, self-damnation involves (1) the process of giving my 'self' a global negative rating and (2) 'devil-ifying' my 'self' as being bad or less worthy (Dryden, 1984b). The rational and healthy alternative to self-damnation is self-acceptance, which involves refusing to give our 'self' a single rating (because it is an impossible task, due to our complexity and fluidity, and because it normally interferes with attaining our basic goals and purposes) and acknowledging our fallibility.

In discomfort disturbance, the person again makes demands on self, others and the world, which are related to dogmatic commands that comfort and comfortable life conditions must exist. When these demands are not met in the past, present or future, the person becomes disturbed. Tolerating discomfort in order to aid goal attainment and long-range happiness is the healthy and rational alternative to demands for immediate gratification.

Thus, as will be shown later, self-acceptance and a high level of frustration tolerance are two of the main cornerstones of the rational–emotive image of the psychologically healthy human being (Ellis, 1979a).

The ABCs of RET: An Expanded Framework

When RET was originally established, Ellis employed a simple ABC assessment framework to conceptualise clients' psychological problems (Ellis, 1962). In this schema, 'A' stood for the activating event, 'B' represented a person's belief about that event, and 'C' denoted the person's emotional and behavioural responses or consequences to holding the particular beliefs at 'B'. The major advantage of the ABC framework lay in its simplicity. However, its simplicity was also a disadvantage in that important distinctions between different types of cognitive activity were glossed over (Wessler and Wessler, 1980). It is important to note that different RET therapists use different expanded versions of the original ABC framework (compare Wessler and Wessler, 1980; Ellis, 1985a). There is thus no absolutely correct way of conceptualising clients' problems according to such an expanded schema. What is presented below is one version of the expanded ABC framework.

Activating events or activators (As) of cognitive, emotional and behavioural consequences (Cs)

The RET theory of personality and personality disturbances begins with people trying to fulfil their goals (Gs) in some kind of environment and encountering a set of activating events or activators (As) which tend to help them achieve or block these goals. The As they encounter usually are present or current events or their own thoughts, feelings or behaviours about these events, but they may be embedded in memories or thoughts (conscious or unconscious) about past experiences. People are prone to seek out and respond to these As because of (1) their biological or genetic predispositions; (2) their constitutional history; (3) their prior interpersonal and social learning; and (4) their innately predisposed and acquired habit patterns (Ellis, 1976a, 1979a, 1983a).

As (activating events) virtually never exist in a pure or monolithic state, they almost always interact with and partly include Bs and Cs. People bring themselves (their goals, thoughts, desires and psychological propensities) to As.

Beliefs (Bs) about activating events (As)

According to RET theory, people have almost innumerable beliefs (Bs) – cognitions, thoughts or ideas – about their activating events (As); these Bs importantly and directly tend to exert strong influences on their cognitive, emotional and behavioural consequences (Cs). Although As often seem directly to 'cause' or contribute to Cs, this is rarely true, because Bs normally serve as important mediators between As and Cs and therefore more directly 'cause' or 'create' Cs (Ellis, 1962; Goldfried and Davison, 1976; Bard, 1980; Grieger and Boyd, 1980; Wessler and Wessler, 1980). People largely bring their beliefs at A, and they prejudicially view or experience As in the light of these biased beliefs (expectations, evaluations) and also in the light of their emotional consequences (Cs). Therefore, humans virtually never experience A without B and C, but they also rarely experience B and C without A.

Bs take many different forms because people have many kinds of cognitions. In RET, however, we are mainly interested in their rational beliefs (rBs), which we hypothesise lead to their self-helping behaviours, and in their irrational beliefs (iBs), which we theorise lead to their self-defeating (and social-defeating) behaviours. Some of the main (but not the only) kinds of Bs are listed below.

Non-evaluative observations

Example: '(I see)...the man is walking.'

Such observations do not go beyond the available data. They are non-evaluative because they are not relevant to our goals. When such observations are relevant to our goals they become evaluative, for example, when the man walking is my father who has just recovered from a car accident. The evaluative aspects of such 'evaluative observations' are often implicit – for example, '(I am pleased that)...the man is walking'.

Non-evaluative inferences

Example: 'The man who is walking is going to the post office.'

Such cognitions are called 'inferences' because they go beyond the available data. All we are able to observe in this example is a man walking in a certain direction. Although he is proceeding in the direction of the post office, he may or may not be 'going to the post office'. As such, inferences may be viewed as hypotheses about our observations that may or may not be correct. These inferences are non-evaluative when they are not relevant to our goals. When such inferences are relevant to our goals they become evaluative; for example, when the man who may be going to the post office will bring us back our birthday parcels (if indeed he does make a visit). The evaluative aspects of such 'evaluative inferences' are again often implicit – for example, '(it is good that) ... the man who is walking is going to the post office'.

It is helpful to realise for assessment purposes that inferences are frequently chained together (Moore, 1983) and that it is often important to find the most relevant inference in the chain, i.e. the one that overlaps with the person's 'musturbatory' evaluations (i.e. events that are dogmatic in nature and couched in the form of musts, shoulds, oughts and have-to's etc.). Thus, if a client reports experiencing anger at his wife for forgetting the shopping, shopping may not actually be the 'event' that triggers his anger-producing evaluations. The inference chain may be revealed thus: wife forgets shopping → I will mention this to her → she will nag me → I won't be able to watch the football game on TV in peace. Any of these inferences may trigger anger-creating evaluations and it is often important to involve clients as fully as possible in the assessment process by asking questions to help them provide reliable information concerning their most relevant inferences in particular chains.

Positive preferential evaluations

Example: 'I prefer people to approve of me' or 'I like people to approve of me ... (but they do not have to)'.

These cognitions are termed 'positive preferential evaluations' because (1) they are relative and non-absolute (statements such as 'but they do not have to' are rarely stated but are implicit in such cognitions); and (2) they refer to what the person evaluates as positive – 'people approving of me'. They are often termed 'rational' in RET theory because they tend to aid and abet a person's basic goals and purposes.

Let us assume that a man who holds the belief 'I prefer people to approve of me' observes a group of people laughing and infers that they are laughing *with* him. This person may conclude the following based on the positive preferential evaluation that he likes approval and the inference that they are laughing with him:

'(I presume) ... they think I am funny.'
'(I presume) ... they like me.'
'(I presume) ... their liking me has real advantages.'

These cognitions are all positive non-absolute inferences because (1) they go beyond the available data; (2) they are relevant to the person's goal (he is getting what he values); and (3) they are not held with absolute conviction.

'My ability to make them laugh is good.'
'It's pleasant to hear them enjoy themselves.'

The latter are both positive non-absolute evaluations because this man is appraising his ability to make them laugh and their pleasure at laughing in a positive but relative manner.

Positive musturbatory evaluations

Example: 'I must have people approve of me.'

Such cognitions are termed 'positive musturbatory evaluations' because they are absolute and dogmatic and they refer to what the person evaluates as positive in a devout manner. They are often termed 'irrational' in RET theory in that they tend to impede and inhibit a person from achieving his or her other basic goals and purposes.

Let us again assume that a group of people are laughing with a man and presumably like him. He may conclude the following based on his positive musturbatory evaluations – thinking errors are categorised in parentheses:

'I am a great, noble person!' (overgeneralisation)
'My life will be completely wonderful!' (overgeneralisation)
'I deserve to have only fine and wonderful things happen to me!' (demandingness and deification)

These are all positive absolute evaluations. The evaluations of 'I' and the world are positive and grossly exaggerated.

'I am sure they will always like me' (delusions of certainty)
'I am convinced that I will always please them' (delusions of certainty)

The latter are both positive absolute inferences because: (1) they go beyond the data at hand; (2) are positively relevant to the person's goal; and (3) are held with absolute conviction.

Negative preferential evaluations

Example: 'I prefer people not to disapprove of me ...' or 'I dislike people disapproving of me ... (but there's no reason why they must not disapprove of me)'.

These cognitions are termed 'negative preferential evaluations' because, once again, (1) they are relative and non-absolute (statements such as 'but there's no reason why they must not ...' are also rarely stated but are again implicit in such beliefs) and (2) they refer to what the person evaluates as negative – 'people disapproving of me'. They are also termed 'rational' in RET theory because they again tend to aid and abet a person's basic goals and purposes.

This time let us assume that a man who holds the belief 'I prefer people not to disapprove of me' observes a group of people laughing but infers that they are laughing *at* him. This man may conclude the following based on the negative preferential evaluations:

> '(I presume) ... they think I am stupid.'
> '(I presume) ... they don't like me.'
> '(I presume) ... that their not liking me has real disadvantages.'

These are all negative non-absolute inferences because (1) they go beyond the data at hand; (2) they are relevant to the person's goal (he is getting what he dislikes); and (3) they are not held with absolute conviction.

This man may further conclude:

> 'It's unfortunate that they are laughing at me.'
> 'It would be bad if I have some unfortunate trait.'

These are both negative non-absolute evaluations. The evaluations of his 'situation' and of his 'unfortunate trait' are negative and non-devout (i.e. not absolutistic).

Negative musturbatory evaluations

Example: 'I must not have people disapprove of me.'

Such cognitions are termed 'negative musturbatory evaluations' because (1) they are absolute and dogmatic and (2) they refer to what the person evaluates as negative in a devout manner. They are further examples of 'irrational' beliefs in that they tend to impede the achievement of a person's basic goals and purposes.

If we assume that a group of people are laughing at a man and presumably disapprove of him, he may conclude the following based on the above negative musturbatory evaluations – again, the categories of thinking errors are listed in brackets.

'I am an incompetent, rotten person!' (overgeneralisation, self-downing)
'My life will be completely miserable!' (overgeneralisation, awfulising)
'The world is a totally crummy place!' (overgeneralisation, awfulising)
'I deserve to have only bad or good things happen to me!' (demandingness and damnation)
'This is awful, horrible, and terrible!' (awfulising, catastrophising)
'I can't bear it!' (I-can't-stand-it-itis)

These are all examples of negative absolute evaluations. The people and things appraised are all evaluated in a negative and grossly exaggerated manner.

'I will always act incompetently and have significant people disapprove of me' (overgeneralisation)
'They know that I am no good and will always be incompetent' (non-sequitur, jumping to conclusions, mind-reading)
'They will keep laughing at me and will always despise me' (non-sequitur, jumping to conclusions, fortune-telling)
'They only despise me and see nothing good in me' (focusing on the negative, overgeneralisation)
'When they laugh with me and see me favourably that is only because they are in a good mood and do not see that I am fooling them' (disqualifying the positive, non-sequitur, phonyism)
'Their laughing at me and disliking me will definitely make me lose my job and lose all my friends' (catastrophising, magnification)
'They could only be laughing because of some foolish thing I have done and could not possibly be laughing for any other reason' (personalising, non-sequitur, overgeneralisation)

The above seven are all examples of negative absolute inferences because (1) they go beyond the data at hand; (2) they tend to sabotage the person's goal; and (3) they are held with absolute conviction.

Consequences (Cs) of activating events (As) and beliefs (Bs) about As

Cs (cognitive, affective and behavioural consequences) follow from the interaction of As and Bs. We can say, mathematically, that $A \times B = C$, but this formula may actually be too simple and we may require a more complex one to express the relationship adequately. C is almost always significantly affected or influenced but not exactly 'caused' by A, because humans naturally to some degree react to stimuli in their environments. Moreover, when A is powerful (e.g. a set of starvation conditions or an earthquake) it tends to affect C profoundly.

When C consists of emotional disturbance (e.g. severe feelings of anxiety, depression, hostility, self-deprecation and self-pity), B usually (but not

always) mainly or more directly creates or 'causes' C. Emotional disturbance, however, may at times stem from powerful As – for example, from
environmental disasters such as floods or wars. Emotional disturbance may
also follow from factors in the organism – for example, hormonal or disease
factors – that are somewhat independent of yet may actually 'cause' consequences (Cs).

When strong or unusual As significantly contribute to or 'cause' Cs, or
when physiological factors 'create' Cs, they are usually accompanied by
contributory Bs as well. Thus, if people are caught in an earthquake or if
they experience powerful hormonal changes and they 'therefore' become
depressed, their As and their physiological processes probably are strongly
influencing them to create irrational beliefs (iBs), such as, 'This earthquake
shouldn't have occurred! Isn't it awful! I can't stand it!'. These iBs, in turn,
add to or help create their feelings of depression at C.

Cs usually consist of feelings and behaviours but may also consist of
thoughts (e.g. obsessions). Cs (consequences) which follow from As and Bs
are virtually never pure or monolithic but also partially include and
inevitably interact with A and B. Thus, if A is an obnoxious event (e.g. a job
refusal) and B is, first, a rational belief (e.g. 'I hope I don't get rejected for
this job!'), as well as, second, an irrational belief (e.g. 'I must have this job!
I'm no good if I don't get it!'), C tends to be, first, healthy feelings of frustration and disappointment and, secondly, unhealthy feelings of severe
anxiety, inadequacy and depression.

So A × B = C. But people also *bring* feelings (as well as hopes, goals and
purposes) to A. They would not keep a job unless they desired or favourably
evaluated it or unless they enjoyed some aspect of it. Their A therefore partially includes their B and C. The three, from the beginning, are related
rather than completely disparate.

At the same time, people's beliefs (Bs) also partly or intrinsically
relate to and include their As and their Cs. Thus, if they tell themselves,
at B, 'I want to get a good job', they partly create the activating event
at A (going for a job interview), and they partly create their emotional
and behavioural consequences at C (feeling disappointed when they
encounter a job rejection). Without their evaluation of a job as good,
they would not try for it nor have any particular feeling about being rejected.

A, B and C, then, are all closely related and none of them tends to exist
without the other.

The Nature of Psychological Disturbance and Health

Psychological disturbance

Rational–emotive theory, then, posits that at the heart of psychological
disturbance lies the tendency of humans to make devout, absolutistic

evaluations of the perceived events in their lives. As has been shown, these evaluations are couched in the form of dogmatic 'musts', 'shoulds', 'have to's', 'got to's' and 'oughts'. We hypothesise that these absolutistic cognitions are at the core of a philosophy of religiosity which is the central feature of human emotional and behavioural disturbance (compare Ellis, 1983a). These beliefs are deemed to be irrational in RET theory in that they usually (but not invariably) impede and obstruct people in the pursuit of their basic goals and purposes. Absolute musts do not invariably lead to psychological disturbance because it is possible for a person to believe devoutly 'I must succeed at all important projects', have confidence that he or she will be successful in these respects, and actually succeed in them and thereby not experience psychological disturbance. However, the person remains vulnerable in this respect because there is always the possibility that he or she may fail in the future. So whilst on probabilistic grounds RET theory argues that an absolutistic philosophy will frequently lead to such disturbance, it does not claim that this is absolutely so. Thus, even with respect to its view of the nature of human disturbance, RET adopts an anti-absolutistic position.

RET theory goes on to posit that if humans adhere to a philosophy of 'musturbation' they will strongly tend to make a number of core irrational conclusions that are deemed to be derivatives of these 'musts'. These major derivatives are viewed as irrational because they too tend to sabotage a person's basic goals and purposes.

The first major derivative is known as '*awfulising*'. This occurs when a perceived event is rated as being more than 100% bad – a truly exaggerated and magical conclusion that stems from the belief: 'This must not be as bad as it is.'

The second major derivative is known as '*I-can't-stand-it-itis*'. This means believing that it is impossible to experience virtually any happiness at all, under any conditions, if an event that 'must' not happen actually occurs or threatens to occur.

The third major derivative, known as '*damnation*', represents a tendency for humans to rate themselves and other people as 'subhuman' or 'undeserving' if self or another does something that they 'must' not do or fail to do something that they 'must' do. 'Damnation' can also be applied to world or life conditions that are rated as being 'rotten' for failing to give the person what he or she must have.

Whilst RET holds that 'awfulising', 'I-can't-stand-it-itis' and 'damnation' are secondary irrational processes in that they stem from the philosophy of 'musts', these processes can sometimes be primary (Ellis, 1984a). Indeed, Wessler (1984) has argued that they are more likely to be primary and that 'musts' are derived from them. However, the philosophy of 'musts', on the one hand, and those of 'awfulising', 'I-can't-stand-it-itis' and 'damnation', on the other, are in all probability interdependent processes and often seem to be different sides of the same 'cognitive' coin.

RET notes that humans also make numerous kinds of illogicalities when they are disturbed (Ellis, 1984a, 1985a). In this respect RET agrees with cognitive therapists (Beck et al., 1979; Burns, 1980) that such cognitive distortions are a feature of psychological disturbance. However, RET theory holds that such distortions almost always stem from the 'musts'. Some of the most frequent of them are:

1. *All-or-none-thinking*: 'If I fail at any important task, as I *must* not, I'm a *total* failure and *completely* unlovable!'
2. *Jumping to conclusions and negative non-sequiturs*: 'Since they have seen me dismally fail, as I *should* not have done, they will view me as an incompetent worm.'
3. *Fortune-telling*: 'Because they are laughing at me for failing, they know that I *should* have succeeded, and they will despise me forever.'
4. *Focusing on the negative*: 'Because I *can't stand* things going wrong, as they *must* not, I can't see any good that is happening in my life.'
5. *Disqualifying the positive*: 'When they compliment me on the good things I have done, they are only being kind to me and forgetting the foolish things that I *should* not have done.'
6. *Allness and neverness*: 'Because conditions of living ought to be good and actually are so bad and so intolerable, they'll *always* be this way and I'll *never* have any happiness.'
7. *Minimisation*: 'My good shots in this game were lucky and unimportant. But my bad shots, which I *should* never have made, were as bad as could be and were totally unforgivable.'
8. *Emotional reasoning*: 'Because I have performed so poorly, as I *should* not have done, I feel like a total nincompoop, and my strong feeling proves that I *am* no damned good!'
9. *Labelling and overgeneralisation*: 'Because I *must* not fail at important work and have done so, I am a complete loser and failure!'
10. *Personalising*: 'Since I am acting far worse than I *should* act and they are laughing, I am sure they are only laughing at me, and that is *awful*!'
11. *Phonyism*: 'When I don't do as well as I *ought* to do and they still praise and accept me, I am a real phony and will soon fall on my face and show them how despicable I am!'
12. *Perfectionism*: 'I realise that I did fairly well, but I *should* have done perfectly well on a task like this and am therefore really an incompetent!'

Although RET clinicians at times discover all the illogicalities just listed – and a number of others that are less frequently found with clients – they particularly focus on the unconditional 'shoulds', 'oughts' and 'musts' which seem to constitute the philosophical core of irrational beliefs that lead to emotional disturbance. They hold that if they do not get to and help clients surrender these core beliefs, the clients will most probably keep holding them and create new irrational derivatives from them.

RET practitioners also particularly look for 'awfulising', 'I-can't-stand-it-itis' and 'damnation', and they show clients how these almost invariably stem from their 'musts' and can be surrendered if they give up their absolutistic demands on themselves, or other people, and on the universe. At the same time, rational–emotive therapists usually encourage their clients to have strong and persistent desires, wishes and preferences, and to avoid feelings of detachment, withdrawal and lack of involvement (Ellis, 1972a, 1973, 1984a).

More importantly, RET holds that unrealistic and illogical beliefs do not *in themselves* create emotional disturbance. Why? Because it is quite possible for people to unrealistically believe, 'Because I frequently fail I always do' and it is possible for them also to believe illogically, 'Because I have frequently failed, I always will'. But they can, in both these instances, rationally conclude, 'Too bad! Even though I always fail, there is no reason why I *must* succeed. I would *prefer to* but I never *have to* do well. So I'll manage to be as happy as I can be even *with* my constantly failing'. They would then rarely be emotionally disturbed.

To reiterate, the essence of human emotional disturbance, according to RET, consists of the absolutistic 'musts' and 'must nots' that people think *about* their failure, *about* their rejections, *about* their poor treatment by others, and *about* life's frustrations and losses. RET therefore differs from other cognitive–behavioural therapies – such as those of Beck (1967, 1976), Bandura (1969, 1977), Goldfried and Davison (1976), Lazarus (1981), Mahoney (1977), Meichenbaum (1977), Janis (1983) and Maultsby (1984) – in that it particularly stresses therapists looking for clients' dogmatic, unconditional 'musts', differentiating them from their preferences, and teaching them how to surrender the former and retain the latter (Ellis, 1962, 1984a, 1985a; Ellis and Harper, 1975; Bard, 1980; Grieger and Boyd, 1980; Walen, DiGiuseppe and Wessler, 1980; Wessler and Wessler, 1980; Ellis and Becker, 1982; Grieger and Grieger, 1982; Phadke, 1982).

Psychological health

If the philosophy of musturbation is at the core of much psychological disturbance, then what philosophy is characteristic of psychological health? RET theory argues that a philosophy of relativism or 'desiring' is a central feature of psychologically healthy humans. This philosophy acknowledges that humans have a large variety of desires, wishes, wants, preferences etc., but if they refuse to escalate these non-absolute values into grandiose dogmas and demands they will not become psychologically disturbed. They will, however, experience appropriate negative emotions (e.g. sadness, regret, disappointment, annoyance) whenever their desires are not fulfilled. These emotions are considered to have constructive motivational properties in that they both help people to remove obstacles to goal attainment and help them to make constructive adjustments when their desires cannot be met.

Three major derivatives of the philosophy of desiring are postulated by rational–emotive theory. They are deemed to be rational in that they tend to help people reach their goals or formulate new goals if their old ones cannot be realised.

The first major derivative, known as '*rating or evaluating badness*', is the rational alternative to 'awfulising'. Here, if a person does not get what she wants she acknowledges that this is bad. However, because she does not believe 'I have to get what I want', she contains her evaluation along a 0–100% continuum of badness and does not therefore rate this situation as 'awful' – a magical rating that is placed on a nonsensical 101%–infinity continuum. In general, when the person adheres to the desiring philosophy, the stronger her desire the greater her rating of badness will be when she does not get what she wants.

The second major derivative is known as '*tolerance*' and is the rational alternative to 'I-can't-stand-it-itis'. Here the person: (1) acknowledges that an undesirable event has happened (or may happen); (2) believes that the event should empirically occur if it does; (3) rates the event along the badness continuum; (4) attempts to change the undesired event or accepts the 'grim' reality if it cannot be modified; and (5) actively pursues other goals even though the situation cannot be altered.

The third major derivative, known as '*acceptance*', is the rational alternative to 'damnation'. Here the person accepts herself and others as fallible human beings who do not have to act other than they do and as too complex and fluid to be given any legitimate or global rating. In addition, life conditions are accepted as they exist. People who have the philosophy of acceptance fully acknowledge that the world is highly complex and exists according to laws that are often outside their personal control. It is important to emphasise here that acceptance does not imply resignation. A rational philosophy of acceptance means that the person acknowledges that whatever exists empirically should exist but does not absolutely have to exist forever. This prompts the person to make active attempts to change reality. The person who is resigned to a situation usually does not attempt to modify it.

RET theory also puts forward the following 13 criteria of psychological health.

Self-interest

Sensible and emotionally healthy people tend to be first or primarily interested in themselves and to put their own interests at least a little above the interests of others. They sacrifice themselves to some degree for those for whom they care, but not overwhelmingly or completely.

Social interest

Social interest is usually rational and self-helping because most people choose to live and enjoy themselves in a social group or community; if they do not act morally, protect the rights of others, and abet social survival, it is unlikely that they will create the kind of world in which they themselves can live comfortably and happily.

Self-direction

Healthy people tend mainly to assume responsibility for their own lives while simultaneously preferring to cooperate with others. They do not need or demand considerable support or succouring from others.

High frustration tolerance

Rational individuals give both themselves and others the right to be wrong. Even when they intensely dislike their own and others' behaviour, they refrain from damning themselves or others, as persons, for unacceptable or obnoxious behaviour. People who are not plagued with debilitating emotional distress tend to go along with St Francis and Reinhold Niebuhr by changing obnoxious conditions they can change, accepting those they cannot, and having the wisdom to know the difference between the two.

Flexibility

Healthy and mature individuals tend to be flexible in their thinking, open to change, and unbigoted and pluralistic in their view of other people. They do not make rigid, invariant rules for themselves and others.

Acceptance of uncertainty

Healthy men and women tend to acknowledge and accept the idea that we seem to live in a world of probability and chance where absolute certainties do not, and probably never will, exist. They realise that it is often fascinating and exciting, and definitely not horrible, to live in this kind of probabilistic and uncertain world. They enjoy a good degree of order but do not demand to know exactly what the future will bring or what will happen to them.

Commitment to creative pursuits

Most people tend to be healthier and happier when they are vitally absorbed in something outside themselves and preferably have at least one powerful creative interest, as well as some major human involvement, that they consider so important that they structure a good part of their daily existence around it.

Scientific thinking

Non-disturbed individuals tend to be more objective, rational and scientific than more disturbed ones. They are able to feel deeply and act concertedly, but they tend to regulate their emotions and actions by reflecting on them and evaluating their consequences in terms of the extent to which they lead to the attainment of short-term and long-term goals.

Self-acceptance

Healthy people are usually glad to be alive and accept themselves just because they are alive and have some capacity to enjoy themselves. They refuse to measure their intrinsic worth by their extrinsic achievements or by what others think of them. They frankly choose to accept themselves unconditionally, and they try to avoid rating themselves completely – their totality or their being. They attempt to enjoy rather than to prove themselves (Ellis, 1973, 1984a; Ellis and Harper, 1975).

Risk-taking

Emotionally healthy people tend to take a fair amount of risk and try to do what they want to do, even when there is a good chance that they may fail. They tend to be adventurous but not foolhardy.

Long-range hedonism

Well-adjusted people tend to seek both the pleasures of the moment and those of the future and do not often court future pain for present gain. They are hedonistic, i.e. happiness-seeking and pain-avoidant, but they assume that they will probably live for quite a few years and that they had therefore better think of both today and tomorrow, and not be obsessed with immediate gratification.

Non-utopianism

Healthy people accept the fact that utopias are probably unachievable and that they are never likely to get everything they want and to avoid all pain. They refuse to strive unrealistically for total joy, happiness or perfection, or for total lack of anxiety, depression, self-downing and hostility.

Self-responsibility for own emotional disturbance

Healthy individuals tend to accept a great deal of responsibility for their own disturbance rather than defensively blame others or social conditions for their self-defeating thoughts, feelings and behaviours.

Distinction between appropriate and inappropriate negative emotions

Rational–emotive theory argues that people can hold rational and irrational beliefs at the same time. They can easily escalate their desires into demands. Thus I may rationally believe, 'I want you to love me' and simultaneously believe that 'since I want you to love me, you must do so'. Thus, it is important for therapists to discriminate between their clients' rational and irrational beliefs. When such distinctions are made it is easier to distinguish between appropriate and inappropriate negative emotions. Appropriate negative emotions are deemed to be associated with rational beliefs and inappropriate negative emotions with irrational beliefs. (See Chapter 2 for an extended discussion of this issue.)

Acquisition and Perpetuation of Psychological Disturbance

Rational–emotive theory does not put forward an elaborate view concerning the acquisition of psychological disturbance. This partly follows from the hypothesis that humans have a distinct biological tendency to think and act irrationally, but it also reflects the RET viewpoint that theories of acquisition do not necessarily suggest therapeutic interventions. Whilst RET holds that humans' tendencies towards irrational thinking are biologically rooted, it also acknowledges that environmental variables do contribute to psychological disturbance and thus encourage people to make their biologically based demands (Ellis, 1976a, 1979a). Thus, Ellis has said, 'Parents and culture usually teach children *which* superstitions, taboos and prejudices to abide by, but they do not originate their basic tendency to superstitions, ritualism and bigotry' (Ellis, 1984b, p. 209).

Rational–emotive theory also posits that humans vary in their disturbability. Some people emerge relatively unscathed psychologically from being raised by uncaring or overprotective parents, whilst others emerge emotionally damaged from more 'healthy' child-bearing regimes (Werner and Smith, 1982). In this respect, RET claims that 'individuals with serious aberrations are more innately predisposed to have rigid and crooked thinking than those with lesser aberrations, and that consequently they are likely to make lesser advances' (Ellis, 1984b, p. 223). Thus, the RET theory of acquisition can be summed up in the view that as humans we are not made disturbed simply by our experiences; rather, we bring our ability to disturb ourselves to our experiences.

While rational–emotive theory does not posit an elaborate view to explain the acquisition of psychological disturbance, it does deal more extensively with how such disturbance is perpetuated. First, people tend to maintain their psychological problems by their own 'naïve' theories concerning the nature of these problems and to what they can be attributed. They lack what RET calls 'RET insight no. 1': that psychological disturbance is primarily determined by the absolutistic beliefs that people hold about negative life events (B determines C). Rather, they consider that their disturbances are caused by these situations (A causes C). Since people make incorrect hypotheses about the major determinants of their problems, they consequently attempt to change A rather than B. Secondly, people may have insight no. 1 but lack 'RET insight no. 2': that people remain disturbed by reindoctrinating themselves *in the present* with their absolutistic beliefs. Whilst they may see that their problems are determined by their beliefs, they may distract themselves and thus perpetuate their problems by searching for the historical antecedents of these beliefs instead of directing themselves to change them as currently held. Thirdly, people may have insights no. 1 and no. 2 but still sustain their disturbance because they lack 'RET insight no. 3': that only if people diligently work and practise in the present as well as in the future to think, feel and act against their irrational beliefs are they likely to change them and make themselves significantly less disturbed. People who have all three insights clearly see that it is in their interests persistently and strongly to challenge their beliefs cognitively, emotively and behaviourally to break the perpetuation of the disturbance cycle. Merely acknowledging that a belief is irrational is usually insufficient to effect change (Ellis, 1979a).

RET contends that the major reason why people perpetuate their psychological problems is that they adhere to a *philosophy of low frustration tolerance* (LFT) (Ellis, 1979a, 1980a). Such people believe that they *must* be comfortable and thus do not work to effect change because such work involves experiencing discomfort. They are short-range hedonists in that they are motivated to avoid short-term discomfort even though accepting and working against their temporary uncomfortable feelings would probably help them to reach their long-range goals. Such people rate cognitive and behavioural therapeutic tasks as 'too painful', even more painful than the psychological disturbance to which they have achieved some measure of habituation. They prefer to remain with their 'comfortable' discomfort rather than face the 'change-related' discomfort that they believe they must not experience. Maultsby (1975) has argued that people often back away from change because they are afraid they they will not feel right about it. He calls this the 'neurotic fear of feeling a phony' and actively shows clients that these feelings of 'unnaturalness' are natural concomitants of relearning. Another prevalent form of LFT is 'anxiety about anxiety'. Here, individuals believe that they must not be anxious and thus do not expose themselves to anxiety-provoking situations because they might become anxious if they did so – an experience they would rate as 'awful'. As such, they perpetuate their problems and overly restrict their lives to avoid experiencing anxiety.

'Anxiety about anxiety' constitutes an example of the clinical fact that people often make themselves *disturbed about their disturbance*. Having created secondary (and sometimes tertiary) disturbances about their original disturbance, they become preoccupied with these 'problems about problems' and thus find it difficult to get back to solving the original problem. Humans are often very inventive in this respect. They can make themselves depressed about their depression, guilty about being angry (as well as anxious about their anxiety) etc. Consequently, people are often advised to tackle their disturbances about their disturbances before they can successfully solve their original problems (Ellis, 1979b, 1980a).

RET theory endorses the Freudian view of human defensiveness in explaining how people perpetuate their psychological problems (Freud, 1937). Thus, people maintain their problems by employing various defence mechanisms (e.g. rationalisation, avoidance) that are designed to help deny the existence of these problems or to minimise their severity. The RET view is that these defences are used to ward off self-damnation tendencies and that under such circumstances if these people were honestly to take responsibility for their problems they would severely denigrate themselves for having them. In addition, these defence mechanisms are also employed to ward off discomfort anxiety, because if, again, such people admitted their problems they would rate them as 'too hard to bear' or 'too difficult to overcome'.

Ellis has noted that people sometimes experience a form of perceived pay-off for their psychological problems other than avoidance of discomfort (Ellis, 1979a). The existence of these pay-offs serves to perpetuate these problems. Thus, a woman who claims to want to overcome her procrastination may avoid tackling the problem because she is afraid that should she become successful she might then be criticised by others as being 'too masculine', a situation she would evaluate as 'terrible'. Her procrastination serves to protect her (in her mind) from this 'terrible' state of affairs. I have noted that 'rational–emotive therapists stress the phenomenological nature of these pay-offs, i.e. it is the person's view of the pay-off that is important in determining its impact, not the events delineated in the person's description' (Dryden, 1984a, p. 244).

Finally, the well-documented 'self-fulfilling prophecy' phenomenon helps to explain why people perpetuate their psychological problems (Jones, 1977; Wachtel, 1977). Here, people act according to their evaluations and consequent predictions and thus often elicit from themselves or from others responses that they then interpret in a manner that confirms their initial hypotheses. Thus, a socially anxious man may believe that other people would not want to get to know 'a worthless individual such as I truly am'. He then attends a social function and acts as if he were worthless, avoiding eye contact and keeping away from others. Unsurprisingly, such social behaviour does not invite approaches from others, a lack of response that he interprets and evaluates thus: 'You see I was right. Other people don't want to know me, I really am no good.'

In conclusion, RET theory holds that people 'naturally tend to perpetuate their problems and have a strong innate tendency to cling to self-defeating, habitual patterns and thereby resist basic change. Helping clients change, then, poses quite a challenge for RET practitioners (Dryden, 1984a, pp. 244–245).

The Theory of Therapeutic Change

It has been argued that the rational–emotive view of the person is basically an optimistic one, because although it posits that humans have a distinct biological tendency to think irrationally, it also holds that they have the capacity to *choose* to work towards changing this irrational thinking and its self-defeating effects.

There are various levels of change. Rational–emotive theory holds that the most elegant and long-lasting changes which humans can effect are ones that involve philosophical restructuring of irrational beliefs. Change at this level can be specific or general. Specific philosophical change means that individuals change their irrational absolutistic demands ('musts', 'shoulds') about *given* situations to rational relative preferences. General philosophical change involves people adopting a non-devout attitude towards life events in general.

To effect a philosophical change at either the specific or general level, people are advised to do the following:

1. First, realise that they create, to a large degree, their own psychological disturbances and that while environmental conditions can contribute to their problems they are in general of secondary consideration in the change process.
2. Fully recognise that they do have the ability to change these disturbances significantly.
3. Understand that emotional and behavioural disturbances stem largely from irrational, absolutistic dogmatic beliefs.
4. Detect their irrational beliefs and discriminate them from their rational alternatives.
5. Dispute these irrational beliefs using the logico-empirical methods of science.
6. Work towards the internalisation of their new rational beliefs by employing cognitive, emotive and behavioural methods of change.
7. Continue this process of challenging irrational beliefs and using multimodal methods of change for the rest of their lives.

When people effect a philosophical change at B in the ABC model they often are able spontaneously to correct their distorted inferences of reality (overgeneralisations, faulty attributions etc.). However, they can often benefit from challenging these distorted inferences more directly, as RET has always emphasised (Ellis and Harper, 1961a, b; Ellis, 1962, 1971a, 1973), and as Beck et al. (1979) have also stressed.

Whilst rational–emotive theory argues that irrational beliefs are the breeding ground for the development and maintenance of inferential distortions, it is possible for people to effect inferentially based changes without making a profound philosophical change. Thus, they may regard their inferences as hunches about reality rather than facts, may generate alternative hypotheses, and may seek evidence and/or carry out experiments that test out each hypothesis. They may then accept the hypothesis that represents the 'best bet' of those available.

Consider a man who thinks that his co-workers view him as a fool. To test this hypothesis he might first specify their negative reactions to him. These constitute the data from which he quickly draws the conclusion, 'They think I'm a fool'. He might then realise that what he has interpreted to be negative responses to him might not be negative. If they seem to be negative, he might then carry out an experiment to test out the meaning he attributes to their responses. Thus, he might enlist the help of a colleague whom he trusts to carry out a 'secret ballot' of others' opinions of him; or he could test his hunch more explicitly by directly asking them for their view of him. As a result of these strategies this person may conclude that his co-workers find some of his actions foolish rather then considering him to be a complete fool. His mood may lift because his inference of the situation has changed, but he may still believe, 'If others think I'm a fool, they're right, I am a fool and that would be awful'. Thus, he has made an inferential change but not a philosophical one. If this person were to attempt to make a philosophical change, he would *first* assume that his inference was true, *then* address himself to his evaluations about this inference and hence challenge these if they were discovered to be irrational (i.e. musturbatory evaluations). Thus he might conclude: 'Even if I act foolishly that makes me a *person with* foolish behaviour, not a *foolish person*. And even if they deem me a total idiot, that is simply *their* view, with which I can choose to disagree.' Rational–emotive therapists hypothesise that people are more likely to make a profound philosophical change if they first assume that their inferences are true and then challenge their irrational beliefs, rather than if they first correct their inferential distortions and then challenge their underlying irrational beliefs. However, this hypothesis awaits full empirical enquiry.

People can also make direct changes of the situation at A. Thus, in the example quoted above the man could leave his job or distract himself from the reactions of his colleagues by taking on extra work and devoting himself to this. Or he might carry out relaxation exercises whenever he comes in contact with his co-workers and thus distract himself once again from their perceived reactions. Additionally, the man might have a word with his supervisor, who might then instruct the other workers to change their behaviour towards the man.

When we use this model to consider behavioural change, it is apparent that a person can change his or her behaviour to effect inferential and/or philosophical change. Thus, again using the above example, a man whose co-workers view him as a fool might change his own behaviour towards them and thus elicit a different set of responses from them that would lead him to reinterpret his previous inference (behaviour change to effect inferential change). However, if it could be determined that they did indeed consider him to be a fool, then the man could actively seek them out and show himself that he could stand the situation and that just because they think him a fool does not make him one, i.e. he learns to accept himself in the face of their views while exposing himself to their negative reactions (behaviour change to effect philosophical change).

Whilst rational–emotive therapists prefer to help their clients make profound philosophical changes at B, they do not dogmatically insist that their clients make such changes. If it becomes apparent that clients are not able at any given time to change their irrational beliefs, then RET therapists would endeavour to help them either to change A directly (by avoiding the troublesome situation or by behaving differently) or to change their distorted inferences about the situation.

Chapter 2
Understanding Clients' Problems

It is important for the reader to understand at the outset of this chapter that rational-emotive theory uses 'feeling' words in a precise way; a major purpose of this chapter is to show how RET defines such feelings by clarifying their cognitive correlates. Because clients often use the same words in different ways from their rational-emotive counsellors (e.g. what a client means by anxiety may be different from its meaning in rational-emotive theory), the latter seek to adopt a shared meaning framework with their clients concerning emotions. This often involves teaching clients the rational-emotive language of emotions but can also involve using the clients' own feeling language but in a way that helps them to differentiate between the rational and irrational versions of these emotions (e.g. rational anxiety vs irrational anxiety). (Please note in this chapter that the client is referred to as 'she' throughout.)

Anxiety

Inferences

Typically, in anxiety, a person makes inferences that a threat exists to her personal domain, by which is meant those objects - tangible and intangible - in which a person has an involvement (Beck, 1976). The threat refers generally to a future event, or to future implications of a current event.

Beliefs

RET theory states that anxiety results when a person believes: 'This threat must not occur and it would be terrible if it did' (irrational belief).

First published in 1987.

Action tendencies and response options

When a person is anxious, her major action tendencies are to avoid or to withdraw from the inferred threat in order to obtain short-term relief from anxiety. As will be shown, the person is more likely to avoid or withdraw from the threat when she cannot respond constructively to it. In addition to keeping away from, or physically withdrawing from a threat, people often engage in various forms of behaviour which serve the purpose of obtaining short-term relief from anxiety, but which also have long-term destructive effects on the person's growth.

Thus, clients who present with anxiety often also report problems of self-discipline, e.g. procrastination, alcohol and drug abuse etc. (specific responses which actualise the action tendency to avoid or to withdraw). Another action tendency associated with anxiety can be described as attempting to 'ward off' the threat. This may, for example, involve the use of obsessive and/or compulsive patterns of behaviour and thought. Such tactics serve to perpetuate anxiety and the dysfunctional cognitions upon which the anxiety is based. Seeking reassurance is another response that some individuals tend to make when they are anxious. Here a person looks to other people for guarantees that threats to their personal domain will not happen. When reassurance is given, the person gains short-term relief from anxiety, but once again, the dysfunctional cognitions which underpin the anxious experience are perpetuated. Finally, some people who experience anxiety have an action tendency that encourages them to expose themselves to *more* dangerous instances of the threat. This is known as 'counterphobic behaviour'.

Typically, in anxiety, the person considers that she could not deal with the threat if it occurred. She may judge that there are no viable responses that she can make in the situation; she does not have the sufficient competence to execute such responses; or the responses which she could make would not nullify the threat. Because the person judges that she cannot deal effectively with the threat, she tends to assume that she will be overwhelmed by it.

Other issues

Ellis (1979b, 1980a) has distinguished between two types of anxiety. One occurs when the person has irrational beliefs about threats to her self-worth (ego anxiety), and the other occurs when she has such beliefs about threats to her level of personal comfort (discomfort anxiety). These two types of anxiety often interact leading to the spiralling effect of mounting anxiety or panic. A feature of this spiralling effect is that the person tends to experience very unpleasant bodily sensations which are, as recent research has found, exacerbated by a process called 'overbreathing' (an increase in the rate and depth of respiratory ventilation which occurs particularly when the individual is under stress; Clark, Salkovskis and Chalkley, 1985). Thus, while helping people to overcome anxiety, rational–emotive counsellors not only have to help them to change their inferences and beliefs about the threat but also may usefully help those vulnerable to 'overbreathing' to utilise effective controlled breathing techniques when they experience anxiety.

Concern: The rational alternative to anxiety

In rational–emotive theory, concern is the rational alternative to anxiety. In concern, a person again makes an inference that a threat exists to her personal domain, but her belief about this is rational: 'I don't want this threat to occur, but there is no reason why it must not happen. If it occurs, it is undesirable but not terrible.'

When a person is concerned but not anxious about an inferred threat to her personal domain, she tends to consider that she can deal with the threat, i.e. she can execute successfully assertive and/or coping options from her response repertoire. She is thus able to actualise her action tendency to confront and deal successfully with the threat, and not avoid or withdraw from it, as in anxiety.

Shame and Embarrassment

Inferences

In shame, a person tends to infer that (1) she has revealed a personal weakness (or acted stupidly) in public, and (2) others will notice this display and will evaluate her negatively. In embarrassment, the same types of inferences are made as in shame, with the exception that the personal weakness is regarded by the person as less serious than in shame (e.g. spilling coffee vs stammering).

Beliefs

Both shame and embarrassment tend to result when the person agrees with the negative evaluations that she infers others have made of her, e.g. 'They're right, I am worthless for revealing my weakness'. Such conclusions tend to stem from such irrational beliefs as: 'I must not reveal my weakness in public', and 'I must not be disapproved of by others'. Thus self-devaluation is a core cognitive process in both shame and embarrassment.

Action tendencies and response options

When a person is feeling ashamed or embarrassed, her major action tendency is to remove herself from the 'social spotlight', or the gaze of others, e.g. through avoiding eye contact or through physical withdrawal from the social situation. When the person remains in the situation she feels awkward ('I don't know what to do with myself') yet still feels as if she wants to withdraw ('I want the ground to open up and swallow me'). Remaining in the situation, the person may paradoxically display further signs that may draw attention to herself, e.g. through blushing or becoming agitated.

However, as Duck (1986) has shown, other people may come to the person's rescue, particularly when her social 'gaffe' is not too serious, e.g. by disclosing that similar incidents have happened to them, or by reassuring the person that no harm has been done. Yet, when the person is in a self-devaluing frame of mind and considers that others are unsympathetic to her, she may not be able to use such cues to restore the social equilibrium, and may indeed draw further attention to herself by failing to take advantage of such help.

Regret: The rational alternative to shame/embarrassment

In rational-emotive theory, regret is the rational alternative to shame and embarrassment. In regret, a person again makes an inference that she has revealed a personal weakness or acted stupidly in public and that others will notice this and may evaluate her negatively, but her belief about this is rational: 'I don't like the fact that I've acted in this way and the fact that others may think badly of me, but there's no reason why I must not have committed this 'shameful' or 'embarrassing act', and there's no reason why people must not think badly of me. It's a pity that this has happened, but not terrible, and I choose to accept myself as a fallible human being for acting in this way.'

When a person experiences regret, but not shame or embarrassment, about revealing a personal weakness in public, she tends to consider that she can choose to focus on the humour implicit in the event, if it exists, or to apologise without desperation for inconveniencing others, if this is relevant. She is also able to utilise the attempts of others to help her to restore the social equilibrium. She is thus able to actualise her action tendency to continue to participate actively in social interactions.

Depression

Inferences

According to the rational-emotive model, depression tends to occur when a person makes inferences that she has experienced a significant loss to her personal domain (Beck, 1976). The loss might be the death of a significant other, the loss of a love relationship, the loss of a limb, the loss of personal functioning or the loss associated with failure to achieve a valued goal.

Beliefs

However, whilst inferences of loss tend to be present when the person is psychologically depressed, according to rational–emotive theory, they do not by themselves account for the person's depression. Rather, the person has to hold irrational beliefs about the loss, e.g. when a man believes: 'I absolutely should have not experienced this loss' he tends to conclude that the loss 'is terrible and unbearable', and the loss means either that 'I'm no good' or that 'the world and other people are no good for allowing the loss to occur'. Such irrational beliefs tend to underpin the fact that depressed people are often hopeless about the future.

Action tendencies and response options

When a person is depressed, her major action tendency is to withdraw from experiences that were previously reinforcing to her, or from other people who were previously valued. The person tends to withdraw 'into herself' and to become immobilised. Another behavioural pattern which often accompanies less severe psychological depression is related to problems of self-discipline. Thus, for example, a person may start drinking when depressed, or may get involved in other self-defeating activities in order to escape from the pain of depression, e.g. promiscuous sexual relationships and drug taking.

Typically, in depression, the person considers that she is unable to execute appropriate responses to the loss ('helplessness'), or that nothing she could do will improve the situation ('hopelessness').

Other issues

As in anxiety, depression can be related to losses in self-worth (ego depression) or losses in personal comfort (discomfort depression). Again, both types of depression often interact and people can experience ego depression and their discomfort depression and vice versa (Teasdale, 1985).

Hauck (1971) has discussed two types of depression that are prominently featured in rational–emotive theory (his third type will be discussed in the section on 'Hurt'). First, Hauck argues, as shown above, that depression can occur because the person has a negative view of self. Thus, a client may become depressed because she concludes: 'I am unworthy (or less worthy) because I did not achieve a valued goal as I should have done.' This is depression based on self-devaluation or ego depression. Secondly, depression may be related to 'other pity' which, in my opinion, occurs less frequently in clinical practice than ego depression. Here the person focuses on the misfortunes or losses of others and believes: 'Such misfortunes or losses should not have occurred. It is terrible that the world allows such things to happen.'

Sadness: The rational alternative to depression

In rational-emotive theory, sadness is the rational alternative to depression. In sadness, the person again makes an inference that she has experienced a significant loss to her personal domain, but her belief about this is rational: 'I didn't want this loss to occur, but there is no reason why it should not have happened. It is bad that it has occurred but not terrible.' In this respect healthy grief is seen in rational-emotive theory as profound sadness.

When a person is sad but not depressed about a loss to her personal domain, she tends to consider that she can engage in constructive actions from her response repertoire. She is able to actualise her action tendency to express her feelings about her loss and to talk about it with significant others and not withdraw into herself, as in depression.

Guilt

Inferences

Typically, in guilt, a person infers that she has broken her personal code of moral values either by doing something that she considers to be 'bad' (the 'sin' of commission) or not doing something she considers to be 'good' (the 'sin' of omission).

Beliefs

Rational-emotive theory states that guilt results when a person believes: 'I absolutely should not have done what I did (or should have done what I did not). I am a damnable individual for doing so (or not doing so) and should be punished.'

Action tendencies and response options

When a person is feeling guilty, her major action tendencies involve: (1) 'undoing' - this process which aims to 'right the wrong' is often unproductive, e.g. attempting to repair 'broken relationships' by desperately begging forgiveness from others (often accompanied by statements of self-loathing); (2) self-punishment, where the person may harm herself in a physical way, or involve herself in activities that may lead her to harm because she believes that she deserves punishment; (3) attempting to anaesthetise herself from the pain of guilt, usually in a self-defeating manner by taking drugs or alcohol; or (4) avoiding responsibility, by making defensive excuses whereby the person claims that she did not do wrong, or blames others for her actions.

Typically, in guilt, because the person is in a self-condemnatory frame of mind, she is likely to choose options from her response repertoire which tend to make it more likely that she will 'sin' in future. For example, a common pattern in eating disorders involves the person resolving to diet, establishing a strict dieting regime, breaking this regime, condemning herself, and eating to take away the pain of guilt.

If the person experiencing guilt considers that she has wronged another, she is likely to make unrealistic promises to the other to the effect that 'I will never do that again', without attempting to understand the factors which led her to act that way. She thus finds it difficult to learn from her errors, and thus tends not to be able to keep such promises. Thus, people who experience guilt are often so preoccupied with 'purging' their badness, or with self-punishment, that they tend not to look for explanations for their behaviour other than those that involve internal attributions of badness.

Remorse: The rational alternative to guilt

In rational–emotive theory, remorse, or sorrow, is the rational alternative to guilt. In remorse, a person again infers that she has violated her personal code for moral values, but her belief about this is rational: 'I don't like what I did, or didn't do, but there's no reason why I must not have done it. I'm a fallible human being who did the wrong thing and therefore not damnable.'

When a person feels remorse, but not guilt, about breaking her personal code of moral values, she tends to take responsibility for her actions without damning her 'self' and tries to understand why she acted or failed to act as she did. If others are involved, the person may choose to communicate to them the reasons for her actions and apologise, without desperation, to them for 'causing' them pain. She is thus able to repair 'broken' relationships in a rational manner, i.e. while accepting self and others, and to make reparation where appropriate.

Other issues

It is important to distinguish between 'feeling' guilt (i.e. condemning self for acting badly) and acknowledging that you are guilty of doing something wrong – better termed 'accepting responsibility for your actions'. When a rational–emotive counsellor asks whether the client wishes to overcome her feelings of guilt, the client often thinks that she is being asked to consider that she hasn't broken her moral code rather than to consider the option of accepting herself as a fallible human being for transgressing this code (the latter strategy represents the counsellor's actual intent).

As noted above, clients often consider that having guilty feelings will prevent them from breaking their moral code in the future. However, often the reverse is true. Since guilt involves the belief 'I am bad', a self-fulfilling prophecy often comes into play because a person who considers herself 'bad' will tend to act 'badly' in the future.

Anger

The term 'anger' has several meanings in the counselling literature. Rational–emotive theory differentiates damning anger, which tends to be an irrational emotion, from non-damning anger, which tends to be a rational emotion. Here I will use the term 'anger' to refer to damning anger, and annoyance to refer to its non-damning counterpart.

Inferences

There appear to be three major inference patterns in anger. First, a person may make an inference that a frustrating circumstance exists which serves to block her from achieving goals which she deems important in her personal domain. As Wessler and Wessler (1980) note: 'The source of frustration can be external or internal, so anger can be directed at other people, the world in general or oneself' (p. 98).

Secondly, a person may make an inference that another person, an institution, e.g. a company, a tax office or university, or the person herself has transgressed a personal rule deemed important in her personal domain. When the transgressor of the rule is yourself, the rule in anger tends to be non-moral in contrast to guilt when the rule is in the moral domain. Whilst Wessler and Wessler (1980) observe that transgression of personal rules represents a major source of inferred frustration, I prefer to see the rule-transgression inference pattern as separate from inference patterns associated with frustration, because it occurs frequently in counselling practice.

Thirdly, in a certain type of anger that I call 'self-defence' anger, a person makes an inference that the actions of another person, or the responses of an institution, threaten her 'self-esteem' (see 'Other issues' below).

Belief

Rational–emotive theory states that whilst inferences of frustration, rule transgression or threat to self-esteem tend to be present when the person is angry, they do not, by themselves, account for anger; rather, the person tends to hold irrational beliefs about these inferences, e.g. 'You must not act in this way and you are damnable for doing so'. It is important to stress then that damning another person, an institution or yourself is an important cognitive dynamic in anger.

Action tendencies and response options

When a person is feeling angry, her major action tendency is to attack either physically or verbally the relevant source of the frustration, rule-breaking or threat to self-esteem in some way. This attack often has a retaliatory intent. If this attack cannot be mounted directly, as strict social rules often restrict the expression of aggression, the person may tend to displace her attack onto another person, usually of lower status or less powerful that the original source, an animal ('kicking the cat') or an object. Another major action tendency associated with anger is withdrawal, as when a person 'storms' out of a meeting.

Typically, in anger, a person tends to choose options from her response repertoire that are characterised by retaliation. The person seeks to get even in some way by choosing, for example, to respond to another person's criticism with damning criticism of that other person in return. When the person's anger is passive–aggressive, this retaliation is expressed indirectly and without the recipient necessarily knowing where the attack has come from, e.g. sending anonymous poison-pen letters, because the person tends also to be anxious of attacking the other directly.

Whilst the person who is angry could theoretically choose to engage in productive responses from her response repertoire, e.g. honest non-damning communication, the fact that she is in a 'damning' frame of mind makes this unlikely. This explains why rational–emotive counsellors seek to help clients to work to overcome their anger before helping them to communicate constructively with others (Dryden, 1985a).

Other issues

It is often difficult to help people to overcome their anger because anger tends to have positive short-term results. Thus anger often helps people to 'feel' powerful and it may, in certain circumstances, help them to get what they want from others, at least initially. However, anger tends also to have negative long-term consequences for the person. Thus anger tends to encourage the deterioration and disintegration of relationships and tends to lead to high blood pressure and other cardiovascular disorders (Chesney and Rosenman, 1985).

As noted earlier, anger can form an entry point or a 'gateway' to the experience of other emotions such as anxiety or hurt. For example, a client may be angry with her husband for forgetting her birthday, not just because the other person has broken a personal rule and should be punished (although there is that element to the experience), but because she infers that her husband has acted in an uncaring manner. In this example, hurt underpins the experience of anger, i.e. the woman believes that it is terrible to be treated in a way she did not deserve. Another example of anger as a 'gateway' emotion occurred when I once became angry when a friend enquired about the progress of a writing project. I responded with anger, not because I believed that my friend should not have made this enquiry, but because he should not have reminded me of my sense of personal inadequacy due to the fact that the project was not going well (threat to my self-esteem). If I was more accepting of myself on that occasion when being reminded of my poor performance, I would still have been annoyed because I would not have liked being reminded of my inadequacy, but I would not have been angry.

Annoyance: The rational alternative to anger

In rational–emotive theory, annoyance is the rational alternative to anger. In annoyance, a person again makes an inference that concerns frustration, rule-breaking or threat to self-esteem, but her beliefs about these are rational, e.g. 'I don't like your behaviour and I prefer you didn't act in this way. But there's no reason why you must not act in this bad manner. You are not damnable but a fallible human being who, in my opinion, is acting badly.' Thus, acceptance of the other or yourself as 'fallible' is an important cognitive dynamic in annoyance.

When a person is annoyed but not angry, she tends to actualise her tendency to remain in the situation and deal with it constructively by choosing responses from her repertoire that may include assertion and requesting (but not demanding!) behavioural change from others. As in remorse, the person who is annoyed at her own behaviour tends to take responsibility for her own actions, tries to understand her reasons for breaking her own, non-moral rule, and takes corrective action in the future.

Hurt

Inferences

Typically, in hurt, a person infers that a significant other has acted towards her in an 'unfair' manner. The other might have ignored the person or disregarded her desires, acted in a non-caring way towards the person or betrayed the person in some way. Another important inference pattern in hurt, which often accompanies the inferences referred to above, involves the person considering that she is undeserving of such treatment.

Beliefs

Rational–emotive theory states that hurt results when a person believes: 'The other person absolutely should not have treated me in this unfair manner'. Typical conclusions which follow from this irrational premise can be three-fold:

1. 'It's terrible to be treated in this way, particularly as I do not deserve it. Poor me! The world is a rotten place for allowing this to happen.' This can be referred to as 'self-pitying hurt'.
2. 'I'm no good for being treated this way.' This can be referred to as 'depressed hurt'.

3. 'You are no good for treating me in this way.' This can be referred to as 'angry hurt'.

Often, in hurt, the person has a blend of these three irrational beliefs.

When deservingness is an issue for the person when she is hurt, she tends to believe: 'I must get what I deserve' or 'I must not get what I do not deserve'.

Action tendencies and response options

When a person is feeling hurt, her major action tendencies involve withdrawing and closing communication channels with the person who has 'hurt' her (colloquially referred to as 'sulking'), and criticising the other person normally without disclosing what she feels hurt about. Both often serve the purpose of getting even with the other. Other action tendencies in 'depressed hurt' and 'angry hurt' are similar to those associated with depression and anger.

Typically, in hurt, the person, as noted above, often chooses to withdraw from the other who has 'hurt' her. She may also choose responses which are intended to encourage the other person to feel guilty, e.g. 'If you really cared about me you would know what you did to hurt me'. Underlying this notion is the person's magical belief that the other person should be able to read one's mind, or know the meaning underlying one's distress. When the person is hurt in a depressed or angry way, she tends to choose response options similar to those selected in depression and anger.

Disappointment: The rational alternative to hurt

In rational-emotive theory, disappointment is the rational alternative to hurt. In disappointment, a person again infers that another has acted unfairly towards her, but her belief about this is rational: 'I prefer to be treated fairly (or not to be treated unfairly), but there's no reason why I must be treated in the way that I prefer (even though I may "deserve" it). I do not have to get what I deserve.' Typical conclusions that follow from this rational premise are: 'It's bad (but not terrible) to be treated in this way.' 'Being treated in this way does not affect my worth. I'm a fallible human being no matter how I am treated.' Here the person's disappointment is tinged with sadness, 'I don't like your behaviour but you are a fallible human being for acting unfairly. You are not damnable.' Here the person's disappointment is tinged with annoyance.

When a person feels disappointment but not hurt about being treated unfairly, she tends to choose options from her response repertoire which actualise her action tendency to influence the other person to act in a 'fairer' manner. She communicates her feelings clearly, directly and assertively to the other person.

Morbid Jealousy

In this section, I will focus on romantic jealousy, because clients are most likely to seek counselling help for this type of jealousy.

Inferences

In morbid jealousy, a person can make a number of inferences including: (1) that the loss of her partner to another is imminent or has occurred; (2) that she does not have the exclusive love or attention of her partner; (3) that she is not the most important aspect of her partner's life; and (4) that her partner is acting in a way that violates her property rights (when she views her partner as her 'property'). These inferences are often linked to inferred threats to the jealous person's self-esteem.

Whilst many people are jealous of their partner's actual or imagined sexual involvement with another person, others allow their partner to have sex with other people and only get jealous when their partner becomes emotionally involved with another person. This suggests that people differ in their jealousy 'rules' (Duck, 1986).

Beliefs

Whilst one or more of the above inferences tend to occur when the person is morbidly jealous, they again do not, by themselves, account for the person's destructive jealous feelings. Rather, the person has to hold irrational beliefs about these inferences, e.g. when a woman believes 'My husband must only be interested in me. If he shows interest in another woman that would be awful'. She may then conclude either: 'His interest in someone else proves that I am worthless' (morbid jealousy tinged with depression) or 'He is no good [and/or the other woman is no good] for doing this to me' (morbid jealousy tinged with anger).

Action tendencies and response options

When a person is morbidly jealous, her action tendencies include monitoring the actions and feelings of her partner, e.g. constantly asking her partner for assurances that she is loved, or phoning her partner at work to check on his movements; searching for evidence that her partner is involved with somebody else, e.g. checking his car for signs of sexual activity or accusing her partner of engaging in extramarital affairs; attempting to place restrictions on the movements of her partner, e.g. not allowing her partner to talk to other women at social gatherings; and retaliating, e.g. becoming sexually involved with another person to 'get even' with her partner for his actual or presumed infidelity, or angrily condemning her partner for his 'infidelity'.

As shown above, people who experience morbid jealousy often act in self- and relationship-defeating ways. Because they are anxious about losing their relationship and are yet convinced that this loss is imminent, they often hasten the end of the relationship by their checking, accusatory and prescriptive behaviour towards their partner, thus displaying the self-fulfilling prophecy effect commonly found in cases of morbid jealousy.

Non-morbid jealousy: The rational alternative to morbid jealousy

In non-morbid jealousy, the person may again make similar inferences as in morbid jealousy, but her beliefs about these are rational, e.g. 'I want my husband to be only interested in me, but there's no reason why I must have his exclusive interest. If he shows interest in another woman it would be bad, but not awful'. She may then conclude either 'I am still a fallible human being even if he shows interest in someone else' or 'He [and/or the other woman] is a fallible human being who is acting against my interests'. Ellis (1985b) has argued that non-morbid jealousy encourages a person to act and express herself in a loving manner towards her partner rather than taking him for granted; to do something effective to try and win her partner back if that is what she wants; to express her distress assertively and without anger and to ask her partner to set limits on his outside involvement; and to reorganise her life constructively without her partner if he leaves her, or if she decides to terminate the relationship given that it no longer meets her deepest desires.

Whilst there is no research on the subject, rational–emotive theory would predict that the person who experiences non-morbid jealousy is less likely to consider that her partner has outside romantic interests in the absence of such evidence than the person who experiences morbid jealousy.

Problems of Self-discipline

Clients sometimes seek counselling for help with problems of self-discipline, such as procrastination, eating disorders and addictions to, say, alcohol or drugs. Also such problems may also be involved in other emotional disorders – for instance, alcoholism is often a feature of aggression.

According to the framework presented in this book, problems of self-discipline are seen here in terms of the conversion of action tendencies into fixed patterns of response which have become habitual. It is important to note that self-discipline problems involve a complex interaction of ego disturbance, discomfort disturbance and responses chosen to actualise action tendencies, the main purpose of which is often to gain relief from immediate feelings of distress. One example will suffice.

People with drink problems often originally have ego anxiety, e.g. 'I must do well and I'm worthless if I don't'. They then experience discomfort anxiety about such ego anxiety, e.g. 'I can't stand being so anxious' and thence drink to rid themselves of their anxiety. In the next part of the chain they may have irrational beliefs about their drinking and/or about the results of their drinking – because alcohol often disrupts performance, e.g. 'I'm no good for doing so poorly' or 'I must not drink this much'. They then make themselves anxious about this ego anxiety and once again drink to rid themselves of these anxious feelings. It should be apparent then that such people set up and maintain a vicious circle of disturbance, while often simultaneously and paradoxically denying that they have a problem. This process of denial probably accounts for the reluctance often shown by such individuals to seek help for their problems.

Wessler and Wessler (1980) have argued that problems of self-discipline serve three major functions:

1. A *relief function*, whereby the person either abuses alcohol, food or drugs, or procrastinates to gain relief from immediate emotional disturbance, or to prevent such distress occurring
2. A *self-protective function*, whereby the person uses her self-defeating behaviour as a protection against possible self-condemnation, e.g. the woman who overeats to make herself unattractive to men thus attributing any rejection to her weight rather than to her inherent worthlessness
3. A *'spurious' self-enhancement function* whereby a person engages in self-defeating behaviour in order to obtain something positive that she believes she needs, e.g. the man who gambles compulsively in order to finance his entry into an elite social group to which he aspires, and which he thinks he must join.

To this list we can add a fourth function, what I call a *'positive feeling function'* whereby the person engages in self-defeating behaviour, such as alcohol, drugs etc., in order to get quick intense positive feelings, or a state of relaxation, rather than to avoid negative feelings such as anxiety.

It is apparent, then, that people with problems of self-discipline adhere to a philosophy of low frustration tolerance (LFT) in that they believe they must get what they want, or must not get what they do not want, quickly and easily. Thus a major feature of rational–emotive counselling with such individuals is to help them to raise their level of frustration tolerance.

Additional Issues

I conclude this chapter by considering briefly some additional issues in understanding clients' problems.

A mixture of emotions

Although I have considered emotional problems separately, it is not uncommon in counselling practice for clients to describe a mixture of emotions.

For example, some clients report feeling simultaneously depressed and guilty. In practice, it is often helpful to separate these emotions and deal with them one at a time. Also clients sometimes report experiencing 'blended' emotions as in 'hurt anger' or 'jealous anger'. Because as has been shown, there are various types of anger, it is helpful to determine the nature of the emotional blend for assessment purposes, particularly when clients only refer to 'feeling angry': the cognitions which underpin 'hurt anger' are somewhat different from those underlying 'jealous anger'.

'False' emotions

It is important to bear in mind that clients may report emotions that they do not, in fact, experience, or emotions that are less important to their actual problems than other feelings that they do not disclose. Clients who report emotions that they do not experience sometimes do so because they think that they are supposed to have these emotions (DiGiuseppe, 1984). Clients who report emotions peripheral to their real concerns do so for similar reasons and, in addition, may feel ashamed about their real emotions, e.g. clients who report feeling depressed rather than their true feelings of anger. As Snyder and Smith (1982) have shown, some clients use emotions for impression management purposes. For example, some clients present with 'false' feelings of depression based on self-devaluation in order to elicit pity from other people or to ward off attack from other people. In the latter instance, such clients are often anxious about being criticised and ward off criticism by seeming to put themselves down before they are put down by others (most people will not criticise those who are already criticising themselves; indeed others are likely to boost the ego of those who are actively condemning themselves). It is difficult for counsellors to identify clients' 'false' emotions, at least initially. However, they should be alert to their existence, particularly when 'something does not seem to ring true' about clients' accounts of their emotional experiences.

Strength vs rationality of negative emotions

Some counsellors who misinterpret rational–emotive theory consider that strong negative emotions are reliable signs that these emotions are irrational. This is not necessarily the case. Thus we can experience mild anger (irrational emotion) and strong annoyance (rational emotion). Strong rational emotions occur when the person does not get what she strongly prefers, or gets what she strongly prefers not to get. Weak irrational emotions occur when the person demands weakly that she gets what she wants, or that she does not get what she does not want.

The clue to whether an emotion is rational or irrational is whether or not the person demands that her desires are met. Thus, counsellors who try to help clients to reduce the strength of their rational emotions make the unfortunate mistake of encouraging them to deny the strength of their desires.

Part II
Basic RET Practice

Chapter 3
The Basic Practice of RET

The Therapeutic Relationship

RET is an active–directive form of psychotherapy in that therapists are active in directing their clients to identify the philosophical source of their psychological problems and in showing them that they can challenge and change their irrational, musturbatory evaluations. As such, RET is an educational form of therapy. Ellis has sometimes conceptualised the role of the effective RET therapist as that of an authoritative (but not authoritarian!) and encouraging teacher who strives to teach his or her clients how to be their own therapists once formal therapy sessions have ended (Ellis, 1979c, 1984b).

Therapeutic conditions

Given the above role, RET therapists strive to *accept unconditionally* their clients as fallible human beings who often act self-defeatingly but who are never essentially bad (or good). No matter how badly clients behave in therapy, the RET therapist attempts to accept them as people but will frequently, if appropriate, let them know his or her reactions to the client's negative behaviour (Ellis, 1973).

In our role as therapists, we strive to be as open as therapeutically feasible and will not hesitate to give highly personal information about ourselves should our clients ask for it, except when we judge that clients would use such information against themselves. RET therapists often disclose examples from their own lives concerning how they experienced similar problems and, more importantly, how they have gone about solving these problems. Thus, they strive to be *therapeutically genuine* in conducting sessions.

Written with Albert Ellis; first published in 1987.

RET therapists tend to be *appropriately humorous* with most of their clients because they think that much emotional disturbance stems from the fact that clients take themselves and their problems, other people and the world too seriously. RET therapists thus strive to model for their clients the therapeutic advantages of taking a serious, but humorously ironic, attitude to life. They endeavour, however, not to poke fun at the clients themselves but at their self-defeating thoughts, feelings and actions (Ellis, 1977a, b, 1981b). In the same vein, and for similar purposes, RET therapists tend to be informal and easy-going with most of their clients. However, RET opposes therapists unethically indulging themselves in order to enjoy therapy sessions at their clients' expense (Ellis, 1983b).

RET therapists show their clients a special kind of empathy. They not only offer them 'affective' empathy (i.e. communicating that they understand how their clients feel), but also offer them *philosophical empathy* (i.e. showing them that they understand the philosophies that underlie these feelings).

Thus, with certain modifications, they agree with Rogers' (1957) views concerning therapist empathy, genuineness and unconditional positive regard. However, rational–emotive therapists are very wary of showing the vast majority of their clients undue warmth. RET holds that if RET therapists get really close to their clients and give them considerable warmth, attention, caring and support, as well as unconditional acceptance, then these therapists run two major risks (Ellis, 1977c, 1982b): the first major risk is that therapists may unwittingly reinforce their clients' dire needs for love and approval – two irrational ideas that are at the core of much human disturbance. When this happens, clients appear to improve because their therapists are indeed giving them what they believe they must have. They begin to 'feel better', but do not necessarily 'get better' (Ellis, 1972a). Their 'improvement' is illusory because their irrational philosophies are being reinforced. Because they seem to improve, their therapists have restricted opportunities to identify these ideas, show them how they relate to their problems, and help them challenge and change them. Consequently, whilst such clients are helped by their therapists, they are not shown how they can help themselves and are thus vulnerable to future upset.

The second major risk is that therapists may unwittingly reinforce their clients' philosophy of low frustration tolerance (LFT), a major form of discomfort disturbance. Clients with LFT problems 'almost always try to seek interminable help from others instead of coping with life's difficulties themselves. Any kind of therapy that does not specifically persuade them to stop their puerile whining and to accept responsibility for their own happiness tends to confirm their belief that others *must* help them. Close relationship therapy is frequently the worst offender in this respect and thereby does considerable harm' (Ellis, 1977c, p. 15).

However, because RET is relative in nature and is against the formulation of absolute, dogmatic therapeutic rules, it does recognise that under certain conditions (e.g. where a client is extremely depressed, accompanied by powerful suicidal ideation etc.), distinct therapist warmth may be positively indicated for a restricted period of time (Ellis, 1985c; see Chapter 8).

Therapeutic style

I recommend that RET therapists adopt an active–directive style with most clients and a particularly forceful version of that style with some very disturbed and resistant clients (Ellis, 1979d). However, not all RET therapists concur with this view. Some recommend a more passive, gentle approach under specific or most conditions with clients (e.g. Young, 1974a, 1977; Garcia, 1977). Eschenroeder (1979) notes that it is important to ask in RET, 'Which therapeutic style is most effective with which kind of client?' (p. 5). In the same vein, recent proponents of eclectic forms of therapy argue that style of therapeutic interaction had better be varied to meet the special situations of individual clients (Lazarus, 1981; Beutler, 1983). Whilst this is a scantily researched area in RET, it may be best for RET therapists to avoid: (1) an overly friendly, emotionally charged style of interaction with 'hysterical' clients; (2) an overly intellectual style with 'obsessive–compulsive' clients; (3) an overly directive style with clients whose sense of autonomy is easily threatened (Beutler, 1983); and (4) an overly active style with clients who easily retreat into passivity. This line of reasoning fits well with the notion of flexibility that rational–emotive therapists advocate as a desirable therapeutic quality. Varying one's therapeutic style in RET does not mean departing from the theoretical principles on which the content of therapy is based. As Eschenroeder (1979) points out, in RET 'there is no one-to-one relationship between theory and practice' (p. 3).

Personal qualities of effective rational–emotive therapists

Unfortunately, no research studies have been carried out to determine the personal qualities of effective rational–emotive therapists. Rational–emotive theory, however, does put forward a number of hypotheses concerning this topic (Ellis, 1978a), but it is important to regard these as both tentative and awaiting empirical study.

1. Due to the fact that RET is a fairly structured form of therapy, its effective practitioners are usually comfortable with structure, but flexible enough to work in a less structured manner when the need arises.
2. RET practitioners tend to be intellectually, cognitively or philosophically inclined and become attracted to RET because the approach provides them with opportunities to express this tendency fully.

3. Because RET has often to be conducted in a strong active-directive manner, effective RET practitioners are usually comfortable operating in this mode. Nevertheless, they have the flexibility to modify their interpersonal style with clients so that they provide the optimum conditions to facilitate client change.

4. RET emphasises that it it important for clients to put their therapy-derived insights into practice in their everyday lives. As a result, effective practitioners of RET are usually comfortable with behavioural instruction and teaching, and with providing the active prompting that clients often require if they are to follow through on homework assignments.

5. Effective rational-emotive therapists tend to have little fear of failure themselves. Their personal worth is not invested in their client's improvement. They do not need their client's love and/or approval and are thus not afraid of taking calculated risks if therapeutic impasses occur. They tend to accept both themselves and their clients as fallible human beings and are therefore tolerant of their own mistakes and the irresponsible acts of their clients. They tend to have, or persistently work towards acquiring, a philosophy of high frustration tolerance, and they do not get discouraged when clients improve at a slower rate than they desire. Thus, effective practitioners tend to score highly on most of the criteria of positive mental health outlined in Chapter 1, and they serve as healthy role-models for their clients.

6. RET strives to be scientific, empirical, anti-absolutistic and undevout in its approach to people's selecting and achieving their own goals (Ellis, 1978a). Thus, effective practitioners of RET tend to show similar traits and are definitely not mystical, anti-intellectual or magical in their beliefs.

7. RET advocates the use of techniques in a number of different modalities (cognitive, imagery, emotive, behavioural and interpersonal). Its effective practitioners are thus comfortable with a multimodal approach to treatment and tend not to be people who like to stick rigidly to any one modality.

Finally, Ellis has noted that some rational-emotive therapists often modify the preferred practice of RET according to their own natural personality characteristics (Ellis, 1978a). Thus, for example, some therapists practise RET in a slow-moving passive manner, do little disputing, and focus therapy on the relationship between them and their clients. Whether such modification of the preferred practice of RET is effective is a question awaiting empirical enquiry.

Inducting Clients into RET

When clients seek help from rational-emotive therapists they vary concerning how much they already know about the type of therapeutic process they are likely to encounter. Some may approach the therapist because they know he or she is a practitioner of RET, whilst others may know nothing about this therapeutic method. In any event, it is often beneficial to explore clients' expectations for therapy at the outset of the process. Duckro, Beal and George (1979) have argued that it is important to distinguish between preferences and anticipations when expectations are assessed. Clients' preferences for therapy concern what kind of experience they want, whilst anticipations concern what service they think they will receive. Clients who have realistic anticipations for the RET therapeutic process and have a preference for this process require, in general, far less induction into rational–emotive therapy than clients who have unrealistic anticipations of the process and/or preferences for a different type of therapeutic experience.

Induction procedures, in general, involve showing clients that RET is an active–directive structured therapy oriented to discussion about clients' present and future problems and one that requires clients to play an active role in the change process. Induction can take a number of different forms. First, therapists may develop and use a number of pre-therapy role-induction procedures where a typical course of RET is outlined and productive client behaviours demonstrated (Macaskill and Macaskill, 1983). Secondly, therapists may give a short lecture at the outset of therapy concerning the nature and process of rational–emotive therapy. Thirdly, therapists may employ induction-related explanations in the initial therapy sessions using client problem material to illustrate how these problems may be tackled in RET and to outline the respective roles of client and therapist.

Assessment of Clients' Problems

The next stage of therapy concerns assessment. Assessment of the kind and degree of emotional disturbance of clients is held to be important in RET for several reasons:

- To determine how seriously disturbed clients are, so that therapists can see how likely they are to benefit from any form of therapy, including RET, and so that they can also decide which RET techniques (of the many possible ones available) may be most suitably employed (and which techniques avoided) with each particular client under the conditions in which he or she may be expected to live.
- To determine – or at least guess with a fair degree of accuracy – how difficult clients are likely to be, how they will probably take to the main RET procedures and how long psychotherapy with each of them is likely to be required.
- To discover which type of therapist involvement, e.g. a more or less active or a more or less passive and supportive kind, is likely to help the individual client.

- To discover what types of skill deficiencies clients have and what kinds of training (either in the course of RET or outside of therapy) they might best undertake to remedy some of their skill deficiencies. Thus, on the basis of this assessment, certain kinds of skill training, such as assertiveness, social skills, communication or vocational training, may be recommended for specific clients.

RET practitioners are at liberty to use all kinds of assessment procedures but generally favour the types of cognitive–behavioural interventions described in Kendall and Hollon (1980). They tend to take a dimmer view of diagnostic procedures such as the Rorschach and other projective techniques, than they do of more objective personality questionnaires and behavioural tests, largely because the former often have dubious validity, incorporate questionable psychoanalytical and psychodynamic interpretations and, usually, are not particularly relatable to effective treatment processes.

Together with many other RET practitioners, Ellis and I take the view that, although assessment interviews and some standard diagnostic tests may at times be useful in exploring clients' disturbances, perhaps the best form of assessment consists of having several RET sessions with the client. Some of the advantages of this kind of therapy-oriented assessment are:

1. In the course of such an assessment procedure, clients can get to work almost immediately on their problems; they can gain therapeutically while being assessed; and they can be helped to suffer less pain, hardship and expense while undergoing treatment.

2. The preferred techniques to be used with different clients are often best determined mainly through experimenting with some of these techniques in the course of the therapeutic process. While the use of standard personality tests, such as the Minnesota Multiphasic Personality Inventory (MMPI), may help the therapist start off with some RET methods rather than other methods with a given client, only by actually experimenting with certain specific methods is the therapist likely to see how the client reacts to them and consequently how they had better be continued or discontinued.

3. Assessment procedures divorced from ongoing psychotherapy (such as giving a whole battery of tests prior to beginning therapy) may be iatrogenic for a number of clients. During this testing process, especially if the assessment procedures are long-winded and take some time to complete, clients may imagine 'horrors' about themselves that lead them astray and make it more difficult for them to benefit from therapy.

4. Certain conventional assessment procedures – for example, the Rorschach and TAT – may wrongly predict problems, symptoms and dynamics that many clients do not really have, and may help lead their therapist up the garden path and away from more scientifically based evaluations.

5. Clients sometimes take diagnoses obtained from complicated assessment procedures as the gospel truth, feel that they have thereby received a valid 'explanation' of what ails them, and wrongly conclude that they have been helped by this 'explanation'. RET assessment procedures, including using therapy itself as an integral part of the assessment process, primarily focus on what clients had better do to change rather than emphasise clever diagnostic 'explanations' of what ails them.

Due to the fact that RET is strongly cognitive, emotive and behavioural, it not only assesses clients' irrational beliefs but also their inappropriate feelings and their self-defeating behaviours. The usual RET assessment process almost always includes the following:

1. Clients are helped to acknowledge and describe their inappropriate feelings (e.g. anxiety, depression, anger and self-hatred), and these are clearly differentiated from their negative appropriate feelings (e.g. disappointment, sadness, frustration and displeasure).
2. They are led to acknowledge and delineate their self-defeating behaviours (e.g. compulsions, addictions, phobias and procrastination) rather then to overemphasise idiosyncratic but non-deleterious behaviours (e.g. unusual devotion to socialising, sex, study or work).
3. They are asked to point out specific activating events in their lives that tend to occur just prior to their experienced disturbed feelings and behaviours.
4. Their rational beliefs which accompany their activating events and which lead to undisturbed consequences are assessed and discussed.
5. Their rational beliefs which accompany their activating events and which lead to disturbed consequences are assessed and discussed.
6. Their rational beliefs which involve absolutistic 'musts' and grandiose demands on themselves, others and the universe are particularly determined.
7. Their second-level irrational beliefs which tend to be derived from their absolutistic 'shoulds' and 'musts' – i.e. their 'awfulising', their 'I-can't-stand-it-itis', their 'damning' of themselves and others, and their unrealistic overgeneralisation – are also revealed.
8. Their irrational beliefs which lead to their disturbance about their disturbances, i.e. their anxiety about their anxiety and their depression about being depressed, are particularly revealed and discussed.

As these specialised RET assessment and diagnostic procedures are instituted, specific treatment plans are made, normally in close collaboration with the clients, to work first on the most important and self-sabotaging emotional and behavioural symptoms that they present and later on related and possibly less important symptoms. RET practitioners, however, always try to maintain an exceptionally open-minded, sceptical and experimental atttude towards clients and their problems, so that what at first seem to be

Consultation Center

Institute for Advanced Study in Rational Psychotherapy

45 East 65th Street • New York, N. Y. 10021

Personality Data Form — Part 2

Instructions: Read each of the following items and circle after each one the word STRONGLY, MODERATELY, or WEAKLY to indicate how much you believe in the statement described in the item. Thus, if you strongly believe that it is awful to make a mistake when other people are watching, circle the word STRONGLY in item 1; and if you weakly believe that it is intolerable to be disapproved by others, circle the word WEAKLY in item 2. DO NOT SKIP ANY ITEMS. Be as honest as you can possibly be.

Acceptance

1. I believe that it is awful to make a mistake when other people are watching — STRONGLY MODERATELY WEAKLY

2. I believe that it is intolerable to be disapproved of by others — STRONGLY MODERATELY WEAKLY

3. I believe that it is awful for people to know certain undesirable things about one's family or one's background — STRONGLY MODERATELY WEAKLY

4. I believe that it is shameful to be looked down upon by people for having less than they have — STRONGLY MODERATELY WEAKLY

5. I believe that it is horrible to be the center of attention of others who may be highly critical — STRONGLY MODERATELY WEAKLY

6. I believe it is terribly painful when one is criticized by a person one respects — STRONGLY MODERATELY WEAKLY

7. I believe that it is awful to have people disapprove of the way one looks or dresses — STRONGLY MODERATELY WEAKLY

8. I believe that it is very embarrassing if people discover what one really is like — STRONGLY MODERATELY WEAKLY

9. I believe that it is awful to be alone — STRONGLY MODERATELY WEAKLY

10. I believe that it is horrible if one does not have the love or approval of certain special people who are important to one — STRONGLY MODERATELY WEAKLY

11. I believe that one must have others on whom one can always depend for help — STRONGLY MODERATELY WEAKLY

Frustration

12. I believe that it is intolerable to have things go along slowly and not be settled quickly — STRONGLY MODERATELY WEAKLY

13. I believe that it's too hard to get down to work at things it often would be better for one to do — STRONGLY MODERATELY WEAKLY

14. I believe that it is terrible that life is so full of inconveniences and frustrations — STRONGLY MODERATELY WEAKLY

15. I believe that people who keep one waiting frequently are pretty worthless and deserve to be boycotted — STRONGLY MODERATELY WEAKLY

16. I believe that it is terrible if one lacks desirable traits that other people possess — STRONGLY MODERATELY WEAKLY

17. I believe that it is intolerable when other people do not do one's bidding or give one what one wants — STRONGLY MODERATELY WEAKLY

18. I believe that some people are unbearably stupid or nasty and that one must get them to change — STRONGLY MODERATELY WEAKLY

19. I believe that it is too hard for one to accept serious responsibility — STRONGLY MODERATELY WEAKLY

20. I believe that it is dreadful that one cannot get what one wants without making a real effort to get it — STRONGLY MODERATELY WEAKLY

21. I believe that things are too rough in this world and that therefore it is legitimate for one to feel sorry for oneself — STRONGLY MODERATELY WEAKLY

22. I believe that it is too hard to persist at many of the things one starts, especially when the going gets rough — STRONGLY MODERATELY WEAKLY

23. I believe it is terrible that life is so unexciting and boring — STRONGLY MODERATELY WEAKLY

24. I believe it is awful for one to have to discipline oneself — STRONGLY MODERATELY WEAKLY

Figure 3.1 Personality data form. (Reproduced with the permission of the Institute for Rational–Emotive Therapy, New York, USA.)

56

Injustice

25. I believe that people who do wrong things should suffer strong revenge for their acts — STRONGLY / MODERATELY / WEAKLY

26. I believe that wrong doers and immoral people should be severely condemned — STRONGLY / MODERATELY / WEAKLY

27. I believe that people who commit unjust acts are bastards and that they should be severely punished — STRONGLY / MODERATELY / WEAKLY

Achievement

28. I believe that it is horrible for one to perform poorly — STRONGLY / MODERATELY / WEAKLY

29. I believe that it is awful if one fails at important things — STRONGLY / MODERATELY / WEAKLY

30. I believe that it is terrible for one to make a mistake when one has to make important decisions — STRONGLY / MODERATELY / WEAKLY

31. I believe that it is terrifying for one to take risks or to try new things — STRONGLY / MODERATELY / WEAKLY

Worth

32. I believe that some of one's thoughts or actions are unforgivable — STRONGLY / MODERATELY / WEAKLY

33. I believe that if one keeps failing at things one is a pretty worthless person — STRONGLY / MODERATELY / WEAKLY

34. I believe that killing oneself is preferable to a miserable life of failure — STRONGLY / MODERATELY / WEAKLY

35. I believe that things are so ghastly that one cannot help feel like crying much of the time — STRONGLY / MODERATELY / WEAKLY

36. I believe that it is frightfully hard for one to stand up for oneself and not give in too easily to others — STRONGLY / MODERATELY / WEAKLY

37. I believe that when one has shown poor personality traits for a long time, it is hopeless for one to change — STRONGLY / MODERATELY / WEAKLY

38. I believe that if one does not usually see things clearly and act well on them, one is hopelessly stupid — STRONGLY / MODERATELY / WEAKLY

39. I believe that it is awful to have no good meaning or purpose in life — STRONGLY / MODERATELY / WEAKLY

57

Control

40. I believe that one cannot enjoy himself today because of his poor early life
STRONGLY MODERATELY WEAKLY

41. I believe that if one kept failing at important things in the past, one must inevitably keep failing in the future
STRONGLY MODERATELY WEAKLY

42. I believe that once one's parents train one to act and feel in certain ways, there is little one can do to act or feel better
STRONGLY MODERATELY WEAKLY

43. I believe that strong emotions like anxiety and rage are caused by external conditions and events and that one has little or no control over them
STRONGLY MODERATELY WEAKLY

Certainty

44. I believe it would be terrible if there were no higher being or purpose on which to rely
STRONGLY MODERATELY WEAKLY

45. I believe that if one does not keep doing certain things over and over again something bad will happen if one stops
STRONGLY MODERATELY WEAKLY

46. I believe that things must be in good order for one to be comfortable
STRONGLY MODERATELY WEAKLY

Catastrophizing

47. I believe that it is awful if one's future is not guaranteed
STRONGLY MODERATELY WEAKLY

48. I believe that it is frightening that there are no guarantees that accidents and serious illnesses will not occur
STRONGLY MODERATELY WEAKLY

49. I believe that it is terrifying for one to go to new places or meet a new group of people
STRONGLY MODERATELY WEAKLY

50. I believe that it is ghastly for one to be faced with the possibility of dying
STRONGLY MODERATELY WEAKLY

Figure 3.1 (continued)

their crucial and most debilitating ideas, feelings and actions may later be seen in a different light, and emphasis may be changed to working on other equally or more pernicious irrationalities which might not be evident during the clients' early sessions.

RET therapists, in general, spend little time gathering background information on their clients, although they may ask them to fill out forms designed to assess which irrational ideas they spontaneously endorse at the outset of therapy (Figure 3.1). Rather, they are likely to ask clients for a description of their major problems(s). As clients describe their problems, RET therapists intervene fairly early to break these down into their ABC components. If clients begin by describing 'A' (the activating event) then the therapists ask for 'C' (their emotional and/or behavioural reactions). However, if clients begin by outlining C, therapists ask for a brief description of A.

In RET, A and C are normally assessed before B and are usually assessed in the order that clients report them. C refers to both emotional and behavioural consequences of the preferential or musturbatory evaluations made at B. Careful assessment of emotional Cs is advocated in RET, because they serve as a major indicator of what type of evaluations are to be found at B. In this regard, it is important to reiterate that 'appropriate' negative emotions are different from 'inappropriate' negative emotions. Emotions such as sadness, regret, annoyance and concern are termed 'appropriate' in RET in that they are deemed to stem from rational, preferential evaluations at B and encourage people to attempt to change, for the better, obnoxious situations at A. The 'inappropriate' versions of the above emotional states are depression, guilt, anger and anxiety. These are deemed to stem from irrational, musturbatory evaluations at B and tend to interfere with people's constructive attempts to change undesirable situations.

When emotional Cs are being assessed, it is important to realise three important points. First, clients do not necessarily use affective terminology in the same way RET therapists do. It is often helpful to inform them about the nature of the unique discriminations made between 'appropriate' and 'inappropriate' negative emotional states so that therapist and client can come to use a shared emotional 'language'. Secondly, emotional Cs are often 'chained' together. For example, anger is frequently chained to anxiety in that anger can be experienced to 'cover up' feelings of inadequacy. Also we can feel depressed after a threat to our self-esteem emerges (Wessler, 1981). Finally, rational–emotive therapists had better realise that clients do not always want to change every 'inappropriate' negative emotion as defined by RET theory, i.e. they may not see a particular 'inappropriate' emotion (e.g. anger) as being truly 'inappropriate' or self-defeating. Thus, a good deal of flexibility and clinical acumen is called for in the assessment of emotional Cs to be targeted for change.

Whilst C is assessed mainly by the client's verbal report, occasionally clients experience difficulty in accurately reporting their emotional and behavioural problems. When this occurs, RET therapists may use a number of methods to facilitate this part of the assessment process. Thus a variety of emotive (e.g. gestalt two-chair dialogue, psychodrama), imagery, and other techniques (e.g. keeping an emotive/behaviour diary) can be used in this respect (Dryden, 1984b).

Whilst I have chosen to highlight the assessment of emotional Cs, similar points can be made about the assessment of behavioural Cs. As noted earlier, withdrawal, procrastination, alcoholism and substance abuse are generally regarded as dysfunctional behaviours and related to irrational, musturbatory evaluations at B (Ellis, 1982c).

When B is assessed, some rational–emotive therapists prefer to assess fully the client's inferences in search of the most relevant inference that is linked to the client's musturbatory evaluations, given that C is self-defeating. This is known as *inference chaining* (Moore, 1983). An example of this procedure is described below:

Therapist: So what was your major feeling here?
Client: I guess I was angry.
Therapist: Angry about what? (Here the therapist has obtained C and is probing for A.)
Client: I was angry that he did not send me a birthday card. (Client provides inference about A.)
Therapist: And what was anger-provoking about that? (Probing to see whether this is the most relevant inference in the chain.)
Client: Well ... He promised me he would remember. (Inference 2.)
Therapist: And because he broke his promise? (Probing for relevance of inference 2.)
Client: I felt that he didn't care enough about me. (Inference 3.)
Therapist: But let's assume that for a moment. What would be distressing about that? (Probing for relevance of inference 3.)
Client: Well, he might leave me. (Inference 4.)
Therapist: And if he did? (Probing for relevance of inference 4.)
Client: I'd be left alone. (Inference 5.)
Therapist: And if you were alone? (Probing for relevance of inference 5.)
Client: I couldn't stand that. (Irrational belief.)
Therapist: OK, so let's back up a minute. What would be most distressing for you, the birthday card incident, the broken promise, the fact that he doesn't care, being left by your husband or being alone? (Therapist checks to see which inference is most relevant in the chain.)
Client: Definitely being alone.

This example shows that not only are inferences chained together but, as mentioned earlier, emotions are too. Here anger was chained with anxiety about being alone. Whilst this rational–emotive therapist chose then to dispute the client's irrational belief underlying her anxiety, he still has to deal with her anger-creating belief. Other rational–emotive therapists may have chosen to take the first element in the chain (anger about the missing birthday card) and disputed the irrational belief related to anger. Skilful RET therapists do succeed in discovering the hidden issues underlying the 'presenting problem' during the disputing process. It is important for RET therapists to assess correctly *all* relevant issues related to a presenting problem. How they do this depends upon personal style and how particular clients react to different assessment procedures.

When irrational musturbatory beliefs are assessed clients are helped to see the link between these irrational beliefs and their 'inappropriate' affective and behavioural consequences at C. Some rational–emotive therapists like to give a short lecture at this point on the role of the 'musts' in emotional disturbance and how they can be distinguished from 'preferences'. Ellis, for example, often uses the following teaching dialogue:

Ellis: Imagine that you prefer to have a minimum $11 in your pocket at all times and you discover you only have $10. How will you feel?

Client: Frustrated.

Ellis: Right. Or you'd feel concerned or sad but you wouldn't kill yourself. Right?

Client: Right.

Ellis: OK. Now this time imagine that you absolutely *have to* have a minimum of $11 in your pocket at all times. You *must* have it, it is a *necessity*. You *must*, you *must*, you *must*, have a minimum of $11 and again you look and you find you only have $10. How will you feel?

Client: Very anxious.

Ellis: Right, or depressed. Right. Now remember it's the same $11 but a different belief. OK, now this time you still have that same belief. You *have to* have a minimum of $11 at all times, you *must*. It's absolutely *essential*. But this time you look in your pocket and find that you've got $12. How will you feel?

Client: Relieved, content.

Ellis: Right. But with that same belief – you *have to* have a minimum of $11 at all times – something will soon occur to you to scare you shitless. What do you think that would be?

Client: What if I lose $2?

Ellis: Right. What if I lose $2, what if I spend $2, what if I get robbed? That's right. Now the moral of this model – which applies to all humans, rich or poor, black or white, male or female, young or old, in the past or in the future, assuming that humans are still human – is: People make themselves miserable if they don't get what they think they *must* but they are also panicked when they do – because of the *must*. For even if they have what they think they *must*, they could always lose it.

Client: So I have no chance to be happy when I don't have what I think I *must* – and little chance of remaining unanxious when I do have it?

Ellis: Right? Your *must*urbation will get you nowhere – except depressed or panicked!

An important goal of the assessment stage of RET is to help clients distinguish between their primary problems (e.g. depression, anxiety, withdrawal, addiction) and their secondary problems, i.e. their problems about their primary problems (e.g. depression about depression, anxiety about anxiety, shame about withdrawal and guilt about addiction). Rational–emotive therapists often assess secondary problems before primary problems because these often require prior therapeutic attention – because, for example, clients frequently find it difficult to focus on their original problem of anxiety when, for example, they are severely blaming themselves for being anxious. Secondary problems are assessed in the same manner as primary problems.

When particular problems have been adequately assessed according to the ABC model and clients clearly see the link between their irrational beliefs and their dysfunctional emotional and behavioural consequences, then therapists can proceed to the disputing stage. The initial purpose of disputing is to help clients gain *intellectual insight* into the fact that there is no evidence in support of the existence of their absolutistic demands, or the irrational derivatives of these demands ('awfulising', 'I-can't-stand-it-itis', and 'damnation'). There exists only evidence that if they stay with their non-absolutistic preferences and if these are not fulfilled, they will get unfortunate or 'bad' results whilst if they are fulfilled they will get desirable or 'good' results. Intellectual insight in RET is defined as an acknowledgement that an irrational belief frequently leads to emotional disturbance and dysfunctional behaviour and that a rational belief almost always abets emotional health. But when people see and hold rational beliefs only weakly and occasionally, they have intellectual insight that may not help them change (Ellis, 1963, 1985a). So RET does not stop with intellectual insight but uses it as a springboard for the working-through phase of RET. In this phase clients are encouraged to use a large variety of cognitive, emotive and behavioural techniques designed to help them achieve emotional insight. Emotional insight in RET is defined as a very strong and frequently held belief that an irrational idea is dysfunctional and that a rational idea is helpful (Ellis, 1963). When a person has achieved emotional insight he or she thinks–feels–behaves according to the rational belief.

Two other points relevant to the assessment stage of RET bear mention. First, therapists had better be alert to problems in *both* areas: ego and discomfort disturbance. In particular, ego and discomfort disturbance often interact, and careful assessment is frequently required to disentangle one from the other. Secondly, RET practitioners pay particular attention to other ways in which humans perpetuate their psychological problems and attempt to assess these carefully in therapy. Thus, humans often seek to defend themselves from threats to their 'ego' and sense of comfort. Therapists are often aware that much dysfunctional behaviour is defensive and help their clients to identify the irrational beliefs that underlie such defensive dysfunctional behaviour. In addition, psychological problems are sometimes perpetuated because the person defines their consequences as pay-offs. These pay-offs also require careful assessment if productive therapeutic strategies are to be implemented.

Treatment Strategies in RET

There are two forms of RET – preferential and general (Ellis, 1980b). General RET is synonymous with cognitive-behaviour therapy (CBT), whilst preferential RET is unique in a number of important respects. Because a major aim of this book is to present the distinctive features of RET, the emphasis here will be on preferential RET (although it should be noted that RET therapists routinely use strategies derived from both forms of RET). The major goal of preferential RET is an ambitious one: to encourage clients to make a profound philosophical change in the two main areas of ego disturbance and discomfort disturbance. This involves helping clients, as far as is humanly possible, to give up their irrational musturbatory thinking processes and to replace them with rational non-absolute thinking as discussed in Chapter 1.

In preferential RET, the major goals are to help clients pursue their long-range basic goals and purposes and to help them do so as effectively as possible by fully accepting themselves and tolerating unchangeable uncomfortable life conditions. Practitioners of preferential RET further strive to help clients obtain the skills that they can use to prevent the development of future disturbance. In encouraging clients to achieve and maintain this profound philosophical change, rational–emotive therapists implement the following strategies. They help their clients see that:

1. Emotional and behavioural disturbances have cognitive antecedents, and these cognitions normally take the form of absolutistic devout evaluations. RET practitioners train their clients to observe their own psychological disturbances and to trace these back to their ideological roots.
2. People have a distinct measure of self-determination and can thus *choose* to work at undisturbing themselves. Thus, clients are shown that they are not slaves to their biologically based irrational thinking processes.
3. People can implement their choices and maximise their freedom by actively working at changing their irrational musturbatory beliefs. This is best achieved by employing cognitive, emotive and behavioural methods – often in quite a forceful and vigorous manner (Ellis, 1979d).

With the majority of clients, from the first session onward RET therapists are likely to use strategies designed to effect profound philosophical change. The therapist begins therapy with the hypothesis that this particular client may be able to achieve such change and thus begins preferential RET, which he or she will abandon after collecting sufficient data to reject the initial hypothesis. I regularly implement this viewpoint, which is based on the notion that the client's response to therapy is the best indicator of his or her prognosis. It is not known what proportion of RET therapists share and regularly implement this position.

When it is clear that the client is not able to achieve philosophical change, whether on a particular issue or in general, the therapist often switches to general RET and uses methods to effect inferential and behaviourally based change. A good example of this change in strategy is one reported by a therapist of our acquaintance. He was working with a middle-aged married woman who reported feeling furious every time her ageing father telephoned her and enquired 'Noo, what's doing?'. She inferred that this was a gross invasion of her privacy and absolutistically insisted that he had no right to do so. The therapist initially intervened with a preferential RET strategy by attempting to dispute this client's dogmatic belief and tried to help her see that there was no law in the universe that stated that he *must* not do such a thing. Meeting initial resistance, the therapist persisted with different variations of this theme, all to no avail. Changing tack, he began to implement a general RET strategy designed to help the client question her inference that her father was actually invading her privacy. Given her father's age, the therapist enquired, was it more likely that his question represented his usual manner of beginning telephone conversations rather than an intense desire to pry into her affairs? This enquiry proved successful in that the client's rage subsided because she began to reinterpret her father's motives. Interestingly enough, although he returned to the specialised strategy later, the therapist never succeeded in helping this client to give up her irrational musturbatory belief! However, some clients are more amenable to re-evaluating their irrational musturbatory beliefs *after* they have been helped to correct distorted inferences. We had better do research on this topic if we are to answer the question, 'Which strategy is most appropriate for which clients at which stage in therapy?'. Meanwhile, it is important to note that RET therapists, if they follow our lead, are unique in that they are more likely to challenge musturbatory cognitions and to dispute these self-defeating beliefs of their clients much earlier in the therapeutic process than do other cognitive–behavioural therapists. Further differences between preferential RET and general RET (or cognitive–behaviour therapy) will be discussed in Chapter 20.

Major Treatment Techniques in RET

RET represents a major form of eclecticism known as 'theoretically consistent eclecticism' (Dryden, 1987a) in that techniques are liberally borrowed from other therapeutic systems but employed for purposes usually consistent with RET's underlying theory. In particular, RET therapists are mindful of the short-term and long-term effects of particular therapeutic techniques and will rarely employ a technique that has beneficial immediate but harmful long-range consequences. Whilst rational–emotive therapists employ a large number of cognitive, emotive and behavioural techniques, only the major ones will be discussed here. It should be noted at the outset that probably all the following techniques have cognitive, emotive and behavioural elements to them and that 'pure' techniques (e.g. purely cognitive) probably do not exist. Techniques are grouped below to show which psychological process predominates.

Cognitive techniques

Probably the most common technique employed by RET therapists with the majority of their clients is the *disputing of irrational beliefs*. There are three subcategories of disputing (Phadke, 1982): *detecting* consists of looking for irrational beliefs – particularly 'musts', 'shoulds', 'oughts' and 'have to's' – that lead to self-defeating emotions and behaviours. *Debating* consists of the therapist asking a number of questions that are designed to help the client give up irrational beliefs. Questions such as 'Where is the evidence ...?', 'In what way does this belief have truth or falseness?' and 'What makes it so?' are frequently employed. The therapist proceeds with such questioning until the client acknowledges the falseness of his or her irrational belief and, in addition, acknowledges the truth of its rational alternative. *Discriminating* involves the therapist helping the client to clearly distinguish between his or her non-absolute values (his or her wants, preferences, likes and desires) and his or her absolutistic values (his or her needs, demands and imperatives). Rational–emotive therapists are often very creative in their use of disputing sequences (e.g. Young, 1984a, b, c) and sometimes employ such methods in a highly dramatic fashion (Dryden, 1984b). A formal version of disputing that includes some of its main components is known as DIBS (disputing irrational beliefs). Ellis has outlined its form thus:

Question 1:   What irrational belief do I want to dispute and surrender?
Answer: I must be as effective and sexually fulfilled as most other women.
Question 2:   Can I rationally support this belief?
Answer: ....
Question 3:   What evidence exists of the truth of this belief?
Answer: ....
Question 4:   What evidence exists of the falseness of my belief that I must be as orgasmic as other women are?
Answer: ....
Question 5:   What are the worst possible things that could actually happen to me if I never achieved the orgasm that I think I must achieve?
Answer: ....
Question 6:   What good things could happen or could I make happen if I never achieved the heights of orgasm that I think I must achieve?
Answer: ....

(Ellis, 1979c, pp. 79–80)

DIBS is one example of *cognitive homework* that is frequently given to clients to do between sessions after the client has been trained to use them. Other examples appear in Figures 3.2 and 3.3. The purpose of these forms is to provide a clear framework for clients to do disputing for themselves.

Clients can also use audio cassettes as an aid to the disputing process. They can listen to audio tapes of therapy sessions and also dispute their own irrational beliefs on tape (*disputing on tape*). Here they initiate and sustain a dialogue between the rational and irrational parts of themselves (Ellis, 1987).

Clients who do not have the intellectual skills necessary to perform cognitive disputing are usually helped to develop *rational self-statements* that they can memorise or write out on 3 inch 3 5 inch cards and repeat at various times between sessions. An example developed by me with a client was: 'Just because my being overweight is bad doesn't mean that I am bad. My overeating makes me too heavy and is therefore wrong, but I can correct it and get better results.'

Three cognitive methods that therapists often suggest to their clients to help them reinforce that new rational philosophy are: (1) *bibliotherapy*, where clients are given self-help books and materials to read (e.g. Young, 1974b; Ellis and Harper, 1975; Ellis and Becker, 1982); (2) listening to *audio cassettes of RET lectures* on various themes (e.g. Ellis, 1971b, 1972b, 1976b); and (3) *using RET with others*, where clients use RET to help their friends and relatives with their problems. In doing so they gain practice at using rational arguments (Ellis and Abrahms, 1978).

A number of semantic methods are also employed in RET. *Defining* techniques are sometimes employed, the purpose of which is to help clients use language in a less self-defeating manner. Thus, instead of 'I can't ...' clients are urged to use 'I haven't yet...'. *Referenting* techniques are also employed (Danysh, 1974). Here, clients are encouraged to list both the negative and positive referents of a particular concept such as 'smoking'. This method is employed to counteract clients' tendencies to focus on the positive aspects of a harmful habit and to neglect its negative aspects.

RET therapists also employ a number of imagery techniques. Thus, *rational–emotive imagery* (Maultsby and Ellis, 1974; Ellis, 1979c); is often employed. Clients thereby gain practice at changing their 'inappropriate' negative emotions to 'appropriate' ones (C) while maintaining a vivid image of the negative event at A. Here, they are in fact learning to change their self-defeating emotions by changing their underlying beliefs at B. *Time projection* imagery methods are also employed in RET (Lazarus, 1984). Thus, a client may say that a particular event would be 'awful' if it occurred. Rather than directly challenging this irrational belief at this stage, the therapist may temporarily go along with this but help the client to picture what life might be like at regular intervals after the 'awful' event has occurred. In this way clients are indirectly helped to change their irrational belief because they come to 'see' that life goes on after the 'awful' event, that they will usually recover from it, and that they can continue to pursue their original goals or develop new ones. Such realisations encourage the person to re-evaluate his or her irrational beliefs. Finally, a number of therapists have successfully employed RET in a *hypnosis* paradigm (e.g. Boutin and Tosi, 1983; Golden, 1983).

Emotive techniques

Rational–emotive therapy has often been falsely criticised for neglecting emotive aspects of psychotherapy. However, this is far from the truth, and

RET SELF-HELP FORM

Institute for Rational-Emotive Therapy
45 East 65th Street, New York, N.Y. 10021
(212) 535-0822

(A) ACTIVATING EVENTS, thoughts, or feelings that happened just before I felt emotionally disturbed or acted self-defeatingly: _____

(C) CONSEQUENCE or CONDITION—disturbed feeling or self-defeating behavior—that I produced and would like to change: _____

(B) BELIEFS—Irrational BELIEFS (IBs) leading to my CONSEQUENCE (emotional disturbance or self-defeating behavior). Circle all that apply to these ACTIVATING EVENTS (A).	(D) DISPUTES for each circled IRRATIONAL BELIEF. Examples: "Why MUST I do very well?" "Where is it written that I am a BAD PERSON?" "Where is the evidence that I MUST be approved or accepted?"	(E) EFFECTIVE RATIONAL BELIEFS (RBs) to replace my IRRATIONAL BELIEFS (IBs). Examples: "I'd PREFER to do very well but I don't HAVE TO." "I am a PERSON WHO acted badly, not a BAD PERSON." "There is no evidence that I HAVE TO be approved, though I would LIKE to be."
1. I MUST do well or very well!	....	....
2. I am a BAD OR WORTHLESS PERSON when I act weakly or stupidly.	....	....

3. I MUST be approved or accepted by people I find important!

....

4. I am a BAD, UNLOVABLE PERSON if I get rejected.

....

5. People MUST treat me fairly and give me what I NEED!

....

6. People who act immorally are undeserving, ROTTEN PEOPLE!

....

7. People MUST live up to my expectations or it is TERRIBLE!

....

8. My life MUST have few major hassles or troubles.

....

9. I CAN'T STAND really bad things or very difficult people!

....

Figure 3.2   RET self-help form. (Reproduced with the permission of the Institute for Rational–Emotive Therapy, NEW York, USA.)

(OVER)

10. It's **AWFUL** or **HORRIBLE** when major things don't go my way!

11. **I CAN'T STAND IT** when life is really unfair!

12. **I NEED** to be loved by someone who matters to me a lot!

13. **I NEED** a good deal of immediate gratification and **HAVE TO** feel miserable when I don't get it!

<u>Additional Irrational Beliefs:</u>

14.

15.

16.

17.

18.

(F) FEELINGS and BEHAVIORS I experienced after arriving at my EFFECTIVE RATIONAL BELIEFS: _____

I WILL WORK HARD TO REPEAT MY EFFECTIVE RATIONAL BELIEFS FORCEFULLY TO MYSELF ON MANY OCCASIONS SO THAT I CAN MAKE MYSELF LESS DISTURBED NOW AND ACT LESS SELF-DEFEATINGLY IN THE FUTURE.

Joyce Sichel, Ph.D. and Albert Ellis, Ph.D.

Copyright © 1984 by the Institute for Rational-Emotive Therapy.

Figure 3.2 (continued)

100 forms $10.00
1000 forms $80.00

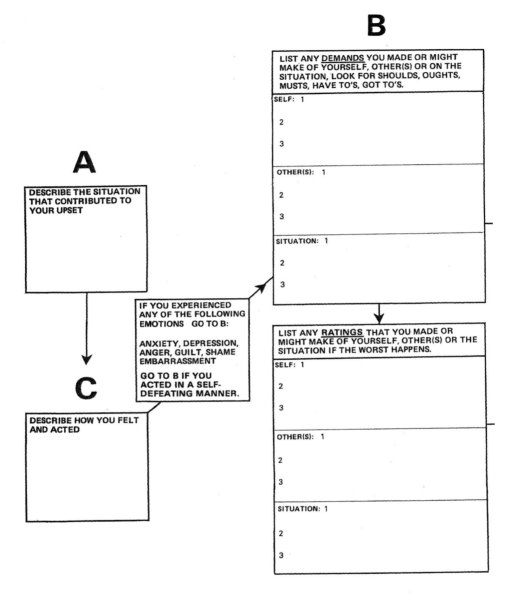

B

LIST ANY <u>DEMANDS</u> YOU MADE OR MIGHT MAKE OF YOURSELF, OTHER(S) OR ON THE SITUATION, LOOK FOR SHOULDS, OUGHTS, MUSTS, HAVE TO'S, GOT TO'S.

SELF: 1

2

3

OTHER(S): 1

2

3

SITUATION: 1

2

3

A

DESCRIBE THE SITUATION THAT CONTRIBUTED TO YOUR UPSET

IF YOU EXPERIENCED ANY OF THE FOLLOWING EMOTIONS   GO TO B:

ANXIETY, DEPRESSION, ANGER, GUILT, SHAME EMBARRASSMENT

GO TO B IF YOU ACTED IN A SELF-DEFEATING MANNER.

C

DESCRIBE HOW YOU FELT AND ACTED

LIST ANY <u>RATINGS</u> THAT YOU MADE OR MIGHT MAKE OF YOURSELF, OTHER(S) OR THE SITUATION IF THE WORST HAPPENS.

SELF: 1

2

3

OTHER(S): 1

2

3

SITUATION: 1

2

3

Figure 3.3   A guide for solving your emotional and behavioural problems by re-examining your self-defeating thoughts and attitudes.

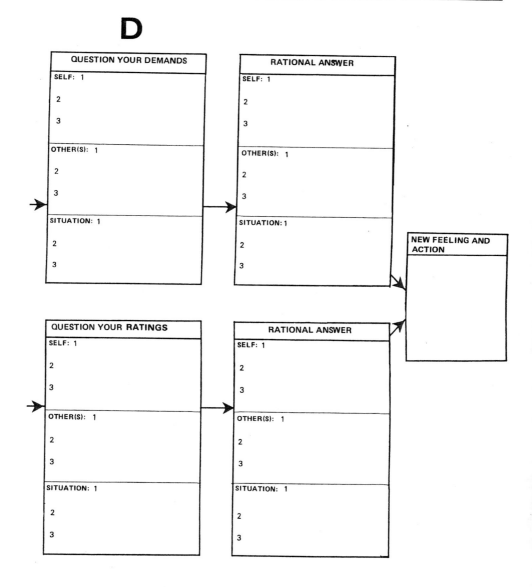

Figure 3.3 (continued)

RET therapists frequently employ a number of emotive techniques. As has already been shown, RET therapists offer their clients the emotional attitude of *unconditional acceptance*. No matter how badly clients behave, their therapists strive to accept them as fallible humans but do not go along with their bad behaviour. RET therapists use a variety of emotive techniques that are designed to help their clients challenge their irrational beliefs. First, a number of *humorous* methods are employed to encourage clients to think rationally by not taking themselves too seriously (Ellis, 1977a, b). Secondly, RET therapists do not hesitate to model a rational philosophy through *self-disclosure*. They honestly admit that they have had similar problems and show that they overcame them by using RET. Thus I frequently tell clients that I used to feel ashamed of my stammer. I then relate how I accepted myself with my speech impediment and how I forced myself to tolerate the discomfort of speaking in public whenever the opportunity arose (see Chapter 9). Thirdly, RET therapists frequently use a number of *stories, mottoes, parables, witticisms, poems* and *aphorisms* as adjuncts to cognitive disputing techniques (Wessler and Wessler, 1980). Fourthly, Ellis and I have written a number of rational humorous songs that are designed to present philosophies in an amusing and memorable format (Ellis, 1977a, b, 1981b). The following is a rational humorous song written by me to the tune of 'God Save the Queen':

God save my precious spleen
Send me a life serene
God save my spleen!
Protect me from things odious
Give me a life melodious
And if things get too onerous
I'll whine, bawl, and scream!

In an important paper, Ellis first advocated the use of force and energy in the practice of psychotherapy (Ellis, 1979d). RET is unique among the cognitive–behavioural therapies in emphasising the employment of such interventions that fully involve clients' emotions. Thus, RET therapists suggest that clients can help themselves go from intellectual to emotional insight by *vigorously disputing* their irrational beliefs. Vigour is often employed by clients in *rational role-reversal* where they forcefully and dramatically adopt the role of their rational 'self', whose goal is successfully to dispute self-defeating beliefs as articulated by their irrational 'self'. Force and energy also play a significant part in RET's now famous *shame-attacking exercises* (Ellis, 1969; Ellis and Becker, 1982). Here clients deliberately seek to act 'shamefully' in public in order to accept themselves and to tolerate the ensuing discomfort. Because clients had better neither harm themselves nor other people, minor infractions of social rules often serve as appropriate shame-attacking exercises (e.g. calling out the time in a crowded department store, wearing bizarre clothes designed to attract public attention, and going into a hardware store and asking if they sell tobacco). *Risk-taking exercises* come into the same category. Here clients deliberately force themselves to take calculated risks in areas where they wish to make changes. Whilst disputing relevant irrational beliefs, Ellis overcame his anxiety about approaching women by deliberately forcing himself to speak to 100 women in the Bronx Botanical Gardens. I pushed myself to speak on national and local radio as part of a campaign to overcome my public-speaking anxiety. Both of us took these risks while showing ourselves that nothing 'awful' would result from such experiences. *Repeating rational self-statements in a positive and forceful manner* is also often used in conjunction with such exercises (Ellis, 1985a).

Behavioural techniques

RET has advocated the use of behavioural techniques (particularly *homework assignments*) from its inception in 1955 because it is realised that cognitive change is very often facilitated by behavioural change (Emmelkamp, Kuipers and Eggeraat, 1978). Because RET therapists are concerned to help clients raise their level of frustration tolerance, they encourage them to carry out homework assignments based on in vivo *desensitisation* and *flooding* paradigms rather then those that are based on the gradual desensitisation paradigm (Ellis and Grieger, 1977; Ellis and Abrahms, 1978; Ellis, 1979c; Ellis and Becker, 1982). However, pragmatic considerations do have to be considered, and some clients refuse to carry out such assignments. When this occurs, RET therapists would negotiate a compromise encouraging such clients to undertake tasks that are sufficiently challenging for them but that are not overwhelming, given their present status (Dryden, 1985b).

Other behavioural methods frequently employed in RET include (1) '*Stay in there*' *activities* (Grieger and Boyd, 1980), which present clients with opportunities to tolerate chronic discomfort while remaining in '*uncomfortable*' situations for a long period of time; (2) *antiprocrastination exercises*, where clients are encouraged to push themselves to start tasks sooner rather than later, while again tolerating the discomfort of breaking the 'mañana' habit; (3) the use of *rewards and penalties*, which are employed to encourage clients to undertake uncomfortable assignments in the pursuit of their long-range goals (Ellis, 1979c) (stiff penalties are found to be particularly helpful with chronically resistant clients – Ellis, 1985a); and (4) Kelly's *fixed role therapy*, sometimes employed in RET, where clients are encouraged to act 'as if' they already think rationally, to enable them to get the experience that change is possible.

A number of other behavioural methods are employed in both preferential and general RET (e.g. various forms of *skills training methods*). When these are used in preferential RET they are done to encourage philosophical change, whereas in general RET they are employed to teach clients skills that are absent from their repertoire. When skill training is the goal in preferential RET, it is employed *along with* disputing of irrational beliefs and while some measure of philosophical change is being sought.

Techniques that are avoided in RET

By now it will be clear that RET is a multimodal form of therapy that advocates the employment of techniques in the cognitive, emotive and behavioural modalities. However, because the choice of therapeutic techniques is inspired by RET theory, the following available therapeutic techniques are avoided or used sparingly in the practice of RET (Ellis, 1979c, 1983c, 1984b).

- Techniques that help people become more dependent (e.g. undue therapist warmth as strong reinforcement and the creation and analysis of a transference neurosis).
- Techniques that encourage people to become more gullible and suggestible (e.g. pollyannaish positive thinking).
- Techniques that are long-winded and inefficient (e.g. psychoanalytical methods in general and free association in particular, encouraging clients to give lengthy descriptions of activating experiences at A).
- Methods that help people feel better in the short term rather than get better in the long term (Ellis, 1972a) (e.g. some experiential techniques such as fully expressing one's feelings in a dramatic, cathartic and abreactive manner, i.e. some gestalt methods and primal techniques. The danger here is that such methods may encourage people to practise irrational philosophies underlying such emotions as anger).
- Techniques that distract clients from working on their irrational philosophies (e.g. relaxation methods, yoga and other cognitive distraction methods). These methods may be employed, however, *along with* cognitive disputing designed to yield some philosophical change.
- Methods that may unwittingly reinforce clients' philosophy of low frustration tolerance (e.g. gradual desensitisation).
- Techniques that include an antiscientific philosophy (e.g. faith healing and mysticism).
- Techniques that attempt to change activating events (A) before or without showing clients how to change their irrational beliefs (B) (e.g. some strategic family systems techniques).
- Techniques that have dubious validity (e.g. neurolinguistic programming).

Finally, to reiterate, RET therapists do not absolutistically avoid using the above methods. They may on certain occasions with certain clients utilise such techniques, particularly for pragmatic purposes. For example, if faith healing is the only method that will prevent some clients from harming themselves, then RET therapists might either employ it themselves or, more probably, refer such clients to a faith healer (Ellis, 1985a).

Overcoming Obstacles to Client Progress

When RET is practised efficiently and effectively and when clients understand and are prepared continually to implement its basic concepts, then it can achieve remarkable results. However, frequently (and perhaps more frequently than most therapists are prepared to admit!) various obstacles to client progress are encountered in the practice of RET (and indeed all other forms of therapy). Three major forms of obstacles are deemed to occur in RET: (1) 'relationship' obstacles, (2) therapist obstacles and (3) client obstacles (Ellis, 1985d).

'Relationship' obstacles to client progress

These can be first attributed to poor therapist–client matching. Such mismatching may occur for many reasons. Thus, clients 'may have a therapist who, according to their idiosyncratic tastes or preferences, is too young or too old, too liberal or too conservative, too active or too passive' (Ellis, 1983d, p. 29). If these 'relationship match' obstacles persist, then it is preferable for that client to be transferred to a therapist with more suitable traits. Other relationship obstacles may occur because the therapist and client may get on 'too well' and get distracted from the more mundane tasks of therapy. In such cases, the paradox is that if the client improves, the 'life' of the satisfactory relationship is threatened. As a result, collusion may occur between therapist and client to avoid making therapy as effective an endeavour as it might otherwise be. This problem can be largely overcome if the therapist helps first himself or herself and then the client to overcome the philosophy of low frustration tolerance implicit in this collusive short-range hedonism.

Therapist obstacles to client progress

There are two major types of therapist obstacles: skill-oriented obstacles and disturbance-oriented obstacles. When obstacles to client progress can be mainly attributed to therapist skill deficits, these may appear in a variety of forms, but most commonly therapists may impede client progress by the following:

1. Improperly inducting clients into therapy and failing to correct unrealistic expectations such as 'my therapist will solve my problems for me'.
2. Incorrectly assessing clients' problems and thus working on 'problems' that clients do not have.

3. Failing to show clients that their problems have ideological roots and that C is largely (but not exclusively) determined by B and not by A. Inexpert therapists often fail to persist with this strategy or persist with an ineffective strategy.

4. Failing to show clients that the ideological roots of their problems are most frequently expressed in the form of devout, absolutistic 'musts' or one of the three main derivatives of 'musturbation'. Instead, inexpert RET therapists frequently dwell too long on their clients' anti-empirical or inferentially distorted thinking.

5. Assuming that clients will automatically change their absolute thinking once they have identified it. Inexpert RET therapists either fail to dispute such thinking at all or use disputing methods sparingly and/or with insufficient vigour. In addition, inexpert therapists routinely fail to (1) give their clients homework assignments, which provide them with opportunities to practise disputing their irrational beliefs, (2) check on their clients' progress on these assignments and (3) help their clients to identify and change their philosophical obstacles to continually working at self-change.

6. Failing to realise that clients often have problems about their problems and thus working only on a primary problem when the client is preoccupied with a secondary problem.

7. Frequently switching from ego to discomfort disturbance issues within a given session so that clients get confused and thus distracted from working on either issue.

8. Working at a pace and a level inappropriate to the learning abilities of clients so that these clients are insufficiently involved in the therapeutic process due to confusion or boredom.

For these reasons it is highly desirable for RET therapists to strive to improve their skills continually by involving themselves in ongoing supervision and training activities (Wessler and Ellis, 1980, 1983; Dryden, 1983).

Client progress can also be hindered because therapists may bring their own disturbances to the therapeutic process. Ellis has outlined five major irrational beliefs that lead to therapeutic inefficiency (Ellis, 1983b):

1. 'I *have* to be successful with all my clients practically all of the time.'

2. 'I *must* be an outstanding therapist, clearly better than other therapists I know or hear about.'

3. 'I *have* to be greatly respected and loved by all my clients.'

4. 'Since I am doing my best and working so hard as a therapist, my clients *should* be equally hardworking and responsible, *should* listen to me carefully and *should* always push themselves to change.'

5. 'Because I am a person in my own right, I *must* be able to enjoy myself during therapy sessions and to use these sessions to solve my personal problems as much as to help clients with their difficulties.'

In such cases, it is recommended that RET therapists apply RET principles and methods to search for and dispute their own self- and client-defeating beliefs, which may (1) impede them from confronting their clients; (2) distract them and their clients from getting the therapeutic job done; (3) foster undue therapist anxiety and anger; and (4) encourage inappropriate behaviour that is anathema to the practice of effective and ethical therapy.

Client obstacles to client progress

In order to really benefit from RET, clients had better achieve three forms of insight, namely: (1) psychological disturbance is mainly determined by the absolutistic beliefs that they hold about themselves, others and the world; (2) even when people acquired and created their irrational beliefs in their early lives, they perpetuate their disturbance by reindoctrinating themselves in the present with these beliefs; (3) only if they constantly work and practise in the present and future to think, feel and act against these irrational beliefs are clients likely to surrender their irrationalities and make themselves significantly less disturbed.

In a study by Ellis on the characteristics of clients who 'failed' in RET, the following findings emerged:

1. Clients who did poorly in RET failed to do consistent *cognitive* self-disputation. They were characterised, among other factors, by extreme disturbance, grandiosity, lack of organisation and plain refusal to do these cognitive assignments.
2. 'Failure' clients, who refused to accept responsibility for their 'inappropriate' emotions and refused to change forcefully and *emotively* their beliefs and actions, were more clingy, more severely depressed and inactive, more often grandiose, and more frequently stubbornly rebellious than clients who benefited from RET.
3. 'Failure' clients who did poorly in the *behavioural* aspects of RET showed 'abysmally low frustration tolerance, had serious behavioral addictions, led disorganized lives, refrained from doing their activity homework assignments, were more frequently psychotic and generally refused to work at therapy' (Ellis, 1983e, p. 165).

Thus, clients' own extreme level of disturbance is a significant obstacle to their own progress. Whilst a full discussion of what 'special' therapeutic methods and techniques to employ with such clients is outside the scope of this chapter (see Ellis, 1985a), therapists can adopt a number of strategies to enhance therapeutic effectiveness with these DCs ('difficult customers'). Among other tactics, therapists, first, are advised to be consistently and forcefully encouraging in their therapeutic interactions with these clients, showing them that they can do better if they try. Secondly, therapists would be wise to keep vigorously showing these resistant clients that they, the therapists, do, in fact, unconditionally accept them with all their psychological difficulties and that they can indeed accept themselves in the same way. Thirdly, therapists can often be successful with such clients by consistently showing them that their refusal to work on their problems will generally lead to bad consequences and needless suffering. Fourthly, therapists are advised to be flexible in experimenting with a wide range of therapeutic techniques (including some unusual ones!) in their persistent efforts to help their 'difficult' clients. Above all, rational–emotive therapists should preferably be good representatives of their therapeutic system and accept themselves and tolerate the discomfort of working with difficult clients while sticking to the therapeutic task!

Termination preferably takes place in RET when clients have made some significant progress and when they have become proficient in RET's self-change techniques. Thus, terminating clients should preferably be able to: (1) acknowledge that they experience 'inappropriate' negative emotions and act dysfunctionally when they do; (2) detect the irrational beliefs that underpin these experiences; (3) discriminate their irrational beliefs from their rational alternatives; (4) challenge these irrational beliefs; and (5) counteract them by using cognitive, emotive and behavioural self-change methods. In addition, it is often helpful for therapists to arrange for their clients to attend a series of follow-up sessions after termination to monitor their progress and deal with any remaining obstacles to sustained improvement.

Chapter 4
The Rational–Emotive
Treatment Sequence

While training and supervising novice rational–emotive therapists it has been my experience that these therapists are frequently confused concerning the steps that need to be taken in helping their clients solve specific psychological problems. As a result I developed the RET treatment sequence which outlines these steps in the order in which creative RET therapists most often carry them out.

It is important, at the outset, to note that this treatment sequence applies when dealing with a *given* client problem. I will consider how to deal with the situation where a client has several problems in the next chapter.

When reading this chapter, please note that the creative execution of the RET treatment sequence is done within the context of developing and maintaining a productive therapeutic alliance between you and your client, an issue which will be considered in detail in Chapter 7.

The Sequence

Step 1: Ask for a problem

After you have greeted your client (in this case female), help her to discuss her reasons for coming for therapy and to talk about her problems in a fairly open-ended manner, and show empathic understanding of her position. Then ask her for a specific problem to work on. This might be the client's major problem or the problem that she wishes to start on first.

Step 2: Define and agree the target problem

It is important for you and your client to have a common understanding of what this particular problem is, and a shared understanding that this problem will be the focus for initial therapeutic exploration. The more

First published in 1990.

specifically you can help your client to identify the nature of the problem, the more likely it is that you will then be successful in carrying out an assessment of this problem (in steps 3, 4 and 7). This is accomplished by using the ABC framework of RET, where 'A' equals the activating event, or the client's inference about this event. 'B' stands for the client's beliefs about the event, and 'C' stands for the client's emotional and behavioural consequences of holding the belief at B.

Step 3: Assess C

This step in the RET sequence involves the assessment of C, the client's emotions and behaviour. It is important at this stage that you help her to focus on an inappropriate negative emotion, such as anger, depression, anxiety or feelings of hurt etc. You would also be advised to be on the look-out for self-defeating actions or behaviour, such as procrastination, addictions and so on. However, clients who report experiencing concern, or sadness in response to a loss, annoyance or some other kind of disappointment, and who are taking effective action and leading self-disciplined lives, are in fact handling themselves constructively. This follows from the observation that it is generally regarded as unrealistic for human beings to have neutral or positive feelings about negative events in their lives. Thus, it is important at this point to help your client to identify a self-defeating negative emotion, not a constructive negative emotion. At this step you can also assess your client's motivation to change her inappropriate negative emotion and encourage her to strive towards experiencing the more constructive negative appropriate emotion. This, however, can be done elsewhere in the assessment part of the sequence (i.e. between steps 3 and 6).

Step 4: Assess A

Once you have clarified what C is, you are now in a position to find out what your client specifically was disturbed about in the actual example you are assessing. It is important to realise that, when you assess A, you are not only trying to assess the objective aspects of that situation. This involves looking for your client's interpretations or inferences about A. Your major task here is to identify the most relevant interpretation or inference involved, the particular inference which triggered the client's emotional beliefs that in turn led to her disturbed feelings or behaviours at C (see Chapter 3).

Step 5: Determine the presence of secondary emotional problems and assess if necessary

It often transpires that clients have secondary emotional problems about their original emotional problems. For example, clients can often feel guilty about their anger, ashamed about their depression, anxious about their anxiety, guilty about their procrastination etc. Therefore, at this point in the sequence, or earlier if appropriate, it is important to determine whether or not your client does have a secondary emotional problem about her primary emotional problem. If she does have a secondary problem, then it is important to target this problem for treatment first before proceeding to deal with the primary problem if you consider that the secondary problem is going to interfere significantly with your work on the primary problem. So, if your client is feeling ashamed about her anger, for example, then those feelings of shame may interfere with and possibly block effective work on helping her overcome her anger, and thus shame (the secondary emotional problem) would be dealt with first in this case.

Step 6: Teach the B–C connection

Whether you are proceeding with your client's primary emotional problem, or whether you have switched and are now in the process of assessing a secondary emotional problem, the next stage in the RET treatment sequence is to help the client to understand the connection between her emotions and her beliefs. Specifically strive to help your client to understand that her emotions do not stem from the activating event which she is discussing, or her interpretations of this event, but from her beliefs and evaluations about these events or interpretations. If you fail to do this, your client will be puzzled by your emphasis on assessing her irrational beliefs. It is important, therefore, to bring out the connection between the Bs and Cs at the right stage in the RET treatment sequence.

Step 7: Assess irrational beliefs

Assuming that you have successfully assessed A and C, you are now in a position to help your client to identify the particular irrational beliefs that she has about the event or situation that brought about her problem at C. In particular, be on the lookout for the following.

'Demandingness'

Here your client will be making absolute demands about A in the form of 'musts', 'shoulds', 'oughts', 'have to's' etc.

'Awfulising'

Here, your client will be saying things like, 'It's awful that A occurred, and that's terrible, or horrible'.

Low frustration tolerance

Help your client to look for beliefs indicative of low frustration tolerance, or an attitude of 'I can't stand it'. Your client will frequently say that something was intolerable, or unbearable, or too hard to put up with etc.

Statements of damnation

Under this heading you will hear your client making global negative evaluations of herself, other people and/or the life conditions she is living under. These global statements of evaluation can be extreme, such as, 'I am a rotten person', or they may be less extreme but still basically irrational and insupportable because they involve a total, or global, evaluation of the self – which is, in reality, far too complex to be given such a rating or indeed, as you will see later, *any* kind of rating whatever. Thus, your client may, to use a less extreme example, insist that she is less worthy or less lovable as a result of what happened at A. This is still a global kind of rating, however, and if it occurs you will note it for later discussion.

Step 8: Connect irrational beliefs with C

Before proceeding to encourage your client to challenge her irrational beliefs, it is important, first of all, to help her to see the connection between her irrational beliefs and her disturbed emotions and behaviours at point C. If this is not done, or not done adequately, your client will not understand why you are now proceeding to encourage her to question her irrational beliefs. Even if you discussed the general connection between B and C at step 6, you still need to help your client to understand the specific connection between irrational beliefs and C at step 8.

Step 9: Dispute irrational beliefs

The major goals of disputing at this point in the RET treatment process is to encourage your client to understand that her irrational beliefs are unproductive, i.e. that they lead to self-defeating emotions which are illogical and inconsistent with reality. Moreover, these irrational beliefs cannot be supported by any factual evidence or scientific reasoning. By contrast, rational alternatives to these beliefs are productive, logical, consistent with reality and self-helping. They will not get the client into trouble, but instead, help her to achieve her goals in life with the minimum of emotional and behavioural upsets. More specifically, the goals of disputing are to help your client to understand the following.

Musts

There is no evidence in support of her absolute demands, while evidence does exist for her preferences.

'Awfulising'

What your client has defined as awful, i.e. 100 per cent bad, cannot be upheld and that in reality it will lie within a scale of badness from 0 to 99.9. Only one thing could be regarded as totally bad, and that is death itself; but even that is debatable since it is possible to regard death as preferable to dying slowly in excruciating agony with no hope whatsoever of relief. Often when you are helping your client to understand that, if she rates something as 100 per cent bad, she is really saying that nothing else in the world could possibly be worse. Once your client can see that this is absurd, she can more readily accept that her evaluation is greatly exaggerated.

Low frustration tolerance

Your client can always stand what she thinks she cannot stand, and can be reasonably happy, although not as happy as she would be if the difficult situation she has outlined at point A changed for the better.

Damnation or making global negative ratings of self, others or the world

This cannot legitimately be done because humans are human, i.e. fallible beings, and are not in any way damnable no matter what they do or do not do. Further, human beings are too complex to be given a single global rating that completely summarises their total being. Statements such as 'I am worthless', for example, mean that I am totally without worth or value to myself or to anybody else and possess no redeeming features whatever. How could this ever be substantiated? Obviously, it could not. Similarly, the world, too, is not damnable and contains a mixture of good, bad and other complex aspects which cannot possibly be given some kind of global rating. Once you can get your client to understand and accept this, she will become less inclined to deify or devilify herself or others, and more able to accept herself and others as fallible, but non-damnable, human beings.

At the end of step 9, if you have been successful in helping your client to dispute her irrational beliefs, you will perceive a new awareness in your client of the lack of any real evidence to support her previously held irrational beliefs and an acceptance of these beliefs and evaluations as illogical and both self- and relationship-defeating. At the same time, you will observe the gradual emergence of the client's appreciation of why the new rational beliefs are logical, reality based and self-helping, as well as potentially relationship enhancing with others. A word of caution, however. Your client's newly acquired rational beliefs are unlikely to become deep, solid convictions overnight. She may say things like, 'I understand what you are saying, and I think I believe it, but I don't yet feel it in my gut'. It takes time for your client's new beliefs about herself and the world to sink in, so to speak, and to become an integral part of her psychological make-up. For that reason, the remaining steps in the RET sequence are devised to help your client internalise her rational beliefs to the point that she can say with conviction, 'Yes, I now understand what you are saying in my gut as well as in my head and I can now act on this rational understanding'.

Step 10: Prepare your client to deepen her conviction in her rational beliefs

At this point, before you encourage your client to put into practice her new learning, it is important to help her to understand that long-term therapeutic change does involve a good deal of hard work on her part if she is ever going to deepen her new rational convictions to the point that they become virtually a new rational philosophy of living.

Step 11: Encourage your client to put her learning into practice

You are now in a position to help your client to put into practice a variety of cognitive, emotive, imagery and behavioural homework assignments. These are discussed with your client and she plays an active role in choosing assignments that are most relevant for her. For further information on such assignments see Chapter 3.

Step 12: Check the homework assignment

The next step in the RET sequence is for you to check your client's reactions to doing the homework assignment you set. This may have been a shame-attacking exercise, or some other activity which your client has been reluctant to face because of some emotional block arising from irrational beliefs concerning the situation. It is important to ascertain if she faced the situation that she agreed to face and whether or not she changed her irrational beliefs in the process of doing so. If the assignment was not carried out satisfactorily, reassign the task after verifying whether your client's failure was due to the continuing existence in her mind of those irrational beliefs and evaluations which the exercise was designed to undermine in the first place. Should that turn out to be the case, once more invite your client to identify and challenge the irrational beliefs that side-tracked her from carrying out the assigned task. When this has been done, reassign the task and monitor the result (see Chapter 5).

Step 13: Facilitate the working-through process

Once your client has achieved a measure of success in changing some of her core irrational beliefs by successfully executing the relevant homework assignments, go on from there to help your client to develop other assignments designed to help her gain experience in behaving in accordance with her emerging new rational philosophy. Thus, if your client has successfully challenged the irrational beliefs concerning public disapproval in social situations, help her to maximise her gains by designing homework assignments aimed at helping her to recognise and dispute any irrational beliefs she might have about disapproval in other situations, such as work relations with colleagues or personal relations with significant others. Your aim is to help your client not only to recognise and rip up her irrational beliefs about whatever situation or problem is currently troubling her, but to show her how to generalise her new learning to any future problem that she might experience. Once your client has gained experience and achieved success at challenging and disputing the irrational beliefs underlying one particular problem, she is more likely to be able to take on greater responsibility for initiating the RET sequence with other problems. At the end of rational–emotive therapy, the degree of success achieved by both you and your client may be gauged by the extent to which she demonstrates the ability to live a more satisfying life with few, if any, of the emotional hang-ups with which she began therapy originally.

However, even the brightest and most enthusiastic of clients may, on occasions, slip back into their old self-defeating ways. The answer? Back to basics you go! It is on occasions like this that you will see the emergence of what I referred to previously as secondary problems. Here, your client upsets herself because she has experienced some kind of a relapse. For example, your client may have felt guilty over some act of commission or omission and is now denigrating herself for feeling guilty. 'How stupid of me to upset myself again, and after all I've learned about RET! Boy, what a dumbo that makes me!'

If your client reports a relapse, consider it as normal, as par for the course. In any case, nobody is completely rational. We can think, feel and behave rationally most of the time and rarely upset ourselves over the various hassles and problems of living in a complex world. But can we realistically expect to be like that all of the time? Hardly! Assure your client, therefore, that to take two steps forward and then one back, is the common experience. Do not waste time overly commiserating with your client. Instead, repeat the 13-step RET treatment sequence. Help your client to understand that staying emotionally healthy does not come about automatically, but requires continuous work and practice before the RET philosophy she has been trying hard to assimilate actually becomes an integral part of her life.

Show your client that there is no reason why she absolutely must not feel ashamed or dejected because some old emotional problem has returned to plague her. Encourage her to accept that this is normal, a natural part of our human fallibility. Emphasise (once more) that we all have innate tendencies to think in absolutistic, *mus*turbatory ways and that we are all naturally crooked thinkers; it comes easily to us! At this point retrace your steps and use the ABC framework to re-orient your client back to the task of disputing her irrational beliefs. Your client already knows that her previous problem(s) become established through her habitually thinking the irrational thoughts that created it. So, go after those irrational beliefs with your client. Get your client to identify, challenge and dispute them until she is thoroughly convinced of their falseness. Encourage her to look for variations of the main irrational beliefs and to understand *why* they are irrational and cannot be accepted as true, regardless of what form they are presented in. Help your client to keep looking, and looking, for her absolutistic demands upon herself and others, the *shoulds*, *oughts* and *musts*, and to replace them with flexible, non-dogmatic desires and preferences.

Finally, stress the importance, once more, of your client acting against her irrational beliefs until she becomes comfortable doing what she was unrealistically afraid to try. Show your client how she can put muscle into her newly acquired RET philosophy by means of self-management techniques, rational–emotive imagery exercises and shame-attacking exercises until she convinces herself that she really can make headway against even her most stubborn self-defeating beliefs and habits. When your client reaches the stage where she can easily recognise and distinguish her appropriate from her inappropriate feelings, understand why the difference is important, and demonstrate that she can uproot the shoulds, oughts and musts that underlie her inappropriate feelings, you may assume that your client is well on her way to regaining effective emotional control of her life.

Chapter 5
The Process of
Rational–Emotive Therapy

Whilst it is impossible to differentiate clearly between different stages of the therapy, for the sake of clarity I will consider the beginning, middle and ending stages of RET.

The Beginning Stage

Establish a therapeutic alliance

The first task of a rational–emotive therapist is to greet your client (in this case male) and to begin to establish a productive therapeutic alliance with him (see also Chapter 7). This will normally involve discussing his reasons for seeking help, his expectations for therapy and correcting any obvious misconceptions he has about the therapeutic process. You will also want to deal with such practicalities as fees and frequency and length of sessions. However, your main task at the outset is to encourage your client to talk about his concerns, initially in an open-ended way, while you communicate your understanding of his problem. It is important that you (1) show your client that you understand his concerns, (2) demonstrate an unconditional acceptance of him as a person and (3) establish your credibility as an effective therapist. In RET, establishing credibility is best done if a problem-solving approach to your client's concerns is adopted from the outset. In doing so you should preferably communicate to your client that you intend to help him as quickly as possible and that you take seriously the problems for which he is seeking help. This means that you quickly come to an agreed understanding with your client concerning which of his problems you are both going to address first. In order to establish credibility with your client, it is also important for you to provide him with a clear rationale which

First published in 1990.

makes the purpose of your intentions clear. You need to be flexible at this point because clients differ concerning the degree to which they benefit from a problem-focused approach to psychotherapy. You are advised to accommodate to your client's expectations on this point. For example, with some clients you may need to explore with them, in detail, their life situation, and also perhaps the historical determinants of their problem before adopting a problem-solving focus. With other clients, however, you may enhance the therapeutic alliance by becoming problem-focused from the beginning. Here, as elsewhere, I suggest that you show a high degree of flexibility in modifying your approach to take into account both the treatment expectations of your client and the preferred mode of practice in RET (i.e. an early focus on problem solving).

There are 13 major steps that you need to follow in dealing with any one of your client's given problems (see Chapter 4). However, here I want to stress that it is important to adjust your mode of therapeutic participation according to the client with whom you are working. In doing so, you will strengthen the therapeutic alliance. Thus, you may need to vary the pace of your interventions with different clients. Some clients think very quickly and will therefore respond to a fairly rapid intervention approach. Others, however, process information much more slowly and with these clients you need to reduce the speed at which you talk and the pace of your interventions. Because RET is first and foremost an educational approach to therapy, you should respect your client's pace and way of learning, and adjust your therapeutic interventions accordingly. If you work quite slowly with a client who would respond better to a more rapid exchange, then that client may become frustrated and may conclude that you are not helping him quickly enough. However, another client may find that you talk too quickly and deal with concepts too rapidly and consequently may experience confusion at the outset. You should realise that it is basically your responsibility to tailor your therapeutic delivery to the client you have before you. Do not expect that your client, when confused because he does not understand the points you are making, will readily disclose this to you. Thus, like all good therapists, you need to be alert to your client's non-verbal cues to gauge his level of understanding.

Also, bear in mind that, at the beginning of the therapy process, it is important to meet your client's preferences concerning your therapeutic style. Clients vary concerning the value that they place on different therapeutic styles. Some clients, for example, respond best to therapists who are self-disclosing and friendly. Other clients, however, will respond better to greater therapist formality. Such clients are more concerned with the therapist's expertise and value a more distant, 'professional' style.

My own approach to determining how best to meet clients' preferences concerning my therapeutic style is based on a number of factors (see also Chapter 7). First, I have found it valuable in an initial session to ask clients questions concerning their prior experiences of receiving formal psychotherapy and of being helped more informally with their psychological problems. In doing so, I focus the discussion on the factors that clients have found both helpful and unhelpful in such 'therapeutic encounters'. I also ask them directly which particular style they would like me to adopt with them. As Tracey (1984) has argued, it is important to meet clients' initial preferences for therapist behaviour if you are to develop a productive therapeutic alliance with them. Other rational-emotive therapists obtain similar information from standard forms that they may use at the outset of psychotherapy: for example, some employ Lazarus's (1981) Life History Questionnaire, which contains the following questions:

1. In a few words what do you think therapy is all about?
2. How long do you think therapy should last?
3. How do you think a therapist should interact with his or her clients?
4. What personal qualities do you think the ideal therapist for you should possess?

Despite the use of such questions, it should be realised that the issue of adjusting your therapeutic style according to the unique requirements of particular clients is very much a matter of trial and error.

Some therapists are uneasy about changing their therapeutic style with different clients. However, it should be borne in mind that in your daily life it is very likely that you vary your interactive style with different people. It is likely that you interact differently with your family, strangers whom you might encounter, colleagues at work and dignitaries whom you may meet in a formal setting. So you are probably familiar with the concept of being flexible in interactive style. In the same way I encourage the adoption of a stance of therapeutic flexibility and a variation of therapy style according to the productive desires of your client. I stress the word productive here because, of course, not all clients' preferences for therapist behaviour are necessarily therapeutic. For example, in RET it is important to avoid doing all the therapeutic work for your clients, to avoid meeting your clients outside therapy sessions for social purposes and to avoid letting your clients lay on a couch while encouraging them to free associate.

Teach the ABCs of RET

Another task which you have at the outset of RET involves teaching your client the rational-emotive model of emotional disturbance. First, encourage your client to understand that his emotional problems are determined largely by his irrational beliefs rather then by the troublesome events in his life. Secondly, help your client to understand that in order to change his dysfunctional emotions he needs to challenge the beliefs that he holds now, in the present, rather than engaging him in overly long exploration of the historical determinants of such beliefs. However, as I noted earlier, some historical exploration can be helpful, if only to strengthen the therapeutic alliance between you and your client. Thirdly, encourage your client to see that if he wants to gain lasting benefits from psychotherapy he needs to put into practice what he learns during therapy sessions. This involves working repeatedly at changing his irrational beliefs and acting according to his newly acquired rational beliefs. You will have to go over these three major RET insights repeatedly before your client internalises them to the extent that he acts on them in his everyday life.

At this stage of therapy your client is unlikely to be knowledgeable about the ABCs of RET. You thus need to take a focused active–directive approach to helping your clients learn the rational–emotive model of emotional disturbance. Wherever possible, encourage your client to think for himself by engaging him in a Socratic dialogue. Using this type of exchange helps him understand that his emotional problems are largely determined by his irrational beliefs. However, at times you will need to use a didactic style of teaching your client the ABCs of RET. Whenever you do this at length, you should check whether or not your client has understood the points you have made.

Given that RET has an educational focus, it is important that your client is clear concerning what you are trying to teach him (either Socratically or didactically). As such, it is important to remain focused on one problem at a time. Switching from problem to problem when your client has several emotional problems can be quite confusing for him and may interfere with the major points you wish your client to learn.

By the end of the initial stage, your client should have learned that it is his irrational beliefs that largely determine his emotional and behavioural problems. He should have had initial experience of detecting the irrational beliefs that underpin his initial target problem. He should be able to discriminate his rational beliefs from his irrational beliefs, and should have had some initial experience at disputing these irrational beliefs, using logical, empirical and pragmatic arguments.

This learning should be reinforced by homework assignments. At this stage, such homework assignments may involve your client reading specific chapters concerning the ABCs of RET in one of the available RET self-help books (e.g. Ellis and Harper, 1975; Ellis and Becker, 1982; Ellis, 1988; Dryden and Gordon, 1990). In addition, you may ask your client to fill in one of the available rational–emotive self-help forms (see Chapter 3).

Deal with your client's doubts

Given that clients have a wide variety of preferences concerning which approaches to psychotherapy may be helpful to them, you may find at this stage that some of your clients may express doubts concerning the usefulness of RET to help them overcome their problems. One approach to handling such doubts is to encourage your client to persist with an open mind at using rational–emotive methods of change for a given time period (e.g. five sessions) at the end of which you will review his experiences in using the approach. If, at the end of this period, your client continues to be doubtful concerning the usefulness of RET to his problem, discuss his views concerning which type of therapy approach he thinks may be helpful to him. A judicious referral at this stage may be more helpful to your client than encouraging him to persist with an approach to psychotherapy about which he has serious doubts.

The Middle Stage

By the middle stage of RET, your client should have gained some experience at disputing the irrational beliefs which underpin his target problem. Your client should have become accustomed to the idea that homework assignments are an important component of the rational–emotive therapy process, and may have had some experience of changing his irrational beliefs to their rational alternatives. Whilst it is desirable for you to keep on track with a given problem (namely, the target problem) and to help your client through steps 1–12 of the rational–emotive therapy sequence, this is not always possible.

When to change tack

When your client has several problems, one of the problems other than his target problem may become more pressing during the middle stage of therapy. Whilst it may be desirable to persist with the initial target problem until your client has reached a reasonable level of coping on that problem, to ignore the client's desire to work on a different and, to him, more salient problem may unduly threaten the therapeutic alliance and you should avoid this if possible.

In my experience, there are a number of good reasons to switch tack and to deal with a different client problem before he has attained coping criterion on the target problem. The first indication that a productive shift in problem emphasis is indicated is when the client reports a crisis with the new problem. For example, imagine that your client's initial target problem is public speaking anxiety. If he reports a crisis, namely that he has been physically abused by a family member and is experiencing emotional distress about this, then it is important to switch and to deal with this new problem. However, having made the switch, encourage your client to remain with the second problem until he has gone through steps 1–12 of the rational–emotive therapy sequence and has achieved the coping criterion.

A second indication that it is important to switch to a second problem is when your client becomes emotionally disturbed in the session about his second problem and cannot concentrate on work on the target problem. If you try to continue to help him with his initial target problem, you will rarely succeed and you will create the impression that you are more concerned with following your approach to therapy than you are with being empathic and responsive to the client's experience. Once again, when you have switched to the second problem help your client to reach the coping criterion on that problem by proceeding through steps 1–12 of the rational–emotive therapy sequence.

A final reason to switch to a different problem before you have helped your client to reach the coping criterion on the initial target problem is when one of your client's other problems has become more pervasive than the target problem, i.e. it pervades a greater number of areas of your client's life than does the target problem. Once you have switched to the new problem, again persist with it until your client has reached the coping criterion.

If your client has several problems and wishes to deal with different ones before he has attained the coping criterion on any one problem, give him a plausible rationale for remaining with one problem and for working on it until the coping criterion has been reached. If your client still wishes to switch between different problems even after hearing your rationale, then do so to preserve the therapeutic alliance. However, if you suspect that your client is switching between different problems in order to avoid dealing with any one problem, then put this forward as a hypothesis for further exploration with your client. Once again bear in mind that whilst you may prefer to help your client to reach the coping criterion on any one given problem before tackling a second or subsequent problem, you may have to be flexible to avoid unduly threatening the therapeutic alliance which by now you have established with your client.

Identify core irrational beliefs

Whether you deal with your client's problems one at a time, switching from one to another when the client has reached the coping criterion on any given problem, or whether you have to compromise this ideal way of working and switch from problem to problem in order to engage your client fully in therapy, it is important that you look for common themes among the irrational beliefs that underpin his problems. Thus, if your client has discussed public speaking anxiety, procrastination, anxiety about approaching women and fear of being criticised by his work superior, begin to form hypotheses concerning the presence of core irrational beliefs that may be common across these problems. Thus, in the example that I have given, it may be that your client's problems concern ego anxiety related to the need for approval. If this is the case, then as you work on a number of these problems you may suggest to the client that there may be a similarity between these problems with respect to the underlying cognitive dynamics. However, guard against making the assumption that all of your client's problems can be explained with reference to one core irrational belief because this is rare. More common is the clinical fact that your client may have two or three core irrational beliefs. These more non-specific issues should become the focus for therapeutic exploration during this middle stage of therapy.

Encourage your client to engage in relevant tasks

As noted above, your major goal during the middle stage of RET is to engage your client to strengthen his conviction in his rational beliefs. This involves both you and your client using a variety of cognitive, emotive, imagery and behavioural techniques which are all designed to encourage him to internalise his new rational philosophy (see Chapters 3 and 12).

When considering the use of techniques it is important to note that as a therapist you need to help your client:

1. To understand what his tasks are in therapy and how the execution of these tasks will help him to achieve his therapeutic goals.
2. To identify and overcome his doubts about his ability to execute his tasks.
3. To understand what your tasks are in RET and to see how your tasks relate to his therapeutic goals.
4. To undertake tasks that he can realistically be expected to carry out.
5. To use therapeutic tasks in the sessions before you can expect him to put these into practice outside sessions.
6. To use techniques which are potent enough to help him to achieve his therapeutic goals.

Due to the fact that the main burden of responsibility for promoting client change rests on your client carrying out homework assignments between sessions, it is important that you prepare him adequately to execute such assignments. Thus, you need to:

1. Provide a persuasive rationale for the importance of executing homework assignments in RET.
2. Negotiate with your client appropriate homework assignments rather than unilaterally suggest what these assignments should be.
3. Negotiate assignments which are relevant to your client achieving his goals.
4. Negotiate assignments which follow on naturally from what has been discussed in therapy sessions.
5. Specify as fully as possible what these assignments will be, when your client is going to do them, and where and how he is going to execute them.
6. Elicit a firm commitment from your client that he will execute these homework assignments.

7. Encourage your client, whenever possible, to rehearse the particular homework assignments in the sessions. Your client is more likely to execute homework assignments successfully when he can picture himself doing so in imagery.
8. Identify and overcome potential obstacles that may prevent your client from putting into practice particular homework assignments.
9. Negotiate homework assignments which are not too time-consuming for your client.
10. Suggest assignments which are challenging at a particular time for your client but not overwhelming for him.

Because the successful execution of homework assignments is such an important part of therapy, it is very important that you check what your client's experiences were in executing these assignments:

- Ask your client to report what he learned or did not learn from carrying out the assignments.
- Reinforce his success at executing assignments and, where necessary, reinforce his attempts at executing these assignments.
- Identify and correct errors that your client made in carrying out his homework assignments.
- Identify, assess and deal with your client's reasons for not attempting or not completing his homework assignments. In particular help him to dispute his resistance-creating irrational beliefs.
- Encourage him to re-do the assignment (if relevant).

You will frequently have no way of knowing in advance which assignments your client will find helpful, and therefore you should use a trial and error approach to find this out. Also discuss with your client your intention to discover which techniques work and do not work for him, otherwise he may become discouraged when he uses a technique that does not lead to progress.

Due to the fact that your main goal during this stage is to encourage your client to internalise a new rational philosophy, you and your client need to determine reasons for therapeutic change. Ideally, your client should be effecting change by disputing his irrational beliefs rather than by changing his inferences about life events or the events themselves or by changing his behaviour. If you discover that your client has demonstrated therapeutic change without changing his irrational beliefs, reinforce his efforts but point out to him the importance of changing his irrational beliefs. Remind him of the rational–emotive hypothesis that long-term change is best achieved by philosophical change.

Deal with obstacles to change

It is during the middle stage of RET that clients show most resistance to change. Assuming that your client has understood that his irrational beliefs do determine his emotional and behavioural problems and that he has gained some initial success at disputing his irrational beliefs, it is likely that his resistance to change can be attributed to his philosophy of low frustration tolerance (LFT). Frequently clients do not follow through on their initial successful change because they believe that 'Change must not be difficult' or 'I should not have to work so hard in therapy'. It is very important for you to be alert to the possibility that your client has a philosophy of LFT about change and, if so, you need to help him to challenge and change the irrational beliefs implicit in such a philosophy. Otherwise, these beliefs will interfere with your client's attempts to internalise a new rational philosophy.

Maultsby (1984) has argued that change itself can be an uncomfortable experience for clients. He refers to a state called 'cognitive–emotional dissonance' during which clients feel 'strange' as they work at strengthening their conviction in their rational beliefs. Encourage your client to accept that this feeling of 'strangeness' is a natural part of change and if necessary dispute any ideas that he must feel natural and comfortable all the time. Grieger and Boyd (1980) have called this concern the 'I won't be me' syndrome.

You will encounter a minority of clients who internalise the theory of RET as a body of knowledge, but who will not work towards putting this knowledge into practice. Such clients are often very knowledgeable about the theory and can quote extensively from various RET books, but they often have an implicit philosophy of low frustration tolerance which stops them from putting their knowledge into practice. They may also believe that their knowledge is sufficient for them to effect lasting emotional and behavioural changes. As with other clients, the ideas which stop them from putting their knowledge into practice need to be identified, challenged and changed.

Encourage your client to maintain and enhance his gains

It is in the middle stage of therapy that your client will experience greatest variability in the progress he makes, sometimes going forward, sometimes backsliding. As a result you need to help him stay fully engaged in therapy by helping him (1) to deal with set-backs, (2) to maintain his progress and later (3) to enhance his gains. Ellis (1984c) has written an excellent pamphlet on this issue. I refer this to you for the variety of points made and suggest that you give a copy to your clients when the issues raised by Ellis become salient.

Encourage your client to become his own therapist

Another important task which you have as a rational–emotive therapist in the middle stage of therapy is to encourage your client to work towards becoming his own therapist. I noted in the previous section on the beginning stage of RET that you will often have to take an active–directive stance in helping your client to learn the ABCs of RET and to understand why his irrational belief is self-defeating and the rational alternative is more constructive. As you move into the middle stage of therapy, you will need to review such points. However, the more you do so the more you should encourage your client to take the lead in the exploration.

When you first discuss a particular problem with your client, you should be active and directive, but as you work more on this problem, gradually reduce the level of your directiveness and encourage your client to practise self-therapy. As you work together with your client on a particular problem over the course of therapy, help him to internalise the rational–emotive problem-solving method. Encourage him to learn to identify troublesome emotions and behaviours, help him to relate these to particular activating events, and from there identify his major core irrational beliefs. Then encourage him to dispute these beliefs for himself and to develop plausible rational alternatives to these beliefs. Your client's major task during this stage of therapy is to weaken his conviction in his irrational beliefs and strengthen his conviction in his rational beliefs.

Not only should you encourage your client to internalise the RET process of change, but you should also encourage him to look for links between his problems, particularly those that involve core irrational beliefs. Your goal should be to help your client to identify his core irrational beliefs across a number of settings and to dispute these beliefs. As noted above, whilst you should reduce the level of your directiveness as you help your client to deal with a particular problem, you may have to go back to becoming active and directive when the focus of therapeutic exploration shifts to a new problem. However, as a major goal of this stage is to encourage your client to begin to become his own therapist, you should endeavour, even when working on a new problem, to encourage your client to take the lead in the exploration of this new problem.

During this stage of RET, you should increasingly use Socratic dialogue to encourage your client to do most of the work and you should keep didactic teaching to a minimum. In particular, you should use short, probing, Socratic questions to check on your client's progress. Thus, when your client discusses his experiences in dealing with his problem between sessions you may ask questions such as the following:

- 'How did you feel?'
- 'What was going through your mind?'
- 'How did you dispute that?'
- 'How could you have disputed that?'
- 'Did you believe the new rational belief?'
- 'Why not?'

- 'What could you believe instead?'
- 'How would you know that this belief was true?'
- 'If you believe that how would you act?'
- 'Could you try that for next week?' etc.

When your client responds successfully to your decreased level of directiveness over a period of weeks, then you may begin to start thinking of working towards termination (see next section).

The Ending Stage

The question of ending rational–emotive therapy arises when your client has made significant progress overcoming the problems for which he originally sought therapy and has shown evidence that he has been able to utilise the rational–emotive problem-solving method in approaching his problems. Discussion about termination may be raised by either you or your client. When you both decide that you will work towards termination of therapy this may be done either by decreasing the frequency of sessions over time or by setting a definite termination date. During this stage, you can usefully encourage your client to anticipate future problems and to imagine how he would apply the skills which he has learned during the rational–emotive therapy process to these problems. Your goal should be to encourage your client to view himself as his own major source of problem solving and discussions should centre on how he can apply his problem-solving skills in a variety of settings.

Clients who have done well during RET may well have ambivalent feelings towards ending the process. You may need, for example, to assess whether or not your client believes that he needs your ongoing help. This may be expressed by your client casting doubts on his ability to cope on his own or by him reporting a relapse before termination. The best way of dealing with your client's belief 'I must have the ongoing support of my therapist, because I cannot cope on my own' is as follows. First, encourage him to dispute this irrational belief in the usual way. Then urge him to conduct an experiment to see whether or not it is true that he cannot cope on his own. Help him to specify which aspects of his life he thinks he cannot cope with on his own and then encourage him to test this out as a homework assignment.

Whether you are working with your client towards a phased or definite ending, you should build in well-spaced-out, follow-up sessions so that you and your client can monitor his future progress. In one respect, there is no absolute end to the rational–emotive therapy process because, in most cases, you would probably want to encourage your client to contact you for further help if he has struggled for a reasonably long time to put into practice the rational–emotive problem-solving method without success.

When RET has been successful and you are working towards a termination with your client, bear in mind that what has been a significant relationship for your client and perhaps for you is coming towards an end. Thus, it is highly appropriate for both you and your client to feel sad about the dissolution of this relationship. I believe it is important for you to encourage your client to express this sadness and in doing so he may express feelings of gratitude for your help. Whilst you may wish to encourage your client to attribute most of his progress to his own efforts (this is undoubtedly true because he had the major responsibility for carrying out homework assignments between sessions), if you believe you have done a good job then it is appropriate for you to say this to your client.

Sometimes your client may offer you a gift in recognition for the help that you have given him. My own practice is to accept a gift with gratitude as long as its value in monetary terms is not highly disproportionate to the occasion. Appropriate gifts in this regard are perhaps a bottle of alcohol, some flowers or a small figurine. Some clients, however, do have difficulty saying goodbye and difficulty in experiencing and expressing sadness about the end of a relationship. They may, for example, cancel their final session or try to introduce a light-hearted tone into the final session. Whilst extending therapy at this stage for too long is not to be recommended, I do suggest that in such instances you first look for possible irrational beliefs that your client may have about saying goodbye and about experiencing and expressing sadness concerning losing an important relationship. Then, encourage him to use his skills to identify, challenge and change the relevant irrational beliefs that underpin these difficulties. Be problem-focused to the very end!

Chapter 6
Some Misconceptions about Rational-Emotive Therapy

Whenever workshops in rational-emotive therapy are conducted workshop participants have made the following criticisms about RET. These tend to be misconceptions about this therapeutic method and here some of the more common of these are outlined and corrected.

RET is brainwashing

The idea that rational-emotive therapy is brainwashing is a misconception because RET therapists encourage their clients to think for themselves rather than telling them what to think. RET therapists adopt the Socratic method of challenging the core irrational philosophies their clients hold about themselves, other people and the world that underly their problems. RET therapists encourage their clients to question their irrational beliefs for their own benefit and not for their therapists' benefit. RET therapists try to teach their clients the scientific method of logically examining their beliefs, to look for evidence in support of them and to learn the difference between beliefs that are rational and those that are irrational, i.e. unrealistic, illogical, dogmatic and self-defeating. They try to show their clients how thoughts, emotions and behaviour are all interrelated, and that the consequences of holding irrational, unsustainable beliefs are disturbed emotions and dysfunctional behaviours. RET therapists do not unequivocally tell clients that their irrational beliefs are inconsistent with reality, are illogical and are self-defeating. Instead, they try to teach their clients, through Socratic dialogue, how to apply the methods of science to their beliefs and see for themselves that some stoutly held beliefs are simply not viable, and therefore are largely unproductive or self-defeating in the long term.

Written with Jack Gordon; first published in 1990.

RET therapists tell their clients what to feel and how to act

This criticism is misconceived because, rather than tell their clients what their goals in life should be, RET therapists help them to identify their own basic goals and purposes. RET therapists assume that clients come to therapy in the first instance because they are not achieving their basic goals and because they have developed habitual dysfunctional behavioural patterns which keep getting them into trouble. For example, clients may repeatedly respond to both normal and unusual stimuli by overreacting, or underreacting, emotionally and may be quite unaware that their psychological problems arise from their faulty interpretations and mistaken ideas about what they perceive is happening to them. Even when they know that they are behaving poorly, clients will keep repeating non-adjustive or inappropriate responses to environmental situations. It follows that, unless some inroads can be made into helping these clients change their self-defeating and maladaptive behaviours, their emotional and behavioural problems will persist, often with unfortunate consequences to themselves and to others.

RET therapists help clients to identify their own idiosyncratic ways of enjoying life and, given that these are the clients' goals, help them to evaluate whether or not certain irrational beliefs that they cling to will aid or block them in the process of achieving their goals. Once the clients are in agreement that their irrational beliefs are sabotaging the realisation of their goals, then RET therapists demonstrate exactly how they can forthrightly question and challenge these beliefs, and induce them to work at uprooting these ideas and to replace them with scientifically testable hypotheses about self, other people and the world which are unlikely to get them into future emotional difficulties. This process is achieved again through the use of Socratic dialogue where RET therapists encourage their clients to set their own feeling and behavioural goals and help them to maximise these through the use of rational thinking. It is not done by RET therapists unilaterally telling clients what they should feel or how they should act.

RET is not concerned with clients' emotions

Originally, rational–emotive therapy was called rational therapy, but Ellis changed the name of the therapy to rational–emotive therapy in response to critics' comments that RET therapists do not concern themselves with their clients' emotions. By now it is hoped that you will have realised that RET is essentially, and fundamentally, concerned with clients' emotions; indeed, the whole aim of the therapy is to help clients overcome their emotional problems and, by recognising and uprooting the irrational cognitions underlying their problems, to help them to experience appropriate emotions in response to life's happenings, and to lead less frustrating and happier lives.

RET holds that there are virtually no legitimate reasons why we need make ourselves emotionally disturbed about anything, but allows us full leeway to experience strong constructive negative emotions such as sorrow, regret, displeasure, annoyance and determination to change obnoxious social or environmental conditions. RET maintains, however, that when we experience certain self-defeating and inappropriate emotions (such as guilt, depression, anxiety, worthlessness or rage), we are adding an unverifiable element to our rational view that some things in the world are bad and had better be changed. Moreover, so long as we cling to these negative, inappropriate emotions, our ability to change unpleasant conditions will be hindered, rather than helped.

The essence of RET is that emotions are valuable – they motivate us to action, but we had better favour constructive, rather than destructive, emotions if we are to survive happily in this world. It is the hallmark of RET that we actually have enormous but not perfect control over our destructive emotions *if* we choose to work at changing the bigoted and unscientific notions which we employ to create them.

RET is just concerned with changing people's beliefs

While I have focused in this book on RET's distinctive features, RET therapists are also concerned with helping clients to change the negative events in their lives so that they gain more positive experiences. This frequently involves changing the negative activating events of their lives (the As), and this is best done, as argued above, by changing the irrational beliefs clients may hold about these events, and replacing them with reality-based convictions. When, however, negative events cannot for the moment be changed, RET therapists will help clients constructively to adjust to these negative situations by encouraging them to change their thinking.

Thus, if a male client is rejected after going for a job interview, the therapist will show the client that he can still accept himself, that the situation is unfortunate but not terrible, and that by refusing to down himself because of this failure to land a job this time, he can keep trying to find another job with better chance of success than if he sat around and felt miserable. The therapist could even teach the client better interview skills. As we have stated above, appropriate negative emotions can be motivating. Consequently, good RET therapists will encourage their clients to rid themselves of their irrational ideas which create those self-defeating negative emotions that tend to sabotage clients' efforts to achieve their goals. But good RET therapists will also encourage clients to take constructive action, learn more effective coping and other skills, and to attempt to change negative life events.

RET encourages clients to become unfeeling robots

Nothing could be further from the truth! Indeed, RET is one of the few therapies that help clients to discriminate between their inappropriate and self-defeating negative emotions and their appropriate and constructive negative emotions. When clients are faced with negative life events, such as the loss of loved ones, RET therapists encourage such clients to feel keenly appropriate emotions, such as sorrow, sadness and grief. An emotion-free existence, even if it could be achieved, has no place in the RET view of things. Such an existence would seem a very dull, sterile sort of state in which to 'live' and could only be achieved by the abandoment of all desire and the creation of an attitude of total indifference to the world. That would be, indeed, the exact opposite of the RET philosophy, and no good RET therapist would ever attempt to do any such thing.

A consideration of two philosophical objections to RET

How is a criterion of rationality determined?

This raises the question of who or what decides whether or not the client is being irrational, and that this contention is largely definitional. We can imagine some contending that the client is neither irrational nor disturbed, because he *should* be anxious or enraged and *should* actually enjoy these feelings, or others might argue that it is good for the client to be irrational because certain human values are enhanced by irrationality. We would agree, therefore, that definitions of rationality and irrationality are some-what arbitrary – in *any* of the main contemporary systems of therapy, and not just in RET. However, clients come to therapy because they, and not the therapist, think their life is not going well, and want help to change their ways and learn how to live a happier more self-fulfilling existence. In effect, clients come to therapy and say: 'My way of doing things hasn't been work-ing too well for me. Now, let's see if you can help me do better.' This is then what RET therapists will help clients to do. Note that the definition that the clients' behaviour has been irrational and self-defeating up to this point is jointly accepted as such by client and therapist: the definition has not been thrust upon the client.

The idea that other people cannot affect you adversely

This criticism contends that RET therapists encourage their clients to treat the responses of others as of little consequence and results in creating an illusion in the client of virtual impregnability to the world outside himself. In fact, RET therapists teach their clients that other people can certainly affect them adversely in significant ways. Clients can be fired from their job, rejected in love or ostracised for supporting unpopular social and political causes. However, RET therapists do try to help their clients to see the dif-ference between being rejected by other people and rejecting oneself. We teach clients to see that their 'ego' or self-regarding attitude *cannot* be adversely affected by others unless they take these others too seriously and by doing so give these others a power over their 'self' that they otherwise do not have. In other words, when you are rejected, that does not necessarily make you a rejectee. You can refuse to allow your self-regarding attitude to be affected by others' positive or negative attitude towards you, whilst accepting that others have the power to harm or frustrate you as a human organism.

In conclusion, RET therapists encourage their client to face both direct and indirect threats to their well-being squarely. For example, RET therapists would agree with their clients that *concern* over hijacking, bomb threats, air pollution, political repression and racial injustice is legitimate and helpful in motivating people to change these things. But *overconcern* or panic is not constructive, and if clients can stop defining themselves as worthless individuals who cannot cope and if they can face these threats and difficulties with due concern, they will stand a much better chance of tackling them successfully.

Part III
Vicissitudes of the
Therapeutic Relationship
in RET

Chapter 7
The Therapeutic Alliance in Rational–Emotive Therapy

Bordin's Concept of the Therapeutic Alliance

As a rational–emotive therapist I have found the work of Ed Bordin (1979) on the concept of the therapeutic alliance particularly helpful in developing a basic framework for the conduct of RET. Bordin argues that the therapeutic alliance refers to the complex of attachments and shared understandings formed and activities undertaken by therapists and clients as the former attempt to help the latter with their psychological problems.

As discussed in Chapter 3 Bordin has stressed that there are three major components of the therapeutic alliance: (1) bonds - which refer to the interpersonal connectedness between therapist and client; (2) goals - which refer to the aims of both therapist and client; and (3) tasks - which are activities carried out by both therapist and client in the service of the latter's goals.

I will consider each of these components separately and show that rational–emotive therapists have important clinical decisions to make in each of the three alliance domains so as to individualise therapy for each client and thus maximise therapeutic benefit.

At the outset it should be noted that Bordin (1979) has speculated that effective therapy occurs when therapist and client (1) have an appropriately bonded working relationship; (2) mutually agree on the goals of the therapeutic enterprise; and (3) both understand their own and the other person's therapeutic tasks and agree to carry these out to implement the client's goals.

Bonds

The major concern of rational–emotive therapists in the bond domain should be to establish and maintain an appropriately bonded relationship

First published in 1987.

that will encourage each individual client to implement his or her goal-directed therapeutic tasks. It should be underlined that there is no single effective bond that can be formed with clients in RET; different clients require different bonds. This observation became clear to me when, on a 6 months' sabbatical at the Center for Cognitive Therapy in Philadelphia in 1981, I saw two clients on the same afternoon who benefited from a different bonded relationship with me. At 4 p.m. I saw Mrs G., a 50-year-old married business woman, who was impressed with my British professional qualifications and whose responses to initial questions indicated that she anticipated and preferred a very formal relationship with her therapist. I provided such a relationship by using formal language, citing the research literature whenever appropriate, wearing a suit, shirt and tie and by referring to myself as Dr Dryden and to my client as Mrs G. On one occasion I inadvertently used her first name and was put firmly in my place concerning the protocol of professional relationships. On another occasion I disclosed a piece of personal information in order to make a therapeutic point and was told in no uncertain terms: 'Young man, I am not paying you good money to hear about your problems.' Here, a therapist is faced with the choice of respecting and meeting a client's bond anticipations and preferences or examining the reasons why, for example, this client was so adamantly against her therapist's informality. In my experience the latter strategy is rarely productive and rational–emotive therapists are recommended to fulfil their clients' preferences for therapy style as long as doing so does not reinforce the client's psychological problems.

At 5 p.m. on the same afternoon I regularly saw Mr B., a 42-year-old male nurse who indicated that he did not respond well to his previous therapist's neutrality and formality. Our therapy sessions were thus characterised by an informal bond. Before seeing him I would remove my jacket and tie that I wore for Mrs G.; in sessions we would use our first names and would both have our feet up on my desk. We also developed the habit of taking turns to bring in cans of soda and my client referred to our meetings as 'rap sessions' while I conceptualised my work as therapy within an informal context.

I maintain that Mrs G. would not have responded well to an informal therapy relationship nor would Mr B. have done as well with a highly formal mode of therapy. Thus, I argue that it is important that rational–emotive therapists pay attention to the question: 'Which bond is likely to be most effective with a particular client at a given time in the therapeutic process?' Drawing upon social–psychological principles, certain writers have argued that some clients show more progress when the therapeutic bond is based on liking and trustworthiness, whilst others flourish more when the bond emphasises therapist credibility and expertness (Strong and Claiborn, 1982; Beutler, 1983; Dorn, 1984). Future research in RET could fruitfully address the issue of which bond is effective with which clients. However, until we have such data, therapists could make decisions about which type of bond to foster on the basis of an early assessment of the client's anticipations and preferences in the bond domain and to try to meet such expectations, at least initially. This is one reason why I would caution novice therapists against emulating the therapy style of leading RET practitioners whose bond with clients may be based mainly on prestige and expertness. Rational–emotive therapists should thus be prepared to emphasise different aspects of themselves with different clients in the bond domain, without adopting an inauthentic façade, and to monitor transactions in this domain throughout therapy.

How can this best be done? One way would be to administer a modified portion of Lazarus's (1981) Life History Questionnaire which focuses on client's expectations regarding therapy. The items: 'How do you think a therapist should interact with his or her clients?' and 'What personal qualities do you think the ideal therapist for you should possess?' are particularly relevant and could usefully provide impetus for further exploration of this issue at the outset of therapy. If the client has had therapy previously, the current therapist could usefully explore which aspects of the previous therapist(s') interactive style and behaviour were deemed by the client to be both helpful and unhelpful. Particular emphasis should be placed on the exploration of the instrumental nature of previous therapeutic bonds since statements such as 'He was warm and caring' are of little use unless the client evaluated these qualities positively and attributed therapeutic progress to these factors.

Furthermore, and for similar reasons, I have found it helpful to explore clients' accounts of people in their lives who have had both positive and negative therapeutic influence on their personal development. Such exploration may provide the therapist with important clues concerning which types of therapeutic bonds to promote actively with certain clients and which bonds to avoid developing with others.

Therapeutic style is another aspect of the bond domain which requires attention. Interpersonally oriented therapists (e.g. Anchin and Kiesler, 1982) have argued that practitioners need to be aware that therapeutic styles have a 'for better or worse' impact on different clients. Rational–emotive therapists tend to be active and directive in their style of conducting therapy. This therapy style may not be entirely productive with both passive clients and, as Beutler (1983) has argued, clients who are highly reactive to interpersonal influence. Clients who tend to be passive in their interpersonal style of relating may 'pull' an increasingly active style from their therapists who may in turn reinforce these clients' passivity with their increased activity. Clients whose psychological problems are intrinsically bound up with a passive style of relating are particularly vulnerable in this regard. It is important that rational–emotive therapists need to engage their clients productively at a level which constructively encourages increased activity on their part but without threatening them through the use of an overly passive style of practising RET.

Beutler (1983) has argued that all approaches to psychotherapy can be viewed as a process of persuasion and this is particularly true of RET practitioners who aim to 'persuade' clients to re-evaluate and change their irrational beliefs. As such, rational–emotive therapists need to be especially careful in working with clients for whom such persuasive attempts may be perceived as especially threatening (i.e. highly reactant clients). Here it is important that therapists execute their strategies with due regard to helping such clients to preserve their sense of autonomy, emphasising throughout that these clients are in control of their own thought processes and decisions concerning whether or not to change them. At present, the above suggestions are speculative and await full empirical enquiry, but my clinical work has led me to question the desirability of establishing the same therapeutic bond with all clients and of practising rational–emotive therapy in an unchanging therapeutic style.

Goals

The major concern of rational–emotive therapists in the goal domain of the alliance is to ensure that there is agreement between therapist and client on the client's outcome goals for change. A prerequisite of such agreement concerns client and therapist arriving at a shared understanding of the client's most relevant problems as defined by the client (Meichenbaum and Gilmore, 1982). Difficulties may occur here when the therapist uncritically accepts the client's initial accounts of his or her problem because such accounts may well be biased by the client's internalised values, e.g. the views of significant others in the client's life. In addition, although most rational–emotive therapists consider that early goal-setting with the client is important, clients' initial statements about their goals for change may well be coloured by their psychological disturbance as well as by their internalised values concerning what these goals should be. Rational–emotive therapists need to walk a fine line between uncritically accepting clients' initial goals for change and disregarding them altogether. A helpful solution here involves establishment and maintenance of a channel of communication between client and therapist which deals with metatherapy issues (i.e. issues concerning matters relating to therapy itself). I have referred to the activities that occur within this channel as involving negotiations and renegotiations about therapeutic issues (Dryden and Hunt, 1985). Rational–emotive therapists need to take the main responsibility for keeping this communication channel open in order to monitor clients' goals over time and to determine the reasons for shifts in these goals.

Pinsof and Catherall (1986) have made the important point that clients' goals occur (implicitly or explicitly) in reference to their most important relationships and their therapists need to be mindful of the impact that these systems are likely to have on both the selection of such goals and the client's degree of progress towards goal attainment. Adopting this focus may well possibly mean involving parts of the client's interpersonal system in therapy itself. It also suggests that future theorising in RET could profitably assign a more central role to interpersonal issues (compare Safran, 1984; Kwee and Lazarus, 1986).

Tasks

Rational-emotive practitioners tend to subscribe to the following therapeutic process. Initially, having agreed to offer help to the client, the therapist attempts to structure the therapeutic process for the client and begins both to assess his or her problems in rational-emotive terms and also to help the client to view his or her problems within this framework. Goals are elicited based on a rational-emotive assessment, and therapeutic strategies and techniques are implemented to effect the desired changes. Finally, obstacles to client change are analysed and, it is hoped, overcome, and therapeutic gains are stabilised and maintained.

Therapists have tasks to execute at each stage in the rational-emotive therapeutic process and these will now be outlined.

Structuring

Effective RET depends in part on each participant clearly understanding their respective responsibilities in the therapeutic endeavour and upon each agreeing to discharge these responsibilities in the form of carrying out therapeutic tasks. It is the therapist's major responsibility to help the client to make sense of this process by providing an overall structure of mutual responsibilities and tasks. It is important to stress that structuring occurs throughout therapy and not just at the outset of the process. Sensitive therapists who pay attention to alliance issues will structure the process using language which the client can understand and analogies which make sense to each individual person. Thus, it is often helpful to discover clients' hobbies and interests so that apt and personally meaningful structuring statements can be made. Thus, if a client is interested in golf, ascertaining how that person learned the game may be valuable in drawing parallels between the processes of learning coping skills and learning golfing skills. Both involve practice and failures can be realistically anticipated in each activity.

Assessment and conceptualisation of clients' problems

During the assessment process, rational-emotive therapists traditionally attempt to gain a full understanding of the cognitive and behavioural variables that are maintaining their clients' problems. During this stage two issues become salient from an alliance theory perspective. First, it is important for therapist and client to arrive at a shared definition of the client's problems (i.e. what these problems are). Secondly, as Meichenbaum and Gilmore (1982) have noted, it is important for them to negotiate a shared conceptualisation of the client's problems (i.e. an explanation of what accounts for the existence of these problems) so that they can work productively together in the intervention stage of therapy.

When working towards shared problem conceptualisation, I argue that it is important for RET practitioners to use, wherever possible, the client's own language and concepts, particularly when providing alternative explanations of their problems. This helps therapists to work within the range of what clients will accept as plausible conceptualisations of their problems. If clients' own ideas about the origins of their problems and more particularly what maintain them are ignored, then they may well resist accepting their therapists' conceptualisations. As Golden (1985) has noted, sometimes therapists often have to accept initially, for pragmatic purposes, a client's different (i.e. to the therapist's) conceptualisation of his or her problems in order to arrive later at a shared one. In addition, rational–emotive therapists may well privately (i.e. to themselves) conceptualise a client's problems in rational–emotive terms (irrational beliefs) whilst publicly (to the client) using the client's conceptualisation (e.g. negative self-hypnosis). To what extent the effectiveness of RET is based on negotiation or on the unilateral persuasion attempts of the therapist is a matter for future empirical enquiry.

Change tactics

Once the therapist and client have come to a mutually agreed understanding of the client's problems, the therapist then discusses with the client a variety of techniques that the client can use to reach his or her goals. Here it is important to realise that both client and therapist have tasks to execute.

Effective RET in the task domain tends to occur when:

1. Clients understand what their tasks are.
2. Clients understand how executing their tasks will help them achieve their goals.
3. Clients are, in fact, capable of executing their tasks and believe that they have this capability.
4. Clients understand that change comes about through repeated execution of their tasks.
5. Clients understand the tasks of their therapists and can see the link between their therapists' tasks, their own tasks and their goals.
6. Therapists adequately prepare their clients to understand and execute the latter's tasks.
7. Therapists effectively execute their tasks (i.e. they are skilled in the techniques of RET) and use a wide range of techniques appropriately.
8. Therapists employ techniques which are congruent with their clients'

learning styles. Whilst some clients learn best through action, others learn best through reading bibliotherapy texts etc.

9. Therapists employ techniques that clients have selected (from a range of possible procedures) rather than unilaterally selecting techniques without client participation.

10. Therapists pace their interventions appropriately.

11. Therapists employ techniques which are potent enough to help clients achieve their goals (e.g. using exposure methods with clients with agoraphobic problems – Emmelkamp, Kuipers and Eggeraat, 1978).

Failures in RET

I have been practising RET now for over 15 years in a variety of settings. I have worked in (1) a university therapy service; (2) a general practice; (3) a National Health Service psychiatric clinic; (4) a local marriage guidance council; and (5) private practice. I have seen in these settings a wide range of moderately to severely disturbed individuals who were deemed to be able to benefit from weekly counselling or psychotherapy. Whilst I do not have any hard data to substantiate the point, I have found rational–emotive therapy to be a highly effective method of individual psychotherapy with a wide range of client problems.

However, I have of course had my therapeutic failures, and I would like, in this final section, to outline some of the factors that in my opinion have accounted for these failures. I will again use Bordin's (1979) useful concept of the therapeutic working alliance as a framework in this respect.

Goals

I have generally been unsuccessful with clients who have devoutly clung to goals where changes in other people were desired. (In this regard, I have also failed to involve these others in therapy.) I have not been able to show or to persuade these clients that they make themselves emotionally disturbed and that it would be better if they were to work to change themselves before attempting to negotiate changes in their relationships with others. It is the devoutness of their beliefs which seems to me to be the problem here.

Bonds

Unlike the majority of therapists of my acquaintance, I do not regard the relationship between therapist and client to be the sine qua non of effective therapy. I strive to accept my clients as fallible human beings and am prepared to work concertedly to help them overcome their problems, but do not endeavour to form very close, warm relationships with them. In the main, my clients do not appear to want such a relationship with me (preferring to become close and intimate with their significant others). However, occasionally I get clients who do wish to become (non-sexually) intimate with me. Some of these clients (who devoutly believe they need my love) leave therapy disappointed after I have failed to get them to give up their dire need for love or refused to give them what they think they need.

Tasks

In this analysis I will assume throughout that therapists are practising RET effectively and thus the emphasis will be on client variables.

My basic thesis here is that when therapist and client agree concerning (1) the view of psychological disturbance as stated in rational–emotive theory, (2) the rational–emotive view on the acquisition and perpetuation of psychological disturbance, and (3) the rational–emotive view of therapeutic change, such agreements are likely to enhance good therapeutic outcome. Furthermore, the greater the disagreement between the two participants on such matters, the greater the threat that exists to the therapeutic alliance with all the negative implications that this has for good therapeutic outcome. I should say at the outset that this hypothesis has yet to be tested and should thus be viewed sceptically.

I will illustrate my points by using clinical examples from my experience as a therapist.

Conceptualisation of psychological disturbance

Rational–emotive theory states that much psychological disturbance can be attributed to clients' devout, absolutistic evaluations (irrational beliefs) about themselves, other people and life events. RET practitioners assume that most clients do not enter therapy sharing this viewpoint and, thus, one of the therapist's major tasks is to persuade the client to adopt this viewpoint if effective RET is to ensue. Of course, not all clients will be so persuaded because they have their own (different) ideas about the nature of their psychological problems and what causes them and are not prepared to relinquish these. In my experience, the following clients are not good candidates for RET unless they change their ideas about the determinants of their problems: those who believe that their problems are caused by (1) external events (including events that happened in childhood), (2) physical, dietary or biochemical factors, (3) repressed basic human impulses, (4) fate or astrological factors and (5) blockages in the body.

I once had a referral from a social worker who confused RET with Reichian therapy. The client specifically wanted to work on his character armour blockages which he considered were at the source of his problems. I explained that an error had been made and that I was a rational–emotive therapist and gave him a brief outline of the rational–emotive view of his problems. He responded with incredulity, saying that he hadn't heard such intellectualised clap-trap in a long while and asked me whether I knew of anyone who could really help him. I referred him to a local bioenergetics therapist who, apparently, helped him considerably.

Acquisition and perpetuation of psychological disturbance

Rational–emotive theory de-emphasises the value of understanding acquisition variables in helping clients change. Rather, it stresses the importance of understanding how people perpetuate their psychological problems. This is because the theory hypothesises that whilst past events may well have contributed to clients' psychological disturbance, these did not make them disturbed, since people bring their tendency to make themselves disturbed to these events and experiences. Thus, clients who come to therapy in order to trace their psychological problems back to their roots tend not to benefit greatly from the present-centred and future-oriented focus of RET. Clients who are prepared to look for and challenge their currently held irrational beliefs do much better in RET than clients who are preoccupied with discovering how they came to hold such beliefs in the first place.

A 60-year-old woman with agoraphobic and panic problems was firmly convinced that the origins of her panic lay in buried childhood feelings towards her parents, who while kindly disposed to my client, had placed undue burdens on her as a child. Not only did we have different views concerning the 'cause' of her present problems, but we differed as to the most appropriate time focus for the therapy. I did discuss her childhood with her, but as a stimulus to help her re-focus on her present disturbance-perpetuating beliefs, but to no avail. She quit therapy with me and started consulting a Jungian therapist who has seen her now for 2 years with little impact on her panic disorder.

Views on therapeutic change

RET can be viewed as a therapeutic system which has a 'Protestant Ethic' view of therapeutic change. Clients are urged to 'work and practise' their way to emotional health by using a variety of cognitive, emotive and behavioural methods designed to help them to change their irrational beliefs. Clients who are not prepared to put in the necessary hard work usually have less successful therapeutic outcomes than clients who challenge repeatedly their irrational beliefs in thought, feeling and deed.

It follows from the above that RET places most emphasis on the activities that clients initiate and sustain outside therapy as the major agent of change. Clients who consider that change will occur primarily from therapy sessions usually do not gain as much from RET as clients who are in accord with the rational–emotive viewpoint on this matter.

During my 6 months stay at the Center for Cognitive Therapy in

Philadelphia, I saw briefly a client who had heard of cognitive therapy for depression and wished to try it. I was learning this approach at the time and was keen to do it 'by the book'. The client had recently moved to Philadelphia from Los Angeles where she had consulted an experiential therapist with whom she had had a very close relationship which, in my opinion, had encouraged her to be more dependent on love and approval than she was before she consulted him. The client had come to believe that therapeutic change depended on a very warm, close therapeutic relationship in which completing homework assignments and 'Daily Record of Dysfunctional Thoughts' sheets had no place. Despite my attempts to change her views on such matters, she left cognitive therapy to seek another experiential therapist.

Ellis's study on failure in RET

Ellis (1983) has published some interesting data which tend to corroborate my own experiences of therapeutic failure in RET. He chose 50 of his clients who were seen in individual and/or group RET and were rated by him, and where appropriate by his associate group therapist, as 'failures'. In some ways, this sample consisted of fairly ideal RET clients in that they were individuals (1) of above average or of superior intelligence (in Ellis's judgement and that of their other group therapist); (2) who seemed really to understand RET and who were often effective (especially in group therapy) in helping others to learn and use it; (3) who in some ways made therapeutic progress and felt that they benefited by having RET but who still retained one or more serious presenting symptoms, such as severe depression, acute anxiety, overwhelming hostility or extreme lack of self-discipline; and (4) who had at least 1 year of individual and/or group RET sessions, and sometimes considerably more.

   This group was compared to clients who were selected on the same four criteria but who seemed to benefit greatly from RET. While a complete account of this study – which, of course, has its methodological flaws – can be found in Ellis (1983), the following results are most pertinent:

1. In its cognitive aspects, RET emphasises the persistent use of reason, logic and the scientific method to uproot clients' irrational beliefs. Consequently, it ideally requires intelligence, concentration and high-level, consistent cognitive self-disputation and self-persuasion. These therapeutic behaviours would tend to be disrupted or blocked by extreme disturbance, by lack of organisation, by grandiosity, by organic disruption and by refusal to do RET-type disputing of irrational ideas. All these characteristics proved to be present in significantly more failures than in those clients who responded favourably to RET.
2. RET also, to be quite successful, involves clients' forcefully and emotive-

ly changing their beliefs and actions, and their being stubbornly determined to accept responsibility for their own inappropriate feelings and vigorously work at changing these feelings (Ellis and Abrahms, 1978; Ellis and Whiteley, 1979). But the failure clients in this study were significantly more angry than those who responded well to RET; more of them were severely depressed and inactive, they were more often grandiose, and they were more frequently stubbornly resistant and rebellious. All these characteristics would presumably tend to interfere with the kind of emotive processes and changes that RET espouses.

3. RET strongly advocates that clients, in order to improve, do in vivo activity homework assignments, deliberately force themselves to engage in many uncomfortable activities until they make themselves comfortable, and notably work and practise its multimodal techniques. But the group of clients who signally failed in this study showed abysmally low frustration tolerance, had serious behavioural addictions, led disorganised lives, refrained from doing their activity homework assignments, were more frequently psychotic and generally refused to work at therapy. All these characteristics, which were found significantly more frequently than were found in the clients who responded quite well to RET, would tend to interfere with clients using the behavioural methods or RET.

Thus it appears from the above analysis that the old adage of psychotherapy applies to RET: namely that clients who could most use therapy are precisely those individuals whose disturbance interferes with their benefiting from it.

Chapter 8
Dilemmas in Giving Warmth or Love to Clients:
An Interview with Albert Ellis

Windy Dryden: Could you put the dilemma that you wish to talk about in your own words.

Albert Ellis: First, it is the dilemma of how warmly to relate to clients in general; and, secondly, how warm to be with very vulnerable clients in particular.

Windy Dryden: Let's take the general case first.

Albert Ellis: I first confronted the general principle years ago when I was questioning orthodox psychoanalytical thought, which holds that early childhood experiences are crucial in determining later disturbance and that clients have to understand and work through these experiences and have a 'corrective emotional experience', as Franz Alexander (Alexander and French, 1946) called it, with an analyst who passively listens to their present and past experiences and feelings.

After seeing that this doesn't bring good results, I experimented with Ferenczi's (1952-55) method of active psychoanalysis. He and other people, such as Izette de Forrest (1954) and Ian Suttie (1948), held that a person's early childhood is even more crucial than Freud thought. Ferenczi claimed that if your parents, and particularly your mother, did not give you enough love, you become emotionally damaged as a result of this lack. Therefore, what an analyst has to be is highly active and really show you the warmth, kindness and love that your parents failed to give you. You will then get that 'corrective emotional experience' and will significantly improve. I experimented with Ferenczi's method in the early 1950s and persisted with it for about a year.

Freud was horrified with Ferenczi's (1952-55) method and said that the next thing Ferenczi would do was to get on the sofa with his clients, particularly with the young attractive females. Whilst I thought that Freud's

First published in 1985.

objection was exaggerated, I made sure that the warmth I gave my clients was purely verbal. I didn't touch them at all and I gave verbal warmth to my male and female clients alike.

Accordingly, I really went out of my way to tell my clients that they had excellent traits, that I liked them, and that I was sure that they could get over their problems because of their fine traits. I thereby made up for the love they had presumably missed in early childhood. Indeed, many of them actually had been treated unlovingly by their parents. I believed, since I still thought in psychoanalytical terms, that their parents were delinquent and had not given them sufficient love. Since that time I have come to realise that some of these clients were probably obnoxious as children and encouraged their parents' lack of feeling. Also their parents may have been biologically prone to disturbance and may have passed on this tendency to the children genetically.

However, in those days I accepted the hypothesis that these clients were disturbed as a result of lack of parental love, so I gave them a good deal of verbal affection, approval and acclaim. I discovered very quickly that they thoroughly liked this. A good many of them started asking for extra sessions, which they had not asked for before. They also began to show greater warmth towards me and to refer their friends to me for therapy. In addition, I integrated Ferenczi's (1952–55) method with Harry Stack Sullivan's (1953) interpersonal approach. I asked my clients about their feelings towards me and talked about my feelings towards them. In talking about my feelings towards them I would include positive appraisals. I did not outrightly lie, but I downplayed my negative feelings towards my clients and emphasised their positive qualities. They loved that!

After 6–8 months of conducting therapy in this way, I realised, however, that my clients were becoming unusually dependent on me. In psychoanalysis, they became dependent anyway, but with Ferenczi's (1952–55) method they become much more so. I also saw that they were improving very little. Some of them seemed even to be getting sicker, more into themselves and our relationship, rather than involved in their external life.

Windy Dryden: And yet they claimed to be benefiting from therapy.

Albert Ellis: They felt marvellous. They would say such things as: 'I have never felt so good in all my life.' My 'leaven of love' therapy – as Izette de Forrest called it – sometimes helped them feel less depressed, so it was good in that way. However, it didn't help them with their anxiety. They incessantly kept worrying, especially about whether other people loved them. They related well to me and perhaps to a few others. But they didn't improve on their jobs and weren't really doing very well in life. So I started thinking that perhaps this therapeutic method had distinct drawbacks. In fact, as a result of these experiences I first developed the concept which I wrote a paper on years later about clients *feeling* better but not *getting* better. In fact sometimes they got distinctly worse; not all of them, to be sure, but certainly some of them.

Windy Dryden: What was the dilemma at that time for you?

Albert Ellis: The dilemma involved a conflict between therapeutic and practical considerations. On the one hand, these clients were saying how much they were being helped by this warmth method and they were referring many other people to me. Because I was in private practice at that time, and could use their patronage, I knew that if I stopped giving them active approval and acclaim, they would probably drop out of therapy. On the other hand, if I continued in the same vein I would be going against what I felt was therapeutic for them in the long run. So I finally decided to stop giving them so much active approval and some clients did quit fairly soon thereafter. They were no longer getting reinforced, as reinforcement theory would say.

I went on to do a different type of active–directive therapy. I started giving homework assignments and eventually went on to establish RET. Incidentally, the same dilemma arose years later when I had therapists working with me here at the Institute. Some of these therapists seemed to do very well with their clients by using RET *and* a great deal of warmth and affection. The clients liked it and on the surface it looked good. However, these therapists often got into trouble with their clients. One therapist in particular got into really hot water because several of his female clients fell madly in love with him. One client bribed the superintendent of his building to let her into his office. The therapist found his client naked on a sofa when he arrived, insisting that he joined her because he had led her to believe that he wanted a sex–love affair. He denied that he wanted that, but his warmth towards her had apparently given her this idea. Some of his other clients became overly attached to him and cracked up when he refused to take this relationship further. You see, there is always the danger that some clients will expect more from you, the more warmth you give them.

Anyway, partly for these reasons I formulated RET along less loving lines. But even in RET, I have the problem from time to time about how warm to be with exceptionally vulnerable clients.

Windy Dryden: Before we deal with the more specific form of the dilemma, I want to ask you one question. Did these experiences help you to sharpen up your thinking concerning the distinction between short-term and long-term consequences of therapy?

Albert Ellis: Yes. I think so. Because I found that in the short run clients did feel better when I gave them active approval and acclaim. Some apparently made remarkable changes in a brief period of time. However, they usually fell back and didn't continue to improve. I learned from this that short-term warmth is reinforcing and rewarding and will keep people in therapy. That is a big part of the dilemma. A very warm type of therapy will keep clients in treatment for a while – treatment that they could really use. However, if you hook them with this type of approval and they stay in therapy for a year or two, will you then be able to teach them the hard-core RET – namely to think for themselves, to dispute their irrational beliefs, to take risks and to make themselves *un*comfortable in order later to become comfortable?

Windy Dryden: What has your experience taught you in this respect?

Albert Ellis: My experience is that if you are really warm and nice to clients, it leads many of them, as well as yourself, up the garden path because they become dependent on you. When they do finally work at therapy, they do it mainly for you, the therapist – i.e. for the wrong reasons. They are not really intent on changing their basic philosophy. They may eventually work at therapy, but usually within their old philosophy, which is frequently a philosophy of 'I need your love'. When they think they need their therapist's love and actually get it, they feel good and seemingly improve. But they are not *really* making significant changes.

Windy Dryden: However, if you do not go some way towards satisfying their expectations they drop out of therapy and presumably remain disturbed.

Albert Ellis: This is right. So therefore you had better develop some kind of good rapport with them and show them that you are certainly on their side. The elegant answer to this dilemma is to show clients *un*conditional acceptance. What Ferenczi (1952–55) and his followers really do is accept their clients *conditionally*. They are implying, 'Because you do good acts and are a nice person, therefore I think you are OK'. However, in RET we practise *un*conditional acceptance and try to show our clients that, no matter how badly they act towards the therapist or towards others, we can still unconditionally accept them and teach them to accept themselves unconditionally. So this is a different kind of acceptance which, when it works, doesn't make clients dependent. In fact, it enables them to become more independent because they become less 'needy'.

Windy Dryden: So these experiences helped you to see that when therapists unconditionally accept their clients this has less dramatic short-term but more therapeutic long-term effects on clients than does undue therapist warmth.

Albert Ellis: Yes. I was also helped to see this at that time by reading Paul Tillich's book, *The Courage to Be* (1953). He clearly encouraged people to have the courage to 'be yourself' and not need the approval of others.

Windy Dryden: OK. Now you mentioned earlier that you still sometimes experience this dilemma, particularly with vulnerable people. Can you elaborate on that?

Albert Ellis: Yes. There are some people who are suicidal and others who are very vulnerable who, if you say anything harsh to them or if you try to push them to do uncomfortable things, just don't seem to be able to take it. So at the beginning of therapy with some people, I lean over backwards to be kinder than I might normally be. I still show them the ABCs of RET and encourage them to do active disputing. But I highlight some of their good traits and push them in the direction of hope. I still have a dilemma because I never know exactly where to draw the line.

This reminds me of the experiences of Maxim Young, who worked in the 1960s at Philadelphia General Hospital, which at that time was a short-stay receiving hospital. Max was using RET with the clients there, some of whom were extremely disturbed. Now Max was very soft sell. He didn't debate or argue with his patients as much as I would do but he was still very educational in his approach to RET. While he reported quite remarkable success with even some of his most disturbed clients, there was one group that he failed to help and who sometimes got worse. These were clients who previously had a very warm therapist who had been very nice to them, who never confronted them and who strongly complimented them. These clients resisted RET even when taught in Max's toned-down style. They sometimes became more depressed because they couldn't take being even mildly challenged.

I have had similar experiences with clients who also had a very warm therapist for 3, 5, some even 10 years. I have been amazed to discover how little they had progressed during therapy. Yet they spoke enthusiastically about their therapist and told me how much they had learned. However, when I asked them specifically what they had learned, their answers were very vague and they couldn't really point to anything. My experience with these clients yielded more evidence that therapist warmth helps people feel better but tends to leave them far from the point that I would like to see them reach after a reasonable period of therapy.

Windy Dryden: Do you have any instances where you got the balance wrong with these vulnerable clients?

Albert Ellis: Well it's hard to say. I still have a peculiarly perfect record with suicidal clients. I have seen hundreds of them over the years and apparently not one of them has committed suicide while I was treating them and only one or two did so years after they stopped seeing me. I'm warm to most of them at the beginning of therapy because they are very vulnerable. Not all of them are vulnerable, though; some of them are quite hard headed and still suicidal. With the vulnerable ones, however, I combine the warm approach with the RET method of getting straight to the main negative things they are telling themselves: 'I am no good! I will *never* get any happiness! It's hopeless!' I very actively reveal these beliefs and vigorously contradict them. But I tend to do so in a warm fashion. With this approach, I find that many clients get over their suicidal feelings in one, two or three sessions, although of course it takes longer to get them over their basic feelings of depression.

However, a number of clients don't continue therapy, perhaps because they think I'm overdoing the warm approach. Some of them tell me to my face: 'Oh you are just saying that because you are a therapist. You don't really like me.' They think I am overly flattering and almost see through what I am trying to do.

Windy Dryden: You seem to be talking about different ways of doing therapy. One type of therapy involves helping clients to get what they want even though this may work against long-term improvement. The other way involves helping clients see, in terms of RET theory, how they are disturbing themselves and how they can get over their disturbance even though this may not coincide with what their own goals are.

Albert Ellis: Well, my own way of doing therapy is first to find out what the client thinks is the problem and start there. I then try to help the client with his or her problem. Then, in subsequent sessions, I usually check on how the client is feeling, how he or she is using RET, and how homework assignments are being carried out. I usually ask questions such as: 'What bothered you most this week?' or 'What do you want to talk about most?'.

The one thing that other therapists often do that I rarely do is to ask the question: 'What do you want to get out of this session?' I think that this is an artificial and pressuring question because the client may easily feel compelled to invent a specific goal. If so, therapists will tend to waste therapeutic time by working on the client's goal that they forced him or her to pick. It sounds like a very democratic, consumer-minded thing to do but it often isn't.

The other aspect of therapeutic consumerism that I am sceptical about is when you as the therapist pretend that you and the client are equal collaborators and that you both equally know the answer to the client's problems. This is often nonsense because, when clients bring up a problem, if you are a competent RET practitioner you can quickly guess what they are telling themselves, how to challenge their irrational beliefs and what rational self-statements clients had better produce. So why should you waste therapeutic time collaborating 50:50 with clients when you can effectively help them quickly zero in on what their philosophical problems are – especially their explicit or implicit *musts*. Indeed, if you do try to maintain a fully collaborative stance, I think you are adopting a hypocritical pretence.

Windy Dryden: Why do you think then that therapists like adopting this 'pretence'?

Albert Ellis: My hypothesis is that many therapists, who are scared shitless of making mistakes in therapy, like 'full collaboration' because they can cop out on taking risks and on doing a great deal of the therapeutic work themselves. They are afraid to do active disputing of irrational beliefs and to teach clients to use the scientific method, which is what good therapy is largely about. They are, in a word, afraid of being directive.

Windy Dryden: Now one criticism that people often make of RET is that you are trying to fit the client to your system as opposed to modifying the system to fit your client.

Albert Ellis: Well, we *are* trying to get the client to fit the system. All therapists do that but many hypocritically deny it. They pretend that they don't use a theoretical Procrustean bed but they really do. Behaviour therapists obviously do and make few bones about it. Rogerian therapists fit clients into their theories about feeling and openness. Gestalt therapists pretend they are spontaneous, but of course try to elicit their clients' presumably spontaneous feelings by their own well-planned and highly directive instructions and exercises.

Windy Dryden: And multimodal therapists?

Albert Ellis: Well, multimodal therapy overlaps significantly with RET, which was always a multimodal form of therapy a decade and a half before Arnold Lazarus invented his system. Multimodal therapists notably put clients into the BASIC ID system, to make sure they are treated in all these modalities. So what therapists don't fit clients to their particular theory or system? None, I would guess. They all do it, honestly or dishonestly. Remember the research studies which showed that Rogerian therapists reinforce their clients with their 'mm-hmms', even when they are ostensibly based on that theory?

Windy Dryden: So what you are unashamedly saying is: 'Yes I do try and fit the client to my theory because I have a good theory and a good therapy that is based on that theory?'

Albert Ellis: Right! I honestly acknowledge that I do. Let's suppose you are a gestalt therapist and your client says: 'I want to talk about my past.' Or you are a psychoanalyst and your client says: 'I only want to stick to the present. I don't want to talk about my parents.' What do you do?

Windy Dryden: I suppose you have the choice of trying to persuade them to your point of view or referring them on.

Albert Ellis: That's right. If you can't persuade them, you refer them elsewhere. So you only stick with your system. Now some systems are more eclectic than others. RET is eclectic in its techniques but not in its theory. It has a theory which states that disturbed people have basic irrationalities, which therapists can identify and can help clients identify very quickly. It also has a theory which holds that to minimise these irrationalities, therapists require many cognitive, emotive and behavioural techniques and not the same ones for each client. Different clients may require different techniques.

Windy Dryden: So, again, if a client comes in and wants something which you regard as bad for them, you would have no hesitation in trying to talk them out of it.

Albert Ellis: Right. Take for example, hypnosis. I have had my Boards in Clinical Hypnosis for many years and I used hypnosis before I began to practise RET. I have merged RET and hypnotic methods for many years – and so have Don Tosi, Bill Golden and other RET therapists. However, when people ask me for hypnosis I often talk them out of it. Why? Because they have usually read somewhere that it does magic and it will help them enormously with very little work on their part. I therefore try to help them see that this isn't so and try to get them to use RET without hypnosis. However, in certain selected cases, I do combine the two and give them RET within a hypnotic framework.

Windy Dryden: What you seem to be saying is this: 'I am prepared to take the risk and lose clients by not giving them what they ask for, because I often have a clear idea of how they disturb themselves and how they can get over their disturbance and what may sidetrack them from doing this successfully.'

Albert Ellis: Yes. I try to talk them *into* something that I believe on theoretical and practical grounds is therapeutic. I don't always succeed. Some of them go off to other forms of therapy, especially inefficient modes such as psychoanalysis. Too bad! I do take the risk of losing clients because I don't believe in pandering to consumerism in therapy. If I were a grocer, I would hardly sell my customers poisoned food even if they believed that it would magically help them. If I were a physician, I would not give them drugs, such as amphetamines, even though these might temporarily make them feel better. As a practising therapist I experiment with many techniques, when I think they will work now – and later. But when I have good reason to believe that they will mainly provide temporary relief and do harm later, I do my best to avoid using them. Even when clients whine and beg for their usage!

Let me tell a sad story that epitomises the dilemma we have been discussing. Over 20 years ago, I saw a very healthy 20-year-old woman who was most undisciplined and who had such a dire need for love that she sometimes used a wooden peg leg to get around on (though both her legs were in fine condition), in order to get people to pity her and offer her help. Although I induced her to use RET to overcome her low frustration tolerance finally to graduate from college, and to finish a novel she intended to write but always avoided working on, I could not induce her to surrender her dire love need. She kept insisting that she would only give it up if I, her therapist, was unusually kind to her and showed that I truly loved her. I stuck to my guns, however; showed her that if I acceded to her demands, I would help confirm her irrational belief that she needed adoration to be happy and self-accepting, and tried to get her to use RET more thoroughly. To no avail. After a year, she quit seeing me and for the next 6 years saw a psychoanalyst who was very warm to her and gave her the kind of therapy she was certain she needed. When her analyst died, she had a severe break-down. She married her next analyst, is still a child-wife to him, has never fulfilled her writing or other talents, and still says nasty things to people about me and RET. She keeps sending me carbon copies of letters almost every December showing that she has donated thousands of dollars to various psychoanalytical institutes – and nothing to the Institute for Rational–Emotive Therapy.

Too bad! But I still stubbornly think that I did the right thing by not going along with this client's consumerism and not giving her the love she demanded.

Chapter 9
Therapist Self-disclosure in Rational–Emotive Therapy

Introduction

One of the basic aspects of the therapist's role in RET is to educate the client in the ABCs of his emotions (Dryden, 1987b). As such, however, the therapist will freely disclose her own experiences in the service of making that educational experience a memorable one for her client. (Note that the therapist is referred to as female and the client as male in this chapter.)

In order to understand fully the RET position on therapist self-disclosure, it is first necessary to outline the RET view of human fallibility (Ellis, 1973) because this is central to such understanding. The RET theory of human fallibility states that all humans are equal in humanity, that there are neither good humans nor bad humans and that no human being is more valuable or more worthy than any other. All people are equal in humanity, although they may be unequal in terms of their different traits, behaviours, thoughts, feelings etc. Thus the RET therapist does not see herself as being more valuable than her client, although she will tend to consider that she is more knowledgeable about understanding and dealing with emotional problems.

Given that the effective RET therapist would accept herself for her errors and flaws, and for past and present emotional disturbances, she will, as often as is therapeutically advisable, show her client how she upset herself about experiences similar to those with which her client is concerned and how she used RET to overcome such emotional disturbances. Note that in choosing this mode of self-disclosure, the RET therapist is providing her client with a coping model. The therapist who employs a mastery model approach to self-disclosure will stress that she has never experienced a problem similar to the client's because she has always thought rationally about similar events with which the client is struggling. This approach is

First published in 1990.

unproductive because it unduly emphasises the inequality between therapist and client and de-emphasises their shared humanity.

A coping model of self-disclosure, on the other hand, where the therapist outlines that she too has experienced or is currently experiencing similar emotional disturbances but is able to get over these by using RET methods and techniques, indicates to the client that both therapist and client share the same experiences, although one is more adept at present in overcoming them than the other. Such a coping model emphasises the shared humanity of the therapist and client whilst not belabouring the inequality that exists between therapist and client in the therapeutic enterprise. The therapist who utilises the coping model of self-disclosure can, furthermore, outline the process of solving emotional problems for the client, and as such self-disclosure can often be a powerful therapeutic tool.

Let me use a personal example to illustrate this. I used to have a very bad stammer and was not only ashamed about this but also anxious about speaking in public because I was scared that if I revealed my stammering in public, other people would laugh at me and I would severely condemn myself if this occurred. I often disclose this fact to clients who not only experience similar problems concerning stammering, but who also have problems which are exacerbated by their anxiety that these problems may be revealed publicly. My self-disclosure is often along these lines:

> You know, as we find out more about your problem I am myself reminded of a problem that I used to have which in certain ways is quite similar to yours. I don't know if you've noticed but I stammer [here the client usually says, 'Well yes, I have noticed it but it's really not that noticeable' (indeed, I rarely stammer these days although I still have a slight speech hesitancy)]. I used to have a very bad stammer and hid myself away because I used to tell myself 'I must not stammer in public. It would be terrible if I did and I couldn't stand it if other people were to see me stammer and to think badly of me.' Well I struggled with this problem for many years and received much inadequate help from various speech therapists. However, it wasn't until I heard a radio programme on which a noted entertainer outlined his own approach to overcoming his stammering problem that I started to overcome mine. This man told how he decided to force himself to speak up in public while reminding himself that if he stammered he stammered, too bad. This was the first good piece of advice I'd heard on overcoming anxiety about stammering and I resolved to apply this myself. Indeed, although I did not realise it, I used the principles of RET which I'm now going to teach you. What I did was to force myself to enter situations and speak up, but before I did so I prepared myself by telling myself that there is no reason why I must not stammer and, if I did, too bad. On occasions I would speak more vehemently to myself and say things, such as: 'If I stammer, I stammer, Fuck it!' The more I internalised these beliefs, the more I was able to go into situations and speak up. It certainly wasn't easy and I did have setbacks, but I persisted and now I speak without anxiety in a variety of public situations, including radio and television. I still make myself anxious at times, but when I do, I look for and dispute my irrational beliefs in a very powerful and vigorous way and push myself forward on the basis of my rational beliefs. Even on the odd occasions when I cop out, I refuse to condemn myself

and fully accept myself as a person who has opted out at a given moment. So you see, I too have experienced similar problems but have managed to help myself enormously. So I have a lot of faith that if you apply similar techniques you could also gain a lot of benefit from these methods.

Whilst I have presented this personal self-disclosure in uninterrupted form, in practice parts of it are interspersed with dialogue with the client concerning what he or she can learn from my experience.

It should be noted that this self-disclosure illustrates for the client the rational–emotive approach to therapeutic change. In this personal example I show the client (1) how to identify a personal problem, (2) how to identify the irrational belief which underpins the problem, (3) the importance of repetitive and forceful disputing of this belief in situations in which the problem occurs, (4) that setbacks will occur and that, under certain circumstances, people will choose to avoid rather than to confront their problems and (5) the importance of accepting themselves when this happens. When the therapist discloses personal information for educative purposes, it is important that she asks her client what he can learn from her experience. It should not be forgotten that the purpose of the therapist self-disclosure is to aid the learning process of the client. It is not an opportunity for the therapist to boast about her achievements in overcoming personal problems. Rather, the philosophy that should preferably underpin therapist self-disclosure is: 'You and I are equal in humanity. At the moment I have more experience and skills in overcoming emotional problems but you can learn this too. It is difficult, but if you persist with it you can experience as much benefit as I did.'

Cautions

Whilst therapist self-disclosure does have great therapeutic merits, therapists should not disclose themselves indiscriminately to their clients and I will now outline circumstances in which it may be preferable for therapists not to disclose themselves to their clients.

First, therapist self-disclosure, like any form of therapist communication, needs to be considered within the wider framework of the therapeutic alliance (Bordin, 1979 and see Chapter 7). For example, in my experience it is probably not wise for therapists to disclose their own problems and how they overcame them at a very early stage in the therapeutic process. This is so mainly because clients may not view such early self-disclosure as appropriate therapist behaviour, and this may threaten the therapeutic alliance (Dies, 1974). Some clients will, however, experience benefit from early therapist self-disclosure and therapists need to use their therapeutic judgement and their knowledge of their clients as guides concerning the wisdom of making such disclosures.

Secondly, RET therapists are cautioned against disclosing themselves to clients who seek a formal relationship with their therapist. I made this mistake once when I disclosed a piece of personal information to a client who responded in this way: 'Well, young man, that's all very interesting but I'm not paying you good money to hear about your problems, will you please address yourself to mine.' This client wanted her therapist to act in a formal manner and did not value the use of therapist self-disclosure which parenthetically does seem to be associated with therapist informality. This is perhaps one reason why RET therapists, in general, favour therapist self-disclosure in that they favour adopting, whenever possible, an informal therapeutic role with their clients.

Thirdly, RET therapists should be wary about disclosing themselves to clients who might use such information to harm themselves, or their therapists. For example, there are clients who idealise their therapists and for whom disclosure of therapist fallibility may come as a very painful blow, with the result that such clients may make themselves (albeit needlessly) depressed and anxious about this. Other clients may distort the content and the purpose of therapist self-disclosure to discredit the therapist in his or her community. It is difficult for RET therapists to predict which clients will have such negative responses to therapist self-disclosure, but it is possible to gain such information and certain signs in the clients' psychopathology may provide clues for therapists in this respect. For example, if a client has a history of extreme anger and vengefulness when their view of a person is threatened, this is perhaps a clue that the therapist may not wish to disclose personal information to the client which may threaten the client's view of the therapist. However, it should be noted that, unless there are signs to the contrary, RET therapists do tend to use self-disclosure whenever therapeutically advisable and will often take risks (although not foolhardy risks) in this regard. Of course RET therapists can never guarantee that their self-disclosures will have positive effects. Therapists who demand certainty that their clients will react favourably to their disclosures will probably never self-disclose. Given the fact that RET therapists are not afraid to take calculated risks in therapy, they will take the chance of gaining therapeutic leverage by disclosing their problems and how they overcame them after disputing any demands they may have about this being acceptable to the client.

Now that I have outlined the value and risks of therapist self-disclosure in RET, I would like to emphasise how important it is for therapists to elicit feedback from their clients concerning the impact of their self-disclosures (Beck et al., 1979). Thus, at the end of the session during which I have disclosed to a client some of my problems and how I overcame them, I generally ask the client what impact this had on him, how he felt about my disclosure, what he had learned from my disclosure, and whether or not he would have preferred me to disclose this information. If the therapist establishes her own system of feedback with the client, then it is possible to gauge the likely future benefit of therapist self-disclosure with that client. When a client indicates that therapist self-disclosure is not helpful, then that is perhaps a good guide for the therapist not to disclose her problems and the way she overcame them in future to that client.

Disclosing Personal Reactions to the Client

Whilst I have so far focused on one major feature of therapist self-disclosure, namely disclosure of problems and how these have been overcome, there is another aspect of self-disclosure that I would like to address in this chapter – the issue of providing clients with feedback concerning the therapist's personal reaction to them. When clients talk about such issues as not getting on with people, I look for possible ways in which they may antagonise people by monitoring my own reactions to them in the therapy session. It sometimes occurs that I get a clear indication that a client's mode of interaction with me may, if reproduced with other people, lead these other people to shun the client.

For example, one of my clients developed the habit of putting his feet up on my furniture. His presenting problem was that he felt quite lonely and didn't get on with people. I not only shared with him my reaction of displeasure whenever he did this, but was also keen to show him that while I disapproved of his behaviour, I did accept him as a person. I told him that whilst I did not demand that he must not under any circumstances continue to put his feet on my furniture, I would, if he continued to do so, exercise my rights to terminate the therapeutic relationship. Later on in the therapeutic process he told me that he really valued my feedback on his interpersonal behaviour (although he did not appreciate it at the time!) because he could see in a very clear way the negative impact that he was having on other people.

In this example, I have stressed an important aspect of the RET approach to disclosing personal reactions to clients – namely that it is important to make a distinction between the person's behaviour from the person as a whole and to teach this principle to the client. Whilst the client is encouraged to take responsibility for his behaviour, he is shown that he does not equal his behaviour. Thus, when the therapist brings to the client's attention some problematic aspect of his behaviour, she demonstrates unconditional acceptance of the client as a person but takes a no-nonsense approach to drawing attention to the negative aspects of the client's behaviour.

RET therapists are again advised to use clinical judgement before disclosing their personal reactions to their clients. For example, clients who very easily upset themselves about even minor criticisms need to be quite adept at using RET methods to overcome such strong reactions before therapists disclose their negative reactions to problematic aspects of their clients' interpersonal behaviour. This is true whether or not such clients ask for such feedback.

In general, whenever clients ask me for my opinion of them, I use this as an opportunity to teach them RET, particularly if I do have a negative reaction to them, and I sometimes disclose this reaction without being asked, as in the example provided above. Such disclosures need to be made tactfully and it is important for the therapist to pay attention to the language she uses to disclose her negative reactions to aspects of her clients' behaviour. In addition to showing the client that he does not equal his behaviour, it is also important that the client is shown that, although he is acting in a way that the therapist finds negative, he does not have to continue to act that way and that the therapist has faith and confidence that he can improve his behaviour. I have personally found the combination of *both* disclosing negative reactions about certain aspects of my clients' behaviour in the context of teaching the RET position on (1) the difference between the person and his acts, and (2) the possibility of change *and* providing encouragement, to be especially therapeutic.

Overcoming Obstacles to Therapist Self-disclosure

In this section, I will outline some of the main explanations for avoidance of self-disclosure in RET therapists and what they and their supervisors can do to help them overcome obstacles to therapist self-disclosure.

RET therapists are usually quite willing to disclose not only their problems and how they overcome them, but also their personal reactions to their clients, although, as I have suggested, such disclosure needs to be made in the context of sound clinical decision-making. However, some RET therapists are reluctant to employ self-disclosure in this way and in my experience in supervising such therapists there are three main reasons why this occurs: (1) a need to be seen as thoroughly competent by the client, (2) a need for the client's approval and (3) the belief that therapists absolutely should not have psychological problems.

When RET therapists believe that they have to be competent under all conditions they tend to avoid the appropriate use of therapist self-disclosure because they predict that, if they disclose that they have had emotional problems even though they have overcome them, their clients will judge them as being incompetent; and if this was the case they would condemn themselves for this. While supervising therapists who have this belief, I have used a double-barrelled approach to this problem. First, I encourage the therapist concerned to assume that her worst fear is realised, i.e. that if she discloses herself to her clients then they will indeed see her as being incompetent as a therapist. Having encouraged her to imagine that her worst fear has come true, I then help her to see that it is her beliefs (B) about this situation (A) that lead to her reluctance to self-disclosure at (C). I then help her to identify and to challenge the irrational belief that underpins this experience, namely: 'I must be seen as a competent therapist otherwise I'm unworthy.' When this has been done, the therapist is in a better position to reassess logically the likelihood that her clients will actually see her as incompetent. Here I use both my own example of past self-disclosure to clients (as outlined earlier in this chapter) and the fact that Albert Ellis (the founder of RET) also employs self-disclosure to show that competent RET therapists do self-disclose and that there seems to be little evidence that our clients generally see us as less competent (although some may have done so in the past).

The second reason why RET therapists are reluctant to self-disclose is their need for their clients' approval. This is related to the need to be seen as competent, but here the therapist is more concerned with the approval of her clients rather than with their judgements of her competence. Again I suggest a double-barrelled approach to this issue – helping the therapist first to identify and challenge her irrational beliefs before helping her to re-evaluate the likelihood that her clients will disapprove of her if she does disclose to them some of her personal experiences.

Finally, and this is perhaps more true of novice therapists than more experienced ones, I find that some RET therapists have a dire need to see themselves as thoroughly mentally healthy. This is, in fact, a paradox, because if they demand that they must have perfect mental health, they are in fact disturbed because of the very existence of such a demand. This need to be problem free stems partly from a misunderstanding of what it means to be a therapist. Being a therapist does not mean that one must be free of all psychological problems; rather that one has such problems, but can use RET techniques to overcome them. The approach to helping a therapist overcome this rigidity is quite similar to what has already been outlined in this chapter. I first encourage her to assume that her unrealistic expectation is true, namely that good therapists do not have any emotional problems. Then I help her to see that there is no reason why she must be a good therapist by this criterion and, if she is not, she can still accept herself and continue to overcome her problems. I then help her to re-evaluate her unrealistic expectations and encourage her to see that being a good therapist does not mean being problem free but means, in part, that we can apply what we are teaching others to ourselves and our own life situations. In using RET to help RET therapists in these ways, it is my experience that they become less anxious about disclosing themselves to their clients and do so appropriately and therapeutically during the process of RET.

Part IV
Advances in Theory and Practice

Chapter 10
Language and Meaning in Rational–Emotive Therapy

In this chapter the issues of language and meaning in rational–emotive therapy will be discussed – a topic which has received scant attention in the RET literature. For example, two of the major texts in rational-emotive therapy (Walen, DiGiuseppe and Wessler, 1980; Wessler and Wessler, 1980) devote a little over a page to this issue. Wessler and Wessler (1980, p. 179) make the important point which encapsulates the argument that will be made in this chapter:

> Since all words are abstractions and subject to varying denotations and connotations, it is important that we use a shared vocabulary with a client – specifically, that we define our terms and check out the meanings of the client's terms – and try to keep the dialogue as concrete as possible.

In addition to understanding the client's language, it is especially important that the therapist ensures that the client understands the therapist's use of language. Because therapist language can be best construed as 'A' in the ABC framework, it is then likely to be interpreted idiosyncratically by the client who will then proceed to make evaluations about such interpretations. Thus, the possibilities for misunderstanding are legion. RET is often also misconstrued by fellow professionals given the different meanings that can be attributed to the term 'rational'. Young (1975) has argued that people often construe rational to mean cold, logical and unemotional, whereas in RET rational is defined as 'that which aids and abets our client's basic goals and purposes'. However, this use of the word 'rational' is not commonly held and, if unexplained, will often lead to wrong impressions being created in the minds of both non-RET therapists and clients.

The Language of Feeling

RET theory states that, when people do not get what they want and do not dogmatically insist that they get what they want, then they are still liable to

First published in 1986.

experience negative emotions. To the extent that these emotions stem from rational beliefs and are deemed to motivate people to recover and to set new goals for themselves or to pursue old ones that are blocked, these emotions are deemed to be constructive. In RET terminology, specific words exist for these constructive emotions and these are contrasted with emotions that are deemed to be destructive, not only because they stem from absolutistic musturbatory evaluations (musts, shoulds, oughts, have to's etc.), but also because most of the time they inhibit clients from achieving their basic goals and purposes. Thus in RET, 'anxiety' is considered to be destructive and 'concern' is deemed to be constructive. However, when listening to clients' accounts of their own problems, it is important that RET therapists remember that the ways in which clients use language spontaneously (i.e. before RET), particularly with regard to feeling words, may suggest different meanings to that denoted by RET language.

Thus, opportunities for confusion and misunderstanding which arise when we consider the ways in which feeling words are used by clients and RET therapists are many. Consider the term 'anxiety'! Anxiety in RET terminology is deemed to result when there exists a threat to the client's personal domain, a threat which is absolutistically evaluated as 'terrible' or 'awful' and which absolutely must not occur. Concern is deemed to result when the client does not evaluate this perceived threat in an absolutistic manner, but instead believes: 'I really don't want this threat to occur but if it does, it does.' Such a belief will result in the person concluding that, if the threat does occur, it would be unfortunate and bad rather than (absolutistically) awful and terrible. However, clients do not make this distinction spontaneously. They may, for example, report feeling 'concern' when a cognitive analysis reveals that they are, in RET terms 'anxious'. Conversely, other clients will report feeling 'anxious' when they are, according to RET theory, experiencing strong 'concern', because they do not make absolutistic irrational evaluations. For example, one of my clients consistently used the term 'anxiety' to refer to keenness. Had I assumed that his use of the term 'anxiety' was in fact synonymous with the RET use of the term 'anxiety', I would have wasted a lot of therapeutic time by seeking to find irrational evaluations which did not exist. I might have also assumed that the client was a DC (difficult customer), because he would not admit to such irrational evaluations.

An additional issue needs to be considered when the term 'anxiety' is subjected to an analysis of its meaning. Although a client may agree that his or her feelings of anxiety stem from the irrational belief 'This perceived threat must not occur', the client may not agree with the therapist's position that such feelings are destructive. Indeed, many clients consider that anxiety (in the RET sense) will in fact motivate them to carry out a given task. Whether or not anxiety will motivate them to better performances is, of course, the issue which needs to be addressed. However, for RET therapists to assume that, once anxiety has been elicited, the client will necessarily wish to change feelings of anxiety to those of concern, overlooks an important fact, namely that clients make inferences and evaluations about their feelings. As DiGiuseppe (1984) has shown, some people consider that good things might happen or bad things might not happen as a result of experiencing (in RET terms) destructive negative feelings. This is one good reason why it is often helpful to discuss with clients their goals for change (Wessler and Wessler, 1980). To assume that the client wishes to change a destructive negative emotion without checking that this is the case may be a recipe for therapeutic failure.

Depression, according to RET theory, is a destructive negative emotion which occurs when clients evaluate some loss to their personal domain as absolutistically awful or terrible, conclusions which stem from the belief 'this loss must not occur or must not be as bad as it is'. It is contrasted with the constructive negative emotion, sadness, which occurs when such losses are evaluated as bad but without the concomitant 'must'. Again, clients regularly refer to their own feeling of 'sadness' when they are really, in RET terms, 'depressed' and vice versa. Continuing the analysis outlined above covering the implications of destructive negative feelings, some depressed clients construe this painful emotion as a sign of acute sensitivity (in a productive sense) and may view a therapist's attempts to help them give up their depression as an attempt to make them less sensitive – efforts they would stubbornly resist. Thus, again, it is important for rational–emotive therapists to be aware that some clients create private meanings about their feelings of depression which may refer to positive implications of this emotion rather than the negative implications held by their RET therapists.

Guilt, according to RET theory, occurs when clients break their moral or ethical codes and absolutistically insist that this must not have occurred. Such individuals damn themselves as bad individuals for committing such a 'bad' act. The rational alternative to guilt is often expressed in the RET literature as remorse, regret or sorrow. These emotions are deemed to occur when the bad act is viewed as bad, but when the person concerned does not demand 'I must not have done this bad thing' or conclude 'I am bad for doing it'. Rather, the person accepts him- or herself as a fallible human being without (and this is important) excusing him- or herself from acting badly. Clients often misconstrue their therapists' interventions when the emotion of guilt is targeted for change, particularly when therapists do not check out with their clients that this is a troublesome emotion for them. Thus, some clients may accuse their RET therapist of encouraging them to do bad things or, less problematically, not discouraging them from doing bad things because they use the term 'guilt' in a different way from the therapist. In addition, clients often believe that guilt, in the RET use of the word, will actually protect them from doing bad things in the future rather than, as is argued in RET theory, encouraging them to do bad things. In this latter

analysis, once one damns oneself and regards oneself as bad, this will lead
to the person committing more rather than less bad acts. As Ellis puts it:
'How can a shit be deshitified?'

Anger is a particularly troublesome emotion because it often has several
meanings. Anger, according to RET theory, is regarded as being a destructive negative emotion which stems from an absolutistic evaluation that the
other person must not break my rule or must not act as badly as they do, in
fact, act. It is contrasted with the appropriate feeling alternative – annoyance which is regarded as being constructive and stems from the belief 'I
don't like your bad behaviour but there is no reason why you must not act
in this way and you are not a worm [or any other subhuman term that the
client uses] for acting badly'. It is important to realise, as DiGiuseppe (1984)
has done, that people often consider that if they are not angry they will, by
definition, then allow people to dominate them. In a sense they believe: 'I
have to be angry in order to protect myself from other people's bad influence.' If RET therapists do not clearly distinguish between RET meanings of
anger and annoyance for their clients, then the latter may view the therapist's attempts to change their anger to annoyance as (1) advice to act less
powerfully in the social arena or (2) suggestions that they would be wise to
experience *less* strong emotions and thus to deny the strength of their rational desires. RET theory holds that annoyance is not necessarily less intense
than anger but clients often conclude that it is. This is, of course, not the
true intention of RET therapists, but without discussing these distinctions
before implementing disputing strategies, client 'resistance' is likely to
occur, although, of course, it is not resistance but the results of a poorly
designed therapeutic intervention.

Ellis (personal communication) has advocated that, in order to get over
these semantic problems with respect to the term 'anger', damning anger
(an inappropriate emotion) should be distinguished from non-damning
anger (an appropriate emotion). Again, if this distinction is not made then
the client who positively values 'anger' will be unlikely to give up his or her
'positive' emotion. However, if the therapist can help the person to realise
that there are different types of anger and that non-damning anger is in fact
productive, and damning anger is unproductive, then the client is at least
liable to listen to the therapist, whereas in the previous scenario the client
may well switch off from the therapist who is viewed as a person who is trying to encourage the client to relinquish a 'positive' emotion.

Similar arguments can be used when jealousy is the focus for discussion
and the distinction between morbid and non-morbid jealousy can usefully
be introduced to clients who, while experiencing the negative behavioural,
emotional and interpersonal consequences of morbid jealousy, nevertheless regard their feelings of jealousy as evidence that they really love their
partner. If a therapist encourages such a person to work on giving up feelings of jealousy without making distinctions between its morbid and non-

morbid forms, then the person is likely to 'resist' the therapist, who in their mind is advocating that they relinquish their feelings of love for their partner.

Premise Language

Wessler and Wessler (1980) have argued that a person's belief can be put in the form of a syllogism which contains both a premise and a derivative. Thus, 'I must do well' is a premise and 'If I don't do well I would be worthless' would be the conclusion that is derived from the premise. It is apparent that semantic confusion can often result when RET therapists refer to such terms as 'musts', 'shoulds', 'oughts', 'have-to's' etc. A major problematic area here concerns the conditionality of these terms. Thus, the term 'I must do well in order to pass my exams' is a conditional phrase and not, therefore, irrational because the person is outlining the conditions which have to be met in order for an outcome to be achieved. Indeed, novice RET therapists, who are only too delighted to have identified a 'must' in the client's thinking, wrongly assume that all 'musts' are irrational and, therefore, to be targeted for change. This is certainly not the case. It is to be understood at this point that rational–emotive therapists are only interested in targeting for change irrational 'musts' (i.e. those that are absolutistic in nature), especially when these are implicated in feelings that the client wishes to change. This latter point is important. I have often heard RET therapists doing sound RET but not therapeutic RET. Here the therapists have in fact identified absolutistic musts and are using correct disputational strategies to help the client to give them up, but the problem is that the client does not want to change his or her destructive emotions or dysfunctional behaviour.

The term 'should' is particularly problematic. As Vertes (1971) has shown, the word 'should' has several different semantic meanings. It can mean, of course, I absolutely should. It can also mean, I preferably should. It also has an empirical meaning (e.g. given the conditions that exist in the world at this present time, the sun should come up in the morning). It can also refer to matters of recommendation (e.g. 'You really should go and see *Chariots of Fire*). I have on more than one occasion heard novice RET therapists challenge such non-absolutistic 'shoulds': 'Why must you go and see *Chariots of Fire?*' 'Because I like it' the client replies. 'But why must you have what you like?', retorts the therapist. This elementary therapeutic error would not occur if therapists were to learn not to confuse the word with its meaning.

A particular problem is encountered when the word 'right' is used in therapy in sentences such as 'He has no right to act that way'. I have sometimes heard RET therapists involve themselves in unproductive discussions with their clients concerning the non-absolutistic meaning of the word 'right'. 'You have the right to do anything, you have the right to rape and murder if that's your inclination' is an example. While this is theoretically correct (this statement really means that there is no law in the universe to suggest that the person must not rape or pillage), the word 'right' is extremely problematic, and in my experience will often be construed by clients as meaning that the therapist is either actively advocating these activities or refusing to condemn their 'badness'. Such is the confusion about the term 'right', that RET therapists might well be advised to drop this from their vocabulary, at least in therapy.

Similar problems can occur when relative or rational beliefs are considered. Thus, RET therapists often teach their clients that the rational form of 'must' is 'I want to' or 'I would prefer to'. Whilst this is correct, it is not the only way of expressing a relative belief. Thus, the term 'It would be better' is also a rational belief, but one which does not indicate that the person may actually *want* to carry out the activity in question. Take, for example, students who believe that they absolutely must pass an exam. A therapist, in trying to help such clients discriminate between their preference and demands correctly, helps them to see that they *want* to pass the exam but they do not have to. But what if such clients go on to express an irrational belief about working to pass the exam? The therapist who tries to help them to see that while they do not have to work, they would want to work is likely to be using an unproductive strategy which ignores the notion that a person may not want to do *what would be better*. Rational beliefs can then take the form of a desire and, therefore, a client can be encouraged to undertake an activity because of his or her desire. But a client can also be encouraged to undertake an undesired activity that would be in his or her best interests because he or she wants the results of doing this activity. The desire concerns the outcome of the activity and not the process.

Derivative Language

Semantic problems can occur when the language of derivatives is analysed, particularly when the terms 'horror', 'awful' and 'terrible' are considered. These terms, in RET theory, are distinguished from terms such as 'catastrophe' and 'tragedy' (as in the phrase, tragedies are not awful). In RET terminology, a tragedy is something that occurs which is rated as very bad. 'Terrible' and related terms in RET theory add to the notion of tragedy. 'Terrible' relates to the belief that this tragedy must not occur or must not be as bad as it is. This distinction needs to be made carefully with clients, otherwise they may assume that their therapists are being insensitive to their tragedies by trying to show them that such bad events are not *that* bad. Such clients may ask: 'Are you trying to argue that it wasn't that bad for me to lose all my possessions and my family in that fire?' Indeed, my experience in working with people who have recently experienced tragedies, such as losing a loved one or being raped, has shown me that endeavours to teach the client the difference between tragedy and horror may themselves be viewed as insensitive interventions by clients who regard their destructive negative emotions as highly appropriate to their situation.

Semantic confusion can often arise when the term 'fallible human being' is being discussed in therapy. First, it is important to ascertain that the client actually understands what the term 'fallible' means. One of my former clients in Birmingham (UK) thought it meant 'obese' and was insulted as I tried to encourage her to accept herself as a fallible human being in such circumstances! In addition, clients may construe therapists' attempts to encourage them to accept themselves as fallible, as encouragement for them to condone their bad actions, or as reasons to excuse future bad actions. When clients view the term 'fallible' as having bad connotations, it is hardly surprising when they 'resist' their therapists' attempts to encourage them to accept themselves as fallible human beings. Another problem relating to the attitude of human fallibility is that it may not reflect accurately the source of the client's irrationality. More than one client has said to me 'Yes, I can accept myself as a fallible human being' but, shortly after, implied: 'who *must not* act badly'. It is therefore important when planning disputing strategies to look at *both* premise and derivative forms of syllogisms to ensure that irrationalities are being challenged at both levels.

The associated term 'self-acceptance' also has its semantic problems. 'Acceptance' is a particularly difficult word because it can often be viewed in clients' minds as meaning 'resignation'. Thus, by encouraging clients to accept themselves, their resistance may indicate that they perceive that they are being asked to resign themselves to being forever the slob that they think they are. Acceptance, when viewed as meaning resignation, also conjures up images of inaction whereas in RET, self-acceptance is viewed as encouraging clients towards productive action.

Semantic problems can also arise when issues of self-rating are being discussed with clients. Clients often have their own private ways of rating themselves. It may come as a surprise to most RET therapists that not all clients regard themselves as 'shits'. In supervising a therapy tape, I heard a RET therapist and his client get into a heated argument due to the therapist's insistence that the client was calling himself a 'shit'. The client replied: 'Listen, I have never, ever in my whole life considered myself a shit and I really don't like your attempts to persuade me thus.' Here the client was being more rational than the therapist! Thus the term 'shit', 'bad', 'worthless', 'less worthy' and 'undeserving' are not synonymous and, in fact, I have found it very useful to discover the particular form of negative self-rating that clients use. The resulting shared meaning that I have been able to establish with my client has been facilitative of both therapeutic communication and the therapeutic change programme.

The Language of Change

The language which therapists use when they attempt to help clients change can also lead to semantic confusion and constitute obstacles to therapeutic progress. For example, clients may construe therapists' attempts to have them give up their musts as meaning 'Give up your desire'. Clients may often assume that the opposite of crucial is indifference. In planning such disputing strategies and while disputing irrational musts, therapists are recommended to keep in mind the importance of using the language of desire during this entire process. The term 'homework' can also be extremely problematic because, in some clients' minds, certainly in Britain, homework is associated with school and with negative experiences. I often find it helpful to ask the client to give me a word that would capture the notion of the importance of putting into practice between therapy sessions what has been learned in the sessions. Thus, one client came up with the term 'transfer task' to capture the meaning of the phrase usually referred to as homework.

Whilst urging clients to persist at executing assignments, Ellis often exhorts clients to 'work and practise, work and practise'. This is good advice but can be construed as very negative by clients who already have a high degree of low frustration tolerance. Thus, for some clients, words such as persistence or repetition may capture similar meanings but be less negative in connotation. In addition, one of the hidden dangers of urging clients to 'work and practise' and to 'push themselves hard in therapy' is that some clients may actually consider that their therapists believe that they *have* to do the work or that they *have* to change. In these instances therapists serve as poor role-models in the minds of their clients.

It is important to realise that virtually any word that therapists can use when encouraging people to change may have negative connotations for some clients. Perhaps it is therefore a good idea for RET therapists to ask clients at the end of a therapy session, whether in this context they are using any words that the clients are viewing as negative (Beck et al., 1979). If I were a client in RET or cognitive therapy I would review the term 'agenda' negatively. This is because my mother used to ask me at the beginning of every day 'What's on your agenda today, son?', a term which has come to have negative connotations for me.

Using Words Clients do not Understand

RET is best viewed as an educational therapy. Because good education depends on effective communication, it is important that the therapist uses words that clients can understand. My 7 years' experience working in a working-class community in east Birmingham has taught me to be wary of using a number of words that are in common usage among RET therapists.

I have found the following words to be most problematic among this population: dysfunctional, fallible, evidence, belief, cognition (to be avoided *almost* at all costs), rational etc. Such clients will in fact rarely say to you 'I'm sorry, I don't understand what that means', but will give various non-verbal cues to non-understanding.

1. *The glazed look*: here the client displays a glazed expression often accompanied by a fixed smile.
2. *The automatic head nod*: here clients nod knowingly as if they understand their therapists' RET terminology.

If such nodding goes on for longer than 10 seconds without interruption, this is a sign that clients may not understand what is being said. If this is accompanied by the knowing smile then it is almost guaranteed that the client does not understand a word the therapist is saying!

Towards Shared Meaning in RET

In this concluding section, ways in which RET therapists can strive towards adopting shared meaning frameworks with their clients will be outlined. One important method of checking whether a client has understood the meaning of a concept which the therapist is using is to ask the client for clarification of the client's understanding. Questions such as 'I am not sure whether I am making myself clear on this point. Can you put into your own words what you think I am saying?', can be used to good effect in that they encourage clients to be active in the therapeutic process and to use their own language rather than just parroting the language of the therapist. It is especially important for the therapist to pay attention to the non-verbal aspects of the client's responses to such questions. Also, when the client uses exactly the same language as the therapist, the way in which the client responds can often serve as a guide to whether or not he or she has understood the therapist's communications. When the client uses the same words as the therapist in answer to such enquiries, the therapist can usefully ask 'What do you understand by these words, e.g. awful. What other words in your mind are equivalent to this word?'. I have found asking for synonyms particularly revealing for clients' misunderstandings of the rational concepts I have been endeavouring to teach them. For example, a common 'synonym' that clients use for the term 'awful' is 'very bad'. The latter, of course, is not a synonym for the former in RET theory.

A constructive therapeutic strategy for making clear distinctions between constructive and destructive negative emotions, while ensuring that client and therapist have a shared meaning framework using the same verbal label, is to define terms before implementing disputing strategies. In particular, emotions should be linked with their evaluative beliefs in any exposition of terms. For example, while trying to clarify whether a client is angry (damningly angry) or annoyed (non-damningly), I might say something like this:

> OK, so you say you are angry. Now, when you were experiencing that emotion, what was more likely to be going through your mind? Did you believe, for example, that the person who did that bad thing was no good and absolutely should not have acted that way, or did you believe that, although their behaviour was bad, there was no reason why the person must not have acted that way. Also, did you regard them as bad or just *their behaviour* as bad?

I have found that my clients can often distinguish between the two emotional states more reliably when I include their cognitive definitions than when such definitions are excluded. Clients rarely know spontaneously the RET theoretical distinction between these two emotional states. Thus, when discussing feeling terms with clients (particularly when distinguishing between constructive and destructive emotions), it is advisable to include their cognitive counterparts.

RET therapists have much to learn from the work of George Kelly (1955) and his followers in personal construct therapy (PCT) with respect to discovering clients' idiosyncratic meaning systems. One such strategy derived from PCT concerns asking clients for polar opposites of their feelings. This is particularly useful when planning and carrying out disputing strategies, because it may help the therapist to discover why clients may not in reality wish to change an emotion that they claim they wish to change and which, according to RET theory, is a destructive negative emotion. Thus, as noted on p. 139, I once worked with a depressed client who claimed not to want to be depressed but was resisting my attempts to help her feel sad. I asked her what she associated in her mind as being the opposite of sad, to which she replied 'sensitive'. This highly idiosyncratic use of the word 'sad' as being in some way equivalent to being insensitive helped me to understand why my client resisted my attempts to encourage her to experience what RET theory states is a constructive negative emotion.

In conclusion, I wish to emphasise that therapists should preferably be alert to the idiosyncratic ways in which clients use language and the equally idiosyncratic ways in which they may interpret the rational concepts that RET therapists strive to teach them. It is important for RET therapists to internalise the language system of RET but, in doing so, they should not assume that their clients will magically share the meaning structure implicit in rational–emotive terminology.

Chapter 11
The Use of Chaining in Rational–Emotive Therapy

One of the drawbacks of the ABC* model of RET is that its simplicity obscures the fact that assessing and intervening in clients' problems can be quite difficult. For example, inferences are often chained together, inference and evaluative beliefs are connected in spiralling chains and these two types of cognitions interact with emotions and behaviours. In this chapter I shall outline and illustrate four types of chains that should preferably, when appropriate, become the focus for assessment and intervention during the course of RET.

Inference Chains

As noted above inferences are often chained together. The purpose of assessing these chains is to identify the major inference in clients' emotional episodes, i.e. the one that triggers the irrational belief that creates their targeted emotional or behavioural problems at C. Moore (1983) advises that in inference chaining therapists initiate an enquiry based on 'then what?' and 'why?' questions in search of the client's most relevant inference. When clients report inferences,[†] 'then what?' questions are employed to uncover further inferences in the chain. However, when clients report emotional and/or behavioural consequences and these hold up research for relevant inferences, 'why' questions are used to help clients to continue their elaboration of inferential As. This process is exemplified in the following dialogue.

Client: So I get very scared when I think about going into the coffee bar.
Therapist: What do you think you are scared of?

---

*In this chapter, 'A' refers to activating events and to inferences (i.e. interpretations that go beyond available data) about these events. 'B' is therefore reserved for evaluative beliefs.
†It should be noted that 'Cs' can be treated as inferences and, when they are, 'then what?' questions are again employed to further the inference-based enquiry.
First published in 1989.

Client: I'm scared of my hands shaking when I go to buy a cup of coffee.
Therapist: Because if it happens, then what?
Client: People will notice.
Therapist: And if they do notice, then what?
Client: Well, they'll bring it to each other's attention.
Therapist: And if they do, then what?
Client: I'd panic.
Therapist: Why? [the client's previous response is treated as a C, hence the 'why?' question.]
Client: Because I'm sure I'd drop the cup.
Therapist: And if you do drop the cup, what then?
Client: They'd all start laughing.
Therapist: And if they did?
Client: Oh God! I couldn't stand that.

Inferences that trigger clients' irrational beliefs which, in turn, account for their targeted Cs are often expressed in close proximity to reports of these irrational beliefs (as in the above example). However, this does not always happen, in which case it is helpful to review the entire chain with clients and to ask them which inference in the chain is most relevant to the problem at hand.

It also happens that clients may report inferences that theoretically follow from 'then what?' questions, but which may not be implicated in their problems. Thus, the client in the above example might have reported the following inferences, in the chain after 'they'd start laughing'. 'I'd leave town and never come back' → 'I'd become a hermit'. To assess the relevance of such inferences to the client's problem, the therapist is advised to (1) review the entire chain with the client at the end of the sequence and (2) note the degree of affect expressed by the client when these inferences are reported. Clients often report theoretically possible, but clinically irrelevant, inferences with flat affect or halting puzzlement. Thus, it is important for therapists to realise that the most relevant inference is not necessarily the final inference in the chain, although it frequently is.

Finally, when clients find it difficult to respond to 'then what?' questions with further inferences, it is helpful to include some variant of the target emotion (C) as part of the assessment question. For example:

Client: People will notice.
Therapist: And if they do, then what?
Client: Er, I'm not sure.
Therapist: Well, what would be anxiety-provoking in your mind about them noticing?
Client: Oh. They'll bring it to each other's attention.

Inference–Evaluative Belief Chains

In inference chaining, as has been shown, the therapist assesses the way one inference leads to another. However, in reality, clients often hold implicit evaluative beliefs about each inference in the chain. These beliefs are bypassed in inference chaining, the purpose of which is to discover the most relevant inference in the chain, i.e. the one that triggers the client's irrational belief which accounts for their targeted emotional or behavioural problem at C. However, there are occasions when it is important to assess these implicit evaluative beliefs. This is particularly so in the assessment and treatment of clients' problems where distorted inferences often stem from irrational beliefs (e.g. panic disorders). The principle that unrealistic inferences stem from irrational beliefs is an important but often neglected one in RET. As Ellis (1977d) has noted:

> If you really stayed with desires and preferences, and virtually never escalated them into needs and necessities, you would relatively rarely make antiempirical statements to yourself and others. But just as soon as you make your desires into dire needs, such unrealistic statements almost invariably follow – and follow, frequently in great numbers.
>
> (p. 9)

In inference-evaluative belief chaining, then, therapists are advised to assess both inferences and the irrational beliefs that are held about these inferences and which, in turn, produce further distorted inferences. This pattern is particularly observable in panic disorders. Clark (1986) has outlined a cognitive approach to panic that draws upon the work of Aaron Beck. In his model, Clark argues that people who are prone to panic attacks make increasingly catastrophic interpretations of their bodily sensations. However, he does not set out to distinguish between clients' interpretations (or inferences) and their irrational beliefs about these inferences, beliefs that are held at an implicit level. In the rational-emotive approach to panic disorders, these two types of cognitions are the targets for assessment and intervention. An example of inference-evaluative belief chaining is provided in Table 11.1 to illustrate this point.

Table 11.1   An example of an inference-evaluative belief chain in panic disorder

C	Feeling tense
Inference	I'm going to have trouble breathing
Irrational belief	I must be able to breathe more easily
Inference	I'm getting more anxious. I'm going to choke
Irrational belief	I must be able to control my breathing right now
Inference	I'm going to die
Irrational belief	I must not die in this fashion
C	Panic

Whilst it is technically correct for RET therapists to dispute their clients' irrational beliefs about dying (see the end part of the chain in Table 11.1), the pragmatic purpose of this strategy, in such cases, is first to help clients to understand how their irrational beliefs which occur earlier in the chain actually produce their increasingly distorted inferences later in the chain and then to help them to dispute these evaluative beliefs. If this can be done in the session while the client is tense and beginning to experience the first signs of panic, then this can be a particularly powerful intervention.

At present, the relationship between distorted inferences and irrational beliefs awaits empirical enquiry and remains a fruitful area for future research in RET.

'Disturbance about Disturbance' Chains

One of the unique features of RET is the emphasis that it places on clients' tendencies to make themselves disturbed about their disturbances. This may involve exacerbation of a particular disorder (e.g. anxiety about anxiety; depression about depression) or it may involve several emotional and/or behavioural disorders within a single episode (e.g. guilt about anger; anxiety about procrastination). A typical sequence is illustrated in Table 11.2.

Table 11.2 An example of a 'disturbance about disturbance' chain

A	Sam treated me unfairly
B	He must not treat me unfairly
C	Anger
A	Anger
B	I must not get angry
C	Guilt
A	Guilt
B	There I go again experiencing needless guilt. I must not do this. I'm worthless
C	Depression

It is often quite difficult for novice RET therapists to select the most appropriate part of the 'disturbance about disturbance' chain to target for intervention with clients. My own practice is to keep three points in mind when making such treatment decisions. In general, I suggest that therapists work on the part of the chain that the clients want to start with and encourage their clients to do this for themselves outside the session. There are two exceptions to this general rule. The first occurs when clients actually experience in the session another inappropriate negative emotion that is part of the chain. In this case, I suggest that therapists offer their clients a plausible rationale for switching to that part of the chain (e.g. 'It seems as if right now you are experiencing guilt about your feelings of anger. Let's first work on this until you can give your full attention to working on your anger').

A second exception to the general rule occurs when clients experience outside the therapy session an inappropriate negative emotion that is also part of the chain (e.g. depression) as they attempt to work on overcoming the target emotion (e.g. guilt). In this case, I suggest that therapists encourage their clients to switch to the depression part of the chain, in the example given above, and give a plausible rationale for this (e.g. 'How can you work on your guilt when you are beating yourself over the head for feeling guilty?').

Complex Chains

Clients sometimes present problems that involve a number of cognitive, emotive and behavioural components linked together in a complex chain. I have found it quite helpful to assess such chains carefully in order to help clients (1) understand the process nature of their problems and (2) identify useful points in the chain at which they can intervene to prevent the build-up of these problems. In such cases, it is usually beneficial to encourage clients to intervene at or near the beginning of these complex chains for the following reason. Towards the end of the chain these clients are so over-whelmed by the intensity of their disturbed feelings or so caught up in their self-defeating behaviours that it is unrealistic for their therapist to anticipate that they will successfully initiate a disputing intervention. To illustrate these points, I present in Table 11.3 one example of a complex chain. This arose out of my work with a female client who sought help for what she described as 'uncontrolled binge-eating'.

Table 11.3 An example of a complex chain

A	Working on Master's thesis and experiencing difficulty with 'simple' statistics
B	I must be able to understand this. I'm a real idiot because I can't
C	Anger at self
A	Anger at self experienced as tension
B	I can't stand this tension
C	Anxious pacing around the room
A	Heightened anxiety
B	I've got to get rid of this feeling
C	Goes to the refrigerator and begins to eat a snack
A	Eating a snack
B	Oh God! What am I doing? I shouldn't be doing this
C	Guilt and increased eating (to try to get rid of the bad feeling)
A	Increased eating
B	What a pig I am. I must not binge again
C	Self-loathing and binge-eating

Two points are worth noting with reference to this example. First, when the client had reached the end of this complex chain, she reported that it is as if she is in an altered state of consciousness. Whilst it is theoretically pos-sible for her to intervene at this point and dispute her irrational belief that led her to feelings of self-loathing and binge-eating, in practice she found this enormously difficult. Thus, for pragmatic reasons, she needed to be helped to make a disputing intervention at a much earlier part of the chain.

Secondly, the entire episode which has been detailed in Table 11.3 happened very quickly. The client barely noticed her tension before she headed towards the refrigerator, i.e. she was not aware of her feelings of self-anger or of discomfort anxiety. Consequently, I helped her in the therapy session to review the entire process as if it were happening in slow motion. As a result she began to identify these implicitly felt emotions and associated irrational beliefs and began to see that psychological events (e.g. anger at self for not understanding 'simple' material) served as triggers for her subsequent irrational beliefs and more intense self-defeating emotions and behaviours. She then began to anticipate these early signs and learned to dispute the related irrational beliefs that occurred at the beginning of the chain. She became very adept at doing this and virtually eliminated her binge-eating that was previously associated with such episodes. We could then deal with her irrational beliefs that occurred later in the chain. If I had started at the end of the chain I doubt whether she would have achieved as good a therapeutic outcome as she did in this case.

Outlining complex chains is particularly helpful then when clients are barely aware of disturbed emotions and self-defeating behaviours that occur at the start of the chain and when this non-awareness leads to more intense negative and self-defeating experiences later in the chain.

Therefore, a described above, chaining is a sophisticated skill and, when used sensitively, highlights the complexity that lies behind the simple ABC formulation of clients' problems.

Chapter 12
Vivid Methods in
Rational-Emotive Therapy

The fundamental goal of rational-emotive therapy is to enable clients to live effective lives by helping them change their faulty inferences and irrational evaluations about themselves, other people and the world. Whilst there are many ways of achieving this goal, the purpose of this chapter is to highlight ways in which rational-emotive therapists can make the therapeutic process a more vivid experience for their clients, so that they may be stimulated to identify and change their faulty inferences and irrational evaluations more effectively. A number of rational-emotive and cognitive therapists have already written on the use of vivid methods in therapy (Knaus and Wessler, 1976; Ellis, 1979c; Walen, DiGiuseppe and Wessler, 1980; Wessler and Wessler, 1980; Arnkoff, 1981; Freeman, 1981). However, a comprehensive account of the uses, advantages and limitations of such methods has yet to appear in the literature on rational-emotive therapy. In this chapter, attention will be given to the use of vivid methods in *problem assessment*, vivid *disputing methods*, and vivid ways in which clients may *work through* their emotional and behavioural problems.

Rationale for Vivid Methods in RET

Rational-emotive therapists aim to help clients achieve their goals through the systematic application of cognitive, emotive and behavioural methods. However, therapist and client rely heavily on verbal dialogue in their in-session encounters. The tone of such dialogue in rational-emotive therapy sessions can be rich, stimulating and arousing, but it is far too often dry and mundane (as supervisors of novice rational-emotive therapists will testify). Whilst the role of emotional arousal in the facilitation of attitude change is

First published in this form in 1986.

complex (Hoehn-Saric, 1978), it is my contention that the majority of clients can be helped best to re-examine faulty inferences and irrational beliefs if we, as therapists, gain their full attention and make therapy a memorable experience for them. Whilst there are no studies that address this point in the rational–emotive therapy literature, there is some suggestion from process and outcome studies carried out on client-centred therapy that vivid therapist interventions are associated with successful client outcome and with certain client in-therapy behaviours which have, in turn, been linked to positive outcome (Rice, 1965, 1973; Rice and Wagstaff, 1967; Rice and Gaylin, 1973; Wexler, 1975; Wexler and Butler, 1976). At present we do not know whether any client in-therapy behaviours are associated with successful outcome in RET. Yet, it is possible to hypothesise that such client in-session behaviours as attending to and being fully involved in the therapeutic process and making links between in-session dialogue and out-of-session activities will be associated with therapeutic gain in RET. If this proves correct, then it is my further contention that vivid methods in RET may effectively bring about such client behaviour.

Given the dearth of much-needed studies on these points, anecdotal evidence will have to suffice. This involves feedback from my clients, who have frequently related incidents of (1) how my own vivid therapeutic interventions helped them to re-examine a variety of their dysfunctional cognitions and (2) how they, with my encouragement, improved by making the working-through process a more stimulating experience for themselves.

It should again be stressed at the outset that, whilst there is a place for vivid methods in RET, these are best introduced into therapy at appropriate times and within the context of a good therapeutic alliance between therapist and client (see Chapter 7).

Problem Assessment

Effective rational–emotive therapy depends initially on the therapist gaining a clear understanding of (1) the client's problems in cognitive, emotional and behavioural terms and (2) the contexts in which the client's problems occur. To a great extent, the therapist is dependent on the client's verbal reports in gaining such an understanding. It is in this area that many obstacles to progress may appear. Some clients have great difficulty identifying and/or accurately labelling their emotional experiences. Other clients are in touch with and able to report their emotions but find it hard to relate these to activating events (either external or internal). Yet a further group of clients is easily able to report problematic activating events and emotional experiences but has difficulty seeing how these may relate to mediating cognitions. Vivid methods can be used in a variety of ways to overcome such obstacles to a valid and reliable assessment of client problems.

Vividness in portraying activating events

With some clients, traditional assessment procedures through verbal dialogue do not always yield the desired information. When this occurs, rational–emotive therapists often use imagery methods. They ask clients to conjure up evocative images of activating events. Such evocative imagery often stimulates the client's memory concerning her or his emotional reactions, or indeed in some instances leads to the re-experiencing of these reactions in the session. While focusing on such images, the client can also begin to gain access to cognitive processes below the level of awareness that cannot be easily reached through verbal dialogue.

One particularly effective use of imagery in the assessment of client problems is that of bringing future events into the present. This is illustrated by the following exchange between myself and a client who was terrified that her mother might die, which led her to be extremely unassertive with the mother.

Therapist: So you feel you just can't speak up to her. Because if you did, what might happen?

Client: Well she might have a fit.

Therapist: And what might happen if she did?

Client: She might have a heart attack and die.

Therapist: Well, we know that she is a fit woman, but let's go along with your fear for the moment. Okay?

Client: Okay.

Therapist: What if she did die?

Client: I just can't think...I...I'm sorry.

Therapist: That's okay. I know this is difficult, but I really think it would be helpful if we could get to the bottom of things. Okay? [Client nods.] Look, Marjorie, I want you to imagine that your mother has just died this morning. Can you imagine that? [Client nods and begins to shake.] What are you experiencing?

Client: When you said my mother was dead I began to feel all alone...like there was no one to care for me...no one I could turn to.

Therapist: And if there is no one who cares for you, no one you can turn to...?

Client: Oh, God! I know I couldn't cope on my own.

Instructing clients to imagine vividly something that has been warded off often leads to anxiety itself. It is important to process this anxiety, as it is sometimes related to the client's central problem. Issues such as fear of loss of control, phrenophobia and extreme discomfort anxiety are often revealed when this anxiety is fully assessed. However, some clients do find it difficult to imagine events spontaneously and require therapist assistance.

Whilst imagery methods are now routinely used in cognitive behaviour therapy (e.g. Lazarus, 1978), there has been little written on how therapists can stimulate clients' imagery processes. I have used a number of the following vivid methods to try and help clients utilise their potential for imagining events.

Vivid, connotative therapist language

One effective way of helping clients to use their imagery potential is for the therapist to use rich, colourful and evocative language while aiding clients to set the scene. Unless the therapist has gained prior diagnostic information, he or she is sometimes uncertain about which stimuli in the activating event are particularly related to the client's problem. Thus, it is best to give clients many alternatives. For example, with a socially anxious client I proceeded thus, after attempting without success to get him to use his own potential imagery.

Therapist: So at the moment we are unclear about what you are anxious about. What I'd like to suggest is that we use your imagination to help us. I will help you set the scene based on what we have already discussed. However, since we have yet to discover detailed factors, some of the things I say might not be relevant. Will you bear with me and let me know when what I say touches a nerve in you?

Client: Okay.

Therapist: Fine. Just close your eyes and imagine you are about to walk into the dance. You walk in and some of the guys there glance at you. You can see the *smirks* on their *mocking* faces and one of them *blows* you a kiss. [Here I am testing out a hypothesis based on previously gained information.] You start to *seethe* inside and...

Client: Okay, when you said I started to seethe, that struck a chord. I thought I can't let them get away with that but if I let go I'll just go berserk. I started feeling anxious.

Therapist: And if you went berserk?

Client: I couldn't show my face in there again.

Therapist: What would happen then?

Client: I don't know. I...It's funny – the way I see it, I would never go out again.

Here I was using words such as, 'smirks', 'mocking', 'blows' and 'seethe' deliberately in my attempt to stimulate the client's imagination. It is also important for the therapist to vary his or her tone so that this matches the language employed.

Photographs

I have at times asked clients to bring to interviews photographs of significant others or significant places. These are kept on hand to be used at relevant moments in the assessment process. I have found the use of photographs particularly helpful when the client is discussing an event in the past that is still bothering her or him. Thus, for example, one client who spoke without feeling about being rejected by his father who died 7 years earlier, broke down in tears when I asked him to look at a picture of him and his father standing apart from one another. Feelings of hurt and anger (with their associated cognitions) were expressed, which enabled us to move to the disputing stage.

Other mementoes

In a similar vein, I have sometimes asked clients to bring in mementoes. These may include pictures they have drawn, paintings that have meaning for them, and poems either written by themselves or other people. The important point is that these mementoes are to be related to issues that the client is working on in therapy. A road block to assessment was successfully overcome with one client when I asked her to bring in a memento that reminded her of her mother. She brought in a bottle of perfume that her mother was accustomed to wearing. When I asked her to smell the perfume at a point in therapy when the assessment process through verbal dialogue was again breaking down, the client was helped to identify feelings of jealousy towards her mother, which she experienced whenever her mother left her to go out socialising. Moreover, my client was ashamed of such feelings. This issue was centrally related to her presenting problem of depression.

Another of my clients was depressed about losing her boyfriend. I had great difficulty helping her to identify any related mediating cognitions through traditional assessment procedures. Several tentative guesses on my part also failed to pinpoint relevant cognitive processes. I then asked her to bring to our next session anything that reminded her of her ex-boyfriend. She brought in a record of a popular song that had become known to them as 'our song'. When I played the song at an appropriate point in the interview, my client began to sob and expressed feelings of abandonment, hurt and fear for the future. Again a vivid method had unearthed important assessment material where traditional methods had failed.

It should be noted from these examples that quite often such dramatic methods lead to the expression of strong affective reactions in the session. This is often an important part of the process, because such affective reactions are gateways to the identification of maladaptive cognitive processes that are difficult to identify through more traditional methods of assessment.

The 'interpersonal nightmare' technique

Rational–emotive and cognitive therapists sometimes employ methods originally derived from gestalt therapy and psychodrama to assist them in the assessment phase of therapy. These have been adequately described (Nardi, 1979; Arnkoff, 1981), and will not be discussed here. I would like to describe a related technique I have developed (Dryden, 1980a), which I call the 'interpersonal nightmare' technique. This technique may be best used with clients who are able to specify only sketchily an anticipated 'dreaded' event involving other people but are able neither to specify in any detail the nature of the event nor to specify how they would react if the event were to occur. First the client is given a homework assignment to imagine the 'dreaded' event. He or she is told to write a brief segment of a play about it, specifying the exact words that the protagonists would use. The client is encouraged to give full rein to imagination while focusing on what he or she fears might happen. An example will suffice. The following scenario was developed by a 55-year-old woman with alcohol problems who was terrified of making errors at the office where she worked as a typist.

Scene:	Boss's office where he sits behind a very large desk. He has found out that one of the typists had inadvertently filed a letter wrongly and sends for her. She comes in and is made to stand in front of her boss.
Boss:	Have you anything to say in this matter?
Typist (me):	Only that I apologise and will be more careful in the future.
Boss:	What do you mean by saying you will be more careful in the future – what makes you think you have a future? [At this point he starts banging on the desk.] I have never yet met anyone less competent or less suited to the job than you are. You mark my words, I will make life so uncomfortable for you that you will leave. When I took over this job I intended to have the people I wanted working for me, and you are not on that list. I have already gotten rid of two typists, and I shall see that you are the third. Now get out of my office you stupid, blundering fool, and remember I shall always be watching you and you will never know when I shall be behind you.

I then read over the scene with the client, making enquiries about the tone in which she thought her boss would make these statements and asking her to identify which words the boss would emphasise. I then arranged for a local actor who was the same age as the boss to enact the scene realistically on cassette. In the next session I instructed my client to visualise the room in which the encounter might take place. She briefly described the room, paying particular attention to where her boss would be sitting and where she would be standing. I then played her the cassette, which evoked strong feelings of fear of being physically harmed and humiliated. Again, important data had been collected that traditional assessment procedures had failed to uncover.

These examples have shown how rational–emotive therapists can employ various visual, language and auditory methods to help clients vividly imagine appropriate activating events. This in turn helps them more easily identify maladaptive emotional experiences and related cognitive processes that are not readily identified through the verbal interchange of the psychotherapeutic interview. It is important to note that the use of such methods is not being advocated for its own sake. They are employed with specific purposes in mind.

Rational–emotive problem solving

Knaus and Wessler (1976) have described a method that they call rational–emotive problem solving (REPS). This method involves the therapist creating conditions in the therapy session which approximate those the client encounters in her or his everyday life and which give rise to emotional problems. Knaus and Wessler contend that this method may be used either in a planned or impromptu fashion and is particularly valuable when clients experience difficulty in identifying emotional experiences and related cognitive processes through verbal dialogue with their therapists. I employed this method with a male client who reported difficulty in acting assertively in his life and claimed not to be able to identify the emotions and thoughts that inhibited the expression of assertive responses. During our discussion I began to search around for my pouch of pipe tobacco. Finding it empty, I interrupted my client and asked him if he would drive to town, purchase my favourite tobacco, adding that if he hurried he could return for the last 5 minutes of our interview. He immediately got up, took my money and walked out of my office towards his car. I rushed after him, brought him back into my office and together we processed his reactions to this simulated experience.

It is clear that this technique must be used with therapeutic judgement and that its use may threaten or even destroy the therapeutic alliance between client and therapist. However, because rational–emotive therapists value risk-taking, they are often prepared to use such techniques when more traditional and less risky methods have failed to bring about therapeutic improvement. It is further important, as Beck et al. (1979) have stressed, for the therapist to ask the client for the latter's honest reactions to this procedure, to ascertain whether it may have future therapeutic value for the client. When a client indicates that she or he has found the rational–emotive problem-solving method unhelpful, the therapist is advised to explain the rationale for attempting such a procedure and disclose that he or she intended no harm but was attempting to be helpful. Normally clients respect such disclosures, and in fact the therapist in doing so provides a useful model for the client, namely, that it is possible to acknowledge errors non-defensively without damning oneself. However, with this method, it is apparent that therapists cannot realistically disclose their rationale in advance of initiating the method, because this would detract from its potential therapeutic value.

Dreams

Although Albert Ellis has written a regular column for *Penthouse* magazine providing rational–emotive interpretations for readers' dreams, rational–emotive therapists are not generally noted for using dream material. However, there is no good reason why dream material cannot be used in RET as long as (1) it does not predominate in the therapeutic process and (2) the therapist has a definite purpose in mind in using it.

Freeman (1981, pp. 228–229) has outlined a number of further guidelines for the use of dreams for assessment purposes:

1. The dream needs to be understood in thematic rather than symbolic terms.
2. The thematic content of the dream is idiosyncratic to the dreamer and must be viewed within the context of the dreamer's life.
3. The specific language and imagery are important to the meaning.
4. The affective responses to the dream can be seen as similar to the dreamer's affective responses in waking situations.
5. The particular length of the dream is of lesser import than the content.
6. The dream is a product of and the responsibility of the dreamer.
7. Dreams can be used when the patient appears stuck in therapy.

I inadvertently stumbled on the usefulness of dream material for assessment purposes when working with a 28-year-old depressed student who would frequently reiterate, 'I'm depressed and I don't know why'. I had virtually exhausted all the assessment methods I knew (including those described in this chapter) to help her identify depressogenic thoughts in situations when she experienced depressions, but without success. In a desperate last attempt, I asked her if she could remember any of her dreams, not expecting in the least that this line of enquiry would prove fruitful. To my surprise she said yes, she did have a recurring dream. In this dream she saw herself walking alone along a river bank, and when she peered into the river, she saw a reflection of herself as a very old woman. This image filled her with extreme sadness and depression. On further discussion she said that she believed that this dream meant that she had no prospect of finding any happiness in her life, either in love relationships or in her career and that she was doomed to spend her years alone, ending up as a sad, pathetic, old woman. This account of the dream and subsequent discussion of its meaning enabled me to help her identify a number of inferential distortions and irrational beliefs, which provided the focus for subsequent cognitive restructuring.

Daydreams may also provide important material for assessment purposes. For some people, particular daydreams occur in response to and as compensation for a negative activating event. Thus, one client reported having the daydream of establishing a multinational corporation after failing to sell insurance to prospective customers. The use of such daydreams by clients may not necessarily be dysfunctional but may impede them (as in the preceding example) from getting to the core of their problems. Often daydreams are an expression of our hopes and aspirations, and I have found it valuable to ask clients not only about the content of such material but also what would stop them from actualising their goals. Much important assessment material is gathered in this manner, in particular concerning ideas of low frustration tolerance.

In vivo therapy sessions

Sacco (1981) has outlined the value of conducting therapy sessions in real-life settings in which clients experience difficulties. I have found moving outside the interview room to such settings particularly useful in gaining assessment material when traditional methods have failed to provide such data. For example, I once saw a male student who complained of avoiding social situations. He did so in case others would see his hands tremble. Traditional assessment methods yielded no further data. To overcome this treatment impasse, I suggested to him that we needed to collect more data and we eventually conducted a therapy session in a coffee shop where I asked him to go and get us both a cup of coffee. He refused because he feared that his hands might tremble, but I firmly persisted with my request. He was able to identify a stream of negative cognitions on the way from our table to the service counter. He returned without our coffees but with valuable information, which we processed later in my office. It is important for therapists to explain their rationale for conducting in vivo sessions in advance, in order to gain client cooperation. In addition, obtaining clients' reactions to these sessions is often helpful, particularly if in vivo sessions are planned for use later in the therapeutic process.

Disputing

In this section, various vivid disputing methods will be outlined. The purpose of these methods is (1) to help clients see the untenable basis and dysfunctional nature of their irrational beliefs and to replace them with more rational ones and (2) to help them make more accurate inferences about reality. These methods often demonstrate the rational message powerfully but indirectly, and they do not necessarily call upon the client to answer such questions as 'Where is the evidence...?'.

It is important for the therapist to make certain preparations before initiating vivid disputing methods, because the success of such methods depends upon (1) the client clearly understanding the link between thoughts, feelings and behaviours and (2) the therapist ascertaining particular biographical information about the client.

Preparing for vivid disputing

The thought–feeling–behaviour link

After the therapist has undertaken a thorough assessment of the client's target problem, the next task is to help the client see the connections among thoughts, feelings and behaviours. Here again vivid methods can be employed. Thus, the therapist, while speaking with the client, might pick up a book, drop it on the floor and continue talking to the client. After a while, if the client has made no comment, the therapist can ask for both affective and cognitive reactions to this incident. Thus, the client is given a vivid here-and-now example of the thought–feeling link.

Biographical information

Before initiating the vivid disputing process, I often find it helpful to gather certain information about the client. I like to find out about my client's *interests, hobbies* and *work situation*. I have found this information often helps me adapt my interventions, using phrases that will be meaningful to my client, given her or his idiosyncratic life situation. Thus, if my client is passionately interested in boxing, a message utilising a boxing analogy may well have greater impact than a golfing analogy.

I also find it helpful to discover *who my client admires*. I do this because later I may wish to ask my client how he or she thinks these admired individuals might solve similar problems. This prompts the client to identify with a model to imitate. Lazarus (1978) has employed a similar method with children. For example, I asked a male client to imagine that his admired grandfather experienced public speaking anxiety, and I enquired how he would have overcome it. This helped him identify a coping strategy that he used to overcome his own public speaking anxiety problem. This approach is best used if the client also can acknowledge that the admired individual is fallible and thus prone to human irrationality. In addition, it is important that the client sees the feasibility of imitating the model.

I find it invaluable to ask my clients about their *previous experiences of attitude change*. I try and discern the salient features of such a change for possible replication in my in-session disputing strategies. For example, one anxious female client told me she had changed her mind about fox-hunting after reading a number of personal accounts offering arguments against fox-hunting. As part of my disputing plan, I directed this client to autobiographies of people who had overcome anxiety. Another client claimed she had in the past received help from speaking to people who had experienced problems similar to her own. I arranged for this client to speak to some of my ex-clients who had experienced but overcome comparable problems.

I now propose to outline a number of ways in which rational–emotive therapists can vividly employ disputing techniques. The importance of tailoring interventions to meet the specific, idiosyncratic requirements of clients should be borne in mind throughout.

Vivid disputing methods

Disputing in the presence of vivid stimuli.
In a previous section of this chapter, I outlined a number of ways of vividly portraying activating events to help clients identify their emotional reactions and the cognitive determinants of these reactions. I outlined various visual, language, auditory and olfactory methods. These same methods can be used as context material in the disputing process. For example, one client brought along a drawing of herself and her *mother*. She portrayed her

mother as a very large, menacing figure and herself as a small figure crouching in fear in front of her mother. I asked the client to draw another picture where she and her mother were of the same height, standing face-to-face, looking each other in the eye. When she brought in this drawing, I enquired how her attitude toward her mother differed in the two pictures. This not only provided her with a demonstration that it was possible for her to evaluate her mother differently, but also led to a fruitful discussion in which I disputed some of her irrational beliefs inherent in the first drawing while having her focus on the second.

A similar tactic was employed using the 'interpersonal nightmare' technique with the 55-year-old woman mentioned earlier. After disputing some of the irrational beliefs uncovered when the technique was employed for assessment purposes, I repeatedly played the woman the tape while having her dispute some of the irrational beliefs it revealed. A similar method can be used when in vivo sessions are conducted. Earlier in this chapter I reported the case of a student who was anxious about his hands shaking in public. Both assessment and later disputing of his irrational beliefs were carried out in a coffee bar. Indeed he practised disputing his irrational beliefs while carrying two shaking cups of coffee back from the service counter to our table. Disputing in the presence of vivid stimuli enables the client to build bridges from in-session to out-of-session situations.

Imagery methods

One very effective imagery method that can be used in the disputing of irrational beliefs is that of time projection (Lazarus, 1978). When a client makes grossly exaggerated negative evaluations of an event, he often stops thinking about it and therefore cannot see beyond its 'dreaded' implications. The purpose of time projection is to enable clients to see vividly that time and the world continue after the 'dreaded event' has occurred. Thus, for example, a Malaysian student whose tuition fees were paid for by his village concluded that it would be terrible if he failed his exams because he couldn't bear to face his fellow villagers. I helped him to imagine his return to his village while experiencing shame. I then gradually advanced time forward in imagery. He began to see that it was likely that his fellow villagers would eventually come to adopt a compassionate viewpoint towards him and, even if they did not, he could always live happily in another part of the country or in another part of the world.

Imagery methods which focus on helping clients to think carefully and critically about 'dreaded' events are also extremely valuable. For example, another client who had a fear of other people seeing his hands shake was asked to imagine going into a bar, ordering a drink and drinking while his hands shook. He said that he would be extremely anxious about this because other people in the bar would stare at him. He was asked to imagine how many people would stare at him. Would they stare in unison or would they stare one at a time? He was asked to imagine how often they would stare at him, how long they would stare at him and how often in the evening they would resume staring at him. He concluded that everybody would not stare at him and those who did stare would possibly only stare for about 30 seconds and he could stand that. This and other methods illustrate that it is possible simultaneously to help clients dispute both their faulty inferences and irrational evaluations. Another technique I employed with this same client was 'imagery to exaggeration'. He was asked to imagine his hands shaking while consuming drink and with everybody in the bar staring at him continually for 3 hours. At this point he burst out laughing and realised the exaggerated nature of his inference.

Rational-emotive imagery is a frequently employed technique and has been fully described by Maultsby and Ellis (1974) and Ellis (1979c). It often has dramatic impact and thus qualifies as a vivid method. It is worth while noting at this point that some clients have difficulty conjuring up images and may have to be trained in a stepwise fashion to utilise this ability. Furthermore, whilst helpful, it is probably not necessary for clients to imagine with extreme clarity.

The rational-emotive therapist as raconteur

Wessler and Wessler (1980) have outlined the therapeutic value of relating various stories, parables, witty sayings, poems, aphorisms and jokes to clients. The important factor here is that the therapist modifies the content of these to fit the client's idiosyncratic situation. Telling identical stories to two different clients may well have two different effects. One client may be deeply affected by the story, whilst for another the story may prove meaningless. It is important that rational-emotive therapists become acquainted with a wide variety of these stories and be prepared to modify them from client to client, without introducing unwarranted distortions.

Active visual methods

Active visual methods combine therapist or client activity with a vivid visual presentation. Young (1980) has outlined one such method, which he uses to help clients see the impossibility of assigning a global rating to themselves. He asks a client to describe some of his behaviours, attributes, talents and interests. Every answer the client gives Young writes on a white sticky label and sticks the label on the client. This continues until the client is covered with white sticky labels and can begin to see the impossibility of assigning one global rating to such a complex being. Wessler and Wessler (1980) outline similar active visual methods to communicate a similar point. For example, they ask their client to assign a comprehensive rating to a basket of fruit or a desk. Clients are encouraged to explore actively the components of the fruit basket or desk while attempting to assign a global rating to it.

Visual models

I have previously described the use of visual models I have devised, each of which demonstrates a rational message (Dryden, 1980a). For example, I employ a model called the 'LFT splash'. In the model a young man is seated at the top of a roller coaster with a young woman standing at the bottom. I tell clients that the young man does not move because he is telling himself that he can't stand the splash. Clients are asked to think what the young man would have to tell himself in order to reach the woman. This model is particularly useful in introducing to clients the idea of tolerating acute time-limited discomfort which, if tolerated, would help them achieve their goals.

Flamboyant therapist actions

A common disputing strategy that rational–emotive therapists use in verbal dialogue when clients conclude they are stupid for acting stupidly is to ask some variant of the question 'How are you a stupid person for acting stupidly?'. Alternatively, instead of asking such questions, the therapist could suddenly leap to the floor and start barking like a dog for about 30 seconds, resume her or his seat, and then ask the client to evaluate this action. Clients usually say that the action was stupid. The therapist can then ask whether that stupid action makes him or her a stupid person. Such flamboyant actions often enable clients to discriminate more easily between global self-ratings and rating of behaviours or attributes.

Rational role reversal

Rational role reversal has been described by Kassinove and DiGiuseppe (1975). In this technique, the therapist plays a naïve client with an emotional problem that is usually similar to the client's. The client is encouraged to adopt the role of the rational–emotive therapist and help the 'client' dispute his or her irrational belief. As Kassinove and DiGiuseppe point out, this technique is best used after the client has developed some skill at disputing some of his or her own irrational ideas. A related technique has been devised by Burns (1980), which he calls 'externalisation of voices'. In this technique which is again used after the client has displayed some skill at disputing irrational beliefs, the therapist adopts the irrational part of the client's personality and supplies the client with irrational messages. The client's task is to respond rationally to the irrational messages. When clients show a high level of skill at this, the therapist, in role, can try hard to overwhelm the client with a barrage of quick-fire irrational messages, thus helping the client to develop an automatic ability to respond to his or her own irrational messages. This method also can be used to help clients identify those negative thoughts to which they experience difficulty responding.

Therapist self-disclosure

Some clients find therapist self-disclosure an extremely persuasive method, whilst for others it is contraindicated. One way of attempting to ascertain a client's possible reactions to therapist self-disclosure is to include an appropriate item in a pre-therapy questionnaire. It may well be wise to avoid using therapist self-disclosure with clients who respond negatively to the item. In any case, the therapist had better ascertain the client's reaction to any self-disclosing statements she or he might make. The research literature on this topic indicates that therapists are advised not to disclose personal information about themselves too early in the therapeutic process (Dies, 1973). When therapists do disclose information about themselves, it is my experience that the most effective forms of self-disclosure are those in which they portray themselves as coping rather than mastery models. Thus, for example, it is better for the therapist to say to the client, 'I used to have a similar problem, but this is how I overcame it', rather than say, 'I have never had this problem, because I believe....' (see Chapter 9).

Paradoxical therapist actions

This method is often best used when clients, through their actions, communicate messages about themselves to the therapist that are based on irrational beliefs. For example, I once saw a female client who experienced a lot of rheumatic pain but had an attitude of low frustration tolerance towards it. Her behaviour towards me in sessions indicated the attitude, 'I am a poor soul, feel sorry for me'. This prompted me to adopt an overly sympathetic and diligent stance towards her. Thus, at the beginning of every session I treated her as if she could hardly walk and escorted her by arm to her chair and made frequent enquiries about her comfort. This eventually prompted her to make statements such as, 'Don't treat me like a child', 'I can cope', or 'It's not as bad as all that'. I then helped her to identify and dispute some of the original implicit irrational messages. Whenever she began to lapse back into her self-pitying attitude, I began to behave in an overly solicitous manner again, which provided a timely reminder for her to attend to the behavioural components of her philosophy of low frustration tolerance and then to the philosophy itself.

Paradoxical therapist communications

Ellis (1977a) has written on the use of humour in RET, where the therapist humorously exaggerates clients' irrational beliefs. He points out the importance of using humour against the irrational belief, rather than as an *ad hominem* attack. Taking clients' beliefs and inferences to an absurd conclusion is another paradoxical technique that can be used. Thus, for 'shameful' acts or traits, therapists can take this to its illogical conclusion by saying,

'Well there is no doubt about it, they will find out, then they will tell their friends, some of whom will call up the local television station, and before you know it you will be on the six o'clock news'. Again, it is important that clients perceive that such communications are being directed against their beliefs rather than against them. Thus, feedback from clients on this matter had better be sought.

Rational songs

Ellis (1977a) has written about the use of his now-famous rational songs in therapy. For example, the therapist can hand a client a song sheet and sing, preferably in an outrageous voice, a rational song that has been carefully selected to communicate the rational alternatives to the client's target irrational belief. Because Ellis tends to favour tunes that were written many years ago, it may be more productive for the therapist to rewrite the words to more up-to-date and popular songs, for clients not familiar with some of the 'old favourites'.

In-session inference tests

Clients are likely to make faulty inferences about their therapist similar to those they make about other people in their lives. For example, one of my clients saw me talking to a fellow therapist at the end of one of our sessions. At our next session she told me that she was anxious about this because she was convinced I had been talking about her and laughing about what she had told me in the session (she was not in fact paranoid). I proceeded to pull out two pieces of paper, kept one for myself and gave the other one to her. I told her that I wanted to find out whether she indeed had extraordinary mind-reading powers. I thus wrote down the word 'chicken' on my piece of paper and asked her to concentrate very carefully for the next 3 minutes and to write down what she thought I was thinking about. I said that I would keep thinking about the word I had written down to make it a fair experiment. After the 3 minutes, she wrote down the word 'baseball'. This became known as the 'baseball–chicken' interview, which she recalled frequently when she made arbitrary inferences concerning the meaning of other people's behaviour.

Using the therapist–client relationship

Wessler (1982a) has written that it is important for the rational–emotive therapist to enquire about the nature of his or her client's reaction to him or her, i.e. to examine some of the client's here-and-now attitudes. Little has been written about this approach in the rational–emotive literature, and thus relatively little is known about its potential as a framework for disputing inaccurate inferences and irrational beliefs. Wessler (1982a) also advocates

that therapists give clients frank feedback about their impact on the therapist and explore whether clients have a similar impact on other people.
Such generalisations must of course be made with caution, but such discussion is often a stimulus for clients to become more sensitive to their
impact on other people and often leads them to ask other people about
their interpersonal impact (Anchin and Kiesler, 1982).

The advantage of using the therapist–client relationship in this way is
that it provides both parties with an opportunity to process the client's
inferences and beliefs in an immediate and often vivid fashion. The outcome of such strategies is often more memorable for clients than the outcome of such traditional disputing methods where client inferences and
beliefs about recent past events are processed.

Therapist paralinguistic and non-verbal behaviour

When rational–emotive therapists want to emphasise a point, one important way of doing so is for them to vary their paralinguistic and non-verbal
behaviour. For example, Walen, DiGiuseppe and Wessler (1980, p. 178)
note that, when Ellis in his public demonstrations talks about something
'awful', he drops his voice several notes, stretches out the word and increases his volume, producing a dreary and dramatic sound, for example, 'and
it's AWWWWWFUL that he doesn't like me'. Later, when he changes the
word 'awful' to 'unfortunate' or a 'need' to a 'want', Ellis again pronounces
the words now reflecting rational concepts in a distinct way. He says the
key word slowly, enunciates very clearly, and raises the pitch of his voice as
well as the volume. In addition, the therapist might associate some dramatic
non-verbal behaviour with the paralinguistic clue. For example, when the
word 'awful' is pronounced, the therapist might sink to the floor, holding
his neck as if strangling himself.

Therapeutic markers

Another way of emphasising a point is to draw the client's attention to the
fact that an important point is about to be made. For example, I might say to
a client when I want to emphasise a point, 'Now I want you to listen
extremely carefully to this point because, if you miss it, it would be awww-
ful' (therapist sinks to the floor again). I call such interventions 'therapeutic
markers'. Another way of emphasising statements is to change one's body
position. For example, by moving their torso forward towards clients, therapists can indicate the importance of their following statements. Whenever I
want clients to become aware of important statements they have made, particularly when they make more rational statements at the beginning of the
disputing process, I may, for example, pause and say, 'Excuse me, could you
just repeat what you said – I really want to make a note of this'. If I am

recording a session, I might say, 'Hold on a minute, I really want you to hear what you have just said, I can't believe it myself, I just want to check it out'.

Pragmatic disputes

One major way of encouraging clients to surrender their irrational beliefs in favour of more rational ones is to point out to them, and in this context in dramatic terms, the implications of continued adherence to their irrational beliefs. Ellis counsels that for particularly resistant and difficult clients this tactic is often the most effective (Ellis, 1985a). Quite often I have heard Ellis tell clients something like, 'If you continue to cling to that belief you'll suffer for the rest of your life'. Here, as before, he changes his paralinguistic and non-verbal behaviour when he states the conclusion, 'You'll suffer for the rest of your life'. In similar vein, when clients state that they can't (or, rather, won't) change their beliefs, he points out to them the logical implications of not doing so when he says forcefully, 'So suffer!' In this regard it would be interesting to determine under what conditions pragmatic disputes are more effective than philosophical ones.

Working Through

This section focuses on how therapists can help clients to work vividly through some of their emotional problems. Ellis (1983c) has criticised some popular behavioural techniques on the grounds that they do not necessarily encourage clients to make profound philosophical changes in their lives. In particular he criticises those methods that encourage the client to confront a dreaded event gradually. He posits that this gradualism may indeed reinforce some clients low-frustration-tolerance ideas. Whenever possible, then, rational–emotive therapists encourage their clients to act in dramatic and vivid ways because they believe significant attitude change is more likely to follow the successful completion of such tasks. I will outline the vivid methods that clients can put into practice behaviourally and cognitively in their everyday lives. First, however, rational–emotive therapists face a further problem, which has received insufficient attention in the RET literature: how to encourage clients to carry out their homework assignments.

Vivid cues for encouraging clients to do their homework

Whilst some clients conscientiously do the homework assignments they and their therapists have negotiated, other clients do not. It is true that some clients do not follow through on these assignments because of low-frustration-tolerance ideas; still other clients do not follow through, particularly early on in the working-through process, because they require some vivid reminders to initiate this process. With such clients, I have found it particularly helpful to ask them what they generally find memorable in everyday life experiences. For example, some people find the printed word memorable, whilst others have visual images on which they cue. Yet others focus primarily on auditory stimuli. I find that it is profitable to capitalise on whatever channel the client finds memorable.

Vivid visual cues

There are a number of ways clients can remind themselves to initiate the disputing process. A number of rational–emotive therapists encourage clients to carry around small cards 3 inches × 5 inches with rational self-statements written on them, to which clients can refer at various times. Other therapists have encouraged clients to write reminders to themselves either to initiate a homework assignment or to refer to a rational message. These clients are encouraged to pin such messages at various places around the home or in their work situation. I find it helpful to encourage those clients who find visual images powerful to associate a particular dysfunctional feeling with a visual image that would enable them to initiate the disputing process. Thus one client found it helpful to conjure up a sign in her mind that said 'dispute' when she began to feel anxious. Another client, who was depressed, began to associate the onset of depression with a road sign on which was written 'act now'.

Another strategy I have used is to ascertain from clients what, if any, in-session experiences they have found particularly memorable. I try to help them encapsulate some of these experiences as a cue either to initiate the disputing process or to remind themselves of the relevant rational principle to which this experience referred. One client who was prone to thinking of himself as an idiot for acting idiotically found it memorable when I made strange faces at him to help him get the point that concluding he was an idiot for acting idiotically was an overgeneralisation. Whenever he began to make such an overgeneralisation in everyday life, he would get the image of my making faces and quickly remembered to what this referred. This helped him accept himself regardless of any idiotic act he actually made or thought he might make in the future.

Another client who did virtually no cognitive disputing or behavioural assignments outside therapy sessions was helped in the following manner. First, this issue was made the focus of therapy. Instead of asking her traditional disputing questions, I asked her to imagine what I would say to her were I to respond to her irrational beliefs. She in fact had understood rational principles because her answers were very good. Her problem was that she would not employ these principles. I then asked her if there was any way she could conjure up a picture of me giving her rational messages at various emotionally vulnerable times in her everyday life. She hit on the idea of imagining that I was perched on her shoulder whispering rational messages into her ear. Additionally, she began to carry around a small card that said 'Imagine that Dr Dryden is on your shoulder'. This proved a particularly effective technique where all else had failed.

Vivid language

Wexler and Butler (1976) have argued in favour of therapists using expressive language in therapy. I have found that one of the major benefits of using vivid non-profane language is that clients remember these vivid expressions or catch-phrases and use them as shorthand ways of disputing irrational beliefs in their everyday lives. For example, in the case where I helped a client dispute a particular distorted inference by having her attempt to read my mind (the 'baseball–chicken' interview), whenever the client concluded that other people were making negative inferences about her without supporting data, she would remember the phrase 'baseball and chicken'. This served (1) as a timely reminder that she might be making incorrect conclusions from the data at hand, and (2) as a cue for her to start examining the evidence.

In a related technique, the therapist asks the client to give his or her own distinctive name to a faulty psychological process. Wessler and Wessler (1980) give such an example where a client came to refer to himself as 'Robert the Rule Maker', to describe his tendency to make demands on himself and other people. A knowledge of clients' subcultural values is particularly helpful here. I worked in a working-class area in Birmingham, England, and one word my clients frequently used, which was unfamiliar to me, was the word 'mather'.* I helped one client who was angry with her mother to see her mother as a fallible human being with a worrying problem, and that she could be accepted for this rather than be damned for it. My client suddenly laughed and said, 'Yes! I guess my mother is a matherer'. I encouraged her to remember this catchy phrase whenever she began to feel angry towards her mother.

Auditory cues

Rational–emotive therapists often make tape recordings of their sessions for clients to replay several times between sessions. This often serves to remind clients of rational principles they have understood in the session but may have since forgotten. Using personal recording systems, clients also can be encouraged to develop auditory reminders to initiate either cognitive or behavioural homework assignments. In addition, they can be encouraged to put forceful and emphatic rational statements on cassettes and play these while undertaking behavioural assignments. For example, I once saw a client who was anxious about other people looking at her for

---

*This is pronounced 'my-the' and means to be worried or bothered.

fear they might think her strange. I suggested that she do something in her everyday life which would encourage people to look at her so she could dispute some of her underlying irrational beliefs. She decided to wear a personal stereo system in the street, which she thought would encourage people to look at her. I suggested that while walking she play a tape on which she had recorded the rational message 'Just because I look strange doesn't mean that I am strange'.

The use of rational songs in therapy has already been described. Several of my clients have found that singing a particular rational song at an emotionally vulnerable time has been helpful for them. It has reminded them of a rational message they might not ordinarily have been able to focus on while being emotionally distressed. Another client told me that her sessions with me reminded her of a particular song and, whenever she hummed this song to herself, it helped bring to mind the fact that she could accept herself even though she did not have a man in her life. The song, ironically, was 'You're No One Till Somebody Loves You'. In fact, she rewrote some of the words and changed the title to 'You're Someone Even Though Nobody Loves You'.

Olfactory cues

It is possible for clients to use various aromas as cues to remind themselves to do a homework assignment or to initiate the disputing process. One client said that she found my pipe tobacco particularly aromatic and distinctive. Because we were both seeking a memorable cue, I suggested an experiment whereby she purchased a packet of my favourite tobacco and carried this around with her to smell at various distressing times. This aroma was associated in her mind with a particular rational message. This proved helpful, and indeed my client claimed that by saying to herself the phrase 'Pipe up' she now no longer has to take the tobacco out of her handbag to smell. Just the phrase is enough to remind her of the rational message.

The Working-through Process

From its inception, RET has strongly recommended that clients undertake 'some kind of activity which itself will act as a forceful counterpropagandist agency against the nonsense he believes' (Ellis, 1958a). Ellis has consistently stressed that for clients who will agree to do them, dramatic, forceful and implosive activities remain the best forms of working-through assignments. Such assignments emphasise either cognitively based or behavioural activities.

Cognitive assignments

In cognitive assignments, clients are encouraged to find ways in which they can convince themselves (outside therapy sessions) that rational philosophies which they can acknowledge as correct in therapy sessions are indeed correct and functional for them. Ellis has always urged clients to dispute their ideas vigorously, using aids as written homework forms (Ellis, 1979c). Other vivid cognitive techniques that clients can use include the following.

Rational proselytising (Bard, 1973)

Here clients are encouraged to teach RET to their friends. In teaching others, clients become more convinced themselves of rational philosophies. This technique, however, had better be used with caution, and clients should be warned against playing the role of unwanted therapist to friends and relatives.

Tape-recorded disputing

In this technique, clients are encouraged to put a disputing sequence on tape. They are asked to play both the rational and irrational parts of themselves. Clients are further encouraged to try and make the rational part more persuasive and more forceful in responding to the irrational part.

Passionate statements

For those clients who are intellectually unable to do cognitive disputing in its classic sense, *passionate rational self-statements* can be used. Here client and therapist work together to develop appropriate rational self-statements that the client can actually use in everyday life. Clients are encouraged to repeat these statements in a very forceful manner instead of in their normal voice tone. Another variation of this technique is to have clients say rational self-statements to their reflection in a mirror, using a passionate tone and dramatic gestures again to reinforce the message.

Behavioural techniques

Behavioural techniques which rational–emotive therapists particularly favour have clients do cognitive disputing in actual settings that vividly evoke their fears. The purpose is to enable clients to have the success experience of doing cognitive disputing while exposing themselves to feared stimuli. In addition, dramatic behavioural assignments are recommended to help clients overcome their low-frustration-tolerance ideas. Here the focus is oriented towards clients changing their dysfunctional attitudes towards their internal experiences of anxiety or frustration. Behavioural assignments include the following.

Shame-attacking exercises

Here the client is encouraged to do some act that she or he has previously regarded as 'shameful'. The client is encouraged to act in a way that will encourage other people in the environment to pay attention to her or him without bringing harm to self or other people and without unduly alarming others. She or he is encouraged to engage simultaneously in vigorous disputing, such as, 'I may look weird, but I'm not weird'. In my opinion, one of the drawbacks of encouraging a client to do shame-attacking exercises in a group is that the group serves to reinforce the client positively for doing the exercise. Doing shame-attacking exercises together can become a game that is not taken seriously. However, shame-attacking exercises are extremely valuable in promoting change and, while humour is an important component, my experience is that greater and longer-lasting change is effected when clients do shame-attacking exercises on their own as part of their individual therapy, without the social support of a group.

Risk-taking assignments

In risk-taking assignments clients are encouraged to do something they regard as being 'risky'. For example, a client may be encouraged to ask a waiter to replace a set of cutlery because it is too dirty. In preparing the client for risk-taking exercises, identification and disputing of faulty inferences and consequent irrational evaluations need to be done. The problem, however, is to get the client to prompt the aversive responses from others that he or she predicts will occur. In order for evaluative change to take place, the client is advised to be prepared to do such risk-taking experiences repeatedly over a long period of time so that he or she eventually encounters the 'dire' response. This is because such aversive responses from others occur far less frequently than the client predicts. Again the client is encouraged to undertake cognitive disputing along with the behavioural act.

Step-out-of-character exercise

Wessler (1982a) has modified this exercise from Kelly (1955). Clients are encouraged to identify desired behavioural goals that are not currently enacted with frequency. For example, one group member chose the goal of eating more slowly, which for him was a desirable, non-shameful, non-risky exercise, but one that involved monitoring of eating habits and cognitive disputing of low-frustration-tolerance ideas.

In vivo desensitisation

These methods require clients to confront their fears repeatedly in an implosive manner. For example, clients with elevator phobia are asked to ride in elevators 20–30 times a day at the start of treatment, instead of gradually working their way up to this situation either in imagery or in actuality. Again, simultaneous cognitive disputing is urged. Neuman (1982) has written and presented tapes of short-term, group-oriented treatment of phobias.

In his groups, clients are encouraged to rate their levels of anxiety. The most important goal is for the clients to experience a 'level 10', which is extreme panic. Neuman continually points out to people that it is important to experience 'level 10' because only then can they learn that they can survive and live through such an experience. Similarly, if in-roads to severe phobic conditions are to be made, it is important for rational–emotive therapists to work towards helping clients tolerate extreme forms of anxiety before helping clients to reduce this anxiety.

Stay-in-there activities

Grieger and Boyd (1980) have described a similar technique, which they call 'stay-in-there' activities, the purpose of which is to have clients vividly learn that they can tolerate and put up with uncomfortable experiences. One of my clients wanted to overcome her car-driving phobia. One of the things she feared was that her car would stall at a set of traffic lights and she would be exposed to the wrath of motorists who were stuck behind her. After eliciting and disputing her irrational ideas in traditional verbal dialogue, I encouraged her to turn off her engine at a set of lights and to stay there for about 20 minutes, thus creating the impression her car had broken down. Fortunately, the other car drivers did react in an angry fashion and she was able to practise disputing her dire needs for approval and comfort in a situation in which she remained for fully half an hour.*

Some clients tend to do these dramatic exercises once or twice and then drop them from their repertoire. Therapists are often so glad and so surprised that their clients will actually do these assignments that they do not consistently show them the importance of *continuing* to do them. One of the reasons for continued practice has already been mentioned, namely, that clients are more likely to make inferential changes than evaluative changes by doing these assignments infrequently. This is largely because the 'dreaded' event has a far lower probability of occurring than clients think. However, sooner or later, if clients consistently and persistently put into practice these assignments, they may well encounter such events that will provide a context for disputing of irrational beliefs. Thus, if therapists really want to encourage clients to make changes at 'B' as well as 'A', they had better be prepared to encourage clients consistently to do these dramatic assignments over a long period of time.

Operant conditioning methods

Ellis (1979c) has consistently employed operant conditioning methods to encourage clients to take responsibility for being their own primary agent

---

* Caution need., to be exercised here because, in some parts of England, the police take a dim view of such behaviour.

of change. Here clients are encouraged to identify and employ positive rein-forcements for undertaking working-through assignments, and apply penal-ties when they do not do so. Whilst not all clients require such encourage-ment, difficult and resistant clients, whose resistance is due to low-frustration-tolerance ideas, can be encouraged to take full responsibility for not putting into practice assignments that would stimulate change. Thus, dramatic experiences, such as burning a £10 note, throwing away an eager-ly awaited meal and cleaning a dirty room at the end of a hard day's work, are experiences that are designed to be so aversive that clients would choose to do the assignment previously avoided rather than undergo the penalty. Of course clients can, and often do, refuse to do the assignment and refuse to employ operant conditioning methods. However, many clients who have been resistant in the working-through process have, in my experience, begun to move when the therapist adopts this no-nonsense approach.

Limitations of Vivid Methods in RET

Whilst the basic thesis in this chapter has been to show the possible effica-cy of vivid RET, there are, of course, limitations to such an approach.

First, it is important for therapists to determine the impact on clients of introducing vivid methods into the therapeutic process. Thus, using the guidelines of Beck et al. (1979), it is perhaps wise for the therapist to ask the client at various points in the therapy to give frank feedback concerning the methods and activities used. Whilst the therapist may not always agree not to use such techniques just because a client has a negative reaction to them we had better obtain and understand our clients' negative reactions to our procedures.

Secondly, it is important in the use of vivid dramatic techniques not to overload the client. One vivid and dramatic method carefully introduced into a therapy session at an appropriate time is much more likely to be effective than several dramatic methods employed indiscriminately in a ses-sion.

Thirdly, it is important that rational–emotive therapists be clear about the rationale for using vivid methods and not to see the use of such methods as a goal in itself. The important thing to remember is that vivid methods are to be used as vehicles for promoting client attitude change and not to make the therapeutic process more stimulating for the therapist. It is also extremely important to ascertain what the client has learned from the vivid methods the therapist has employed. The client will not magically come to the conclusion the therapist wants. It is also important that therapists do not promote 'false' change in their clients. Change is 'false' when a client feels better as a result of some of these vivid methods but does not get bet-ter. Ellis (1972a) has written an important article on such a distinction. Thus therapists should invariably ask questions such as, 'What have you learned from doing this vivid method?' and 'How can you strengthen this learning experience for yourself outside of therapy?'.

Fourthly, dramatic and vivid methods are not appropriate for all clients. They are particularly helpful for those clients who use intellectualisation as a defence and/or who use verbal dialogue to tie rational–emotive therapists in knots. Whilst there are no data at the moment to support the following hypothesis, I would speculate that dramatic and vivid methods had better not be used with clients who have overly dramatic and hysterical personalities. It is perhaps more appropriate to assist such clients to reflect in a calm and undramatic manner on their experiences than to overstimulate an already highly stimulated personality.

Part V
Applications of
Rational–Emotive Therapy

Chapter 13
Rational–Emotive Couples Therapy

Introduction

Albert Ellis began his career in the helping professions as a sex, marital and family counsellor in the early 1940s. As a result of his experiences as a marital counsellor, he concluded that 'in most instances disturbed marriages (or pre-marital relationships) were a product of disturbed spouses; and that if people were truly to be helped to live happily with each other they would first have to be shown how they could live peacefully with themselves' (Ellis, 1962, p. 3). This conclusion led Ellis to embark on intensive psychoanalytical training, believing than that psychoanalysis was the preferred mode of treatment for such disturbances. As has already been mentioned (see Chapter 1), in the early 1950s, Ellis became increasingly disillusioned with both the theoretical validity and clinical effectiveness of psychoanalytical treatment and began to see more clearly that human disturbance has profound ideological roots. Drawing upon the work of early Stoic philosophers (e.g. Marcus Aurelius and Epictetus) who stressed that people are disturbed not by events but by their views of these events, he began to develop a therapeutic approach based upon a perspective of human disturbance that stressed philosophical determinants and de-emphasised psychoanalytical psychodynamic ones and applied it to a number of therapeutic modalities including couples therapy.

Rational–emotive couples therapy (RECT) has not developed in a logical, stepwise direction since those early days. Up to the time of writing (1985), there are no professional books or treatment manuals devoted to the application of RET to couple discord. However, a number of rational–emotive therapists have maintained an active interest in the field of RECT and there are a number of events that can be regarded as important in the history of its growth.

First published in 1985.

An early important development was the publication of Ellis's (1957) first book on RET: *How to Live with a Neurotic: At Home and at Work*. In this book he advances the thesis that partners could alleviate couple discord, first, by working to remain undisturbed about their partners' neurotic problems and, then, by experimenting with various solutions to help their partners get over their neurotic difficulties. In a later text written with Robert Harper, entitled *A Guide to Successful Marriage* (Ellis and Harper, 1961b), Ellis developed this thesis and also made an important distinction between couple disturbance and couple dissatisfaction which has remained a cornerstone of RECT ever since. In the same book, Ellis and Harper also wrote on the important role that unrealistic expectations about intimate relationships play in the development and maintenance of both couple dissatisfaction and disturbance. Whilst the term 'expectation' in psychotherapy is problematic in that it does not clearly differentiate between 'hopes', 'assumptions', 'predictions' of varying certitude, and 'absolutistic demands', they made the valid point that there is often a large discrepancy between what actually happens in intimate relationships and what one or both partners assume or predict will happen. Thus, unrealistic expectations are often the breeding ground for the later development of relationship problems.

In 1962, Ellis's seminal book *Reason and Emotion in Psychotherapy* was published. This contained a chapter entitled 'A rational approach to marital problems' which was adapted and expanded from two earlier articles (Ellis, 1958b, 1960). Here, Ellis clearly outlined that one of the major tasks of the marriage counsellor was to 'tackle not the problem of the marriage, nor the neurotic interaction that exists between the marital partners, but the irrational ideas or beliefs that cause the neurosis à deux' (Ellis, 1962, p. 210).

As will be developed later in this chapter, another cornerstone of RECT is its position on the role and treatment of angry and hostile reactions in intimate relationships. In 1976, Ellis published an important paper on this topic (Ellis, 1976c), in which he clearly outlined both the rational–emotive position on anger – namely that it is a dysfunctional emotion which severely interferes with relationship harmony – and its management in therapy.

Apart from Ellis, a number of other rational–emotive therapists have made important contributions to the field of RECT. Among others, the writings of Church (1974) on the application of RET to divorce, McClellan and Stieper (1973) on a structured rational–emotive approach to group marital counselling, and Hauck on (1) the reciprocity theory of love and business theory of marriage (Hauck, 1981, 1983a) and (2) parenting styles (Hauck, 1977, 1983b) are particularly noteworthy. Special mention should be made of Walen, DiGiuseppe and Wessler's (1980) book chapter entitled 'A rational approach to marriage and divorce counseling'. This chapter is unique in that it provides a clear set of procedural and technical guidelines for the practice of RECT. Also, a special issue of the *Journal of Rational-Emotive Therapy* has been devoted to couples therapy (Grieger, 1986). Despite these developments, there still appears to be an important place for a text which provides a comprehensive exposition of the theory and practice of RECT.*

Theory

The nature of disturbed interpersonal relationships

Rational-emotive therapists clearly distinguish between couple dissatisfaction and couple disturbance. Couple dissatisfaction occurs when one or both partners are not getting enough of what they *want* from their partner and/or from being in an intimate relationship. Couple disturbance arises when one or both partners become emotionally disturbed *about* these dissatisfactions. Thus, they may make themselves anxious, angry, hostile, hurt, depressed, ashamed, guilty and jealous – emotions that usually interfere with constructive communication, problem-solving and negotiation processes which aid the solution of couple dissatisfaction problems. In addition, when one or both partners are emotionally disturbed, they generally act in a self- and relationship-defeating manner, thus perpetuating couple disturbance. RECT theory states that, assuming they have the necessary constructive communication, problem-solving and negotiation skills, couples are likely to solve their dissatisfaction problems on their own. Where they are deficient in such skills, the focus of couples therapy is on training them to develop and use these skills. However, once couples are disturbed about their relationship, unless their emotional problems are dealt with, relationship problems usually remain, no matter how skilful one or both partners are in communicating, solving problems and negotiating workable compromises. Couples, interestingly enough, often misdiagnose their own problems. They often conclude that their problems are due to deficits in communication skills, whilst, in reality, they find it difficult to talk to one another when one or both are hurt, angry, depressed, anxious etc.

Couple disturbance

As has been shown in Chapter 1, emotional disturbance (C), according to RET's ABC theory, stems not from events at A, but mainly from a certain type of evaluative thinking or belief at B. This type of thinking, which is absolutistic, devout and grossly exaggerated in nature, is called 'irrational' in RET theory, mainly to denote that it hinders people from actualising their basic goals and purposes. Thus, irrational beliefs which lead to such disturbed emotions as anxiety, anger/hostility, hurt, depression, shame and embarrassment, guilt and jealousy, stem, according to RET theory, from a thinking process known as *musturbation*. In the couple context, this

---

*One such text appeared in 1989 entitled *Rational-Emotive Couples Therapy*, written by Albert Ellis, Joyce Sichel, Ray Yeager, Dom Di Mattia and Ray Giuseppe and published by Pergamon Press.

process is characterised by one partner making *absolute* demands and commands on self, the other partner and/or the relationship situation.

In the main, three further irrational (i.e. self-defeating) and grossly exaggerated thinking processes tend to stem from musturbation (Ellis, 1984a). Once humans absolutistically demand that something, for example, *'must'* not occur, they tend, if that event occurs, to conclude: that the event is 'awful', 'horrible' or 'terrible'; that they 'can't stand it' or ' can't bear it', and that the perpetrator of the event that must not have occurred is 'no good', 'worthless' (or 'less worthy') or 'bad' – whether the perpetrator is self, another person or life conditions in general. Ellis (1983a) recently noted that these four thinking processes, known colloquially in RET literature as (1) musturbation, (2) awfulising, (3) I-can't-stand-it-itis, and (4) damning, represent a philosophy of religiosity or devout belief where the person adopts a God-like position and *insists* (not just desires or prefers) that the world (and the people in it) be as he or she wants it (or them) to be.

The rational (or self-enhancing) alternatives to these absolutistic beliefs are framed within a non-demanding, non-absolute philosophy of desire. Here, in the relationship context, it is acknowledged that couples do have desires, are probably happier when these are met and become dissatisfied when these remain unfulfilled. However, as has been stressed above, dissatisfaction is not synonymous with disturbance and the latter only develops if one or both partners escalate their non-absolute desires into absolute demands. Couple dissatisfaction occurs when one or both partners' important desires are not being fulfilled (and neither is insisting that they get what they want). Couple disturbance occurs when one or both partners demand that their desires must be met. Parenthetically, couples therapy is normally more difficult when both partners are emotionally disturbed about the relationship than when only one partner is thus disturbed.

The rational versions of the four irrational thinking processes are as follows.

Desiring (vs musturbation)

Here the partner acknowledges his or her desires, does not insist that they be met, but is dissatisfied when they are not. Such dissatisfaction often serves to stimulate constructive attempts at problem solving which have a better chance of success with a spouse who is also not 'musturbating'. Rational thinking processes (2), (3) and (4) tend to be derived from non-demanding desiring just as irrational thinking processes (2), (3) and (4) are derived from musturbation.

Rating as bad (vs awfulising)

RET theory holds that 'awful' really means more than 100 per cent bad because such a definition stems from the belief: 'This *must* not be as bad as it is.' Thus 'awful' is seen to be on a different continuum from 'bad'. If a partner is not getting what he or she really wants, but is not insisting upon it, this person will tend to define the deprivation as 'bad' but not 'awful'. The general principle is that the more important the unfulfilled desire, the more 'bad' the definition of the deprivation is likely to be. It is, thus, only under very unusual conditions that an event can be legitimately rated as 100 per cent bad. Non-absolutistically evaluating something as 'bad' but not 'awful' tends to lead the partner to try to ameliorate the 'bad' situation.

Tolerating (vs I-can't-stand-it-itis)

'I can't stand it' literally means disintegrating or dying on the spot. It more often seems to mean not being able to have happiness whatsoever under any conditions, rather than actually dying. However, tolerating something means (1) acknowledging that some unwanted event has occurred and believing that there is no law that says it must not occur, (2) rating it as 'bad' but not 'awful' and (3) determining whether change is possible. If it is possible, constructive attempts are made to produce the desired change, whilst, if change is not possible, the person accepts, but definitely dislikes, this 'grim' reality. When partners are thinking rationally, they are likely to see that, whilst they can tolerate a bad relationship, there is no reason why they have to. Tolerating adverse conditions is an attitude conducive to constructive change attempts while I-can't-stand-it-itis leads to destructive manipulative strategies.

Accepting (vs damning)

This attitude can be applied to self, others and the world. When a woman, for example, unconditionally accepts herself in this way, she recognises that she is a fallible human being who has an 'incurable error-making tendency' (Maultsby, 1984), meaning that she can and will make mistakes. If she is able to accept herself as such, she will more likely be able to acknowledge these errors, regard them as bad if they impede her goals and take responsibility for committing them. Moreover, if she does not *demand* that her partner act well, she will more likely be able to accept him as fallible, dislike the fact that he is acting badly and initiate constructive negotiations for future improvement. Finally, if she does not dogmatically *insist* that her relationship be the way she wants it to be, she will tend to see it as a fallible institution with good and bad components which can only be improved but not perfected.

As Young (1975) has shown, rational thinking can and does (especially in the arena of intimate relationships) lead to strong negative emotions, such as concern, annoyance, sadness, disappointment, regret and dislike.

However, these emotions tend to motivate marital partners to take constructive steps to improve matters if their shared goal is to remain partnered.

Couple dissatisfaction

RECT theory notes that there are two major contributing factors to couple
dissatisfaction – relationship myths and important incompatibilities.

Couple dissatisfaction may occur if partners adhere to one or more myths
(Ellis and Harper, 1961b; Lederer and Jackson, 1968; Lazarus, 1985). Such
myths tend to be unrealistic in that they idealise the state of the relationship
and encourage partners to overestimate what they can realistically expect
to derive from being partnered. Some examples of commonly held relationship myths* that are often implicated in couple dissatisfaction include
the following: love equals good sex; romantic love will endure throughout
partnership; my partner will be able to know what I want without me having to communicate my desires; good sex will always be spontaneous; I will
not suffer any deprivations or penalties as a result of being partnered; my
partner will help me get over my feelings of unworthiness; my partner will
make up for my past frustrations; my mate will make allowances for my bad
behaviour; my partner will always be on my side, always be loyal and always
love me (no matter how badly I behave). If partners do not modify these
myths in line with their experience, they will tend to become dissatisfied,
as reality proves to be discrepant from their assumptions of what is 'expected' to happen in the relationship. Furthermore, it can easily be seen how
such myths can further lead to couple disturbance when linked to a philosophy of musturbation.

Couple dissatisfaction may also occur when partners are revealed to be
incompatible in one or more areas of the relationship. Generally, the more
important the area, the greater the dissatisfaction, especially if negotiations
for compromise fail to resolve the issues.

Couple incompatibility may stem from naïve and superficial partner
selection where partners do not really get to know one another, or may
occur as a result of changes in outlook on the part of one or both of them.
A commonly encountered example of emergent incompatibility occurs
when a woman seeks to develop a more independent lifestyle. If this
exceeds the role expectations of her partner, then neither are likely to get
what they want in a significant area of their relationship. If she does not act
on her newly discovered desire, she is likely to become dissatisfied and act
less responsively towards him so that he becomes dissatisfied. However, if
she spends less time in the house, he becomes dissatisfied, because his
desires for a well-kept house are not being met and, if he begins to nag her,

---

*Partners often express such myths in idiosyncratic form.

she becomes dissatisfied because her desires for support are not met. Dissatisfaction based on emergent incompatibility can often be a stimulus for constructive renegotiation of roles and responsibilities, but equally often, especially if the incompatibility occurs in a centrally important area for one or both partners, it may lead to relationship breakdown even if couple disturbance is not involved. In such a case, one or both partners conclude that the relationship no longer meets a very important desire and is not likely to in the future. If the incompatibility is in a less important area, it may lead to less intrusive dissatisfaction and may hardly affect the relationship, especially if the partners can find expression for the desire elsewhere and this is accepted by the other.

The development and perpetuation of couple disturbance

RECT theory holds that couple disturbance can develop and be perpetuated in a number of different ways. Conflict may occur soon after the relationship has been established if one or both partners are quite disturbed as individuals. Similarly, conflict might develop at various stages of an ongoing relationship when change occurs in the couple system. This change becomes a stimulus for one or both partners to bring their philosophy of musturbation to the new situation. Thus a dissatisfaction can quickly become a disturbance if, for example, a man demands that his mate *must* not ask to see his pay packet or if the woman insists that her mate *must* telephone to tell her that he will be staying late at the office. Here partners give themselves an emotional problem about the problem of dissatisfaction. In addition, partners may give themselves secondary emotional problems about their newly developed primary emotional problems (Ellis, 1984a). Thus, a man may get angry with his mate because he is demanding that she *must* not act in a certain manner; he may then notice his angry reaction and condemn himself for reacting in such a *terrible* manner. He thus becomes guilty for reacting angrily. It is unlikely that constructive communication or problem solving could ensue while he is experiencing anger alone, and doubly unlikely if he adds guilt to his emotional menu.

Irrational anger, stemming from the absolutistic demand that you, my partner, must not act this way either because it is 'wrong' or because it is a threat to my 'self-esteem', is probably the most prominent reason why couple disturbance is perpetuated (Ellis, 1976c). Indeed, when both partners are damning each other, couple disturbance could be perpetuated indefinitely with little chance of a constructive solution being found. Another core reason why couple disturbance is perpetuated is anxiety over confronting basic issues. One or both partners may be scared that, if they shared their feelings of dissatisfaction with one another, something 'awful' would ensue. They thus withdraw from one another and feel lonely, guilty and depressed about the growing distance between them.

Partners with emotional disturbances tend to act in dysfunctional ways (behavioural Cs). These then serve as the stimuli for the second partner's inference (INF). Vicious circles of disturbed couple interaction result when a dysfunctional behaviour (C) on the part of one partner serves as the trigger (INF$_2$) for an irrational belief (B$_2$) of the other partner which in turn leads to disturbed feelings and behaviour (C$_2$). This serves as a new trigger (INF$_3$) for the first partner ... and so on. An example of such a vicious circle is shown in Figure 13.1. As this interaction pattern demonstrates, partners often make inferences about each other's behaviour (which have been included under INF). These inferences may be correct but, especially in the phase of couple disturbance, are likely to be faulty, coloured as they often are by irrational, evaluative thinking. Nevertheless, rational–emotive therapists do draw on Beck's (1976) work on 'cognitive distortions' and note that patterns often make errors in processing interpersonal information and that these errors often serve to perpetuate

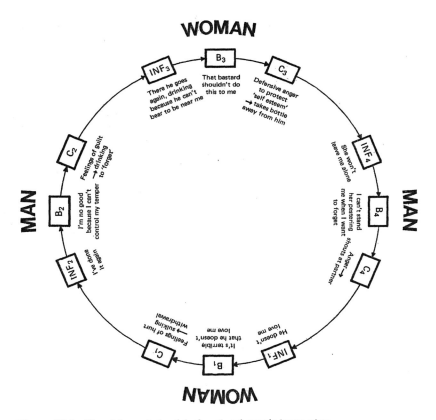

Figure 13.1   The vicious circle of dysfunctional couple interaction.

couple disturbance (see Chapter 1). These also become the focus for therapeutic work, but normally after partners' musturbatory evaluative thinking has been tackled.

Practice

Contextual considerations

Rational-emotive therapists are guided by the principle of flexibility throughout the therapeutic process in working with couples. Thus, there are no absolute rules to guide RECT practitioners concerning whether to see partners conjointly, concurrently or consecutively in individual sessions. Therapeutic decisions concerning the working text are suggested by therapeutic exigencies. Ellis (in Dryden, 1984c) and Bard (1980), for example, consider that the decision whether to see both partners together or separately at the outset of therapy should preferably be made by clients themselves. However, individual sessions may be indicated for three main reasons:

1. When the two partners persist in arguing non-productively in the context of conjoint sessions and thus negate the potential benefit of the therapist's interventions.
2. When the joint presence of the partners in the therapy room unduly inhibits one or both of them. They may be so anxious about the possible negative effects of speaking their minds that they do not disclose significant material in therapy. In such cases, a period of concurrent individual sessions is often helpful.
3. When the goals of the individual partners are sufficiently incongruent to preclude the establishment of a productive therapeutic alliance in conjoint therapy, e.g. when one person wishes to leave the relationship whilst the other wishes to preserve it.

When both partners wish to be seen together, share basically congruent goals, are not inhibited by their joint presence in therapy and can contain their strong angry feelings, then conjoint couples therapy is usually the most beneficial context for productive work.

Some RECT practitioners prefer to work concurrently with the partners in individual sessions in the 'overcoming couple disturbance' phase of treatment. They hypothesise that partners are more likely to disclose their genuinely held 'deep' feelings (e.g. of hurt, jealousy, anger and fear) if they see the therapist alone. Partners can thus give their full attention to the therapeutic process, whilst the therapist helps them to see the connections between their dysfunctional emotions/behavioural patterns and their irrational beliefs and helps them to dispute and change these ideas. Because RECT is by nature an educational process, its practitioners are mindful of choosing environments that best facilitate learning. However, partners *can* learn the ABCs of RECT in the context of conjoint therapy in the 'disturbance' phase. Here, while the therapist works with one partner, helping him or her to identify, challenge and change core irrational beliefs, the 'listening' partner often learns the ABC framework of emotional/behavioural disturbance better than the 'working' partner.*

Whilst RECT practitioners differ concerning their views about the supremacy of conjoint vs concurrent therapy in the 'overcoming couple disturbance' phase of treatment, they generally agree that the presence of both partners is highly desirable in the 'enhancing couple satisfaction' phase. In this phase, both partners have, ideally, made some progress in overcoming their emotional disturbance about their differences and are ready to explore possible ways of improving their relationship, if they have decided to stay together. Rational–emotive therapists use a variety of methods to facilitate such exploration. Communication, problem solving and negotiation training are used in this phase, and the presence of both partners is highly desirable to enable the therapist to instruct them *both* to communicate more effectively, solve problems and negotiate more constructively, so that they can improve the quality of their relationship.

Conjoint RECT is usually conducted with a single therapist, although there are occasions when a co-therapy arrangement would be desirable, particularly if, say, a woman feels unduly adversely affected by the presence of a male therapist. Here a female co-therapist would be helpful to strengthen the therapeutic alliance, and such a four-person arrangement might be particularly desirable in sex therapy.

In conclusion, the conduct of RECT is not bound by strict rules of procedure; flexibility is encouraged and changes in context may occur throughout the therapeutic process. Such changes are made according to therapeutic purposes which are generally made clear and agreed to by clients. It is in keeping with rational–emotive philosophy that RECT practitioners are against dogmatically *insisting* that therapy must be practised in any pre-determined context.

Developing and maintaining a therapeutic alliance

It is important to note, at the outset, that RECT practitioners consider that their therapeutic contract is with the individuals in the relationship and not with the couple system (Walen, DiGiuseppe and Wessler, 1980; Harper, 1981). As Harper argues, the couple system is an abstraction and, as such,

---

*A similar phenomenon often occurs in individual RET. When clients are given audiotape recordings of therapy sessions, they often learn the ABCs of RET better after they have listened to these recordings than when they are in the therapy room. It may be that this is due to the fact that, later, they are less emotionally involved with the material and can thus listen more attentively to what the therapist is saying.

RECT therapists have great difficulty seeing how a therapeutic alliance can be made with it. They prefer, whenever possible, to develop alliances with each of the involved partners. It is preferable if this is made clear to both partners at the outset of couples therapy so that they can see that the therapist is not interested in trying to preserve, or indeed destroy, their relationship. As has already been stressed, a primary objective of RECT therapists is to help both their situation and then help them work on forging a more mutually satisfying relationship, if this is their goal. However, partners often come into couples therapy with overt *and* hidden agendas, and it is often helpful to have separate interviews with each of the partners early in the process, to determine whether the goals of each partner are sufficiently concordant to make conjoint couples therapy – which is the best working forum for partners who have similar objectives – feasible. Because the therapeutic alliance is with the individuals and not with 'the relationship', the most appropriate therapeutic arena is sought to help the individuals actualise their goals.

Due to the fact that therapeutic goals can be based on irrational as well as rational thinking, it is common RECT practice to explain to both partners that they are more likely to make productive decisions about whether to stay partnered (and, if so, what improvements are desired) or to separate, when they are not emotionally disturbed about what is presently happening in the relationship. Thus RECT practitioners prefer to set goals appropriate to particular phases of couples therapy. If the partners are disturbed, attempts are made to have them identify and set goals which involve minimising such disturbance and, if they are dissatisfied, but not disturbed, attempts are made to work on relationship-enhancement goals after a decision has been made by both that they wish to stay partnered. Too often, non-RECT therapy founders because the therapist is working on couple-enhancement goals when one or both partners are emotionally disturbed, with the result that goal sabotaging occurs needlessly.

Another common error made by non-RECT practitioners occurs when the therapist is only prepared to see the partners in conjoint therapy. Thus, if one partner wishes to preserve the relationship whilst the other has a hidden agenda to leave it, but will not declare this openly in the therapeutic triangle, such therapy is either terminated by the latter soon after its inception or is marked by little or no improvement, to the detriment of both partners. RECT therapists would be more likely to identify such a situation earlier in individual assessment interviews.

In the 'overcoming emotional disturbance' phase of RECT, it is important for the therapist to work with each partner individually either in conjoint therapy or in separate interviews. In conjoint therapy, the therapist gives each partner roughly equal amounts of time in order to maintain a productive alliance in the three-person situation – a social system which can easily be destabilised if the therapist, for example, excludes one partner for lengthy periods of time. The therapist explains at the outset of this phase that the goal is to help each of the partners overcome his or her own disturbance (intrapersonal focus) so that they can more productively work on their disagreements later (interpersonal focus). Productive RECT occurs when both partners clearly understand and agree to this *modus operandi*. Highly skilled RECT therapists who can present a convincing rationale concerning this important point are usually, but not always, successful at developing a good therapeutic alliance with both partners when such an alliance is based on this principle. Failure to form a productive alliance with both partners at the outset of therapy usually leads to problems later in the therapeutic process and does not bode well for successful outcome. Such failure is due to either (1) poor therapist skills or (2) various partner factors which include: severe emotional disturbance; rigid adherence to the belief that the other person is totally responsible for relationship problems; or various hidden agendas. In such instances, the therapist is advised to consider changing the therapeutic context or to consider various systems-inspired interventions which are designed to change 'A' factors in the ABC schema.

If the therapist can successfully manage the 'overcoming emotional disturbance' alliance, then the alliance necessary to effect productive change in the 'enhancing couple satisfaction' phase is much easier to manage, because both partners are in a position to make sound decisions about goals and are sufficiently free from emotional disturbance to work towards goal achievement.

Major treatment techniques

RECT is a multimodal form of therapy in that it employs a variety of cognitive (verbal and imagery), emotive and behavioural techniques to help partners overcome their emotional disturbances and relationship dissatisfactions.

'Overcoming couple disturbance' phase

The goal of the RECT practitioner in this phase of couple therapy is to help each partner become relatively undisturbed about their problems so that they can constructively work, if they wish, to improve their level of relationship satisfaction. The therapist helps both partners to think rationally about themselves, their partner and their relationship, which means feeling appropriately frustrated, sorry, annoyed and sad about their predicament when their desires are not met – emotions which will motivate them to work to improve their relationship or separate without needless emotional pain.

In this phase, the RECT practitioner helps both partners to see how they are needlessly upsetting themselves about their problems and often adopts a 'let's assume' approach with both of them. Both partners are encouraged to assume that their inferences about, for example, their partner, are correct, for the time being, to offset unproductive arguments about what actually occurred at 'A' in the ABC framework. In this way, the therapist helps each partner to identify his or her underlying irrational beliefs and replaces them with their rational alternatives. The therapist would be wise to encourage persistently both partners to focus on their own upset if the goals of this phase of treatment are to be achieved. A variety of cognitive methods are used at this stage. Partners are shown how to use the logico-empirical methods of science to dispute their irrational beliefs. They are taught to ask themselves such questions as 'Where is the law of the universe that states that my partner *must* do the housework perfectly well?'; 'How does it follow that she is *bad* for acting badly?'; 'Is it true that I *cannot stand* her behaviour?' etc. They are subsequently helped to see that there is no evidence for such absolute statements, only evidence for their 'preferential' form. A number of clients appear less able to perform this kind of Socratic questioning and here the therapist would help them to develop and employ rational coping statements such as: 'I don't like my partner's behaviour but there's no reason why she must not act badly'; 'She is a fallible human being who is doing the wrong thing'; 'I can stand her behaviour although I may never like it'. These statements can be further written down on index cards and rehearsed between sessions.

Some couples can be shown, similarly, how to dispute each other's irrational beliefs and thus serve as therapists for each other between formal therapy sessions. Other cognitive techniques employed in this phase of RECT include the use of: (1) general semantics methods (Korzybski, 1933); (2) rational self-help forms (see Chapter 3); (3) audio-tape recordings (of the couple's therapy sessions or recorded lectures on rational themes); (4) bibliotherapy, especially the use of books which present the rational–emotive perspective on how to overcome emotional and behavioural disturbance; (5) a variety of imagery techniques (Lazarus, 1984).

Emotively, the therapist can employ several evocative and vivid methods of RET to help change the couple's irrational philosophies (Dryden, 1984a). Such methods include the use of: (1) rational–emotive imagery (Maultsby and Ellis, 1974) – where the partners deliberately imagine 'upsetting events' at 'A', and practise making themselves feel appropriately sad, annoyed, frustrated about these at 'C', which is achieved by spontaneous thinking more rationally at 'B'; (2) vigorous and forceful repetition of rational statements (Ellis, 1979d); (3) role-playing – to uncover hidden feelings which can then be traced back to the relevant irrational beliefs and disputed; (4) shame-attacking exercises – where couples deliberately seek out various 'shameful' experiences and practise accepting themselves for acting 'shamefully; and (5) therapist self-disclosure and humour to help couples not to take themselves and their partners *too* seriously.

Behaviourally, in this phase, partners are encouraged to face and not avoid potential problems so that they may have real-life opportunity to 'stay in' these situations until they have made themselves undisturbed about them (Grieger and Boyd, 1980).

'Enhancing couple satisfaction' phase

Once both partners have made some progress at helping themselves and their partner overcome their emotional disturbances about their dissatisfactory relationship, they are in a position to look constructively at ways of enhancing their degree of relationship satisfaction or to be helped to separate amicably. Assuming that they wish to stay partnered, there are a number of well-established methods that can be used to help them to live more happily together. These include communication training (Guerney, 1977; Crawford, 1982), negotiation training (Stuart, 1980) and a variety of behavioural techniques designed to help them to (1) develop appropriate relating and sexual skills and (2) get more of what they want from each other (Mackay, 1985). Bibliotherapy is often used in conjunction with these methods.

A hallmark of RECT is that homework assignments are negotiated to encourage couples to put into practice what they have learned in therapy. Assuming that such assignments are carefully designed by the therapist and agreed to by both partners, failure to execute them often reveals further emotional disturbance – particularly that which stems from a philosophy of low frustration tolerance (LFT). RECT practitioners are alert to such possibilities and strive to help both partners, if appropriate, overcome their LFT so that they can follow through on the difficult task of changing the nature of their relationship.

A final task for RECT practitioners in this stage is to address the topic of relationship myths (see 'Couple dissatisfaction' above) and help partners develop more realistic perspectives concerning what they can legitimately expect from intimate relationships.

Problems encountered in RECT and their solution

The conduct of couples therapy is fraught with potential problems, no matter which approach the practitioner adopts. The more flexible the practitioner can be, the better and in general it is highly desirable for RECT therapists to dispute their own irrational beliefs concerning how therapy *must* proceed, how clients *must* behave and what harmonious relationships *must* be like. Practitioners would be wise not to be invested in either preserving or destroying relationships, if they are truly to help couples negotiate what is in *their* best interests. Apart from therapist-derived problems the following problems are often encountered in RECT.

Secrets

Due to the fact that RECT therapists conceive their basic task to be one of helping individual partners, rather than the relationship, they will frequently see the partners alone in individual sessions, particularly at the beginning of therapy. Consequently, they will sometimes be called upon to keep 'secrets'. They are prepared to do this and, in order to help both partners disclose what is really on their minds, they will tell clients in individual sessions of their willingness to do so. This tactic also helps therapists to uncover any 'hidden agenda' quickly. Consequently, they are advised to be mindful of what information is confidential to a particular partner and keep a mental note not to disclose this in front of the other. It should again be noted that this is done in order to develop productive contracts with both partners. Some RECT therapists stress to both partners that whatever is discussed in individual sessions is confidential to each partner concerned, so that if directly asked about what occurred in an individual session with the other partner, they can refer to this principle. Moreover, partners are advised to only talk about their individual sessions with each other in general terms rather than in detail.

Persistent other-blaming

It sometimes happens that one or both partners refuse to acknowledge that they make themselves disturbed about their mate's behaviour and cling rigidly to the assertion that their mate is the cause of their upset. In certain of these cases, it transpires that they are anxious that if they admit that they make themselves upset, their mate will not be motivated to change. In other cases, such 'defensiveness' is motivated by fear of self-criticism: 'If I admit that I make myself disturbed, as I *must* not do, then I will condemn myself.' In these two instances, effective RECT practitioners will test out such hypotheses rather than assume that their hunches are correct. Such 'defensiveness' can also be, in certain instances, a sign that the partner is profoundly disturbed. One technique that sometimes helps clients who persistently blame their partner, is to stress that, if they want their partner to change, then one of the most effective ways of achieving this is to change their own behaviour first.

When disputing fails

In certain cases, RECT therapists will fail to encourage one or both partners to identify, challenge and change their irrational beliefs which mediate their disturbance. When this occurs, the practitioner can use some of the methods that are ideally intended for use in the 'enhancing couple satisfaction' phase. In the case where one partner is overcoming his or her emotional disturbance and the other is not, the therapist may focus his or her efforts on encouraging the former to be unusually nice to the disturbed partner to encourage that partner to change. Ellis (1957) originally advocated this tactic in his book, *How to Live with a Neurotic*, and it is one that sometimes proves successful. When both partners remain disturbed after disputing fails, RECT practitioners may use a number of systems-theory-inspired interventions which are designed to change 'A'. Thus, for example, reframing and various paradoxical procedures can be employed to help the couple extricate themselves from a vicious circle of negative interactions. If this is successful, it occasionally provides the stimulus for one or both partners *then* to focus on their disturbance-creating beliefs. However, although such interventions may be successful in the short term, if both partners remain emotionally disturbed they might, as a result, experience more problems later, because unresolved emotional disturbance is the driving force behind the development and maintenance of disturbed interactions.

Extremely hostile interchanges

These are difficult to manage when they occur in couples therapy sessions, and when they become a regular occurrence it is advisable to see the partners individually. However, in dealing with such a situation at a given time, I have found it helpful to do something unusual to gain the couple's attention. Thus, I have, in the midst of a heated interchange, got up and commenced speaking to a picture on the wall, or tried to catch an imaginary mouse. These attention-getting techniques are, in my experience, generally more effective in defusing the situation than trying to shout the couple down which tends to increase the heat in an overly hot kitchen.

The change process

In the same way as a good navigator plots his favourite course but plans several different alternative routes, should they be needed, so do effective RECT therapists have their preferred and alternative game-plans. Because couples differ markedly, the RECT therapist who adheres rigidly to a single game-plan is likely to fail with a number of couple clients.

When therapy goes smoothly, RECT practitioners are able to keep to their preferred game-plan. In cases when this applies, they help both partners see that they have two different kinds of problems: those related to couple disturbance, and those related to couple dissatisfaction. They succeed at: (1) showing the couple that it is better if they work on disturbance issues first; (2) explaining that their disturbance is due in the main to their irrational beliefs about their unsatisfactory relationship; (3) inducing them to work at disputing and changing these irrational beliefs and replacing them with their rational alternatives; (4) inducing them to work at identifying whether or not their differences can be reconciled; and, if so (5) helping them to negotiate more satisfying relationship arrangements; and (6) encouraging them to work to actualise these desired alternatives. When both partners are only dissatisfied and not disturbed, only stages (4), (5) and (6) apply.

Problems still tend to occur even in this smooth change process, and can be generally attributed to one or both partners believing that change *must* be easier than it is (LFT) or to one or both partners testing the solidity of change (Stuart, 1980). Here, the therapist (1) helps the couple to tolerate the discomfort that change almost inevitably brings and to see that change is rarely easily achieved, and (2) explains to the couple (preferably in advance) that 'testing' behaviour is a common occurrence in the change process, i.e. that one or both partners sometimes test out the solidity of change by returning to dysfunctional patterns. When partners are prepared for this eventuality they are less likely to disturb themselves about it. The therapist also explains that change is rarely a linear process because humans easily return to well ingrained but dysfunctional patterns of behaviour, thought and emotion.

When both partners are disturbed at the inception of therapy and only one changes for the better in this respect, the therapist will often, as noted above, encourage that partner to make an extra effort for his or her own sake and for the sake of determining the future prospects of the relationship. This involves being unusually understanding and tolerant of the still disturbed partner, a tactic which often serves as the fulcrum and lever which encourages that partner to begin to change, for it sometimes happens that he or she needs to see that the partner has shown an extra amount of 'good faith' before beginning to work on his or her own disturbance. If such a tactic fails to yield beneficial results for the disturbed partner, then the other partner has useful information when coming to determine the viability of the relationship.

As has also been noted above, when both partners remain disturbed, even as a result of the therapist's interventions in the 'overcoming couple disturbance' phase of treatment, the therapist is prepared to use a variety of behavioural and systems-theory-inspired interventions to change A in the ABC framework even though he or she acknowledges that it is less desirable than producing philosophical change at B (Ellis, 1979c). If these interventions are successful, then the couple have been helped to see that they can extricate themselves from a negative pattern and thus may be encouraged to do so for themselves. There is always the danger, however, that if they re-encounter the original problem situation they will again become disturbed and thus may need further help to change A.

It needs to be reiterated that RECT practitioners tend to be flexible in their use of different therapeutic contexts and thus may suggest changing the therapeutic modality at various points in the process of couples therapy (e.g. from conjoint couples therapy to concurrent individual sessions with each person). Such changes are usually instigated for positive therapeutic reasons, but can also be made if the therapy has become unproductively 'stuck' in a given modality.

The personal qualities of effective RECT therapists

In the practice of couples therapy, effective RECT practitioners will be: (1) comfortable using the structure of RECT, but flexible enough to work in less structured ways when the occasions arise; (2) drawn to adopting an active–directive teaching style and credible enough to teach their client couples the principles of RET in ways appropriate to the learning abilities of the people involved; (3) 'authoritative without being authoritarian; ... bring up discussions of basic values without foisting their personal values on to clients; ... push, coach, persuade, and encourage clients to think and act against their own self-sabotaging tendencies' (Ellis, 1982a, p. 316); and (4) prepared to reveal their own feelings and beliefs and show their clients that they are not scared to take risks in helping them over their relationship difficulties. Moreover, they will tend to be philosophically inclined, scientific, empirical, multimodal and anti-absolutistic in their approach to the problems of their couples, and be drawn to RECT because it allows them to express these tendencies fully. They will be comfortable working with more than one person in therapy and raising difficult issues with both partners, particularly in the area of sexual relations.

Whilst it is not essential for effective RECT therapists to have had first-hand experience of co-habiting relationships, this is probably desirable for a number of reasons. First, they will be able to talk to clients about their difficulties from a more authoritative and credible position, particularly if they have been successful in dealing with some of their own. Secondly, they will tend to have a deeper understanding of the stresses of intimate relationships and see the potential for growth and for harm that such relationships hold. Finally, they will be able to share specific examples from their own experiences to help show their clients the advantages of a rational approach to coupled life. However, it is noted that some RECT practitioners are quite successful without such first-hand experience.

A Typical Case Example of RECT

Mr and Mrs Rogers, married with no children, were seen when I worked as a part-time counselling psychologist for an east Birmingham (England) general practice. Mrs Rogers, a 35-year-old housewife, was initially referred to me for 'depression'. In an initial intake interview, it transpired that she was depressed about what she described as her husband's cold attitude towards her. I decided, with her permission, to invite Mr Rogers to come and see me to determine his opinions about his wife's depression and the marital situation. In cases where one partner is referred to me whose disturbance is rooted in an interpersonal context, I prefer to interview the significant other because this context facilitates their later involvement in therapy if this is indicated. Mr Rogers, a 38-year-old businessman, angrily complained about his wife's 'low mood'. He also expressed concern that he could not 'get through to her'. They both stated in these initial individual interviews that they would be interested to have counselling for their problems. They wanted to stay married, but both stated that they would like to be seen separately at first. I saw no reason to refuse their requests.

'Overcoming couple disturbance' phase

I began by helping Mrs Rogers to see that she was *insisting* in an absolutistic manner that she must have her husband's love and that she was unlovable because he did not seem to love her at present. I showed her that it was this attitude, rather than the assumed lack of love on his part, that determined her feelings of depression, and proceeded to help her to accept herself even if her husband did not love her. I helped her to *dispute* her irrational *need* for love, but encouraged her to keep to her rational *desire* for his love, and showed her that she could be appropriately sad but did not have to be inappropriately depressed if her assumption proved to be correct now and/or in the future.

When working with Mr Rogers, I zeroed in on his demand that his wife *should* not be depressed and helped him to see that this was related to another demand that his wife *must* be supportive which, in turn, was related to his fear of failure at work. His wife used to help him doing important typing and book-keeping and this helped him maintain a high standard of work performance. The fact that she was no longer assisting him in this way confronted him directly with his own anxiety, which, as often occurs, was masked by anger (Wessler, 1981). I encouraged Mr Rogers to face this fear and helped him to dispute his underlying irrational beliefs, namely: 'I *must* do well and continue to do well at work or I'd be inadequate'; and 'I *must* keep getting promoted or I may not be able to improve our living standards which would be terrible'. For good measure, I showed him that, whilst he wanted his wife to support him, there was no law in the universe that decreed that she had to. Consequently, he became more tolerant and sympathetic towards his wife when she became depressed.

At this point, it would have been tempting to bring Mr and Mrs Rogers together for conjoint sessions, because she was becoming less depressed and he was less anxious and angry. However, I decided to see them separately for two more individual sessions each to help them deal more thoroughly with the worst examples of 'A' in the ABC framework that they could imagine. This strategy, in fact, elicited Mrs Rogers' acute fear of divorce. I helped her to identify and challenge her belief that divorce would be 'awful' and helped her to see that she could lead an independent, happy life and therefore was not impelled to stay in the marriage.* I also helped Mr Rogers deal with his morbid fear of unemployment and showed him (1) that his value as a human was not dependent on his work status and (2) that he could become vitally absorbed in other pursuits if he ever faced unemployment.

---

*This procedure, known as 'de-awfulising' divorce, is very helpful in reducing anxiety in partners who feel impelled to stay married out of obligation rather than out of desire.

When I felt satisfied that they had made progress in dealing with their worst fears, I then arranged to see them in conjoint marital therapy, having seen them individually for six sessions each.

'Enhancing couple satisfaction' phase

This phase of treatment began with a review of what Mr and Mrs Rogers had both learned in individual couples therapy. They reiterated their desire to stay together and work towards increased marital satisfaction. At the outset of this phase, Mrs Rogers experienced a greater degree of dissatisfaction than her husband. Although she had made great strides in accepting herself, she stated that, in her opinion, he was still taking her for granted and expected that she would devote much of her life to helping him gain a managerial position to which he had always aspired. She said that she was no longer prepared to devote as much time to helping him in this respect and wanted more time to pursue her own emerging interests. Although Mr Rogers initially appeared to understand her desire for self-actualisation, his actual behaviour in subsequent weeks belied his words.

Despite the fact that I had helped them to negotiate a more equitable allocation of time to different tasks, Mr Rogers failed to keep his part of the bargain. At this point, Mrs Rogers decided to get tough with him. She was able to do this because she was less anxious about the prospect of being alone. When Mr Rogers realised that his wife was really serious about pursuing her own goals he was jolted into realising the implications of continuing to act in an unsupportive way towards her.* At this point, he was able to articulate his fears about what living with an independent woman might mean for him. He feared that she might find another man, whereas in reality Mrs Rogers wanted not only to spend more time pursuing her own interests, but also to spend more time socially with him: 'I no longer want to be a doormat', she said.

At this point, I did some individual work with Mr Rogers in the context of conjoint couples therapy. I helped him to see that he could still accept himself even if his wife did in fact leave him for somebody else, and that he could be relatively happy if this happened. Mrs Rogers tried on several occasions to reassure him that she was not interested in other men, but I showed her and her husband that this was not the central issue and that the real point was that Mr Rogers was anxious about the *prospect* of this happening. As he successfully disputed his irrational beliefs about her leaving him, he calmed down and listened to his wife's desires with greater empathy. At this point, I taught them how to listen accurately and respond to each other's statements, and how to check out their hunches about the

---

*I have often found that this is only when wives are prepared to take drastic action in pursuing their own goals that their husbands are 'shocked' into realising the implications of not listening to them. This 'shock' is often the motivating factor for initiating constructive change.

meaning of such statements rather than assume that their hunches were, indeed, facts (Guerney, 1977). I further helped them to consider the implicit contracts that they had made with each other at the time of their marriage about their roles as husband and wife, and showed them that these role expectations could be renegotiated (Sager, 1976). This led to a full discussion of their aspirations for themselves as individuals and as a couple, and they were able to determine for themselves how they could achieve 'I-goals' and 'We-goals'. At the end of ten conjoint sessions they decided that they had achieved enough to work on 'enhancing couple satisfaction' on their own.

Observations

This example clearly demonstrates the major features of RECT. Issues of couple disturbance were dealt with first, in this instance in individual couples therapy sessions for both partners. Conjoint couples therapy sessions were employed to deal with issues of relationship dissatisfaction. Communication, problem-solving and negotiation training procedures were all employed in this second phase. The case also shows that RECT practitioners are often called upon to deal with further disturbance issues that emerge in the 'enhancing couple satisfaction' phase. As is commonly found, emotional disturbance is often uncovered as a result of the failure of one or both partners to execute carefully negotiated homework assignments. In this case, Mr Rogers' anxiety about his wife having 'affairs' was elicited as a consequence of his failure to follow through on an assignment that was negotiated on two separate occasions. He was helped to see that his 'excuses' were in fact defensive in nature and served to protect him from his own self-condemnation. Mr Rogers confirmed my own hypothesis that it was my early focus on disputing his irrational beliefs in the first phase of treatment that encouraged him to disclose his core fear. In his words: 'I feel that I was helped to acquire the skills to actually deal with this particular fear. I doubt whether I would have revealed it if I felt unable to deal with it.'

Follow-up

I conducted a follow-up session 6 months after treatment was terminated. Mr and Mrs Rogers maintained the gains which they had achieved in therapy and, according to them, were experiencing the most productive period of their marriage. They reported that they were more able to express their desires to one another and be supportive of each other's goals as well as spend more time together. Mrs Rogers had taken up voluntary work, pottery classes and yoga. She spent about an hour a day typing her husband's business correspondence as compared to the 4 hours daily work she used to do for him. She had not experienced any depression episodes since treatment had ended. Mr Rogers had still not acquired his coveted managerial position. He occasionally experienced bouts of panic about this fact, but said on these occasions he was able to identify and dispute the underlying irrational beliefs. He had come to realise that work was not the 'be-all and end-all' of his life and had started to manage a local junior soccer team. He seemed genuinely pleased with his wife's improvement, rarely got angry with her and she felt that he showed sincere interest in her activities. Together they had taken up ballroom dancing lessons and enjoyed regular Saturday evenings at the local dance hall. They reported that they were more able to challenge one another in a constructive way when problems began to emerge and that they were able to resolve matters without undue upset.

Interestingly enough, both Mr and Mrs Rogers pointed to the gains that they had made in the first phase of treatment as the most significant feature of their therapy experiences. Mrs Rogers summed this up well when she said: 'Although it was painful, you helped me most by showing me that divorce wasn't the end of the world. I thought it was, you see. Yes, that really helped. Before, we stayed together more out of fear and obligation than anything else, but now we are together because we want to be together.' That statement beautifully encapsulates the goals and spirit of RECT!

Chapter 14
Rational–Emotive
Conciliation Counselling

Introduction

The last two decades have seen an international move away from 'fault-based' divorce legislation. This, in turn, has led to the adoption of a conciliatory approach to the resolution of disputes arising from separation and divorce, particularly those which centre on children. In Britain there are now around 22 voluntary and statutory agencies affiliating with the National Family Conciliation Council which offers a service to families. The conciliators staffing such agencies are drawn from a variety of disciplines including law, social work and psychology. Many have a background in areas such as marriage guidance or probation. Inevitably, this has resulted in a somewhat eclectic approach to the practice of conciliation, theoretical concepts being drawn from a variety of sources. Parkinson (1985) lists six different perspectives which include psychoanalytical theory, family systems theory, crisis theory, communication theory, attachment theory and conflict management theory. However, it seems that family systems theory is becoming the dominant perspective as it has been argued that, although conciliation is not therapy, the concepts and practices derived from it have much to offer the separating family (Horwill, 1983; Robinson and Parkinson, 1985). Nevertheless, there is a risk that such a perspective can in fact present disputes between separating spouses as being more complex than is necessary by focusing on the whole family system and there is room for alternative models. This chapter puts forward rational–emotive theory as a model from which conciliators can derive useful concepts and practices.

Conciliation

The National Family Conciliation Council (1984) describes the primary aim of conciliation as 'to help those couples involved in the process of

Written with David McLoughlin; first published in 1986.

separation and divorce to reach agreements, or reduce the area of intensity of conflict, on disputes concerning their children'. It is, however, necessarily vague on the question of how this aim should be achieved. Definitions of conciliation have been somewhat legalistic with Saunders (1977) describing it as 'a settling of disputes without litigation' (p. 71). Elsewhere, Saunders (1969) has suggested that 'conciliation' has both a broad sense in which it covers the great variety of methods whereby a dispute is amicably settled, and a narrow sense in which it is a process of formulating proposals of settlement, where, after an investigation of the facts and an offer to reconcile opposing contentions, the parties are left free to accept or reject the proposals formulated. Such a definition allows conciliators broad scope in terms of the practices they can adopt under the heading of conciliation.

There have been attempts to provide clearer definitions of conciliation as it applies to the resolution of disputes arising from separation and divorce. In particular, distinctions have been made between 'mediation' and 'conciliation'. The former is seen as a simple level of effecting change in which the worker attempts to negotiate a limited practical solution to a presenting problem by acting as a go-between and does not deal with aspects of the parties' interaction; whereas conciliation is seen as a more complex process in which the worker acts as a barrier between the parties, preventing them from dealing with each other destructively on the problem (Preston, Ralph and Madison, 1983). In attempting to describe the conciliation task Parkinson (1985) cites Madison's terminology thus:

....conciliation requires an assessment of the interaction between the couple, as a means of understanding the presenting problem. The counsellor works conjointly with the couple and facilitates their own efforts to reduce conflict, communicate and problem solve. The aim is to help the couple reach their own agreement with regard to the dispute and elements of their relationship that promote disputes between them. The method requires expertise in both areas of relationship skills and negotiation.

(Madison, 1983, p. 2)

As Madison was writing as a Director of Counselling within the Australian Family Court where conciliation counsellors are drawn from psychology and social work, and where 'mediation' by workers without expertise in relationship skills is being strongly resisted, such a definition with its focus on interaction and communication skills is understandable. However, his description of conciliation is as close as we have to a working definition, and does fit my understanding of it as practised in voluntary and statutory agencies in Britain. Further, it is a description of the conciliation task for which a number of psychotherapies, but particularly rational–emotive theory, can provide a model for conceptual analysis and practice.

Basic Principles of Rational–Emotive Theory

A major assumption of rational–emotive theory is that emotions are founded upon the evaluative beliefs people hold towards themselves, other people and the world. An important distinction is made between irrational beliefs and rational beliefs.

Irrational beliefs tend to sabotage the person's attempts to pursue constructively his or her basic goals and purposes, and discourage the person from making a healthy adjustment if these cannot be achieved. They are absolutistic and devout in nature. Beliefs are often phrased as two parts of a syllogism: a *premise* and a set of *derivatives*. The premise form of irrational beliefs is often couched in the form of 'musts', 'shoulds' and have-to's' (e.g. 'I must gain custody of my two children'). Typical derivatives that stem from such premises are couched in the form of 'awfulising' (a magical rating that implies that something is more than 100% bad, e.g. 'It would be awful if I did not gain custody of my two children'), 'I-can't-stand-it' (another magical term that implies that I could never be happy again if I do not get what I must, e.g. 'I couldn't stand it if I did not gain custody of my two children'), and 'damning' of self, other(s) and/or the world (e.g. 'I – or my ex-partner – would be no good if I do not gain custody of my two children').

Rational beliefs, however, tend to help the person to pursue constructively his or her basic goals and purposes and encourage the person to adjust if these cannot be achieved. They are relative and non-devout in nature. The premise form of rational beliefs is often couched in the form of 'preferences', 'desires' and 'wants' (e.g. 'I really want to gain custody of my two children, but I do not absolutely have to'). Typical derivatives which stem from such premises are couched in the following forms: 'rating badness' (a realistic evaluation of 'badness' along a 0–100% continuum, e.g. 'It would be very bad if I did not gain custody of my two children, but it would not be awful if I didn't'); 'tolerating' (another realistic term which implies that even very bad situations are tolerable and do not preclude the experience of future happiness, e.g. 'I could tolerate it, but will never like it, if I did not gain custody of my two children'); and 'accepting' self, other(s) and/or the world (e.g. 'If I do not gain custody of my two children, I will still accept myself – or my ex-partner – as a fallible human being').

Another important distinction made by rational–emotive theory concerns that between dysfunctional (or irrational) negative emotions (which tend to impede goal achievement and constructive adjustment) and functional (or rational) negative emotions (which tend to promote goal achievement and constructive adjustment). Furthermore, rational–emotive theory holds that irrational beliefs underpin dysfunctional (or irrational) negative emotions and rational beliefs underpin their functional (or rational) equivalents (Table 14.1).

A further basic principle of rational–emotive theory is that constructive communication, problem solving and negotiation – processes deemed central to successful conciliation – will tend to be impeded when one or both people concerned experience one or more of the dysfunctional (or irrational) negative emotions listed in Table 14.1 (which are underpinned by

Table 14.1 Dysfunctional (irrational) and functional (rational) negative emotions and their cognitive correlates

Inference* related to personal domain†	Type of belief	Emotion	Type of emotion	
Threat or danger	Irrational	Anxiety	Dysfunctional	(Irrational)
Threat or danger	Rational	Concern	Functional	(Rational)
Loss (with implications for future)	Irrational	Depression	Dysfunctional	(Irrational)
Loss (with implications for future)	Rational	Sadness	Functional	(Rational)
Breaking of personal rule (other or self); other threatens self	Irrational	Damning anger	Dysfunctional	(Irrational)
Breaking of personal rule (other or self); other threatens self	Rational	Non-damning anger (or annoyance)	Functional	(Rational)
Breaking of own moral code	Irrational	Guilt	Dysfunctional	(Irrational)
Breaking of own moral code	Rational	Remorse	Functional	(Rational)
Other betrays self (self non-deserving)	Irrational	Hurt	Dysfunctional	(Irrational)
Other betrays self (self non-deserving)	Rational	Disappointment	Functional	(Rational)
Threat to desired exclusive relationship	Irrational	Morbid jealousy	Dysfunctional	(Irrational)
Threat to desired exclusive relationship	Rational	Non-morbid jealousy	Functional	(Rational)
Personal weakness revealed publicly	Irrational	Shame	Dysfunctional	(Irrational)
Personal weakness revealed publicly	Rational	Regret	Functional	(Rational)

*Inference: an interpretation that goes beyond observable reality but that gives meaning to it; may be accurate or inaccurate.
†The objects: tangible and intangible - in which a person has an involvement constitute a person's personal domain (Beck, 1976). Rational–emotive theory distinguishes between ego and comfort aspects of the personal domain although these aspects frequently interact.

irrational beliefs about self, ex-partner and/or the situation). For example, it is difficult for two ex-partners to engage in productive conciliation when one or both are angrily damning the other. Conversely, experiencing functional (or rational) negative emotions as listed in Table 14.1 (which are underpinned by rational beliefs about self, ex-partner and/or the situation) will tend to motivate ex-partners to engage in constructive communication, problem solving and negotiation, given that they both seek a conciliatory solution to their problems.

Finally, rational–emotive theory hypothesises that when a person holds an irrational belief, he or she is likely to make inferences (i.e. interpretations that go beyond the available data) about self and others that are more nega-tively distorted than if the person holds a rational belief. Thus, if a woman believes 'I must at all costs maintain control over access rights to my chil-dren', then she will tend to view her husband's attempts to gain access more negatively than she would if she held a rational equivalent of this belief. It should be noted that this hypothesis awaits empirical enquiry.

Basic Goals of Rational–Emotive Conciliation Counselling

Once it has been established that both ex-partners understand the objectives of conciliation and the role of the conciliation counsellor, and state that they wish to commit themselves to this process, then the counsellor has two basic goals. The first goal is called *overcoming cou-ple disturbance*. This involves helping the clients to overcome their dys-functional (or irrational) negative feelings by having them challenge their irrational beliefs and replace them with their rational alternatives. Once the counsellor has helped both partners make significant progress in this area, they are then, normally, in a better frame of mind to work towards a conciliatory solution to their problems. The second goal is called *promoting constructive couple dialogue*. This involves the con-ciliation counsellor helping the clients to communicate clearly and con-structively, to identify possible solutions to their problems and to nego-tiate fairly with one another. During this process, the conciliation counsellor will also help the clients to correct any distorted inferences that interfere with the promotion of constructive couple dialogue.

It is important to reiterate, at this point, that attempting to promote constructive couple dialogue when one or both clients are experien-cing dysfunctional (or irrational) negative emotions (based on irrational beliefs) is usually unproductive *in the long term*. Whilst it is possible to bypass such emotions in the short term during the conciliation process, and thereby to help the couple establish a given solution to their prob-lems, later sabotage of any such agreements is likely to occur in this cir-cumstance. This tends to happen when one or both ex-partners re-experience dysfunctional (or irrational) negative emotions. Because these have not been dealt with during the conciliation process, the clients do not have the skills of getting over such feelings, i.e. by identi-fying, challenging and changing the irrational beliefs that underpin them. These dysfunctional negative emotions then tend to foster old destructive communication patterns which, when brought into play, in turn tend to destroy the good faith that may have been developed between them during the conciliation sessions.

The Process of Rational–Emotive Conciliation Counselling

Eliciting commitment to the process

When a couple seek conciliation, the rational–emotive conciliation counsellor's initial tasks are to explain the objectives of the process, to correct any misconceptions the couple may have about the enterprise (e.g. it does not seek to effect reconciliation), to outline the likely course the process will take and to explain the role of the conciliation counsellor. This is done to enable the couple to make an informed decision whether or not to commit themselves to the process.

Case illustration

> Mr and Mrs Smith had been separated for 9 months and, until recently, Mr Smith had wanted little contact with Clare, their 5-year-old daughter. He then requested week-end-long access, this being strongly resisted by Mrs Smith. They were referred for conciliation counselling by their respective solicitors.
>
> The conciliation counsellor outlined that his role was to help them to overcome the obstacles that were preventing them from effecting a mutually agreed solution to this current impasse, assured both clients that he would not take sides, and explained that the process normally involves helping both people to get into the right frame of mind to make sound decisions. As with most couples seeking conciliation, Mr and Mrs Smith were somewhat ambivalent about the process. They both wanted a solution to their dispute but did not want to 'lose'. They committed themselves to the process after being assured that this was a common sentiment among couples seeking a conciliatory solution to their disputes.

Overcoming couple disturbance

At this stage, given that such commitment has been elicited, the counsellor helps the clients to: (1) identify any dysfunctional (or irrational) negative emotions that they may be experiencing, (2) see how such emotions will probably sabotage the process of conciliation as well as being self-defeating and (3) commit themselves to work on overcoming their disturbed feelings before working towards an agreed solution to their problems. It is important for the counsellor to stress that the goal of this stage is to help the clients experience functional (or rational) negative emotions which serve as healthy responses to negative events as well as serving as motivating forces to stimulate a conciliatory solution to their problems, rather than to eliminate all feelings about their situation.

The counsellor's next task is to help the clients see the link between their dysfunctional (or irrational) negative emotions and the irrational beliefs that underpin them. Once this has been understood, the counsellor is in a position to help the clients to dispute these beliefs using the methods of Socratic dialogue (Dryden, 1984a). In conciliation counselling, the focus is not only on philosophical disputing (helping the clients learn that there is evidence in support of their rational beliefs, but none in support of their irrational beliefs), but also on pragmatic disputing (helping clients to see that continued adherence to their irrational beliefs will sabotage their own interests as well as the interests of their children).

During this stage, the conciliation counsellor can choose to work conjointly with the couple or see each person individually. This decision is, in part, influenced by the wishes of the couple and the degree to which they can work productively at this stage in conjoint sessions. Thus, if their anger is such that very hostile interchanges ensue or if one or both clients are very withdrawn and refuse to communicate, then it would be wise for the conciliation counsellor to see them separately, at least initially. Otherwise, conjoint sessions are probably indicated.

Case illustration

Mr and Mrs Smith both wanted to be seen separately at the beginning of conciliation counselling and the conciliation counsellor had two individual sessions with each of them.

Mr Smith's 'sudden' desire to have weekend-long access was prompted by his parents' urgings. He felt very guilty about 'neglecting' his daughter and was desperate to 'make up for lost time'. He was helped to see that his feelings of guilt would interfere with his negotiating constructively with his wife, and these were targeted for change. The conciliation counsellor helped him to dispute the irrational belief underlying his guilt – 'I'm bad for neglecting my daughter' – and encouraged him to accept himself as a fallible human being who did the wrong thing. He was then able to understand that his 'neglect' was linked to his past anxiety about being a good father. At the end of the two individual sessions, he was feeling much less guilty and less desperate to make up for lost time with Clare. He still wanted access but was prepared to accept less time than he originally requested.

Mrs Smith was angry about her husband's sudden change of heart towards access to his daughter, but, as often occurs, her anger was underpinned by feelings of anxiety that her daughter might eventually want to live with her father and his parents. Mrs Smith was first asked to assume that her daughter did express such a desire. She was then helped to identify her underlying irrational belief: 'My daughter must not want to live with her father. If she did this would prove that I'm a poor mother and worthless.' She was then helped to dispute this belief and showed that she could accept herself as a fallible human being even if she was deficient as a mother. Once she accepted this she calmed down appreciably, became more open to consider some kind of access arrangement but expressed concern about her husband's competence in looking after Clare.

Promoting constructive couple dialogue

Once both clients have made sufficient progress at replacing their irrational beliefs with their rational alternatives and are experiencing functional (or rational) negative emotions much of the time, the process then shifts to promoting constructive dialogue between ex-partners. The focus here is on the skills of effective communication (empathic listening, 'owning' feelings, 'I' statements etc.), problem solving (brain-storming, evaluating possible solutions etc.), and negotiation (developing compromises, considering the interests of children against self-interest etc.). The counsellor may have to teach one or both clients these skills if these are not in their repertoire. Because this stage of conciliation has a decided interpersonal focus, it is very important that clients are seen in conjoint sessions. Another task of the conciliation counsellor at this stage is to help one or both clients to correct any distorted inferences they may have about themselves, the other person and other involved parties.

It is important to note that the counsellor may have to return occasionally to the tasks of the overcoming disturbance phase during this stage because one or both clients may disturb themselves about what their ex-partner says as they strive to reconcile their differences.

Case illustration

At the beginning of the first conjoint session, the conciliation counsellor summarised what had occurred in the individual sessions. This was done with each client's permission. Both Mr and Mrs Smith were interested to learn that they were, in fact, grappling with a similar issue – self-condemnation for perceived deficits – and could see how this influenced their inferences about each other's motives. Mr Smith had inferred that his wife's refusal to agree to any access arrangements was due to her desire for revenge for him leaving her. Mrs Smith had inferred that her husband wanted to turn Clare against her. Mrs Smith also voiced concern that her 'in-laws' were against her but was assured by Mr Smith that in fact the opposite was the case. This lessened her concern that they were allies in her husband's plot against her.

During the second conjoint session, the conciliation counsellor occasionally had to intervene to aid both clients to negotiate without anger by helping them to see that there was no evidence that the other person must not hold 'wrong' opinions. They were helped to 'own' their opinions (e.g. 'From my perspective, I disagree that your suggestion would be good for Clare') rather than make negative attributions about the other's character (e.g. 'You're callous for suggesting that'). This helped to refocus the couple on the task of problem solving.

With respect to Mr Smith's care-taking ability, Mrs Smith (1) conceded (albeit grudgingly) that his mother was 'good with Clare' and could help him to look after their daughter and (2) agreed to educate her husband concerning Clare's likes and dislikes.

Formulating agreed solutions and trouble-shooting

The next stage of the conciliation process concerns the formulation of agreed solutions to the couple's problems. Ideally, these need to be as detailed as possible and phrased using language and in a form that is acceptable to both partners. The relationship between both sets of solicitors often becomes a focus for discussion at this point.

One additional task, at this stage, concerns the counsellor helping both partners to identify possible future obstacles to maintaining productive communication. These are dealt with by reminding both clients that they can use the cognitive and interpersonal skills that they have developed during conciliation and by asking them to imagine using these skills to overcome the obstacle. Here, the couple are reminded to use the cognitive skills of disputing irrational beliefs before the interpersonal skills when they experience dysfunctional (or irrational) negative emotions. The more the couple can involve themselves in this trouble-shooting task, the more it is likely that they will be able to deal productively with such obstacles if and when they occur in reality.

Case illustration

> In the third conjoint session the couple agreed on the following access arrangements: 'Mr Smith will collect Clare at 10.00 a.m. every other Saturday morning and return her by 6.00 p.m. that day. For the first 3 months Mr Smith's mother will be available to help Mr Smith with looking after Clare.'
>
> The conciliation counsellor helped both clients to identify possible future obstacles which were related to anger and anxiety and reminded them first to dispute their underlying irrational beliefs and then to share their concerns with the other by 'owning' their feelings and opinions.

Reviewing the process

The final stage of conciliation involves the counsellor undertaking with the couple a review of what they have learned from the process. A particular focus here is on underscoring the fact that the couple have not only made agreements on specific issues but have also learned how to restore and maintain channels of constructive communication with one another. This latter point is important because, although they may have divorced, they will continue to have a relationship with one another as parents to their children.

Case illustration

> In the final session, the conciliation counsellor helped Mr and Mrs Smith to see they they had acquired skills which they could use to: (1) dispute irrational beliefs underlying dysfunctional (or irrational) negative emotions; (2) communicate opinions rather than attributing negative traits to the other person; and (3) formulate a mutually agreeable arrangement. They were urged to use these skills to solve further problems that might arise between them *and* in their own separate lives.

Regarding the Involvement of Children

As issues concerning children are those most frequently dealt with in conciliation, their direct involvement in some way is often a necessary prerequisite to dispute resolution. Involving children can be helpful in a number of ways, including providing them with an opportunity to put forward their own perceptions and opinions providing opportunities for the observation of relationships, and facilitating communication between parents and children.

In rational–emotive conciliation counselling, the direct involvement of children can contribute to the process of identifying dysfunctional (or irrational) negative emotions, irrational beliefs and distorted inferences. By involving children directly through separate interviews, or having them participate in sessions with their parents, the irrationality of one or other partner's beliefs and the distorted nature of their inferences can be demonstrated to them. A simple example where inferences can be tested would be a situation in which a mother is denying a father access to his children because she has come to infer that they are afraid of him, and has become anxious about their welfare as a result. Providing such a mother with the opportunity to observe the positive interaction between the children and their father in a 'safe' environment can enable her to question her inference that the children are afraid of their father.

The direct involvement of children does need to be handled carefully, however, because it can place them in a very vulnerable position. They may, for example, wish to say things which will upset one or other partner and have to deal with the threat, real or perceived, of retribution. Even separate interviews with a counsellor do not guarantee children protection because, under present British law, confidentiality cannot be promised as conciliators can be called to give evidence in Court.

Conclusion

We have proposed here that rational–emotive conciliation counselling can effectively deal with disputes arising out of separation and divorce. The illustrative case example shows that both the immediate problem and the underlying beliefs and emotions can be dealt with, despite a relatively short intervention and, as most clients contact with conciliation agencies is short term, this has much to recommend it. Further, the nature of rational–emotive conciliation counselling is such that, whilst dealing with immediate problems, couples are taught skills which will prevent them from becoming entrenched should other disputes arise in the future.

Chapter 15
A Comprehensive Approach to Social Skills Training:
Contributions from Rational–Emotive Therapy

The rational–emotive approach to social skills training stresses that for long-term change, therapists are advised to pay detailed attention to clients' beliefs about themselves, other people and the world. In RET, the targets for change are not only the inferences that patients make about what happens to them at point 'A' (Beck and Emery, 1979), but also the way these events are evaluated at point 'B'.

Rational–emotive theory states that emotional and behavioural consequences at point 'C' are largely determined by these evaluations. Rational–emotive therapists conclude that they do not know their clients' goals in advance but 'encourage people to choose the kinds of basic values and goals they want and to select self-training in the kinds of skills that will probably more appropriately and efficiently abet their chosen values' (Ellis, 1977e, p. 34). It follows that what is *rational* in rational–emotive theory are those processes which aid and abet clients to achieve their own goals and what is *irrational* are those processes which hinder the achievement of these goals. Whilst it may be true that the skills which social skills trainers help their clients acquire may abet their own personally held goals, it is important to recognise that the acquisition of these skills in the therapeutic situation are not sufficient for clients to achieve these goals.

It is possible to look at the concept of rationality/irrationality in a different way. Ellis (1962) has stressed that a major feature of rational beliefs is that they reflect personal preferences, wants or desires. Rational beliefs become irrational when the patient converts these preferences, wants or desires into absolutistic musts, oughts or shoulds. Rational–emotive theory further hypothesises that a *desiring* philosophy is more adaptive and productive than a *demanding* philosophy. Whilst Ellis (1977f) has presented evidence in favour of this theory, it should be pointed out that it is

Written with Peter Trower and Andrew Casey; first published in 1983.

notoriously difficult to operationalise these concepts and, at present, stating that a desiring philosophy is more adaptive and productive than a demanding philosophy should be regarded as a hypothesis rather than a fact. In this section a number of therapeutic issues are addressed. Emphasis will be placed on (1) those beliefs which clients in social skills groups may hold which hinder their long-term change and (2) how to change such beliefs.

Self-acceptance vs Self-esteem

In an up-dated list of common irrational ideas (Ellis, 1977g), one such idea is presented which is central to a rational–emotive approach to social skills training: 'this is the idea that you can give yourself a global rating as a human and that your general worth and self-acceptance depends on the goodness of your performances and the degree that people approve of you.' This idea is considered irrational because rational–emotive theorists claim that it is not possible to give such a complex and constantly changing organism as a human being a single rating. Thus, self-esteem (which is a variant of self-rating) is considered a pernicious rather than a helpful concept in social skills training. Most therapeutic systems do not consider self-esteem as potentially harmful, but rather hold that it is crucial to raise a client's level of self-esteem. This may make it difficult for clinicians to integrate RET into their standard social skills training practice. As a result, clinicians may have to rethink their views on the self-rating/self-acceptance issue and consider the implications of adopting a self-esteem as opposed to a self-acceptance philosophy.

But what is meant in practical terms by the statement that helping a client to improve his self-esteem may be pernicious? To illustrate this, consider John, a patient in a social skills training group. John is assiduous in attending training sessions and shows increasing competence at practising social skills in the therapeutic setting. He is encouraged to go out to practise such skills in his own life setting. He does this by going to a club and engaging a female in conversation for 10 minutes. She responds well to him and he comes back to the next group session in a positive frame of mind which the therapist and his fellow group members reinforce. On the next occasion, John approaches a woman in an optimistic frame of mind. He begins to engage her in conversation but after 2 minutes the woman, who has not responded to him, excuses herself and leaves. John becomes depressed and in a discouraged mood misses the next two group meetings. When he finally returns, exploration of this interaction reveals a number of interesting phenomena. The therapist discovers that John had concluded that because the woman showed no interest in him and excused herself so soon after he initiated the contact, this was proof that he was really unlikeable. Indeed, further exploration revealed that John had concluded that he was likeable when the first female responded to him so warmly. John is thus making global ratings of himself dependent upon the responses he gets from significant others in his environment. In RET, we would uncover and challenge the notion that: (1) it is valid to make such global ratings, and (2) that such self-ratings are dependent upon the responses of significant others. Rather, it is advisable to teach John that he could accept himself as a fallible human being with poor (but improving) social skills, whether or not other people in his social milieu responded well to him. Ellis (1977e) has argued that he '... as an RET practitioner, invariably not only shows shy, non-encountering individuals that they don't *have to* succeed at social relations or view it as *awful or terrible* and themselves as *worthless persons* if they fail, but simultaneously gets them to try various ways of relating so they they will see how they can bear failure and not put themselves down' (p. 31).

The above statement reveals that it is important to prepare clients fully to evaluate themselves rationally when they fail (as they undoubtedly will) to either implement their newly acquired social skills in the outside world or to gain positive responses from others. Indeed, using the technique of reframing (Watzlawick, 1978), rational–emotive therapists can help clients see the positive features in such failure experiences, in that these experiences give them opportunities to accept themselves in the face of adversity. Helping clients to adopt a self-acceptance philosophy rather than a self-esteem philosophy will encourage them to seek out experiences which they might otherwise avoid. However, it is important to state that the hypothesis that therapeutic procedures based on a self-acceptance philosophy are more successful long term than therapeutic procedures based on a self-esteem philosophy, needs to be empirically assessed.

Competence-related Beliefs

In working with clients in social skills training, trainers are usually struck by their strong tendency to evaluate themselves negatively as a consequence of failing to live up to a certain standard of competence in carrying out homework assignments. In believing that they *must* be thoroughly competent at putting their newly acquired social skills into practice, these clients become either very depressed as a result of failing or will avoid the practice that is important in helping them to achieve their social goals. A major task of rational–emotive therapists in this aspect of social skills training is to help clients dispute the belief that they *must* be thoroughly competent. In doing so, therapists are advised to help clients adhere to the more rational belief 'I want to be competent in putting my newly acquired skills into practice, but if I don't it's hardly catastrophic'. It is often observed that, as therapists begin to dispute their irrational beliefs, such clients conclude falsely that 'It doesn't matter whether I succeed or not'. Therapists are advised to watch this drift from defining something as 'all important' to defining it as 'unimportant' and would do well to help clients acknowledge that it does matter whether or not they achieve their standards and as a result will be disappointed in their failure to do so. Consequently, clients will be helped to see that they can be disappointed but not devastated as a result of failing to achieve their own perfectionist standards. At the same time, it is important for therapists to spend a lot of time helping clients to lower their perfectionist standards and thus help them (1) to view themselves as fallible persons who can set themselves more realistic human goals and (2) to accept themselves as fallible persons even if they fail to reach these more realistic goals.

Increased social competence is not just a matter of learning and practising the various component skills which are taught in traditional social skills training. Both the timing of skill responses and the way skills are smoothly put together are important features which may determine whether significant others will respond favourably or not to the clients in everyday life. In order to improve their skills at correctly timing social responses and thus become smoother in the meshing of these component skills, clients had better throw themselves into social interactions at every opportunity. It is hypothesised that, if clients adhere to the rational belief that 'It is unfortunate but hardly catastrophic if I do not achieve the level of competence that I would ideally like', then they will be more likely to persevere in the face of adversity than if they adhere to the irrational standpoint that they *must* achieve their standards. Although clients will be more likely to persevere in practising new social skills if they are able to accept themselves for slower progress than desired, there is another important reason why they may avoid the hard work of practice.

Discomfort-related Beliefs

Ellis (1979b) has made an important contribution to rational–emotive theory by distinguishing between two distinct, but often interrelating, forms of anxiety. The first, ego anxiety (EA), results when patients demand that they must achieve certain standards or gain approval and consequently evaluate themselves negatively for failing to achieve these goals. The two above-mentioned processes, i.e. global self-ratings and demands for competence, are characteristic features of ego anxiety and serve to maintain it. A conceptually different form of anxiety – discomfort anxiety (DA) – results from clients' absolute demand that they achieve a certain level of comfort in their lives. Discomfort anxiety may be present on its own, as in the case of Ron who had gone a long way to accept himself as a fallible human being, but still avoided social encounters because he believed that it was *too* hard to continue to practise his newly acquired skills in everyday life and that it *should* be easier to put them into practice. Discomfort anxiety, however, may interact with ego anxiety as with David who evaluated himself negatively as a result of his failure to maintain a conversation with a woman, started to experience anxiety and consequently defined that anxious feeling as *too* uncomfortable to bear. Thus, discomfort anxiety may serve to interfere with the patient's attempts at disputing his ego anxiety-related beliefs. The task of therapists in this situation is to help such clients deal with their discomfort anxiety-related beliefs before dealing with their ego anxiety-related beliefs. Rational–emotive therapists aim to show their clients that anxiety is uncomfortable, but can be tolerated and often lessened when they adopt an accepting attitude to the experience of that anxiety.

An example will clarify how therapists can help clients who experience both ego and discomfort anxieties. Robert, a university student, who was seen in a university health setting, experienced great social anxiety in conversing with both men and women. He also had poor social skills in a number of areas. The therapist proceeded concurrently to help Robert improve his social skills and dispute the belief that he *must* appear witty and bright and if he didn't then he was an idiot. Robert would characteristically enter social situations and begin to put into practice his newly acquired social skills. However, he would soon excuse himself from such situations when he started to become anxious due to his belief that other people would regard him as a moron because he was not making noteworthy conversation and this indeed would prove that he really was a moron. Robert was helped to dispute such beliefs both in the session, by means of cognitive disputing and imagery-related exercises, to the point where he was adept at disputing such beliefs within the therapeutic setting. However, Robert was not able, at this point, to dispute such beliefs in vivo. Discomfort anxiety prevented Robert from disputing this belief in vivo namely: 'that it would be terrible to experience such anxiety in social situations and I couldn't bear to.' The therapist helped Robert to re-evaluate such anxiety as uncomfortable and to use this feeling of discomfort as a cue to in vivo disputing. This enabled him to remain in the social situation and to take the risk of speaking up and saying something mundane while accepting himself for doing so.

It is important to realise here that clients often switch their goals as a consequence of discomfort anxiety. For example, a client with a fear of approaching and interacting with an attractive woman may have as his therapeutic goal ultimately to be able to do so. What may interfere with his progress towards this goal will be a competing goal of feeling comfortable in social situations and thus he may quickly switch from one goal to the other once he begins to experience anxiety. Rational–emotive therapists may employ several anxiety-reducing methods to help such persons cope with their anxiety, but would not make the error of employing techniques (which are palliative in nature) if they would reinforce the idea that: 'It would be terrible to experience anxiety.' Here, rational–emotive therapists aim to help clients adhere to the more rational belief that: 'It is better not to experience anxiety, it is uncomfortable and inconvenient if I do but it is not horrible or dreadful and I can stand it.'

Discomfort anxiety also arises when clients hold the belief that: 'Things should be easy for me.' As mentioned above, acquiring a sense of timing and smoothness in complex social performance so that clients are more socially reinforcing to persons in their environemn is often an arduous task and involves putting up with a large measure of failure. Clients often deprive themselves of these opportunities precisely because of their discomfort anxiety. A major task of therapists in this situation is to help clients adhere to the more rational: 'It would be nice if it were easier to get what I want (i.e. desired social success) but it is not and that's frustrating. It really is hard and it should be this hard.' Such clients tend to escalate this rational belief to an irrational belief which serves to keep them from the practice that is crucial to goal attainment. An example of such an irrational belief might be: 'Forcing myself into the social world and putting up with failure is *too* hard for me, it would be *dreadful* if I experienced this and thus it is easier if I avoid doing this.' Apart from helping such clients adhere to the more rational belief, it is often helpful to point out to them that they have got their world upside down! When such patients claim that something is *hard* and imply that avoidance is *easy*, they are adopting a short-term time perspective in making such evaluations. Implicit in this viewpoint is that it is in fact *harder* for them, long term, if they continue to avoid and in fact it is *easier*, long term, if they put up with the *hard* work of practice. Thus, therapists can help clients see that what is *hard* is *easy* and what is *easy* is *hard*. Needless to say, this is not an easy task and therapists are advised to overcome their own discomfort anxiety while persisting to help these patients overcome their discomfort anxiety. Ellis (1958a) has observed that helping clients overcome their discomfort anxiety is one of the most difficult tasks in therapy!

Another feature of discomfort anxiety is the demand for a guarantee. Often clients refuse to risk entering a social situation because they do not have the certainty that they will meet with success. Such clients demand a guarantee that things will work out well for them, or that they know in advance what will transpire. A rational–emotive therapist named Lemire has come up with a novel way of helping such clients. When clients reveal that they demand a guarantee, Lemire indicates to them that they are in luck. He just happens to have a guarantee in his drawer; would they like it? Clients usually show obvious interest in this therapeutic manoeuvre and generally accept. Lemire then gives the client an RET guarantee form on which is written 'I guarantee that you will suffer as long as you demand that you have a guarantee'. This point additionally emphasises that clients in their willingness to achieve short-term gain condemn themselves to long-term pain. In addition to helping clients gain a different time perspective on the gain/pain ratio, therapists are advised to help them lessen some of their short-term pain to uncomfortable but manageable proportions.

A somewhat different form of discomfort anxiety has been described by Maultsby (1975) who has written about the 'neurotic fear of feeling a phony'. Maultsby notes that often clients do not persist at practising skills which would ordinarily help them to achieve their goals, because at some point in the skill acquisition process, they claim that 'they don't feel themselves'. Such clients may actually report: 'I feel as if I'm not being me', 'I feel strange and different and I don't like it', 'What sort of person am I turning into?' etc. Therapists who do not address such issues in social skills training may not be helping their client achieve their stated goals. It is often sufficient to provide such clients with examples from their own lives where they have felt awkward, felt unnatural, felt that what they were doing was not really them, but where they persisted and acquired new skills. Helping clients see that this is a temporary phase which, if tolerated as an uncomfortable but bearable experience, enables them to persist until newly acquired skills become more natural.

Discomfort anxiety is often a feature in clients' attitudes towards their progress in social skills training. Often such progress is slower than clients would ideally like and it is important that therapists determine if they are defining such slow progress as 'undesirable' or as 'awful'. In addition, ego anxiety may be implicated here. Clients may evaluate themselves negatively for not progressing as quickly as they 'should'. Figure 15.1 may illustrate how ego anxiety and discomfort anxiety are interwoven in a client's attitude towards slow progress. Here both ego anxiety and discomfort anxiety lead to avoidance of social situations and thus the client deprives him- or herself of important opportunities to practise social skills. The task of therapists in helping clients overcome their ego anxiety or discomfort anxiety, or indeed both, is thus to intervene and help clients (1) re-define slow progress as undesirable but bearable and/or (2) accept themselves for their slow progress.

Figure 15.1 Social skills training.

Approval-related Beliefs

Clients with social difficulties are often over-concerned about gaining approval from other people. This over-concern is reflected at two levels: (1) interpretation/misinterpretation of responses from other people; and (2) evaluation of responses from other people. Clients often misinterpret cues from other people in a number of different ways. One major form of distortion involves the interpretation of a neutral response as negative. Here clients try to engage others in conversation, receive a neutral response and, as a result, conclude that others do not like them. The second major form of distortion occurs when clients receive positive responses from others but distort the message so that the existence of positive responses is denied or explained away. For example, a typical response from clients who receive positive responses from other people is to attribute the other's responses to motives which correspond to their own self-evaluations. To give a clinical example, Ruth was able to talk to a man at a discotheque, yet reported in the following social skills group session that he only spoke to her because he felt sorry for her and wanted to cheer her up. Two major therapeutic strategies are indicated here: first, therapists can use a number of procedures outlined by Beck and Emery (1979)* which aim to teach clients to view their inferences as hypotheses. Clients can, by collecting data from the events that took place and other sources, then test these hypotheses. A second and equally important therapeutic strategy involves helping clients identify the self-evaluations implicit in such perceptual distortions and then to dispute these self-evaluations. Thus, Ruth could be shown that she viewed herself as an 'unlikeable person' and could then be helped to dispute this notion. She could be encouraged to give up self-rating and to accept herself as a person with likeable and unlikeable aspects.

The aforementioned strategies are aimed at helping clients to correct cognitive distortions and are included in a comprehensive approach to RET. Comprehensive RET is sometimes contrasted with classic RET (Walen, DiGiuseppe and Wessler, 1980). In classic RET, therapists begin by agreeing with clients' inferences about the event. Thus, responding to Ruth, the therapist might say: 'OK, let's assume that you are right and he only wanted to cheer you up.' He would then help Ruth identify her emotional experience and hence the beliefs underlying that experience. Thus, in classic RET, therapists aim to identify evaluations and inferences without necessarily challenging the validity of the inference itself. An important research issue emerges here. Does working at the evaluative level, i.e. helping clients to evaluate possible incorrect inferences more rationally, lead to clients making more accurate inferences? Little research has been carried out on this

---

*A comprehensive discussion of procedures which are aimed at helping clients correct their cognitive distortions is beyond the scope of this book. Readers are referred to Beck and Emery (1979).

issue but such studies are crucial if therapists are to be cost-effective in deciding at which level of cognitive activity to intervene – the inferential or the evaluative. It is probable, however, that helping clients make *both* more accurate inferences *and* rational evaluations would be more therapeutically effective than either strategy carried out separately.

Both ego anxiety and discomfort anxiety are often implicated in clients' attitudes towards gaining others' approval. Clients often conclude that gaining others' disapproval means that they are worthless or unlikeable etc. Here, therapists may help the clients to see that others' disapproval could occur for a number of reasons which may provide more information about the evaluators than the evaluated. However, even if the clients have an unlikeable trait or combination of traits which might be evaluated negatively by most people, is this sufficient proof that such clients are totally worthless or totally unlikeable? It is important for therapists to recognise that other people may well reject some clients because of their poor social skills, poor timing of executing such skills and/or an awkwardness of style in social interactions. Thus, it is probable that clients who persist at practising social skills will be rejected as a consequence of the poor timing and relative awkwardness of their social performance. It is thus necessary for therapists to help these clients accept themselves with poor social skills, poor timing and awkwardness of style, if they are to be encouraged to continue to utilise opportunities to overcome these deficits and to become more socially adept.

Discomfort anxiety is implicated when clients indicate that they cannot stand the discomfort of being disliked. Such clients often make continued attempts to regain the approval of others which often has the paradoxical result of further alienating others. In RET, clients are shown that whilst it is uncomfortable and inconvenient to exist in a world where people may dislike them, this hardly constitutes something that they cannot stand unless they foolishly tell themselves that they cannot stand it. Again, it is important to note that clients who struggle to cope with social rejection and disapproval from others often experience both ego and discomfort anxieties, which influence each other often in chain-reaction fashion.

Anger-related Beliefs

In previous sections, we have noted that clients, who endeavour to put into everyday practice the skills that they have learned in their social skills groups, often experience anxiety and depression as a result of failing to (1) achieve their own standards of desired performance and (2) gain desired responses from other people. However, a smaller group of clients experiences anger at themselves, other people and the world as a result of such failures. The tasks of rational–emotive therapists are again to (1) identify the demands which are implicit in such evaluations towards self, others and the world and (2) help clients replace such demands with more

rational preferences. It is important to note that rational–emotive therapists make a crucial theoretical distinction between cognitive determinants of anger and annoyance. Anger is said to follow from *demands* not
being met, whilst annoyance is said to result when *desires* are thwarted.
Thus rational–emotive therapists would not necessarily help clients
change beliefs which underpin annoyance because such beliefs are
deemed rational. Indeed, annoyance is regarded as an appropriate negative emotion, appropriate in the sense that it motivates clients to act and
change what they find annoying.

Anger at self occurs when clients fail to achieve goals which they have
defined as essential to achieve. It is interesting to note that whilst some
clients experience depression as a result of such failure, others experience
anger at themselves. It is thus important for therapists to note clients' own
idiosyncratic emotional 'styles'.

Anger at others often results when clients demand that, because they
have learned and are continuing to practise new social skills, then other
people have to respond in a certain way. Such clients can be shown that,
even though they show diligence at practising their new skills in everyday
life, there is no law which states that they must get (i.e. deserve) what they
would like – i.e. other people to respond favourably to them. It is often
helpful for therapists to explain that, as clients become more socially competent, they will probably gain more favourable responses from others.
However, even though they may become extremely proficient socially,
other people may, and probably will, reject them despite or even because
of this!

Clients sometimes experience anger towards their therapists. Such
clients sometimes put therapists on a pedestal and believe that therapists
have magic wands which when waved will cure all, or that therapists have
some magic called 'social skills training' which, if put into practice in everyday life, will bring clients what they want. Thus, when such clients experience failure, they may put the blame on their therapists because it is their
fault that clients are not getting what they want. Such anger directed
towards therapists is often defensive in nature, in that clients would blame
themselves for failing if they were not to blame their therapists. However,
such anger is not necessarily defensive in nature and may be related to
clients' beliefs about authorities who should be able to deliver what they
have promised, or what they are perceived to have promised.

Lastly, clients may experience general anger towards the world for treating them unfairly in bringing them suffering and denying them favourable
responses from others. A related belief reflects the unfairness concerning
clients' social difficulties. Statements, such as 'Why me?' or 'Why should I
have to be the one to have social problems?', are often heard. Such anger
directed towards the world is based on the core underlying assumption that
the world *should* be fair. If therapists explore this in more detail they often

find that such clients really mean that the world should be fair *to them*! Clients can be shown that whilst inherent fairness or justice in the world would be greatly desired, there is plenty of evidence that such justice does not exist and although this may be frustrating it hardly constitutes a horror unless so defined. Quite often it is helpful to point out that whilst clients focus on certain unfairnesses which are to their disadvantage, they often do not focus on other unfairnesses which are to their advantage. Thus, for example, a client with poor social skills who dwells on the unfairness that *he* is the one who experiences social problems may at the same time be asked to focus on the unfairness that he is more intelligent than most people. It is indeed rare to meet clients in clinical settings who are depressed or angry at the world because they are being treated so (unfairly) well!

In the preceding four sections, it has been shown how clients' inaccurate inferences and irrational evaluations deter them from putting newly acquired social skills into practice in their everyday life. In doing so it was demonstrated how RET in particular can help therapists' understanding of clients who not only approach social situations with poorly developed skills but also with a whole range of cognitions, some which aid, whilst others hinder them reaching their social goals. Suggestions were made to assist therapists in their endeavours to help clients change those cognitions which serve as barriers to goal achievement.

Chapter 16
Problems in Living:
The Friday Night Workshop

Introduction

The role of the counselling psychologist as remedial counsellor/psychotherapist is well defined in the literature, even in Britain where the debate concerning the professional status of counselling psychology continues to rage. But, the role of the counselling psychologist as psychological educator is less well defined. As Nelson-Jones (1982) has argued, psychological education is not a unitary phenomenon and he lists six activities that fall under this general heading. One of the activities concerns educating the public in psychological matters.

In this chapter, we will describe an event pioneered by Albert Ellis that has run continuously for the last 20 years or so. It combines both remedial counselling and that aspect of psychological education which endeavours to educate the public in the rational–emotive view of the nature of psychological disturbance, how people perpetuate their emotional and behavioural problems and how they can overcome them. This event has come to be known as 'The Friday night workshop'.

The Friday Night Workshop

Every Friday night (except when he is 'out of town'), Albert Ellis demonstrates the rational–emotive approach to counselling and psychotherapy by interviewing separately two volunteers from an audience of up to a hundred people at the Institute for Rational-Emotive Therapy in New York. Each volunteer is interviewed for about 30 minutes on a specific psychological problem (or problems), after which the members of the audience who wish to do so are actively encouraged to speak to the volunteer and to the therapist concerning aspects of the volunteer's problem(s) and the

Written with Wouter Backx; first published in 1987.

interview that they have witnessed. The workshop lasts for about 1½ hours and is followed by a coffee hour. Ellis conducts therapy in this format in a very similar manner to how he would conduct therapy in his private office, with the possible exception that he uses more humour in these public demonstrations.

Rational–Emotive Therapy (RET)

RET is well suited to this form of public workshop. It is a non-mystical type of therapy where the therapist is very open about his or her interventions. It is also an educational form of therapy which strives to teach both the volunteer and the members of the audience the ABCs of RET, i.e. it is not 'A' (the event, or the person's inferences about the event) that determines the client's psychological problems (emotional and/or behavioural) at 'C', but rather it is 'B' (the client's irrational beliefs about the event) that seems to more adequately account for the presence of these problems. In the course of the public demonstration, the volunteers are helped to identify, challenge and change their irrational beliefs which take the form of dogmatic musts (shoulds, oughts or have to's) and one of three irrational derivatives. These derivatives take the form of (1) *awfulising* (rating an event as more than 100% bad – an evaluation which stems from the belief: 'This bad event *must* not be as bad as it is'; (2) *I-can't-stand-it-itis* (believing that one cannot tolerate an event and/or that one cannot be happy again as long as the event exists); and (3) *damnation* (giving oneself, other people or the world in general a negative, global damning rating – Dryden, 1984a, 1987b; Ellis, 1985a; Ellis and Dryden, 1987). It is a feature of the Friday night workshop that while Ellis is working intensively with a particular volunteer, the audience is simultaneously being educated concerning the cognitive underpinnings of their emotional and behavioural problems, and how these underpinnings can be identified, challenged and changed.

The Process of a Public Demonstration with a Volunteer

Both Wouter Backx and I have both witnessed dozens of Ellis's interviews conducted in the Friday night workshop and have identified a discernible process to such interviews. First, Ellis elicits the client's major emotional and/or behavioural problem at C. He then links this to a relevant activating event at A. From there he proceeds to identify the client's major irrational beliefs and starts to dispute these in a strong, evocative and often humorous manner (here it is the client's beliefs that are ridiculed, not the client). During this process, Ellis often uses self-disclosure to illustrate a number of points (as is shown in the transcript to be presented later in this chapter). Then, Ellis instructs the client how to use rational–emotive imagery (REI) –

a technique whereby the client vividly imagines the troublesome event at A, is instructed to make him- or herself disturbed at C and then is asked to change this inappropriate (or irrational) emotion (e.g. depression, anxiety, guilt or anger) to an appropriate (or rational) negative emotion (e.g. sadness, concern, regret or annoyance). When the client is successful in using this technique, he or she is practising spontaneously changing irrational beliefs to rational beliefs (which are expressed in the form of non-dogmatic desires and preferences). The client is then asked to practise REI for 10 minutes a day for 30 days and is given what Ellis calls 'operant conditioning' to motivate him or her to carry out this task. In 'operant conditioning', the client forgoes an enjoyable activity until he or she has practised REI and penalised him- or herself if he or she forgoes such practice (e.g. carries out an unpleasant task such as cleaning the toilet). At the end of the counselling session, the audience is invited to ask questions and the client is given a tape of the session for later review. Listening to the tapes of their sessions has two major benefits for clients. First, they often gain increased understanding of issues that were discussed in the public session. This is valuable because talking about one's problems in a public setting can be distracting for some clients. Secondly, clients often learn how to challenge their irrational beliefs more effectively after listening to Ellis's disputing interventions on tape.

Next a verbatim transcript is presented of an interview conducted by Ellis with Wouter Backx in the setting of the Friday night workshop to show this approach in action.

A Public Therapy Session Conducted by Albert Ellis

(Friday Night Workshop 19th of July 1985 in front of an audience of 100 people.)

Therapist   [to the audience]: Please be as compulsively quiet as you can be right now. Later you will get into the act and be able to say anything, but not right now. So shut your big mouths right now or else you'll have to listen in the John, which is a nice place to listen but not as good as in the auditorium. So quiet now and then later you'll be able to talk up and to say practically anything you want.

Therapist: [to client]: OK. Do you want to give me your first name?

Client: Wouter.

Therapist: Woulter, Wouter?

Client: Yes say Walter.

Therapist: Yeah, we would say Walter in English, but W-O-U-T-E-R in your language, right? OK Walter or Wouter, what problem would you like to start with?

Client: Well, I have a problem about doing things on time, especially when I have to take an examination or something like that, and eh...

Therapist: So in plain English you procrastinate, is that right? We call it procrastination; I don't know what you call it in Holland or Germany but we call it procrastination. Right?

Client: That is possible.

Therapist: Give us an example recently when you sat on your ass and procrastinated...

Client: Oh well when I came to the United States I had to finish an essay about the philosophy of science; and eh... well, I had to finish it and I did not make it, I did not get it ready.

Audience: [murmurs to client]

Client: Sorry?

Audience: [says something about the microphone that the client is using not being turned correctly]

Client: Like this?

Therapist: No, no. When you turn to me, it does not turn with you. If you turn around that way, then you face me. But it does not turn your turn. We haven't trained it properly yet. We are training it to turn properly, we are giving it therapy every week on how to turn. But so far we have failed and we may have to give up and kill ourselves. Unless we become rational and stop depressing ourselves about the goddamned mike! Anyway, so this time you could have done the paper...

Client: Yes that is right.

Therapist: ... and you delayed, you procrastinated. Because when you were about to do it and you didn't, what did you say to yourself? What negative self-statement?

Client: Oh, 'I have a lot of time. I'll of that easily'.

Therapist: That's what we call a rationalisation, which means horseshit in English. That is horseshit, because you did not have that much time. You lied to yourself.

Client: That's right.

Therapist: But what was the *reason* underneath the *rationalisation*? You said something about the *hardship* of doing it. What do you think that was?

Client: Well, it could be that I had delayed so much that I did not have sufficient time to do it. So I was afraid to find out. Or realised that it was very difficult, instead of what I originally thought, that it was easy.

Therapist: Yeah...

Client: I was a little bit afraid of not having enough time left in which to do it after I first delayed.

Therapist: Alright, but let us try the issue of difficultness first. Because your not having time enough was *after* you had already delayed. When you started delaying instead of doing it, you were saying, 'It may be difficult to do'. But if you didn't do it, that would be difficult too. Right?

Client: That seems to be – yeah, that is right.

Therapist: Yeah. So therefore you would probably do it. But what were you saying in addition to 'It may be or will be difficult'? You were saying something in addition to that. And what is that?

Client: 'If I fail I'll feel worse, I'll feel bad. I'll feel like a bad person.'

Therapist: So you were putting yourself down in case you failed.

Client: That's right.

Therapist: Alright, we'll start with your fear of failing first. I'll then get back to the difficulty of the task because that is usually important with procrastination – the difficulty of doing it and your reluctance to deal with that. But let us say, let us suppose you do the task quickly and immediately and it is not so hot and you fail. Why would *that* be terrible? Why would you be a bad person, a failure with a capital F for failing?

Client: Well, eh...

Therapist: Yes?

Client: ... that's difficult. Well, I should, must be able to do that!

Therapist: Oh you *should*! That is right: you *should* do it. But why *should* or *must* you?

Client: And it was my fault not to arrange it in a way that I could do it.

Therapist: That is correct, it was your fault. Let us assume that. Nobody made you, put a gun to your head and made you procrastinate. But since it was your fault, your failure, how does it make *you* a failure, a shit, a no goodnick for having that failing?

Client: Now I cannot find a good reason, but...

Therapist: You believe it. You still believe you *must* not fail and are no good if you do.

Client: Yes I do believe it, really. That is ...

Therapist: And as long as you *believe* it you are going to procrastinate.

Client: That is right.

Therapist: You see. Now how can you give up that bloody idea? Not the idea that 'It is my fault if I fail', but the idea that 'I am then a total failure'. How can you *give up* that horseshit?

Client: By telling myself something different.

Therapist: Exactly! What? 'I am a real failure?'

Client: . No, 'I am not a real failure, but I am just failing at this moment'. Or 'I am about to fail this time'.

Therapist: 'If I do it badly' – which you may not, you may do well – 'and I fail, I'll be failing *at this moment* with *this* essay. But I am never a *failing person*. I am never a rotten *individual*.' Right. Now you said the right thing, but you do not really *believe* it? That you could fail at this essay but are not a real failure?

Client: Well, the problem is when I try to tell myself this it is very difficult. I don't make it. I am thinking, 'Well it is not that bad to put it off at this moment'.

Therapist: Yeah.

Client: So I go on delaying it ....

Therapist: Yeah, but that is for the other reason; we'll get to that in a minute, the hardness of it. But could you *really* believe that if you did it steadily and you kept failing, didn't do as well as you could do, do you really believe you would not be a failure, you would not be a worm? Do you *really* believe that?

Client: I think so, to some extent.

Therapist: Yeah to some extent! But how could you believe it *stronger*? Like all these people in the audience believe it about you, but not about themselves. How could you believe it *stronger*? 'I am *never* a failure, a louse, a worm, *even* when I try my best and still fail.' How can you believe that?

Client: Well, I can stop making global evaluations about myself. That's right.

Therapist: Well, eh ...

Client: Because after I fail I can still do very many good things. So it is impossible to say what will be any final or global evaluations or rating of me by the time I die.

Therapist:	Once you fail, you have the possibility to do many successful things in the future.
Client:	That is right.
Therapist:	That is correct. So you are never *a failure*. If you were a failure, that would mean that you always deserve to fail and will fail because you failed this time. Is that correct?
Client:	That's right, yeah. That's right, I would deserve punishment or whatever.
Therapist:	But why *do* you deserve punishment if you fail? If you try your best and you fail this time?
Client:	But I did not try my best.
Therapist:	But suppose you did do your best. Why would you deserve punishment for failing? Why would you?
Client:	No, I don't deserve it. That is right.
Therapist:	Even if you did *not* try, you don't. Suppose you tried very little and you fell on your face. Why would you still *not* deserve punishment for failing?
Client:	Well, I have freedom of choice. I can choose.
Therapist:	You could choose *not* to rate yourself and *not* to consider yourself undeserving. Right. And the universe does not give a shit if you fail. It really does not care.
Client:	Really?
Therapist:	Yeah really. Don't be surprised that the powers up there and the powers down there really don't give a fuck whether you succeed or not. They have their *own* quaint ideas. They are only interested in their own navels, not in your bellybutton. So if you really thought about it you could convince yourself that 'It is bad to fail, it is unfortunate, it is poor behaviour. But I am not *a failure* and I don't *deserve* punishment or anything like that. I just deserve whatever I can get: such as good things in life. And when I get bad things I can live with them.' But now let us go down back to the hardness of doing the essay. You said rightly before that it is easy to put it off till later and to pretend: 'I'll do it later, I'll do it soon. I'll do it when it is easier.' Because it is *hard* to do it right now, right? But it is hard if you *don't* do it right now. In fact it is harder. Is it not?
Client:	Well, sometimes it comes out that it is easier to do it later.
Therapist:	Yeah, *how many* times?
Client:	Yes, well ...
Therapist:	Well, what percentage of times is it *easier* if you put it off?
Client:	Well, I don't ... Ja ...
Therapist:	Yeah, yeah! Out of a hundred times you put it off, how many times does it *really* become easier and a rare delight?
Client:	Ja, that's right. But on the short term it is. That is the problem.
Therapist:	Aah, yeah. That *is* the point. That is what we want you to see. It is easier *in the short run*.
Client:	That's right.
Therapist:	If you would really believe that, and would remind yourself how hard it is in the long run. If you write down on a piece of paper or a card the disadvantages of putting it off instead of the advantages of putting it off, which you have solidly instilled in your head, then you would tend not to put essays and things like that off. Now could you do that? Really write down on a piece of paper the disadvantages of putting it off, of doing it later and the advantages of doing it right now?

Client: I can do that.
Therapist: And would that not help you?
Client: I think so, ja.
Therapist: Is there any other reason which we may have omitted for your not doing the essay? Can you think of any other reason why you don't do it quickly, get it over with and that is that, which is what sensible people like me do?
Client: Well, sometimes I think something like, 'Why do they bother me with this kind of stuff?'.
Therapist: 'Oooooh, oooooh! Those lousy bastards! How could they give a nice guy like me that crummy paper to do?' Right?
Client: That is right!
Therapist: And what is the answer to that question? How *can* they give a nice guy like you that crummy paper to do? How can they?
Client: They are a little bit stupid. They don't know better.
Therapist: They can *easily* do what they do! They have *no trouble* giving you those stupid papers! Do they?
Client: No they don't.
Therapist: And they are surviving very well!
Client: That is right.
Therapist: So you are rebelling and saying to yourself, 'Because it is such a pain in the ass and such a stupid assignment, such a stupid paper to write, therefore they *should* not give it to me!'. But they *should* give it to you! Do you know why they *should* give it to you, that stupid paper?
Client: Because they choose to give it.
Therapist: Yes. Because *that is their nature*, to give out stupid papers! Do you expect them to give out intelligent papers to do or give you sensible things to do? How ridiculous! So you see you have got three major musts to produce your procrastination: One, 'I *must* do it very well and if I don't that would be terrible! I would be no good'. Two, 'They must not give me that goddamned stupid paper! So I'll fix their wagon by not doing it or by doing it later, when I feel like doing it'. And three, 'It is too goddamned hard to do! It *should not* be so hard! Therefore I'll put it off and I hope and pray to God almighty that it becomes easier some day'.
Client: That's right. I do say these things.
Therapist: But that is not working. And you see that your irrational beliefs are all *musts*. 'I must do well! They must treat me well! And conditions, the work itself must be easy!.' You are demanding and commanding that things *must* be your way. Now that is very unlikely!
                  Let me say how I did the opposite, when I was in college. I realised that they gave us term papers, especially in English which was really my major because I took more courses in English than in anything else. So the first day of the term they gave us a list of topics to write a term paper on and everybody else would fart around like you did, till the last day of the term or the day after the last day. But I did my paper immediately. I went to the library to work on it right away. First of all, nobody else was in the library and all the books were there, so that was good. Secondly, I could take any length of time I wanted to do the paper and finish it at my leisure. Thirdly, my professor almost dropped dead when he got the paper the second week of the term, was very grateful to get it so soon and thought I was a very noble person and a scholar. It was the first time in his or her history

that that had ever happened and I could coast for the rest of term, having nothing hanging over my head. No worry, no problems. So I figured out that it was much more advantageous for me to do my term papers that way. So I did them immediately. But you are not figuring what I figured out. You are deluding yourself that it is advantageous to delay your essays. And it very very rarely, practically never, is.

Let us try you with rational-emotive imagery. We have up to now been doing disputing and asking 'Why *must* it be easy and where is it written that you *have to* do a perfect paper?'. And 'Who says that those bastards *must* not give you stupid papers?'. So we have been questioning and challenging your irrational beliefs and you had better keep doing that. But let us also give you rational-emotive imagery. Close your eyes and imagine that the bastards give you another lousy, crummy paper to do which they probably will; and imagine that this paper is really a pain in the ass, it is very stupid that they give it to you, and it is hanging over your head to do. Can you vividly imagine that happening?

Client:	Yes.
Therapist:	How do you feel in your gut as you imagine that paper hanging over your head, the days passing, and you keep telling yourself 'Tomorrow, tomorrow, manana, manana'. How do you feel?
Client:	I feel anger at those people who gave it to me.
Therapist:	Now get in touch with your anger and really make yourself feel very angry at those idiots for giving you this stupid paper. Make yourself feel very angry. Are you feeling very angry with them?
Client:	Right.
Therapist:	All right. Now they are still making you do it, your image is still the same. But make yourself feel only sorry, only disappointed at what they are doing to you. Not angry at them. Tell me when you feel sorry and disappointed, not angry.
Client:	I do.
Therapist:	Open your eyes. That was quick, really quick. Tell us how you changed your feelings. How did you change?
Client:	I eh... first of all turned away from those stupid people and secondly by telling myself, 'Well it is not nice to have to do that paper, but OK I'll do it and I will certainly not die whatever bad things may happen in the world, I can stand it. And when I pass it is OK.'
Therapist:	Alright. Now that was really good. Now all you have to do if you follow this, is every day for the next 30 days you imagine the worst you can think of, make yourself very angry or depressed or anything like that – anger is one of the things that shows how you feel, so that is OK – change it into being sorry and being disappointed the way you did and other ways that may occur to you. Now will you do that for the next 30 days at least once a day? You may do it 10 times a day but do it at least once. Would you really want to do that?
Client:	Let us say before I go to bed?
Therapist:	Well any time in 24 hours once a day, do you want to do it?
Client:	Oh, whether I *want* to do it, I thought you asked when.
Therapist:	Yeah. No, no, I am not telling you that, you can do it any time once a day. Now in case you don't we are going to give you reinforcement – operant conditioning. What do you like to do that you do almost every day in the

	week? What do you really enjoy doing? You enjoy something you do almost every day. What is it?
Client:	Well, reading a book.
Therapist:	Alright. No reading for the next 30 days until after you do that one or two minutes' rational–emotive imagery because that is all it takes you. What do you hate to do that normally you avoid doing because you hate it?
Client:	Doing the laundry and things like that.
Therapist:	Alright. For the next 30 days if bedtime arrives and you have not yet done your rational–emotive imagery you are to stay up another hour to do the laundry. But if you do the rational–emotive imagery you don't have to do the laundry. And if your laundry gets too clean, you can then do your neighbour's laundry!
Client:	I am working at a youth camp, so that won't be difficult to arrange.
Therapist:	That is right! At a youth camp there is plenty of laundry to do! Now, is there anything else about this problem that we may have omitted?
Client:	Well, sometimes I do just the reverse of what you now tell me. When I feel depressed, I do things I like instead of trying to do things ...
Therapist:	... that you don't like?
Client:	Yeah. I do the things that I have to do or that I want to do.
Therapist:	Yeah, that would be all right temporarily, just temporarily for a while. But you could make sure that you later do the things that you don't like to do, in case you avoid performing the rational–emotive imagery. But it would even be better when you are depressed, to do the goddamned things you don't like. They would preoccupy you, help you get distracted from your depression. Also you can then do work at eliminating the depression. Now another thing when you don't do the work, don't write your essays, how do you feel about yourself for procrastinating, for not doing it?
Client:	Well very bad. Shit, shit.
Therapist:	Alright. So some of your depression stems from your self-downing. And you could ask yourself not 'Why am I not doing the work?', but 'Why am I a shit for not doing this work?'. And your answer would be what?
Client:	There is no reason.
Therapist:	Yes, there is no reason. 'I am a fallible fucked up human being who is not doing the work right now. So I'd better move my ass and do it!'

Let us now get the audience's comments and discussion about this problem.

Audience Participation

We have noticed that the types of issues/questions raised by the audience can be placed into a number of categories.

Practical advice

A number of participants offer practical suggestions or advice concerning what the volunteer can do about his or her problem. Thus, good suggestions concerning how to overcome procrastination and how to approach members of the opposite sex, for example, are often put forward. Ellis endorses those practical suggestions that he considers of merit and points out problems in other pieces of advice. However, he generally urges the volunteers (and thus indirectly teaches the audience) to change irrational beliefs before attempting to solve the practical aspects of their problems. In doing so, Ellis highlights an important point in rational–emotive theory that when people are disturbed by holding irrational beliefs about an event, this impedes them from thinking clearly and thus from implementing effective solutions to change the event or to adjust to it.

Challenging inferences

One feature of RET that distinguishes it from other forms of cognitive–behaviour therapy is that RET therapists in general first encourage their clients to assume that their inferences about a situation are true (in order to identify latent irrational beliefs) before challenging these inferences at a later stage. Members of the audience often ask volunteers questions which are directed to the truth or falsity of the latter's negative inferences. Ellis generally endorses such interventions but stresses why it is important to first challenge irrational beliefs before challenging negative inferences.

Assessing the impact of self on others

A number of questions and points are addressed to volunteers concerning the possible impact that their behaviour has on others. These often prove to be valuable interventions because Ellis does not frequently address himself to such material in the course of the 30-minute public demonstration interviews. Thus, volunteers who present with problems of maintaining or developing interpersonal relationships are asked to reflect on the possibility that some aspects of their behaviour impede the quality of their relationships. Some members of the audience are quite astute at picking up cues from the demeanour of volunteers that are worthy of consideration.

Anti-RET viewpoints

Some members of the audience ask questions which are based on therapeutic philosophies that are antithetical to RET. Here Ellis is quick to show the questioner, the volunteer and the rest of the audience the problems which are inherent in such viewpoints. In doing so, Ellis is quite vigorous in his criticisms of opposing viewpoints, for example, labelling them as 'psychoanalytical horseshit' etc. He does this to stress to the audience the dangers he sees in such positions. Whilst some claim that Ellis is dogmatic in his expressed views on these subjects, Ellis defends himself by distinguishing between dogma (which he denies) and strongly held viewpoints (which are non-dogmatically expressed in a powerful manner). After voicing his criticisms, Ellis proceeds to offer the RET position on these issues.

Catching Ellis out

A few members of the audience are extremely knowledgeable in RET theory and practice and delight in pointing out to Ellis that he has omitted some aspect of RET theory and practice in his presentation. Ellis takes these points in very good spirit and uses them to teach the audience the neglected aspect of the rational–emotive approach.

Whilst no systematic research has been done on the effect of the Friday night workshop on audience learning, Ellis claims that members of the audience are often helped by observing such interviews to solve their own problems by using the same methods that they have watched Ellis employ. This would certainly be a fruitful area for future research.

Further Issues

It can be seen from the presented interview that Ellis's approach reflects his New York origins. Several writers have made the point that one does not have to sound like Albert Ellis in order to practise RET effectively (e.g. Meichenbaum, 1977). Indeed, one reason we believe that RET has not attracted a large following among British counsellors and psychotherapists is that these practitioners equate the practice of RET with Ellis's forthright and earthy style. So if a British version of the Friday night workshop were ever to be held, a less forthright and earthy approach may have to be adopted to obviate such negative effects. However, it may be that the British public are less sensitive about such matters than British counsellors and psychotherapists!

Such workshops obviously raise issues concerning confidentiality. Our preference would be to announce at the beginning of such workshops that client material should be respected as confidential and should not be discussed with other people outside the workshop other than in general terms. Certainly no names should be linked to discussions of client material. That Ellis does not make such an announcement is something we would criticise.

It is interesting to observe that disclosing their problems before an audience of strangers does not seem to inhibit the volunteers who choose to discuss their problems in New York. Obviously some material might not be disclosed and it is important to stress at this point that such demonstrations are not designed to replace individual therapy. Indeed, a number of volunteers at Ellis's Friday night workshops later seek help from Ellis himself or from one of the other therapists at the Institute. Whether British people would feel as free to volunteer to discuss their problems in public in such interviews, and whether they will show the same lack of inhibition in their disclosures, remains to be seen.

Part VI
RET in a Broader Therapeutic Context

Chapter 17
Psychoanalytical Psychotherapy for Depressive Patients:
Contributions from Cognitive–Rational Therapy

Whiteley (1981) reported on his experiences of running group therapy sessions with depressive patients along psychoanalytical lines. He concluded that, because the overall experience was an unproductive one, the treatment of depressive patients may still be best carried out using individual therapy. He noted that, in the group therapy sessions, his interpretations were seen as criticisms or confrontations and thus presumably of little value to the group members. Moreover, he hypothesised that his depressive patients' behaviour in the group was motivated by anxiety concerning (1) attack by other group members, (2) being rejected and (3) disapproval. Therapists of many different persuasions have noted the same distorted patterns of cognition in depressive patients. I will argue in this chapter that recent advances in rational–emotive therapy and the cognitive therapy of depression (Beck et al., 1979) may provide important guidelines for the practice of psychoanalytical psychotherapy of depressive patients.

Developing the Observing Self

Weiner (1975) has made an important distinction between the experiencing self, which processes information and has affective reactions consequent to this 'cognitive' activity, and the observing self – the part of the self which can reflect on the experiencing self's psychological processes. Effective therapy involves helping patients to shift between these two 'subselves' as the occasion requires. One of the major problems highlighted in Whiteley's (1981) report may have been his inability, given the treatment context, to help his patients to utilise their observing selves best. It seemed

First published in 1983.

237

to me that his patients were not sufficiently trained to utilise their observing capacities prior to group therapy or, if they were so trained, then the intensity of the treatment context was such as to make utilisation extraordinarily difficult.

Beck et al. (1979) have stressed in their book, *Cognitive Therapy of Depression*, the importance of deliberately and systematically training patients to become expert observers of their cognitive processes because certain cognitive phenomena are deemed to be centrally implicated in their depressive reactions. Initially, cognitive therapists train patients to become aware of their 'stream of consciousness' thoughts, i.e. those that are readily available to identification. These are termed 'automatic thoughts' by Beck et al. Cognitive therapists systematically help patients to develop fully their skills at identifying automatic thoughts and encourage them to regard such thoughts as hypotheses about reality rather than accurate statements about reality. Patients are then trained to examine such thoughts and to respond to them if they prove to be based on cognitive distortions. However, automatic thoughts are but the tip of the 'cognitive iceberg', and are based on underlying evaluative assumptions which are only formulated later on in therapy as part of a joint enterprise between patient and therapist. The formulation of such underlying assumptions depends on the collection of sufficient numbers of automatic thoughts to make such formulation possible. Cognitive therapists then do not generally make interpretations to patients but help patients to collect and examine data (automatic thoughts) and from there to make their own interpretations of the underlying meaning of such data. Although Whiteley's (1981) interpretations may have been accurate, his patients may not have been sufficiently helped to process either the information contained within them or their cognitive reactions to him as group therapist making interpretations. Deliberate attempts to train depressive patients to become skilled observers and examiners of their cognitive processes is best done initially by employing their own experiences *outside* therapy as data for examination. Cognitive therapists help patients talk about and reflect on their weekly outside experiences before dealing with any transference data that may emerge. According to this view, therapy with depressed patients based on making transference interpretations without first training patients to observe and examine their cognitions places much faith in their spontaneous ability to utilise their observing selves in the service of therapy. It is apparent that Whiteley's patients' spontaneous ability to utilise their observing selves was limited.

Group cognitive therapy is generally carried out after depressive patients have had some exposure to individual therapy where such deliberate and systematic training has been carried out. If this group treatment mode is used with patients without individual therapy experience, the initial group sessions are devoted to such training again using members' extra-therapy experiences as data. Here group therapists take quite an active stance to ensure that all patients become competent in the observing-examining process.

Depression and Psychoanalytical Interpretations

Unfortunately, Whiteley (1981) does not provide examples of the specific interpretations that he made in his therapeutic interventions. Whiteley (personal communication) has said, however:

> I think that the only sorts of interpretations I may have made might have concerned defences such as silence or perhaps depression itself, both of which I saw as a form of safety from interference from outside. I might also have interpreted the lack of involvement amongst members of the group with each other as fear of criticism or attack.

It is apparent from his article that patients did react negatively to his interpretation. In terms of the cognitive model of depression:

> Whiteley made an interpretation.... patients made their own negative inferences and evaluations concerning his interpretation and had a concomitant affective response.... Patients made critical comments about Whiteley's interpretation.

Either no attempt was made to help patients reflect on their inferences and evaluations of Whiteley's remarks or further negative cognitive reactions were forthcoming in response to any such attempts. Thus Whiteley is in a bind. If he makes enquiries about such negative reactions (1) patients may not have the ability to reflect on the cognitive determinants of their affective reactions, (2) the intensity of the experience may be such as to make such reflection extremely difficult or (3) Whiteley's interpretation may not account for his patients' depression.

On this last point, because Whiteley was not able to supply me with any specific interpretations he made in his group sessions, I invited a member of the West Midlands Institute of Psychotherapy, a psychoanalytical therapist, to supply me with specific interpretations which had been actually made to depressive patients in the course of their therapy. While I do not wish to generalise from the activity of one psychoanalytical practitioner to others, I do wish to show how such interpretations may not help patients get to the ideological root of their depressive experiences.

Interpretation 1

> I'm inclined to suggest that you've been particularly depressed this week because you've been feeling at odds with various members of your family.

This suggests to the patient that depression is caused by feeling at odds with various family members. Cognitive-rational therapists would disagree and would help the patient distinguish between cognitive evaluations that lead to sadness (e.g. How unfortunate! I wish this was not happening) about the state of affairs and those that lead to depression (e.g. How terrible! I can't stand this conflict!).

Interpretation 2

> I'm thinking now, from what's just been said, that your guilt and depression may be a means by which you try and cope with difficult fantasies about freedom, self-indulgence and escape.

Cognitive-rational therapists would help the patient see the direct relationship between cognitive evaluations about such fantasies and depression/guilt. As an example, the patient may first *infer* that such fantasies are wrong and forbidden and then conclude that he or she was bad for having them. In the actual interpretation made, it is difficult to determine whether the therapist is suggesting that the depression/guilt is a direct response to the fantasies or a way of warding off more dire feelings. If the former, the patient is not helped to see the more direct evaluative link between the fantasies and the feelings of depression and guilt.

Interpretation 3

> It seems from what you just said that you're depressed right now because you think you've undermined our relationship by criticising me last week.

Here the therapist posits that depression stems from the client's inference that the relationship between them has been undermined following the criticism. Cognitive-rational therapists would disagree. They posit that emotions are related to evaluations not inferences and here the client's implicit evaluations are missing. It may be that the client was blaming him- or herself for the inferred event, e.g. 'I undermined the relationship. I'm no good' or 'I undermined the relationship, I can't stand the prospect of being left by my therapist'.

In these three examples, the clients are led to believe that their depression is caused by external events or their inferences. The cognitive-rational perspective suggests that this is incorrect, rather depression is viewed as being determined by cognitive evaluations and that the clients in these examples are being presented with a jigsaw puzzle with the main piece missing.

Interpretation 4

> It sounds as though you're finding it hard to express your anger and disappointment about how your therapy is progressing, and its almost as if the annoyance gets turned in on itself.

Here the therapist implies that feelings have 'agency' properties independent of the person: annoyance gets turned in on itself. This may encourage the client's external locus of control attributions which may perpetuate his or her helplessness. The cognitive-rational therapist may say if he used the interpretation format:

> It sounds as though you're finding it hard to express your anger and disappointment about how your therapy is progressing. Am I right? (If so...) How do you feel about finding expressing such feelings different?

The psychoanalytical therapist's example seems to suggest that annoyance turned inwards leads to depression. Cognitive-rational therapists would say that if the client was depressed about not expressing such feelings he or she *may*, for example, be blaming him- or herself for such difficulty and/or for experiencing the feelings in the first place. Here cognitive evaluations are again stressed in the depressive emotional episode.

Interpretations 5 and 6

> I don't really think you've resolved your feelings about your mother's loss, and suspect your depression is linked with this somehow.
>
> You obviously find it hard to express your mixed feelings about your father since his death, despite the fact that the rest of your family practically curse him. It's almost as if you feel only kindness for him and the others feel only anger ... depression ties up with this.

Here the therapist is making associative links, not causal ones as were made in interpretations (1)-(3). However, he does not show the clients how depression is linked or tied up with the unresolved feelings in interpretation (5) or the difficulty of expressing mixed feelings in interpretation (6). Cognitive-rational therapists would help the client to specify the cognitive evaluations that mediate between the conflict and the depression.

The common thread in the above six interpretations is that, from a cognitive-rational perspective, the therapist has not helped clients to identify the core of their depressing experiences - namely depressive cognitive evaluations. Given different cognitive evaluations, the clients could face the same situations or conflicts and experience less troublesome emotions.

Conclusion

It seems to me that psychoanalytical psychotherapists can learn two important lessons from cognitive-rational therapists to enhance therapeutic effectiveness with depressive patients. First, they would do well to train patients deliberately to become skilled observers and examiners of their cognitive processes in a more systematic fashion than they are accustomed. Secondly, they may need to focus more specifically on cognitive evaluations as the ideological root of the depressive experience.

Acknowledgements

I would like to thank (1) Dr R. Whiteley for responding to my enquiries about the experience described in his article, and (2) the West Midlands Institute of Psychotherapy member who provided me with the interpretations discussed in the present chapter. For reasons of confidentiality, the member will remain anonymous.

Chapter 18
Past Messages and Disputations:
The Client and Significant Others

Rational-emotive therapy is a comprehensive treatment approach which aims to deal with the three basic modalities of human dysfunctioning: cognitive, emotive and behavioural. Indeed, its multimodal focus is what initially attracted me to RET. However, with regard to another important dimension in psychotherapy – time perspective – rational-emotive theory is less comprehensive in its recommendations. In listening to many tapes of RET practitioners and in participating in discussions with Institute faculty, fellows and practicum students, I have noted that the large majority claim (at least within earshot of others!) to follow Ellis's teachings with regard to time perspective:

> The rational therapist for the most part ignores connections between the client's early history and his present disturbances. He does not believe that the client was made neurotic by his past experiences, but by his own unrealistic and over-demanding *interpretations* of these experiences.
>
> (Ellis, 1977h, p. 27)

Thus, when clients have wanted to discuss their past experiences, they are generally instructed by the therapist that the reason they are anxious, depressed, angry or guilty now is because they are *right now* re-indoctrinating themselves with the beliefs they had acquired in the past. Broadly speaking, this is a sound approach and leads the focus of RET practice to be present-centred and future-oriented. However, I am a little concerned with the apparent absolutistic manner in which people have interpreted Ellis in this regard and believe that with *some* clients, therapeutic movement is delayed by the practitioner's strong reluctance to consider past material. This reluctance is also evident in the RET literature; as far as I am aware, only Dombrow (1973) has made a similar plea for working with past material in RET.

First published in 1979.

My first thesis is that, whilst I concur with Ellis's view that 'for the most part' exploring connections between the client's earlier history and his present disturbance may not be particularly helpful, with *some* clients exploring past material can actually enhance therapeutic movement. My second thesis is that this can be effectively done by helping clients to dispute the irrationality implicit in the messages they received in the past from significant others. This has the additional effect of enabling clients to recognise and accept the fallibility of those who were assumed to be infallible or omnipotent. To put this in a theoretical perspective, clients are helped to dispute the irrational belief suggested by Hauck (1967): 'the idea that beliefs held by respected authorities or society must be correct and therefore should not be questioned' (p. 2).

Interestingly enough, I believe that rational–emotive therapists are not loathe to help clients dispute the irrationality implicit in messages they are receiving from people in their lives at present and the messages they may receive from people in the future. Of course, this is not the major focus of therapeutic intervention, because the practitioner will then proceed to help clients to dispute the irrationality implicit in the messages they give themselves in response to the irrational messages received from others. Thus, the principle of disputing the irrationality in others' messages is not altogether foreign to RET practice, although it would be viewed as an inelegant solution. Whilst not foreign to RET practice, this procedure has received little attention in the RET literature. Moreover, whilst at present we have very little research evidence showing the superior effectiveness of elegant over inelegant RET solutions, the possibility may exist that such inelegant solutions may enhance therapeutic movement in some clients and thus deserve consideration.

To illustrate the thesis that helping some clients dispute the irrationality implicit in messages received from people in the past may facilitate therapeutic movement, I will briefly discuss the case of 'Mary'. Mary is a very intelligent, 32-year-old Irish girl whom I saw in a University Health Service setting. Mary had suffered from severe feelings of worthlessness for many years. She had previously received therapeutic help from a kindly Irish psychiatrist who 'boosted her ego' temporarily. However, needless to say, such 'progress' was short-lived. In the traditional manner, I attempted to show Mary that her depression stemmed from the strict demands she placed on herself and the resulting self-downing which accompanied her failures to live up to these demands. However, Mary seemed more interested in talking at length about the inhumane treatment she had received from her parents when she was younger – she was cruelly beaten, often for little reason and particularly when she made mistakes. My repeated and forceful attempts to guide her to the view that her present disturbance was caused by present self-indoctrination did not lead to therapeutic progress. However, movement did occur after I had worked with Mary for a short period of time, helping her to analyse and dispute the irrationality implicit in the messages she had received from her parents in the past. This, in my view, enabled her to become more receptive to the view that it was not the parents' messages of 'A' which caused her disturbance at 'C', but her own interpretations of the messages at 'B' with which she was now re-indoctrinating herself. Mary's response to my change of therapeutic attack was illuminating. She claimed that the occasions when we analysed and disputed her parents' irrationality were helpful in that: 'I felt freed then to look at what I am doing to myself now.'

In conclusion, whilst I have pointed out the advantages of helping some clients to dispute the irrationality implicit in messages received from significant others – (1) it may help initially resistant clients to later respond more favourably to present-centred/future-oriented RET, (2) it has educational value in teaching that significant others are not infallible and have their own irrational beliefs and, finally, (3) it helps make RET even more multimodal in approach – I want to emphasise some potential dangers. First, if not sensitively handled, the client may learn that 'A' really does cause 'C'. Thus, it is important to stress to clients that whatever irrational messages were communicated to them by significant others, they are still responsible for determining their own emotional disturbance by the communication of equally irrational messages to themselves. Secondly, and related to the first issue, clients may begin to severely blame significant others for causing them their problems. This is not a problem if the issue of blame is then handled in the traditional RET manner. Finally, delving into the past may lead the practitioner and his or her client into blind alleys and encourage the former to collude with the latter's attempts to avoid self-responsibility.

Nonetheless, if the above problems are competently handled, it is my contention that the strategy of helping the client to analyse and dispute the irrationality in past (present and future) significant others' messages does have its place in RET practice with certain clients.

Chapter 19
Rational-Emotive Therapy and Cognitive Therapy:
A Critical Comparison

In endeavouring to make a critical comparison between two approaches to psychotherapy, a writer must make clear at the outset to which sources of data he is referring in his comprehensive analysis. In comparing rational-emotive therapy with cognitive therapy I have utilised: (1) the writings of both Aaron Beck and Albert Ellis; (2) other statements by Beck and Ellis which have not appeared in publication form; (3) the views of experienced and highly trained rational-emotive therapists and cognitive therapists; and (4) my own views concerning the differences and similarities between rational-emotive therapy and cognitive therapy based on my experiences of being trained at both the Institute for Rational-Emotive Therapy in New York and the Center for Cognitive Therapy in Philadelphia. My aim in this comparative review is to consider both approaches' (1) developmental history, (2) theoretical and philosophical underpinnings, and (3) practical components.

At the outset it is important to note that Ellis (1979f, 1980b) states that there are two forms of RET: general RET which he claims is synonymous with cognitive-behaviour therapy (Ellis, 1980b), and specialised RET which he claims differs from CBT in several important aspects.* I shall endeavour

---

First published in 1984.

*These ways are 'Cognitively, it has a pronounced philosophic emphasis, includes a humanistic-existentialist outlook, strives for pervasive and long-standing rather than symptomatic change, tries to eliminate all self-ratings, stresses anti*must*urbatory rather than antiempirical disputing methods, recognizes the palliative aspects of cognitive distraction, discourages problem solving that is not accompanied by changes in clients' basic belief system, and emphasizes secondary as well as primary symptoms of emotional disturbance. Emotively it stresses the discrimination of appropriate from inappropriate emotions, emphasizes methods of working directly with and on emotions, encourages forceful emotive interventions, and uses relationship procedures that heavily stress unconditional rather than conditional positive regard. Behaviourally, it favors penalization as well as reinforcement, is partial to in vivo desensitization and flooding and makes sure that skill training is done within a philosophic framework of trying to help clients make basic changes in their irrational beliefs' (Ellis, 1980b).

to make clear at various junctures to which form of RET I am referring in this chapter.

Development

Both rational–emotive therapy and cognitive therapy were developed as a result of their founders' dissatisfaction with psychoanalytical theory and practice. However, whilst Ellis has developed RET mainly outside the formal academic arena, Beck has remained firmly within it. This factor may partially account for the different emphases apparent in the work of Beck and Ellis. Ellis used to be in private practice and is now Executive Director of two non-profit-making institutes. The Institute for Rational–Emotive Therapy has a clinic where lengthy diagnostic interviews are not carried out. Over the years, Ellis and his colleagues have seen patients representing the broad spectrum of emotional disorders. RET, then, has developed without Ellis and his colleagues focusing on any one specific emotional disorder for special and intensive empirical study and without them carrying out rigorously designed outcome studies. Beck and his colleagues, however, have spent much of their time and attention studying the psychological processes of the depressive disorders and have carried out rigorously designed outcome studies on the cognitive therapy of depression. Beck and his team are now adopting a similar approach to the study of anxiety disorders. In their clinic, lengthy diagnostic interviews are carried out.

These differences I think are reflected in the different emphases found in Beck's and Ellis's writings. Ellis has written extensively on a wide variety of psychotherapeutic issues and the whole spectrum of the emotional disorders. He has recently written widely on the philosophical and theoretical underpinnings of RET (e.g. Ellis, 1976a, 1978b, 1979e), has steadily over the years published books and articles on the *general* strategy and specific techniques used in RET (e.g. Ellis, 1958a, 1962, 1971a, 1975, 1979c) but somewhat surprisingly has not written much on the practice of RET over the course of treatment. He has recently published a treatment manual, 23 years after the inception of RET (Ellis and Abrahms, 1978).

In contrast, Beck's writings lack the breadth and variety of Ellis's, but reflect the in-depth study replete with his own group's experimental work which is lacking in the work of Ellis (e.g. Beck, 1964, 1967, 1973; Beck et al., 1979). Beck (1976) has written a more general text on the emotional disorders but, on closer inspection, focuses mainly on the depressive and anxiety disorders. In this publication, anger is covered only briefly while shame and guilt are not given coverage. Beck has not written extensively on the philosophical underpinnings of cognitive therapy but, unlike Ellis, has written on the practice of cognitive therapy over the course of treatment and has published three treatment manuals where therapeutic style, strategy and technique are specifically described.

Any comparison between rational–emotive therapy and cognitive therapy had better be placed in a historical context which illustrates the different interests and emphases in the work of the founding fathers. These differences do, in my opinion, account for some of the differences in the current status of the two approaches.

Theoretical and Philosophical Underpinnings

Image of the person and the acquisition of emotional disturbance

All approaches to psychotherapy are based on either an explicit or implicit image of human beings. Such an image does have a direct influence on the practice of therapy, although this relationship is of course confounded by other variables. Ellis (1976a, 1978b, 1979e) has spelled out in detail the image of the person which underlies his practice of specialised RET. In contrast, Beck does not address himself to this issue in his writings, preferring to focus on the theoretical and experimental factors associated with depression and anxiety.

Ellis (e.g. 1976a, 1978b) has consistently emphasised the biological basis of irrationality which he claims underlies most emotional disturbance. Indeed he writes:

> RET-oriented personality theory hypothesises that probably 80 per cent of the variance of human behaviour rests on biological bases and about 20 per cent on environmental training.
>
> (Ellis, 1978b, p. 304).

It is difficult to determine to what extent this view is shared by rational–emotive therapists and to what extent adhering to this viewpoint influences therapeutic practice.*

Beck's (1967, 1976) earlier work appeared to emphasise important early learning experiences in the development of cognitive schemata which leave a person vulnerable to emotional disorders. However, in his more recent work, more emphasis is given to the influence of premorbid personality (Beck, 1983) and biological factors (Beck, 1982) in the development of emotional disorders.

Both Ellis and Beck have made similar statements concerning the acquisition of emotional disturbance. Ellis (1978b, 1979e) considers there to be a multiplicity of origins of personality and presumably of emotional disturbance. In the same vein, Beck (1983) argues that it is counterproductive to speak of *the* cause of the affective disorders. He argues that there are a host

---

*Throughout this chapter it should be noted that the extent to which rational–emotive therapists and cognitive therapists agree with the views expressed by Ellis and Beck respectively is not known. This remains a fruitful area for research.

of possible predisposing and precipitating factors in the development of depression. While making similar statements concerning the acquisition of emotional disturbance, it is clear that Beck and Ellis differ in their views concerning the *ultimate* determinants of emotional disturbance with Ellis stressing biological factors and Beck stressing significant learning experiences albeit against the background of a specific biological disposition (I. Herman, 1981, personal communication). Such differences show up in how Beck and Ellis talk about the development of emotional disturbance. Whilst Beck talks and writes in terms of human beings *learning* dysfunctional underlying assumptions, Ellis talks in terms of human beings *teaching themselves* irrational beliefs (and being biologically prone to do so). A common Ellis message to his patients is:

> It's got zero to do with your mother and father, you taught yourself that nonsense.

While this phrase is an overexaggeration due to the point which Ellis wishes to make, it does capture his distaste for theories which make significant learning experiences primary in explaining the development of emotional disturbance.

While Ellis stresses humans' biological tendency towards irrationality, he however has an optimistic view of human potential for change.

> People ... have an unusual capacity to change their cognitive and behavioural processes so that they can (a) choose to react differently from the way they usually do, (b) refuse to upset themselves about almost anything that may occur, and (c) train themselves so that they can semi-automatically remain minimally disturbed for the rest of their lives.
>
> (Ellis, 1979g, p. 2)

Thus, as we shall see, if human beings apply themselves they can achieve considerable results.

Whilst Beck, a priori, must have faith in the ability of humans to overcome their emotional problems, he has not written about this potential for change. However, it is difficult for me to imagine him writing in the same vein as Ellis. Whilst Beck's view of this issue seems to me to be a traditional one, i.e. human beings can achieve a fair measure of emotional health, while overcoming significant barriers, Ellis's view is less traditional, i.e. human beings can achieve a considerable measure of emotional health while overcoming gigantic barriers.

The nature of emotional disturbance

Both Beck and Ellis have acquired their reputations for giving cognitive factors primacy in accounting for emotional disturbance and both stress that cognitions, feelings and behaviours interrelate. In addition, both point to underlying cognitive structures as being at the root of emotional disturbance. However, they do not agree as to the nature of these underlying cognitive structures. For Ellis the root of emotional disturbance is a set of 'musturbatory ideologies' towards self, others and life conditions in general (Ellis, 1977d). Such ideologies take the form of evaluations (as opposed to inferences) (Wessler and Wessler, 1980; Wessler, 1982b) and are absolutistic and grandiose in nature. Ellis calls these structures ideologies because he wishes to stress their philosophical nature. Such ideologies, claims Ellis, are responsible for the inferential cognitive distortions that Beck et al. (1979) so carefully document although this claim has yet to be studied. Beck (Kovacs and Beck, 1978; Beck et al., 1979) agrees that maladaptive underlying cognitive structures are responsible for patients' cognitive distortions about one's self, experiences and future, but does not agree with Ellis that these underlying assumptions or cognitive schema are invariably 'musturbatory' and evaluative in nature. Beck (1976) does say that these assumptions tend to be absolute in nature as well as being characterised by such distortions as exaggeration and overgeneralisation. Beck (1976, pp. 255–256) gives nine examples of underlying assumptions – that predispose people to depression. Whilst seven of these assumptions are evaluative in nature, two are inferential statements about reality (i.e. 'If somebody disagrees with me, it means he doesn't like me' and 'If I don't take advantage of every opportunity to advance myself, I will regret it later'). This list is also quoted in Beck et al. (1979) and Coleman and Beck (1981), so it is possible to argue that this is still Beck's viewpoint. Thus, we see that whereas rational–emotive therapists tend to distinguish clearly between inferential (or what Ellis calls observations) and evaluative processes (Wessler and Wessler, 1980; Wessler, 1982b), cognitive therapists do not make such a clear distinction.

Ellis's viewpoint on emotional disturbance is centred around two basic themes. These I call 'ego disturbance' and 'discomfort disturbance'. Emotional disturbance is due to human beings' failure to acknowledge or accept their human fallibility and their failure to adopt a tolerant attitude towards discomfort. Thus, Ellis tends to view disturbance in terms of two fundamental processes. Although Beck and other cognitive therapists (Beck et al., 1979; Burns, 1980) outline a number of faulty information processing styles or cognitive distortions, which are reflected in underlying assumptions, they tend to emphasise the idiosyncratic nature of these assumptions and do not specify such distinct fundamental processes. Thus whilst rational–emotive therapists tend to think in terms of finite clusters of irrational beliefs, cognitive therapists tend to think in terms of an infinite number of underlying assumptions (I. Herman, 1981, personal communication).*

Another difference between rational–emotive therapy and cognitive therapy, which is derived from the writings of Beck and Ellis and my observations, is that Ellis clearly distinguishes between what he calls appropriate

---

*I. Herman's view has recently been challenged by A. Freeman (1982, personal communication) who claims that cognitive therapists think in terms of finite clusters of underlying assumptions, while acknowledging their idiosyncratic nature.

and inappropriate negative emotions and cognitive therapists in general do not. For example, Ellis (1977i) in reviewing Beck's (1976) *Cognitive Therapy and the Emotional Disorders* notes that Beck uses 'sadness' 'as a term for all kinds of states ranging from mild regret to severe self-damning' (p. 295)[*,†] Ellis's clear distinction between appropriate and inappropriate negative feelings stems from his clear distinction between 'healthy' rational beliefs and 'unhealthy' irrational beliefs. Whilst no comparatively simple criteria have been described in the cognitive therapy literature for distinguishing between dysfunctional and functional underlying assumptions, J.E. Young, a cognitive therapist (1982, personal communication), does (as we shall see) employ criteria for distinguishing between functional and dysfunctional thoughts, feelings and behaviours.

Ellis in his writings (e.g. Ellis, 1979e; Ellis and Abrahms, 1978) emphasises that humans often disturb themselves about their disturbance and this is a significant feature of both his theory and his practice. Whilst cognitive therapists acknowledge the prevalence of this process in anxiety disorders (i.e. anxiety about anxiety), the corresponding process in depression (i.e. depression about depression) is not prominently featured.

Beck and cognitive therapists, however, highlight inferential cognitive distortions prominently in their ideas about disturbance and as targets for change in their practical interventions. For example, in depression, negative predictions about the future are regarded as a primary factor in depression and highly influential in the production of suicidal ideations. Ellis does acknowledge the influence of such distortions but these do not occupy a central role in his theorising and practice.

Perpetuation of emotional disturbance

Beck et al. (1979) argue that depressed persons perpetuate their pain-inducing and self-defeating attitudes despite objective evidence of positive features in their lives. They argue that humans utilise cognitive schemata and faulty information processing styles to edit out various potentially disconfirming experiences and distort such experiences to fit in with the activated cognitive schema. As a result alternatives are not explored and new behaviours not attempted. Thus, the person is likely to have familiar experiences which further perpetuate his disturbance (I. Herman, 1981, personal communication). Whilst Ellis would not disagree with this view, his arguments concerning the perpetuation of emotional disturbance highlight the view that 'most people have a natural tendency to resist basic personality change' (Ellis, 1979a, p. 51). Wessler (1978) and Ellis argue that *low frustration tolerance* (LFT) is at the root of such perpetuation. We have already seen that cognitive therapists do not highlight this process in

---

*Beck (1982, personal communication) says that Ellis has misinterpreted him on this point.
†Burns (1980), however, does distinguish between sadness and depression.

their writings. Ellis argues that most human beings have a natural affinity for comfort and thus opt for the relative comfort of short-term, self-defeating goals and in so doing miss out on the potential change-producing but uncomfortable experiences which striving for their long-term self-enhancing goals would afford.

The nature of emotional health and goals of therapy

Ellis's image of the emotionally healthy individual is firmly rooted in a 'clin-ical–humanistic–atheistic' philosophy (Ellis, 1980c). His position is that if human beings are to experience emotional health they had better identify their self-enhancing life goals and work consistently towards them. Furthermore he specifies the subgoals that will enable humans to be successful in their primary goal. These are: (1) self-interest, (2) social interest, (3) self-direction, (4) tolerance, (5) flexibility, (6) acceptance of uncertainty, (7) commitment, (8) scientific thinking, (9) self-acceptance, (10) risk-taking and (11) non-utopianism (Ellis, 1979a, pp. 55–57). Ellis considers that the goals of specialised rational–emotive therapy had better be directed to help patients achieve these eleven subgoals, and thus help them achieve what he calls a 'profound philosophic change', whilst recognising that in a large number of cases the therapist will have to settle for more conservative goals as in general RET. Furthermore, Ellis states that a major goal of RET is to help patients use what he calls 'the scientific method' in the future to test out hypotheses about self, others and the world.

Beck has not addressed himself in detail to describing the characteristics of emotionally healthy individuals. He does say, however, that cognitive therapy techniques are designed to help people 'identify, reality test and correct maladaptive distorted conceptualisations and the dysfunctional beliefs (schemas) underlying those cognitions' (Beck et al., 1979, p. 4). Emotionally healthy individuals are presumably, then, viewed as highly adept at such skills. From this, the goal of cognitive therapy can be seen as helping patients acquire and develop such skills – which is, in my opinion, more ambitious than Beck's subsequent statement: 'the goal of cognitive therapy is to relieve emotional distress and the other symptoms of depression' (Beck et al., 1979, p. 35).

It is doubtful that cognitive therapists generally adhere to a well-organised common philosophical position and consequently do not specify an equivalent list of subgoals. It is doubtful that they would have such aspirations. Indeed as J.E. Young (1982, personal communication) says, cognitive therapists place much more emphasis on modifying expectations than changing philosophies. At times, cognitive therapists share Ellis's views on self-acceptance, i.e. that a person had better accept himself not rate himself, but as Ellis has pointed out, they do not consistently take this position (Ellis, 1977i). However, implicit in their writings is the high regard given to the value of (1) realistic thinking and (2) functionality of thoughts, behaviours and emotions which may prove to be the cornerstone of any future theorising concerning the philosophical underpinnings of cognitive therapy. J.E. Young (1982, personal communication) adopts two major criteria in helping patients determine the functionality of their thoughts, feelings and behaviours: (1) Is it causing the patient unwanted symptoms? (2) Is it hurting others unnecessarily? The overlap between this concept of functionality and Ellis's concept of rationality, which he defines as that which aids and abets one's long-term goals of survival and happiness, is apparent.

Views on change processes

Both Beck and Ellis agree that, for thorough-going cognitive change, repeated rethinking and responding to dysfunctional cognitions is necessary. However, whilst Ellis advises national–emotive therapists to help patients do this forcefully and energetically, Beck does not address himself directly to the issue of force in any of his writings. By implication, however, force is not advocated within the therapeutic style of collaborative empiricism which, as we shall see, is one of the hallmarks of cognitive therapy. Burns (1980), a cognitive therapist, however, does describe and uses freely a technique which he calls 'externalisation of voices'* which does require patients to respond to their own dysfunctional cognitions in an energetic manner.

Whilst both Beck and Ellis stress the importance of behaviour change in effecting cognitive change, Beck and other cognitive therapists have traditionally advocated helping patients to try out new behaviours in a graded fashion, being careful not to expose them to undue discomfort. Cognitive change is deemed to occur when the patient processes and integrates the outcome of these behavioural assignments which are likely to be designed to test out his hypotheses. However, Ellis favours behavioural assignments which repeatedly expose patients 'at a jump' to uncomfortable and feared situations, arguing that for patients who will do it, these experiences bring about the greatest amount of cognitive change and help patients raise their level of frustration tolerance. Because, as we shall see, cognitive therapists value highly the stance of 'collaborative empiricism', they are likely to negotiate behavioural assignments which the patient feels he or she is able to handle. These are unlikely to be too demanding. It is my experience that a number of rational–emotive therapists adopt this approach rather than that of Ellis.

However, Beck, in very recent writings on shame, advocates that the person needs to have 'shameful' experiences in order to begin to see that such experiences are tolerable. Furthermore in a recent statement, Beck (1982,

---

*Alternatively called the 'point–counter point' technique (J.E. Young, 1982, personal communication).

personal communication) has said that whilst graded task assignments are recommended for use with depressed patients, exposure assignments are more effective with anxious patients. (Thus there seems to be a rapprochement in viewpoints on this issue.)

Practical Issues

Therapeutic style

A variety of RET therapists have made the point that it is not necessary to adopt Ellis's forceful style with most patients in order to practise effective RET (Walen, DiGiuseppe and Wessler, 1980; Wessler and Wessler, 1980) and Ellis himself does acknowledge that RET can be practised in many different styles, including one normally associated with client-centred therapists. However, Ellis (1979d) does consider that the preferred therapeutic style of rational–emotive therapists is one that emphasises both active–directiveness and therapeutic forcefulness. One main reason why Ellis advocates forcefulness as a preferred therapeutic style is due to his belief that there is a strong biological basis to human irrationality that had better be forcefully combated. In contrast, whilst Beck stresses that, in short-term treatment of depressed patients, active–directiveness is a preferred style, collaboration, rather than confrontation, is to be regarded as one of the most important hallmarks of cognitive therapy. Indeed as Young and Beck (1982) say, 'cognitive therapy ... consists of a particular therapeutic *style*, as well as a set of techniques'. This therapeutic style is called *collaborative empiricism*. The stance of collaborative empiricism is one in which the therapist ensures that he explains to the patient the rationale for everything that he does. Patient and therapist set an agenda at every session. The therapist helps the patient identify and question maladaptive cognitions through guided discovery. He frequently pauses and asks for feedback from patients to determine the impact of his therapeutic interventions, and basically clues patients into whatever is happening in the therapeutic endeavour. This style has influenced the practice of some rational–emotive therapists (e.g. Wessler and Wessler, 1980). Whenever I have heard Ellis's therapy sessions, whilst he does endeavour to develop a collaborative relationship with his clients, he does not by this definition adhere to the stance of collaborative empiricism. Ellis (1981, personal communication) has said that, with patients who are relatively undisturbed and non-defensive, it is possible to take such a stance in RET, but he would like to know exactly how Beck and his colleagues deal with what he calls 'difficult customers', namely the resistant, disturbed and defensive clients, which he says constitute the bulk of his clinical case-load. He hypothesises that adopting the collaborative empirical stance with such patients would have less effect than adopting a forceful stance. J.E. Young (1982, personal communication), however, has

said that, with patients who are particularly rigid in their thinking, a confrontative style can be employed in cognitive therapy when collaborative
empiricism has been exhausted. Such a confrontative style is used, however, as a last resort.

Therapeutic strategy

Rational–emotive therapists and cognitive therapists differ in the speed
with which therapists and patients move towards the identification and
modification of underlying maladaptive assumptions. In cognitive therapy,
the initial task of the therapist in dealing with a patient's cognitions is to
help him or her identify and correct his or her automatic thoughts. These
thoughts are one which the patient can identify first and constitute the tip
of the cognitive iceberg. This is repeated until tentative hypotheses can be
developed concerning both secondary and primary assumptions which
underlie these automatic thoughts. These hypotheses are either confirmed
or rejected as the result of the collection of more data. Such an approach is
lengthy and is usually reserved for the middle to later stages of therapy. This
entire procedure is based on the principle of *induction* because the cognitive therapist does not claim to know at the outset the nature of the
patient's cognitions that is centrally related to his or her emotional disturbance. He thus chips away from the outer layer of the automatic thoughts
to the inner core of the basic assumption. However, Ellis claims that he can
quickly discern the patient's cognitions which are centrally related to his
problem: namely the absolutistic evaluations which are either couched in
the form of a 'must' or in the form of a grossly exaggerated negative conclusion. Thus, it can be seen that Ellis is operating according to the principle of *deduction*. Ellis tends to refer to the patient's automatic thoughts (as
defined by Beck) only briefly and as a means to identify these irrational
beliefs. Thus, whilst Ellis is likely to go straight for the patient's evaluative
thinking and then deal with any remaining inferential distortions after doing
so, Beck and cognitive therapists in general are more likely to deal with
inferential cognitive distortions initially and only later, if at all, deal with the
patient's evaluative thinking. I say 'if at all' because, as we have seen,
patients' primary underlying assumptions do not in cognitive therapy necessarily take the form of evaluations. I would hypothesise that this difference is a distinguishing feature between rational–emotive therapists and
cognitive therapists in general.

Whilst I have outlined differences between rational–emotive therapists'
and cognitive therapists' typical strategic approaches, it is worth noting
that rational–emotive therapists claim more leeway in deviating from the
typical. In response Beck et al.'s criticism of rational–emotive therapists that
they often do not establish a solid database against which the patient's conclusions can be tested, Ellis says that:

... although RET therapists are not required to do this as you seem to do it, they can easily choose to do so. In many instances I would proceed almost exactly as your therapists did in the dialogue given in this section of the manual; in other instances, I might possibly proceed to discussing the patient's worth or her catastrophising – and in the course of doing so derive the 'solid data base' information. In a few other cases, I might help her to fully accept herself or to stop catastrophising without the data base information brought out in your instance - but with various other kinds of information brought out. RET does *not* have one special way of questioning and disputing.

(Ellis, quoted in Beck et al., 1979, p. 154)

However, it is my view that, in specialised RET, therapists would more probably proceed straight to patients' evaluative beliefs whilst, in general RET, they could and often do proceed as cognitive therapists would. One of the major reasons why cognitive therapists do not deviate from a standardised sequence of treatment procedures is that their outcome studies require standardised treatment. However, both rational–emotive and cognitive therapists need to be more mindful of the question: 'Is an early focus on inferential or evaluative cognitions likely to be more effective with this particular client?'

Therapeutic techniques

There are a number of differences between rational–emotive therapists and cognitive therapists in their use of techniques. Whilst Ellis claims that virtually every behavioural and cognitive technique that has ever been invented is used in general RET and thus presumably all the techniques that cognitive therapists have devised would fall under the rubric of general RET, I shall confine my statements to a comparison between specialised RET and cognitive therapy.

Whilst both rational–emotive therapists and cognitive therapists make use of inductive questioning or the 'Socratic dialogue' method, I have observed that cognitive therapists are likely to persist longer with this method than rational–emotive therapists. Rational–emotive therapists do tend to use explanations more frequently than do cognitive therapists and faced with patients who do not seem to benefit from the 'Socratic dialogue' are likely to dispense with this method sooner than cognitive therapists.

Both rational–emotive therapists and cognitive therapists are well known for asking their patients to look for evidence of their irrational evaluations and faulty inferences respectively. However, and this is a feature of Ellis's practice in particular, rational–emotive therapists are likely to ask for evidence of statements where no corroborating evidence is likely to exist. Thus, when a rational–emotive therapist asks a patient: 'Where is the evidence that you *must* succeed?', he knows, a priori, that there is in all probability no evidence that could corroborate such a statement. There are no behavioural experiments, for example, that a patient and therapist could construct, the results of which could in fact corroborate such a statement. Thus, rational-emotive therapists quite often ask patients for evidence concerning their irrational evaluations - matters which more appropriately belong to the realm of ideology.* These are questions which a patient can in fact answer while sitting in the therapist's armchair using reason alone. Ellis (1982, personal communication) has said that one main reason why he asks patients for evidence supporting their irrational beliefs is because patients often regard such beliefs as facts. However, cognitive therapists are more likely to ask patients for evidence concerning their inferences (hypotheses) where data can be gathered from the outside world to corroborate or falsify the hypotheses.

Thus, if a patient predicts that he will be laughed at when he walks into a room full of people, the cognitive therapist and patient can construct an experiment to test the validity of such an hypothesis. Cognitive therapists are not noted for asking patients for evidence concerning matters belonging to the realm of ideology. They prefer to limit their discussion of such matters to questioning patients concerning the functionality of adhering to such beliefs. Taking this example further, when a rational-emotive therapist asks the patient: 'Where is the evidence that it would be terrible if you are laughed at?' he knows there is in all probability only one answer to this question. He can further show the patient in the session that there is in all probability only one answer. The patient can even acknowledge the 'correct' ideological position. However, paradoxically, the patient will probably only believe in the 'correct' ideological position if he practises adhering to the new position in the outside world.

In my observations of cognitive therapists, it seems to me that one of the most important technical procedures that they have in their armamentarium is the use of the Daily Record of Dysfunctional Thoughts (DRDT) form. This has been verified by I. Herman (1981, personal communication). By contrast, although there are a number of written homework forms that have been devised by rational-emotive therapists, these are neither employed consistently nor seen as a major therapeutic change agent. I believe this may be because rational-emotive therapists do not pay much attention to the role of automatic thoughts in emotional disturbance as do cognitive therapists.

Whilst both Beck and Ellis recommend the use of imagery techniques, Beck and other cognitive therapists employ a wider range of imagery methods than does Ellis who employs mainly rational-emotive imagery (Ellis and Abrahms, 1978) and sexual imagery in the treatment of sexual problems. However, other rational-emotive therapists such as Wessler (Wessler and Wessler, 1980; Wessler, 1982b) are more similar to cognitive therapists in employing a wide variety of imagery procedures.

---

*Here it is again to be noted that Ellis (1977h) refers to such irrational evaluations as 'ideologies'.

As we have seen, rational–emotive therapists and cognitive therapists are likely to favour different types of behavioural assignment. Cognitive therapists are more likely to employ behavioural assignments in the service of helping patients to test faulty inferences or hypotheses (for example, they can be used quite early on in the treatment of a severely withdrawn depressed patient who hypothesises that he could not read even a sentence of a book). Rational–emotive therapists, and Ellis in particular, are likely to employ behavioural assignments, primarily in the service of changing evaluations. As a result, such behavioural assignments often aim to recreate patients' worst fears so as to enable them to see that they can cope with the worst. As we have seen, Ellis often advocates behavioural assignments based on the principle of flooding in order to help patients raise their level of frustration tolerance. He would criticise the use of graded behavioural assignments which are used in cognitive therapy particularly with depressed patients as often doing little to change a patient's philosophy of LFT. In fact he argues that such graded task assignments communicate the implicit message 'Yes, you do need to go slowly, you cannot stand to expose yourself to more discomfort than this' (Ellis, 1983c). Cognitive therapists would counter that to urge most patients (particularly those who are depressed) to full exposure would threaten the therapeutic alliance and be against the spirit of collaborative empiricism. However, cognitive therapists and patients could very well negotiate flooding assignments if so desired within such collaborative guidelines. It is my impression, however, that they do not do so frequently, although they aim to do this in their future work with anxious patients.

Due to the fact that cognitive therapists adhere to the collaborative empiricism stance, this prohibits the use of certain techniques which rational–emotive therapists would employ. For example, paradoxical procedures are not advocated in cognitive therapy because the explanation of the rationale underlying a paradoxical procedure would in fact negate the impact of the procedure. Furthermore cognitive therapists are not encouraged to use the somewhat flamboyant and dramatic interventions rational–emotive therapists sometimes employ which, while possibly having a great amount of therapeutic impact for the patient, may backfire (see Chapter 12). In this regard rational–emotive therapists are greater risk-takers than cognitive therapists. In addition, rational–emotive therapists make more of a concerted effort to use humour in their interventions to help patients take life less seriously. As R. DiGiuseppe (1982, personal communication) has said, rational–emotive therapists are freer than cognitive therapists to use a wide range of educational and social psychological methods to help change maladaptive cognitions and beliefs.

Finally, in the correction of maladaptive basic assumptions, cognitive therapists are likely to emphasise pragmatic arguments to help patients change the nature of these assumptions and are less likely than rational–emotive therapists to help patients see the philosophical errors inherent in their assumptions. Rational-emotive therapists use both pragmatic and philosophical arguments in helping patients to give up their irrational beliefs.

Conclusion

Rational-emotive therapy's strengths lie in the fact that it is based on a well-developed and well-articulated set of philosophical formulations provided primarily by Albert Ellis. Until very recently, rational-emotive therapists have not had recourse to a treatment manual and even now such guidelines as have been provided in these manuals (Ellis and Abrahms, 1978; Walen, DiGiuseppe and Wessler, 1980) lack the specificity of those provided for cognitive therapists (e.g. in Beck et al., 1979), especially over the whole course of therapy.

Cognitive therapy's strengths lie in the careful work that has gone into the development of clear and precise treatment manuals which can be used in outcome studies. Its weaknesses lie in the fact that such practical advances have far outstripped the development of its philosophical underpinnings. This could be a focus for future work.

There are signs that rational-emotive therapists are being influenced by the activities of Beck and his colleagues and also vice versa. In my opinion, one of the strengths of cognitive therapy has been the careful attention that Beck and his colleagues have paid to maximising the use of valuable therapeutic time. Thus agenda setting, careful attention to the development and maintenance of the collaborative working alliance are features which some rational-emotive supervisors are now encouraging their supervisees to employ (Walen, DiGiuseppe and Wessler, 1980; Wessler and Wessler, 1980). Conversely, it is my hypothesis that, as cognitive therapists adopt the same careful study of anxiety disorders as they have of depressive disorders, they will, and there is some evidence that this is already happening, learn the value of encouraging patients to greater behavioural risks in overcoming one of the major bases of anxiety disorders, i.e. discomfort anxiety. Indeed I believe that cognitive therapists have a lot to learn from Albert Ellis about discomfort anxiety, and there are signs that they are beginning to do so. This process of mutual influence will continue given greater contact between rational-emotive therapists and cognitive therapists.

Acknowledgements

I am grateful to the following people with whom I discussed some of the issues which appear in this chapter and/or who gave feedback on earlier drafts: Aaron T. Beck, Ray DiGiuseppe, Albert Ellis, Art Freeman, Ray Harrison, Ira Herman, George Lockwood, Sue Walen, Richard Wessler, Ruth Wessler and Jeff Young. However, only the author is responsible for the chapter's content.

Chapter 20
Compromises in
Rational–Emotive Therapy

Introduction

In this chapter I will discuss the notion that whilst RET therapists prefer to encourage their clients to achieve a profound philosophical change by replacing their irrational beliefs with rational beliefs, this is not always possible. In such cases, RET therapists are advised to make various compromises in helping clients deal with their problems in ways which do not involve philosophical change. These alternative strategies are termed 'compromises' in that, whilst not ideal, they often bear more fruit than the preferred strategies of RET.

I should say at the outset that by RET in this chapter I mean those therapeutic activities which are designed to effect philosophical change – or what Ellis calls 'elegant', 'preferential' or 'specialised' RET. I personally consider that therapeutic activities which are designed to effect other kinds of change (e.g. inferentially based change, behaviourally based change or change in activating events) are best referred to as derived from other approaches to cognitive-behaviour therapy, although Ellis considers such activities to be part of 'inelegant', 'non-preferential' or 'general' RET. Because terms such as 'elegant' vs 'inelegant', 'preferential' vs 'non-preferential' etc. are value-laden and may offend other cognitively oriented practitioners, I prefer to avoid their use and thus distinguish between rational–emotive therapy and other forms of cognitive-behaviour therapy. This distinction is more likely, in my opinion, to promote constructive dialogue among cognitively oriented therapists than the one employed by Ellis (1980b).

Before discussing the various compromises that RET therapists sometimes are called upon to make, it is first important to distinguish between rational–emotive therapy and other approaches to cognitive–behaviour therapy.

First published in 1987.

Differences between Rational–Emotive Therapy and Other Approaches to Cognitive–Behaviour Therapy

As opposed to other approaches to cognitive-behaviour therapy, rational-emotive therapy:

1. Has a distinct philosophical emphasis which is one of its central features and which other forms of cognitive-behaviour therapy appear to omit. Thus, it stresses that humans appraise themselves, others and the world in terms of (a) rational, preferential, flexible and tolerant philosophies and in terms of (b) irrational, musturbatory, rigid, intolerant and absolutistic philosophies.

2. Has an existential-humanistic outlook which is intrinsic to it and which is omitted by most other approaches to cognitive-behaviour therapy. Thus, it sees people 'as holistic, goal directed individuals who have importance in the world just because they are human and alive; it unconditionally accepts them with their limitations, and it particularly focuses upon their experiences and values, including their self-actualising potentialities' (Ellis, 1980b, p. 327). It also shares the views of ethical humanism by encouraging people to emphasise human interest (self and social) over the interests of deities, material objects and lower animals.

3. Favours striving for pervasive and long-lasting (philosophically based) rather than symptomatic change.

4. Attempts to help humans eliminate all self-ratings and views self-esteem as a self-defeating concept which encourages them to make conditional evaluations of self. Instead, it teaches people unconditional self-acceptance (Ellis, 1972a).

5. Considers psychological disturbance to reflect an attitude of taking life 'too' seriously and thus advocates the appropriate use of various humorous therapeutic methods (Ellis, 1977a, 1981b).

6. Stresses the use of antimusturbatory rather than anti-empirical disputing methods. Because it considers that inferential distortions often stem from dogmatic musts, shoulds etc., rational-emotive therapy favours going to the philosophical core of emotional disturbance and disputing the irrational beliefs at this core, rather than merely disputing anti-empirical inferences which are more peripheral. Also rational-emotive therapy favours the use of forceful logico-empirical disputing of irrational beliefs whenever possible, rather than the employment of rationally oriented, coping self-statements. When feasible, rational-emotive therapy teaches clients how to become their own scientists instead of parroting therapist inculcated rational beliefs.

7. Gives a more central explanatory role to the concept of discomfort anxiety in psychological disturbance than do other cognitive- behavioural approaches to psychotherapy. Discomfort anxiety is defined as: 'emotional hypertension that arises when people feel (1) that their life or comfort is threatened, (2) that they *must* not feel uncomfortable and have to feel at ease and (3) that it is awful or terrible (rather than merely inconvenient or disadvantageous) when they don't get what they supposedly must' (Ellis, 1980b, p. 331). Whilst other cognitive–behavioural approaches to psychotherapy recognise specific instances of discomfort anxiety (e.g. 'fear of fear' – Mackay, 1984), they tend not to regard discomfort disturbance to be as centrally implicated in psychological problems as does rational–emotive therapy.

8. Emphasises, more than other approaches to cognitive–behaviour therapy, that humans frequently make themselves disturbed about their original disturbances. Thus, rational–emotive therapists actively look for secondary symptoms of disturbances and encourage clients to work on overcoming these before addressing themselves to the primary disturbance.

9. Has clear-cut theories of disturbance and its treatment, but is eclectic or multimodal in its techniques. However, it favours some techniques (e.g. active disputing) over others (e.g. cognitive distraction) and strives for profound philosophical change where feasible.

10. Discriminates between 'appropriate' and 'inappropriate' negative emotions. Rational–emotive theory considers such negative emotions as sadness, annoyance, concern, regret and disappointment as 'appropriate' affective responses to thwarted desires based on a non-devout philosophy of desires and it views them as healthy when they do not needlessly interfere with people's goals and purposes. However, it sees depression, anger, anxiety, guilt, shame/embarrassment, self-pity and feelings of inadequacy usually as 'inappropriate' emotions based on absolutistic demands about thwarted desires. Rational–emotive therapy considers these latter feelings as symptoms of disturbance because they very frequently (but not always) sabotage people from pursuing constructively their goals and purposes. Other approaches to cognitive–behaviour therapy do not make such fine discriminations between 'appropriate' and 'inappropriate' negative emotions.

11. Advocates therapists giving unconditional acceptance rather than giving warmth or approval to clients. Other cognitive–behaviour therapies tend not to make this distinction. Rational–emotive therapy holds that counsellor warmth and approval have their distinct dangers in that they may unwittingly encourage clients to strengthen their dire needs for love and approval. When RET therapists unconditionally accept their clients, they also serve as good role-models, in that they also help clients to accept themselves unconditionally.

12. Stresses the importance of the use of vigour and force in counteracting irrational philosophies and behaviours (Ellis, 1979c; Dryden, 1984a). Rational-emotive therapy is alone among cognitive-behavioural approaches to psychotherapy in stressing that humans are, for the most part, biologically predisposed to originate and perpetuate their disturbances and often thus experience great difficulty in changing the ideological roots of these problems. Because it holds this view, it urges both therapists and clients to use considerable force and vigour in interrupting clients' irrationalities.

13. Is more selective than most other cognitive-behaviour therapies in choosing behavioural change methods. Thus, it favours the use of penalisation in encouraging resistant clients to change. Often these clients will not change to obtain positive reinforcement, but may be encouraged to change to avoid stiff penalties. Furthermore, rational-emotive practitioners have reservations concerning the use of social reinforcement in psychotherapy. They consider that humans are too reinforceable and that they often do the right thing for the wrong reason. Thus, they may change to please their socially reinforcing therapists, but in doing so they have not been encouraged to think and act for their own sake. RET therapists aim to help clients become maximally non-conformist, non-dependent and individualistic and would thus use social reinforcement techniques sparingly. Finally, rational-emotive therapy favours the use of in vivo desensitisation and flooding methods rather than the use of gradual desensitisation techniques because it argues that the former procedures best help clients to raise their level of frustration tolerance (Ellis, 1983c).

Thus, the major goal of rational-emotive therapy is an ambitious one: to encourage clients to make a profound philosophical change in the two main areas of ego disturbance and discomfort disturbance. This involves helping clients, as far as humanly possible, to give up their irrational beliefs and to replace these with rational beliefs.

In summary, in rational-emotive therapy, the major goals are to help clients pursue their long-range basic goals and purposes and to help them do so as effectively as possible by fully accepting themselves and tolerating unchangeable uncomfortable life conditions. Rational-emotive practitioners further strive to help clients obtain the skills which they can use to prevent the development of future disturbance. In encouraging clients to achieve and maintain this profound philosophical change, rational-emotive therapists implement the following strategies. They help their clients see that:

1. Emotional and behavioural disturbances have cognitive antecedents and that these cognitions normally take the form of absolutistic irrational beliefs. RET therapists train their clients to observe their own psychological disturbances and to trace these back to their ideological roots.

2. People have a distinct measure of self-determination and can thus decide
   to work at undisturbing themselves. Thus, clients are shown that they
   are not slaves to their biologically based irrational thinking processes.
3. People can implement their choices and maximise their freedom by
   actively working at changing their irrational beliefs. This is best achieved
   by employing cognitive, emotive and behavioural methods - often in
   quite a forceful and vigorous manner (Ellis, 1979d).

With the majority of clients, from the first session onwards, RET therapists are likely to use strategies designed to effect profound philosophical
change. The therapist begins the process with the hypothesis that this particular client may be able to achieve such change and thus begins to implement rational-emotive methods which he or she will abandon after collecting sufficient data to reject this initial hypothesis. Rational-emotive
practitioners regularly implement this viewpoint which is based on the
notion that the client's response to therapy is the best indicator of his or her
prognosis.

Compromises

When it is clear that the client is not able to achieve philosophical change,
whether on a particular issue or in general, the rational-emotive therapist
often uses other cognitive-behavioural methods to effect less 'profound'
changes. Because in such cases, these methods yield better results for the
client than can be achieved by standard rational-emotive methods, they are
regarded as compromises yielding an outcome between no change, on the
one hand, and profound philosophical change, on the other.

Inferentially based change

Inferentially based change occurs when clients do not change irrational
beliefs but do succeed in correcting distorted inferences such as negative
predictions, overly negative interpretations of events and of the behaviour
of others etc.

A good example of such change was reported by a therapist of my acquaintance. He was working with a middle-aged woman who reported feeling furious every time her ageing father would telephone her and enquire 'Noo,
what's doing?' She inferred that this was a gross invasion of her privacy and
absolutistically insisted that he had no right to act in this way. The therapist
initially intervened with the usual rational-emotive strategy by attempting to
dispute this client's dogmatic belief and tried to help her see that there was
no law in the universe which stated that he must not invade her privacy.
Meeting initial resistance, the therapist persisted with different variations of
this theme - all to no avail. Changing tack, he began to implement a different
strategy designed to help the client question her inference that her father

was actually invading her privacy. Given her father's age, the therapist enquired, was it not more likely that his question represented his usual manner of beginning telephone conversations rather than an intense desire to pry into her affairs? This enquiry proved successful in that the client's rage subsided because she began to re-interpret her father's motives.

Another example of inferentially based change occurred with one of my clients, Robert, who was anxious lest people would stare at him for spilling his drink. His hands would shake whenever he attempted to drink in public. I first employed the customary philosophically based RET strategy, encouraging him to assume the worst and imagine that people would actually stare at him when he spilled his drink. This yielded his irrational belief: 'If they stare at me, it would prove that I would be a worthless freak.' However, I could not encourage him to dispute this belief successfully and he still adhered strongly to it after my varied disputing efforts. Changing tack, I took him to several pubs and asked him to observe other people's reaction as I deliberately spilled drinks in public. From this, he came to realise that other people in general did not stare at me when I spilled my drinks and this helped him to change his own inference to: 'It is unlikely that most people will stare at me when I spill my drink.' This inferentially based change enabled him to order and consume drink in public and reduce his social anxiety, although he never did change his aforementioned irrational belief.

Interestingly, in both examples, although my fellow therapist and I returned to disputing our clients' irrational beliefs after helping them to modify their distorted inferences, we never succeeded in helping them to change these beliefs. However, some clients are more willing to re-evaluate their irrational beliefs after they have been helped to correct distorted inferences. Rational–emotive theory holds that irrational beliefs are the breeding ground for the development of negative inferences and thus, when clients succeed in changing their irrational beliefs, spontaneous reduction in the negativity of inferences will follow. However, these two examples show that inferentially based change can occur in the absence of philosophically based change.

Behaviourally based change

Behaviourally based change occurs when clients do not change irrational beliefs, but improve by effecting constructive changes in behaviour. Such behaviour change, in my experience, occurs when clients (1) replace dysfunctional behaviour with constructive behaviour and (2) acquire constructive patterns of behaviour which previously have been absent from their skill repertoire. An example of each follows.

Replacing dysfunctional behaviour with constructive behaviour

Sylvia, a first year student, sought therapy for extreme examination anxiety. She predicted that she would fail her first year exams, demanded that she must pass them and concluded that should she fail, this would be the 'end of the world'. No amount of disputing her irrational beliefs yielded any therapeutic gain, so I shifted to her test-taking behaviour. I discovered that Sylvia approached an examination in the following way. She would choose to answer the first question that she knew anything about; she would write everything she knew about that question without first making an answer plan and would often only answer two out of four questions in the entire examination. It thus transpired that her inferences concerning failure were accurate rather than negatively distorted. My subsequent therapeutic approach focused on teaching Sylvia the following examination techniques: allocating sufficient time to answer all questions; analysing the wording of examination questions; making answer plans; answering all parts of a given question; and dealing with 'mind blank' experiences through cognitive distraction. With the help of her department, I arranged for Sylvia to take several 'mock' examinations so that she could practise her newly acquired skills with the result that she performed very well in these examinations. These experiences helped Sylvia to predict success in her 'end-of-year' examinations rather than failure. This led to a significant decrease in her examination anxiety. However, although Sylvia did in fact do very well in her exams, she still held the same irrational beliefs about failure as she did at the outset and did not want to focus on these later as she thought failure to be 'so unlikely that it's not worth considering'.

This example clearly shows that behaviour change often leads to inferentially based change.

Acquiring new skills

Mrs Anderson was referred to me with problems of anger and depression. Her husband and two teenage children expected her to go out to work, do all the housework without help and cater to their every whim. She had done this for several years, but had become increasingly angry and depressed. Her anger was based on the irrational belief that they must not treat her this way and her depression stemmed from the belief that she was no good for failing to please her family. Traditional rational–emotive disputing methods failed to yield any therapeutic gains so I shifted the focus of therapy to a discussion of assertion and the value of politely declining to do the bidding of her family. Through role-play methods it transpired that Mrs Anderson did not have assertive skills in her repertoire because she could only communicate in an aggressive and demanding manner. I thus trained her intensively in polite, negative assertive skills which she was able to put into practice with her family. Surprisingly her family responded quite well to her behaviour, began to share household tasks and made less demands upon her. The result was that Mrs Anderson's depressed mood lifted appreciably and she became far less angry. As in the other examples in this chapter, I returned to disputing her irrational belief as outlined above but again without success.

This example shows that a client's behavioural changes can sometimes elicit constructive behaviour from others leading to healthy changes in the interpersonal system of which the client is a part.

Changing activating events

I concluded the above example with the observation that a client's change in behaviour can promote healthy system-based change. However, this does not always occur. In a similar case to that described above, I had to involve the client's husband and children in therapy and encourage them to change their behaviour towards the depressed client, Mrs Curran, because her own assertive efforts did not on this occasion elicit constructive responses from her family members. Once they changed their behaviour towards Mrs Curran for the better, her mood lifted accordingly. Again disputing efforts aimed at helping Mrs Curran to re-evaluate her irrational beliefs, pre- and post-improvement, did not lead to philosophically based change.

In another example of helping clients by promoting changes in activating events, I helped Mr Brown to overcome his depression by encouraging him to change his vocation from accountancy to law. He was depressed because he believed: 'I have to enjoy my job in order to be happy.' No amount of disputing this belief yielded any therapeutic gain so I switched the focus of the sessions to exploring his vocational interests and aptitudes. This led Mr Brown to conclude that he would be happier working as a solicitor than as an accountant. Accordingly, he decided to go to law school. Years later, after he qualified as a solicitor, I met Mr Brown who had effected a successful career change. He still believed that he had to be vocationally satisfied in order to be happy but since he was happy working in law he considered that there was no need to re-evaluate this irrational belief.

Challenging but not overwhelming: a compromise in negotiating homework assignments

Ellis (1983c) has recently criticised the use of gradual approaches to helping clients overcome their emotional and behavioural problems. His argument is that the use of gradual methods in psychotherapy and behaviour therapy reinforces 'a philosophy that states or implies that (1) emotional change has to be brought about slowly and cannot possibly occur quickly or suddenly; (2) that it must be practically painless as it is occurring; and (3) that it cannot occur with the use of jarring, painful, flooding methods of therapy' (p. 142). Thus, psychotherapeutic gradualism is seen by Ellis as counter-therapeutic in that it basically reinforces clients' discomfort anxiety or philosophy of low frustration tolerance (LFT) which serve to perpetuate rather than ameliorate their problems. He thus prefers wherever possible the use of flooding or 'full-exposure' methods and homework assignments in RET, primarily because they help clients to overcome their discomfort anxiety and to raise their tolerance level for frustration.

However, 'wherever possible' is the important phrase to note here because not all clients will agree to execute flooding or 'full-exposure' homework assignments. That this should be the rational–emotive therapists' initial approach to negotiating homework assignments is not questioned here. In taking this stance, therapists should explain the rationale for this type of homework assignment, emphasise the benefits of such an approach and encourage clients to implement these assignments after thoroughly disputing clients' LFT ideas. What rational–emotive therapists are in fact saying is: 'Such methods are the most efficient means of helping you achieve your therapeutic goals.' It is not surprising that Ellis should recommend such assignments, given his belief in the value of efficiency in psychotherapy (Ellis, 1980d).

However, no matter how therapists try to encourage (or persuade) some clients to execute 'full-exposure' homework assignments, such clients steadfastly refuse to do so. In the face of such opposition, if therapists persist in their persuasive tactics, they will commit two therapeutic errors. First, they will threaten the therapeutic alliance between themselves and their 'resistant' clients. Bordin (1979) has noted that there are three major components of this alliance: goals, bonds and tasks. In such instances, the therapeutic alliance is likely to break down in the *task* domain. Although therapist and client may have a good collaborative relationship (effective bonds) and agree on the client's goals (shared goals), they disagree about the tasks that the client is prepared to do in order to achieve therapeutic goals. Secondly, such overly persistent therapists serve as poor role-models because they tend to believe that clients *must* be 'efficient' in their approach to therapy and do 'full-exposure' assignments. Paradoxically, these therapists, by insisting that clients execute certain types of homework assignments, are in fact being inefficient themselves. A breakdown in the therapeutic alliance often leads to therapeutic impasses which in turn often lead to clients dropping out of treatment.

In such cases, what should therapists preferably do? There is no need to return to therapeutic gradualism, for there is another alternative which allows therapists and clients to effect a working compromise. Whenever I encounter clients who steadfastly refuse to execute 'full-exposure' homework tasks and prefer gradual assignments, I explain this therapeutic compromise. I invite them to choose assignments which are sufficiently *challenging* to discourage reinforcement of their philosophy of low frustration tolerance, but which are not *overwhelming* for them. I explain their choices thus:

> There are three ways you can overcome your fears. The first is like jumping in at the deep end. You expose yourself straight away to the situation you are most afraid of. The advantage here is that if you can learn that nothing terrible will happen then you

will overcome your problems quite quickly. However, the disadvantage is that some people just can't bring themselves to do this and get quite discouraged as a result. The second way is to go very gradually. On the one hand, you only do something that you feel comfortable doing, while on the other, you don't really get an opportunity to face putting up with discomfort which, in my opinion, is a major feature of your problem. Also treatment will take much longer this way. The third way is what I call 'challenging but not overwhelming'. Here you choose an assignment which is sufficiently challenging for you to make progress but which would not be overwhelming for you at any given stage. Here you are likely to make progress more quickly than with the gradual approach but more slowly than with the 'deep end' approach.

I find that when clients are given an opportunity to choose their own rate of progress, the therapeutic alliance is strengthened. Most clients who refuse to execute 'full-exposure' assignments choose the 'challenging but not overwhelming' approach and only very rarely do they opt for gradual desensitisation therapy. When they do so I do try to dissuade them and frequently succeed. In the final analysis, however, I have not found it productive to insist that clients choose a particular way of tackling problems that is against their preferences.

Case example

Mary, a 23-year-old, single woman came to therapy for help in overcoming her anxiety about eating in public. Typically she had both ego and discomfort anxiety-related beliefs (Ellis, 1979b, 1980a), and in the early sessions I helped her to identify and dispute such self-defeating attitudes as: 'I must not be anxious while eating'; 'If other people see me leave my food they will think I'm odd and I need their approval'; 'I am a shameful individual for having this problem'; 'There is something wrong with me because I have a small appetite' and 'I must not make a fuss and draw attention to myself'.

She claimed that her anxiety would be at its peak if she were faced with the prospect of not finishing her food in a crowded, fashionable restaurant. However, although she was successful at verbally disputing both ego and discomfort anxiety-related beliefs about this incident in therapy sessions, she could not initially conceive of putting this into practice in this particular setting even though I presented the rationale for 'full-exposure' homework assignments and emphasised the benefits that she would experience as a result. She literally could not imagine herself doing it (a good sign that such an experience would, in her terms, be too traumatic). She enquired whether there was not a painless method for overcoming her problems. I explained the dangers of such 'painless' methods and introduced her to the idea of 'challenging, but not overwhelming' tasks. She agreed, albeit with some reluctance, to select such an assignment. My hunch was that she would have terminated therapy if I had persisted in persuading her to expose herself fully to her anxieties. Over the following weeks she set herself and successfully executed the following 'challenging, but not overwhelming' tasks while disputing her salient irrational beliefs. These tasks were in temporal order:

1. Eating two squares of chocolate in a public eating place.
2. Eating a meal of fish and chips on her own in a crowded restaurant, full of strangers.

3. Eating out in a snack bar with her boyfriend.
4. Eating out with her parents in a semi-fashionable restaurant.
5. Eating out with her boyfriend in a fashionable restaurant.
6. Deliberately asking for smaller portions in a fashionable restaurant.
7. Eating out with a large group of friends in a very exclusive restaurant, sending back any portions that were too big.

As I have said, each task was seen by the client as 'sufficiently' challenging but not overwhelming and tasks (5), (6) and (7) were initiated by her in a planned break from therapy. This principle allows clients to take responsibility for their therapy quite early on, once they have fully understood it and experienced initial success. On follow-up, she was able to eat out in a variety of settings with a variety of people without anxiety.

Variations on a theme

Whilst I have not used the 'challenging, but not overwhelming' principle in planning a hierarchy of assignments before treatment commences, it can be used in this way. I have not found this necessary because what clients find 'challenging but not overwhelming' changes over time so that the initial hierarchy becomes redundant. Theoretically, therapists could also use SUDS (subjective unit of distress scale) ratings of hierarchy and/or non-hierarchy items, although, again, I have not found this necessary.

Whilst I have used this principle mainly in helping clients set appropriate challenging tasks to overcome their anxiety problems, I have also used it successfully in helping depressed clients set appropriately challenging behavioural tasks. In so doing I stress to clients the importance of defining what is challenging in personal terms in relation to their depressed state rather than in relation to their non-depressed state. The successful execution of small tasks deemed personally challenging by depressed clients when they are depressed, is highly encouraging for such clients and makes them more amenable to the subsequent use of more traditional cognitive changes procedures (Beck et al., 1979).

In conclusion, the negotiation of 'challenging, but not overwhelming' homework assignments is seen as a healthy compromise between therapists and clients when the latter are overly threatened by the prospect of fully exposing themselves to their anxieties. Such tasks enable clients to execute homework assignments without unduly reinforcing their low frustration tolerance ideas and help to preserve the therapeutic alliance between the protagonists. I maintain that in such circumstances it is a highly pragmatic and efficient approach to negotiating homework assignments, in that it provides clients with the best available (acceptable) means to achieve therapeutic ends.

Conclusion

In this chapter I have considered the various compromises that RET therapists may be called upon to make when they cannot help their clients achieve philosophically based change. Rather than persist with traditional rational–emotive methods that do not prove to be effective, RET therapists can still help their clients by encouraging them to change inferences, behaviour or activating events.

There are, of course, problems associated with such compromises:

1. Clients who succeed in changing negative inferences may later encounter events that realise their inferences. As they have not changed their irrational beliefs they make themselves disturbed about such events. Thus, the client of my colleague may later discover that her father in fact had been prying into her affairs and my own client with social anxiety (Robert) may later encounter a group of people who will notice his anxiety and stare at him.

2. Clients who do change their behaviour for the better may still encounter events which serve to activate their latent unchanged irrational beliefs. Thus, Sylvia, my client with examination anxiety, may in the future fail an important examination and Mrs Anderson's family may again make unreasonable demands upon her.

3. Clients who change or remove themselves from problematic activating events may later re-encounter such situations which again may activate their latent unmodified irrational beliefs. Thus, Mrs Curran's family may later mistreat her and Mr Brown's enthusiasm for the law may wane.

4. Clients who overcome their problems by using 'challenging, but not over-whelming' methods are still vulnerable to 'overwhelming' situations.

Whilst I have described cases where productive changes in inferences, behaviour and situations have not led to belief change, other clients do later change their irrational beliefs after effecting such changes. Yet, although RET theory has emphasised the interdependence of ABC factors, I have endeavoured to show here that change, particularly at the level of beliefs ('B'), does not necessarily follow changes achieved at 'A' or 'C'.

The implications of this chapter for empirical study are clear. It would be helpful to research such questions as:

1. 'With which clients, and at which stages of the therapeutic process, are belief change (inference change, behaviour change and situation change) methods appropriate?'

2. 'Under which conditions do changes in inferences, behaviour and situations lead to belief change and when do they not promote such change?'

Finally, given the way I have chosen to distinguish rational–emotive therapy from other approaches to cognitive-behaviour therapy, and given my arguments about 'compromises' in RET, I conclude with the intriguing notion that RET therapists do not only practise RET! Indeed it would be fascinating to research the question: 'When do RET therapists practise RET and when do they not do so?'

Chapter 21
Rational–Emotive Therapy and Eclecticism

Eclecticism has been defined as 'consisting of that which has been selected from diverse sources, systems or styles' (*American Heritage Dictionary of the English Language*, 1971) and much has been recently written on eclectic approaches in psychotherapy (e.g. Lazarus, 1976; Shostrom, 1976; Dryden, 1980b; Garfield, 1980). However, there have been few attempts to clarify the decisions that clinicians make in broadening their therapeutic repertoire by selecting from diverse therapeutic orientation. The aim of this chapter is to show what guides rational–emotive therapists in such endeavours.

Rational–emotive theory states that much emotional disturbance stems from the faulty inferences and irrational evaluations that patients make in endeavouring to make sense of themselves, other people and the world (Wessler and Wessler, 1980). Examples of faulty inferences have been detailed by Beck et al. (1979) and include arbitrary inferences, overgeneralisations and selective abstractions. Irrational evaluations are based on a philosophy of demandingness which hinders patients from achieving their long-term goals and restricts their opportunities to live effectively and creatively in the world. The major task of rational–emotive therapists is to help patients correct their faulty inferences and to replace their demanding philosophy with a desiring philosophy, i.e. one which is characterised by wants, preferences and wishes. To achieve their basic task, rational–emotive therapists focus on cognitive, affective and behavioural factors and consequently RET has been described as a comprehensive system of therapy (Ellis and Abrahms, 1978).

Rational–emotive psychotherapists then are guided by a particular theory of emotional disturbance and personality change (Ellis, 1978b) and thus can be contrasted with eclectic therapists who de-emphasise theory.

First published in 1982.

Theory is considered important by rational–emotive therapists for a number of reasons. First, theory provides testable propositions for empirical study. Secondly, as Frank (1970) has shown theory helps therapists gain emotional support from others with similar views and thus helps sustain the therapist's morale. The third and most important reason is that theory helps guide therapists in their work, helps them correctly select particular therapeutic procedures and gives them a framework for determining the consequences of such procedures. Eysenck (1970) also stresses the need for theory in psychotherapy and warns that without a theoretical framework the practice of eclectic therapists would be characterised by 'a mishmash of theories, a hugger-mugger of procedures, a charivaria of therapies and a gallimaufry of activities having no proper rationale and incapable of being tested or evaluated' (p. 145).

Therapeutic Practice

In the execution of their major task – effecting cognitive change – rational-emotive therapists attempt to engage patients in a concrete and situationally based exploration of their problems. To encourage concreteness, therapists tend to use explicitly an implicit ABCDE framework in exploring their patients' problems. Point 'A' in the framework represents an event or the patients' perceptions and inferences concerning that event. 'B' represents the patient's beliefs or evaluations about the phenomenal event, whilst 'C' stands for the emotional and behavioural consequences of the patient's beliefs. At point 'D' the therapist's task is to help the patient challenge his faulty inferences and irrational evaluations and replace them with more realistic and rational cognitions which leads to emotional and behavioural change at point 'E'.

In practice rational-emotive therapists tend to start at point C. The major goal here is to help patients acknowledge their feelings (without dwelling on them) and to identify their actions. In doing so the therapist may very well use procedures derived from other therapeutic systems. For example, if a patient experiences difficulty in acknowledging feelings, the rational-emotive therapist might employ a gestalt awareness exercise or psychodramatic technique with the specific purpose at this stage of encouraging the patient to acknowledge feelings.

After helping the patient to identify correctly emotional and behavioural responses, the therapist shifts his or her attention to the context in which such responses arise (point A). Exploration at this point involves the therapist paying attention to the patient's description of the relevant context. The patient is helped to describe his perception of the relevant situation fairly briefly. The therapist tends not to dwell upon those events and discourages the patient from presenting too many or problem-irrelevant contexts. The goal of the therapist is to aid the patient in adequately framing the problem so that he or she can assist in the identification and correction of presently held faulty inferences and beliefs. In practice the context tends to be either one that is anticipated or one of recent occurrence and thus RET tends to be a present- and future-oriented approach to therapy. Rational–emotive therapists tend not to focus on events that have occurred in the distant past since it is argued that such exploration does not aid the correction of presently held faulty cognitions (Ellis, 1962). However, I have found that in certain circumstances such exploration does assist the therapist in his or her dissuasion strategies with some patients Dryden (1979). Thus understanding the likely origins of presently held beliefs may motivate such patients to change such beliefs. The point at issue here is that the purpose of exploring such past events is to facilitate the disputing of *presently* held inferences and beliefs.

At point B in the ABCDE framework, the therapist's task is to help the patient identify the irrational evaluations that the latter employs in appraising the relevant context. Here the therapist is not limited to verbal interventions such as: 'What are you saying to yourself?', that are often seen in therapy transcripts. In fact, in the author's experience a common answer to such questions is – 'nothing'. In addition to psychodrama (Nardi, 1979) and gestalt methods, various role-playing and imagery methods may be used as an aid to facilitate the discovery of irrational beliefs. Indeed, person-centred procedures for some patients may be employed. Such patients find the less active–directive style implicit in such procedures helpful in exploring and discovering meanings and beliefs (DiLoreto, 1971). Rather than abandon RET for person-centred therapy, an eclectic rational–emotive therapist would vary his or her therapeutic style but not the theoretical underpinnings of her system.

Point D in the framework is also called the dissuasion process (Wessler and Wessler, 1980). On attempting to dissuade the patient, the therapist may use a wide variety of cognitive, imaginal, affective and behavioural methods, and may suggest similar procedures for the patient to use between sessions as the latter strives to put into practice in everyday life what he or she has learned in therapy (point E).

Theory-inspired Guidelines for Choosing Appropriate Therapeutic Procedures

Thus far it has been argued that rational–emotive therapists may choose from a range of cognitive, experiential and behavioural methods to facilitate their task of working within the ABCDE framework. However, rational–emotive therapists are mindful of possible negative effects of employing certain procedures and by no means would employ all available procedures. There are a number of issues that rational–emotive therapists have in mind when deciding whether or not to employ a particular thera-peutic procedure.

Helping patients get better rather than feel better

One basic aim of rational–emotive therapists is to promote long-term philo-sophically based change as opposed to helping patients feel better in the short term (Ellis, 1972a). Thus rational–emotive therapists may deliberately avoid being unduly warm towards their patients and would be wary of employing cathartic methods. The hazard of undue therapist warmth is that it may lead to increased long-term dependence in patients who may then believe that they are worth while because the therapist is acting very warm-ly towards them. However, if the therapist or other significant people act coldly towards the patient, he or she may then conclude that he or she is worthless. Thus, undue therapist warmth, although patients feel better when so exposed, tends to distract them from dealing with the more diffi-cult task of accepting themselves unconditionally (Ellis, 1977c). For this reason an intense relationship between therapist and patient is generally avoided. The therapist strives to establish and maintain a working relation-ship with the patient and strives to accept the patient as a fallible human being without being unduly warm towards him or her.

Cathartic methods have the short-term value of encouraging relief of pent-up feelings, but in the long term, if not employed sparingly and briefly, often encourage patients to practise their already well-ingrained irrational philosophies. For example, cathartic procedures which place emphasis on the ventilation of intense angry feelings (e.g. pounding a cushion) run the risk of encouraging processes of blaming which are, according to rational-emotive theory, a feature of the irrational philosophy underlying anger. Rational–emotive therapists might employ such procedures when they wish to help patients to acknowledge their feelings, but the patient would then be quickly encouraged to consider the philosophy underlying such feelings.

Self-esteem vs self-acceptance

In RET, self-esteem is defined as a form of global self-rating and is to be avoided since according to rational–emotive theory it has problematic long-term implications for patients. Procedures based on self-esteem notions encourage patients to define themselves as worth while or competent so long as they gain approval or succeed at valued tasks. They are thus prone to defining themselves as worthless and incompetent if they receive disap-proval or fail at the same task. Furthermore, rational–emotive theory states that it is nonsensical to give humans global ratings since they are on-going, complex, ever-changing organisms who defy such ratings. As an alternative, rational–emotive therapists urge patients to accept themselves as on-going, complex, ever-changing fallible human beings but also encourage them to rate their traits, aspects and behaviour but not their selves. Many procedures do not in fact discourage patients from making such global self-ratings. For example, many therapists give patients homework assignments which are designed to encourage the patient to succeed. Thus a patient who succeeds at approaching a woman at a discotheque may conclude that because he has been able to do this, perhaps he is not worthless after all. The implication would be that if he failed in his assignment then this would be a confirmation of his worthlessness. Rational–emotive therapists, by contrast, may at times encourage patients deliberately to go out and fail since such a failure experience presents them with opportunities to work on accepting themselves as fallible humans rather than subhumans when they fail. In reality, rational–emotive therapists suggest both success and failure-oriented homework assignments to their patients.

Anger vs annoyance

Rational–emotive theory clearly distinguishes between anger and annoyance. Annoyance results when something occurs that we view as a trespass on our personal domain, which we strongly dislike but which we refrain from demanding should not have happened. There is an absence of blaming of self, other or the world for the deed, i.e. the deed is rated but the perpetrator of the deed is accepted. In contrast anger stems from the jehovian demand that the trespass absolutely should not have occurred and the trespasser is damnable. Counsellors from other persuasions often do not make such a clear distinction and thus the therapy procedures which they employ may encourage the full expression and ventilation of anger rather than annoyance. If this occurs then rational–emotive therapists would avoid using these procedures. As mentioned earlier, whilst the full expression and ventilation of anger helps the person feel better it often encourages adherence to a long-term and damaging anger-creating philosophy. In RET, procedures are used to help patients to acknowledge their anger fully but then they are encouraged to dispute the underlying philosophy.

Desensitisation vs implosion

Rational–emotive therapists face a choice between two different approaches when the issue of suggesting homework assignments to patients arises (however, see Chapter 20 for a third approach). They can either suggest that patients gradually face their fears and overcome their problems in a slow stepwise fashion while minimising discomfort (desensitisation), or they can suggest that patients take a risk and forcefully confront their fears and their problems while tolerating discomfort (implosion). Rational–emotive therapists very definitely favour implosion-based assignments because they help patients overcome their 'low frustration tolerance' (LFT) or 'discomfort anxiety', constructs which, according to rational–emotive theory, play a central role in preventing change (Wessler, 1978; Ellis, 1979b). Consequently such therapists would avoid helping patients to overcome gradually and painlessly their problems because such procedures are viewed as encouraging patients to cling to their philosophy of LFT which actually decreases their chances of maintaining therapeutic improvement and increases the possibility of relapse (Ellis, 1979b).

Due to the somewhat unusual stance taken on the above issues rational–emotive therapy has proved rather difficult to combine with other methods derived from different theoretical origins. Garfield and Kurtz (1977) make a similar observation, noting in their study of 154 clinicians' eclectic views that RET was occasionally combined with learning theory-based approaches but was not combined with psychoanalytical, neo-analytical, Rogerian, humanistic or Sullivanian orientations.

Therapeutic Style

Ellis (1976a) speaking for rational–emotive theory argues that humans have great difficulty maintaining, in the long term, the changes that they make more easily in the short term because of the strong biological basis to irrational thinking. Because of this difficulty, Ellis urges rational–emotive therapists to adopt an active–directive, forceful and persistent therapeutic style and also encourage their patients to be equally active, forceful and persistent with themselves. However, is such a style beneficial with a wide range of patients? Or should rational–emotive therapists vary their therapeutic style with different patients? If the latter is to be advised, what criteria should be employed to assist rational–emotive therapists in these important decisions?

The first question remains unanswered since there is a lack of research which has systematically studied the effects of active–directive RET across a wide range of patients. There is, however, some research evidence concerning different therapeutic styles with different patients which has relevance for RET practitioners. DiLoreto (1971) in a study using socially anxious patients found that active–directive RET was more effective with introverts than with extroverts in the sample whilst person-centred therapy was more effective with extroverts. This suggests that RET practitioners might effectively adopt a less directive, more reflective style of RET, when working with socially anxious extroverts. Morley and Watkins (1974) carried out a treatment study with speech anxious patients. They found that active–directive RET benefited external locus of control patients most, whilst internal locus of control patients profited most from a modified RET approach where rational and irrational beliefs relevant to speech anxiety were merely presented and not challenged in the usual fashion. To what extent these findings can be generalised to other patient populations remains unclear. We must also wait for studies to consider Ellis's point often made in practice that the stronger patients adhere to irrational philosophies the more forceful the therapist had better be.

Carson (1969) advocates an interpersonally based system to help the therapist vary his or her interpersonal style according to the patient's own style. Unproductive interlocking interactional patterns arise when the therapist adopts a manner of relating which confirms the patient in his own self-defeating style. The therapist's task is to adopt an interpersonal style which (1) does not reinforce the patient's dysfunctional style and (2) provides a disconfirming experience for the patient. For example, with a passive patient, it would be important for the rational–emotive therapist to refrain from adopting a very active style which might reinforce the patient's self-defeating passivity.

Thus, rational-emotive therapists had better be mindful of Eschen-roeder's (1979) question: 'Which therapeutic style is most effective with what kind of patient?' (p. 5).

Therapeutic Modalities

Rational-emotive theory holds that the important modalities of human experience – cognitive (verbal and imaginal), affective and behavioural – are overlapping rather than separate systems (Ellis, 1962). However, it may be important for RET practitioners to vary the emphasis they place in working within the various modalities with different patients. Which criteria might be important as guides to decision-making in this area bearing in mind that the ultimate goal is a common one (i.e. to effect philosophical changes)? One set of criteria might be the ability of patients to handle verbal concepts. My own experience of working as a counselling psychologist in a working-class region is that with those patients who find it difficult using words it is important for therapists to focus on the behavioural modality both within and between sessions. When teaching rational concepts, important with such patients, then it is essential to use the visual mode of communication as an adjunct to the verbal mode. Thus, I use pen and paper a lot, sketching diagrams to facilitate such patients' understanding of difficult rational concepts. In addition, I have devised a number of visual models to illustrate rational concepts (Dryden, 1980a). When patients employ words to protect themselves from emotional experience, i.e. when they employ intellectualisation as a major defensive style, then rational-emotive therapists might more effectively focus on the experiential modality helping such patients to acquaint themselves with that mode of experience from which they have shielded themselves. If therapists spend too much time engaging such patients in traditional rational-emotive Socratic dialogue then they may well reinforce their patients' defensive style. Such speculations of course need to be tested.

Beutler (1979) has suggested a system which combines therapeutic modalities and styles in determining whether certain approaches to therapy are more effective than others with patients on three major patient dimensions. The first dimension is symptom complexity. If symptoms are circumscribed Beutler (1979) hypothesises that a greater behavioural focus would be more effective, whereas if they are more complex a greater cognitive focus is needed. The second dimension is defensive style. According to Beutler, if the patient utilises an external defensive style, the therapist needs to emphasise the behavioural modality in therapy whereas cognitive interventions are required with patients utilising an internal defensive style. The third dimension – reactance – taps the degree to which external events are construed as representing a threat to the person's autonomy. If the patient is high on the reactance dimension, i.e. if he or she is predisposed to view external events as autonomy-endangering, then the therapist would be more productive if he or she adopted a less directive, more experiential, therapeutic style. If the patient is low on this dimension then greater therapist direction with a more behavioural focus is needed. Beutler (1979) reviewed empirical studies relevant to his hypotheses but found only meagre to moderate support for these hypotheses. However, these hypotheses were not tested *directly* and Beutler's system remains a promising one in that it provides the rational–emotive therapist with some guidelines as to possible variations in style and modality focus with different patients.

In conclusion, it has been shown how RET practitioners employ rational–emotive theory as a guide in their choice of a wide array of therapeutic interventions. In addition, the argument was advanced that RET practitioners are advised to take into account patient characteristics in making decisions concerning therapeutic style and modality focus. However, the central purpose of the eclectic RET practitioner remains the modification of faulty inferences and irrational beliefs.

Chapter 22
Theoretically Consistent Eclecticism:
Humanising a Computer 'Addict'

My Unique Brand of Theoretically Consistent Eclecticism

Theoretically consistent eclectics are therapists who have a particular theoretical perspective on human psychological disturbance but are prepared to use particular techniques developed by other therapeutic schools (Dryden, 1984d). In doing so they do not subscribe to the schools' theoretical postulates, but use techniques spawned by these schools for therapeutic purposes consistent with their own orientation. Although I consider myself a rational–emotive therapist in that I am in basic agreement with the theoretical tenets of RET, I also consider myself 'eclectic' in that, in the *practice* of therapy, I select what appears to be best from diverse therapeutic sources, systems and styles to help my clients. The therapeutic practice of theoretically consistent eclectics is likely to be quite individualistic in that these therapists will draw from the aforementioned sources, systems, and styles what *they*, individually, consider to be best. What guides them in their choices is as yet unknown, and this area would be a fruitful one for research.

Before describing the case I have selected here, I wish to outline the major elements that constitute my own brand of theoretically consistent eclecticism.

Rational–emotive therapy: My theoretical base

I am in basic agreement with the ideas of Albert Ellis (1984a) concerning the foundations of psychological disturbance. RET posits that although emotions, cognitions and behaviours are interdependent processes, much human disturbance seems to stem from absolutistic, evaluative cognitions

First published in 1987.

that profoundly affect how humans feel and act. These cognitions, which are often couched in the form of 'musts', 'absolute shoulds', 'oughts', 'have to's' etc., are termed 'irrational' by RET theory in that they frequently impede people from reaching their basic goals and purposes. One of the major tasks of RET practitioners is to help clients change their absolutistic evaluative cognitions to those which are non-absolutistic in nature. These latter cognitions are frequently couched in the form of 'wants', 'wishes', 'desires', 'preferences' etc., and basically help people achieve their basic goals and purposes and adapt constructively when these cannot be met.

RET therapists have invented a whole range of cognitive, emotive and behavioural techniques that they routinely employ in therapy, but RET-oriented theoretically consistent eclectics, as mentioned above, go further and employ a number of techniques derived from other therapeutic schools to help clients effect a profound philosophical change, i.e. from devout absolute beliefs to non-devout relative beliefs. In my case, I often use methods and techniques derived from gestalt therapy, transactional analysis, personal construct therapy, behavioural therapy, person-centred therapy and Adlerian therapy, to name but a few. However, and this should be emphasised, I use RET as a guiding framework for the selection of appropriate techniques. In addition, RET helps me decide which techniques *not* to choose (Dryden, 1984a). In the case that follows I attempt to show how I use RET as part of my therapeutic decision-making in this regard.

Therapeutic alliance theory

The second major element in my brand of theoretically consistent eclecticism concerns the application of what has come to be known as 'therapeutic alliance theory'. Although the term 'therapeutic alliance' has been in use in the literature for over 50 years, the concept has recently been reformulated by Ed Bordin (1979). Bordin has argued that there are three major components of the alliance between therapist and client: *bonds, goals* and *tasks.*

Alliance theory proposes that effective therapy occurs when the bonds between therapist and client are strong enough for the work of therapy to be executed. My overriding concern here is to develop a type of bond with a particular client that will enable me to help that person without unwittingly perpetuating his or her problems. There are two important elements here. First, most clients (if not all) come into therapy with implicit (or explicit) preferences for a particular type of relationship with their therapist. Some, for example, seek a formal type of relationship, whereas others prefer one that is more personal and intimate. I seek to meet a client's preferences to the extent that they do not perpetuate his or her problems. As will be shown in the case to be described, the client sought a formal type of relationship with me, which, if offered, would have rendered me a less potent change agent. The second element, the relationship between the client's interpersonal style and his problems, is to be found in the writings of interpersonal psychotherapists (e.g. Anchin and Kiesler, 1982). These theorists argue that clients bring a preferred interpersonal style to therapy and 'pull' a complementary response style from their (unsuspecting) therapists, which, in turn, reinforces both their own self-defeating style and their psychological problems. Thus, a client who presents herself as 'helpless' in therapy may well 'pull' an overly active–directive stance from her therapist, which renders her more 'helpless'. Thus, I ask myself: 'What interpersonal style will enable me to keep this client in therapy [clients' disconfirmed expectations here may lead to premature termination] while at the same time helping him (or her) to escape his (or her) self-imposed vicious cycles?'

Secondly, the *goals* of the enterprise must be considered. Effective therapy is deemed to occur when therapist and client agree on the latter's goals. Agreement on goals can occur at three levels:

1. Client and therapist can set *outcome goals*, which represent what the client wishes to achieve at the end of therapy.
2. *Mediating goals* can be set. These are the goals that the client needs to achieve before outcome goals can be reached. For example, a client may have to become proficient in a number of social skills before realistically being able to achieve the outcome goals of finding a partner.
3. Client and therapist can set goals for a particular session (i.e. *session goals*).

Alliance theory predicts that effective therapy is facilitated by the participants' agreements on each of these goals (where appropriate) and when they both can see the progressive link between the three levels (i.e. session goals → mediating goals → outcome goals).

Thirdly, therapeutic *tasks* must be considered. Both therapist and client have tasks to carry out in therapy. Alliance theory predicts that effective therapy is facilitated when each person: (1) understands which tasks he or she has to execute; (2) can see the relevance of the other person's tasks; (3) is able to execute his or her respective tasks; and (4) acknowledges that the execution of these promotes the attainment of the client's goals. In addition, the tasks must have sufficient therapeutic potency to facilitate goal achievement. Thus, as a theoretically consistent eclectic, I need to know that the techniques I select from other therapeutic schools are sufficiently powerful vehicles to promote therapeutic change. For example, exposure methods may well help clients overcome phobic reactions, but Gendlin's (1978) focusing techniques probably will not.

Finally, a channel of communication needs to be established between therapist and client so that alliance issues can be discussed and problems in the alliance resolved.

Challenging but not overwhelming

The third major feature of my eclectic approach is based on a principle that I have come to call 'challenging but not overwhelming' (Dryden, 1985b). I believe that people learn best in an atmosphere of creative challenge, and I try to develop such an environment for my clients in therapy (Hoehn-Saric, 1978). Conversely, people will not learn as much in a situation that either challenges them insufficiently or overwhelms them. In this respect, Hoehn-Saric (1978) has shown that a productive level of emotional arousal facilitates therapeutic learning. For example, some clients are emotionally over-stimulated, and hence the therapeutic task is to create a learning environment that decreases their emotional tension to a level where they can adequately reflect on their experiences. With these clients, I make use of a lot of cognitive techniques and adopt an interpersonal style that aims to decrease affect. This style may be either formal or informal in character. These strategies are particularly appropriate with clients who have a 'hysterical' style of functioning. However, other clients require a more emotionally charged learning atmosphere. Such clients often use 'intellectualisation' as a major defence and are used to denying feelings (see the case to be described). With such clients I attempt to inject a productive level of affect into the therapeutic session and employ emotive techniques, self-disclosure and a good deal of humour. These 'challenging' strategies are best introduced gradually so as not to overwhelm clients with an environment they are not accustomed to utilising. However, before deciding on which interpersonal style to emphasise with clients, I routinely gain information from them concerning how they learn best. Some clients learn best directly through experience whereas for others vicarious experiences seem to be more productive. I try to develop a learning profile for each of my clients and use this information to help me plan my therapeutic strategies and choose techniques designed to implement these strategies. Care needs to be taken, however, that the therapist does not use a mode of learning that may perpetuate the client's problems.

The 'challenging but not overwhelming' principle extends to Ellis's (1979b, 1980a) writings on 'discomfort anxiety'. Ellis has argued that many clients perpetuate their problems and deprive themselves of learning experiences because they believe that they *must* be comfortable. Thus, a major therapeutic task here is to help such clients challenge this belief and carry out assignments, while tolerating their uncomfortable feelings. Although this is a sound theoretical principle, I have found that it needs to be modified for pragmatic purposes. It may be desirable for a client who is anxious about eating in public to go to an expensive restaurant and challenge her anxiety-creating cognitions in a situation where her worst fears may be realised, but many clients will not do this. When I provide a rationale for homework assignments, I do so in a way that incorporates the 'challenging but not overwhelming' principle and contrasts it with gradual desensitisation and implosion methods:

> There are three ways you can overcome your fears. The first is like jumping in at the deep end; you expose yourself straightaway to the situation you are most afraid of. The advantage here is that if you can learn that nothing terrible will happen, then you will overcome your problems quite quickly. However, the disadvantage is that some people just can't bring themselves to do this and get quite discouraged as a result. The second way is to go very gradually. Here, on the one hand, you only do something that you feel comfortable doing, while, on the other, you don't really get an opportunity to face putting up with discomfort, which in my opinion is a major feature of your problem. Also, treatment will take much longer this way. The third way is what I call 'challenging but not overwhelming'. Here you choose an assignment which is sufficiently challenging for you to make progress but not one which you feel would be overwhelming for you at any given stage. Here you are likely to make progress more quickly than with the gradual approach but more slowly than with the deep-end approach.

I find that when clients are given an opportunity to choose their own rate of progress, the therapeutic alliance is strengthened. Most clients choose the 'challenging but not overwhelming' approach, and only very rarely do they opt for the gradual desensitisation approach. When they do so, I try to dissuade them and frequently succeed. In the final analysis, however, I have not found it productive to insist that clients choose a particular way of tackling problems that is against their preferences.

Having outlined the major elements of my eclectic approach, I shall now describe the case I have selected to demonstrate my approach in action.

The Client

The client, whom I shall call Eric, was a 31-year-old, white, unmarried man. He was born in the south of England, an only child of Peter and Margaret. His father was a ranking officer in the British Army and his mother did not work outside the home. At the time of treatment, Eric lived alone in a flat in Birmingham and worked as a computer programmer in a middle-sized business institution that manufactures electronic equipment. He was educated at a leading British university and has a master's degree in computer studies.

Eric sought therapeutic help because he had increasingly come to feel that his life lacked direction and he had recently become concerned about his level of alcohol intake. This was the first time that he had sought help and there was no evidence of any psychiatric history. He enjoyed good physical health.

He initially reported his childhood to be uneventful; he saw his father infrequently because of the latter's Army commitments and described his relationship with his mother as 'cordial but rather distant'. He was sent to boarding school at the age of 10 where he remained until age 18, when he went to university. He said that he had many acquaintances at boarding school and university, but no real friends. He dated infrequently and reported no intimate relationships with women. He was sexually inexperienced and recently lost his virginity after having sex with a local prostitute. Describing this experience, he said, 'It was time, I thought, that I had sex with a woman; I felt a bit stupid being a 30-year-old virgin. I didn't enjoy it and wondered what all the fuss was about.' His main interest was in computers. He was fascinated by them and often worked late into the night trying to solve a problem posed by the latest program he was working on. Of late, however, he said, 'I can't seem to dredge up the enthusiasm any more.'

He was recommended to see me by his local GP, who gave him the name of a number of therapists in the area. Explaining his choice of therapist, Eric said: 'I chose to come and see you because I was attracted by the name rational–emotive therapy. I see myself as basically rational, but there seems to be a breakdown in my logic at the moment. I'm hoping you can isolate the bugs in the system.' Perhaps not surprisingly, Eric's language reflected his interest in computers. My immediate impression of this tall, well-groomed man was that he had almost become an extension of the computer he had recently lost interest in. His speech was very precise and his language lacked emotionally toned words. He was almost devoid of affect apart from allowing himself a little laugh when he drew attention to the fact that his surname was the same as a leading computer company.

His expectations for therapy were as follows. He anticipated that we would have an orderly discussion of his life's goals and why he had become 'stuck'. He further hoped we would find out why he had started drinking more heavily than was his custom. He was pleased that I was not going to ask him to lie on the couch: 'I like to see who I am talking to.' I was left with the initial impression that here was a man who kept a very tight rein over his feelings from which he had become increasingly divorced. He seemed to employ intellectualisation as a major defence in his life. Yet the cracks were beginning to appear. This marked the end of the initial interview, at which time I offered to accept him for therapy. We would review progress after five sessions, which would give him an opportunity to determine whether I was the kind of person who could help him. He accepted this contract.

The Therapy

What I shall do is to give an account of my work with Eric over the 17 sessions I saw him. I will include at various points (1) my thoughts as a therapist, which will help the reader understand my eclectic approach, and (2) verbatim transcripts of our interchanges to illustrate (a) Eric's mode of functioning, (b) two critical incidents, and (c) how I dealt with an incident concerning Eric's resistance to experiencing feelings.

Initial phase (sessions 1–4)

Initially I asked Eric to help me understand more deeply his predicament and what he would like to achieve from therapy. He reiterated the theme first raised in the intake session, namely, that he wanted to regain his enthusiasm for his computer interest and was puzzled about what had been going wrong.

Initially I wanted to test my hypothesis that his difficulties lay in the feeling domain, so I decided to ask him to fill out a structural profile (Lazarus, 1981) to test this and to demonstrate to Eric how he saw himself as a person.

Session 1 transcript (client functioning)

Windy: Okay, Eric, now throughout therapy I'll be sharing some hunches with you, and it would be good if you could help us both by giving me honest reactions to these hunches. I see you and myself as a team joining together to figure out what has gone wrong in your life and how you can find a more meaningful direction for you. How does that seem?

Eric: Fine.

W: Now, human beings have seven basic aspects. These aspects interact with one another to be sure, but I want to understand how you see yourself on these aspects. I want to use a rating scale from 0 to 10, 0 being an absence of this modality and 10 being a high score on it. Now these modalities are behaviour, affect, sensation, imagery, cognition, interpersonal relationships and biological factors.* Now taking behaviour first...

I then spent some time developing the structural profile with Eric (Figure 22.1).

W: Okay, what's your reaction to this profile?

E: What do you mean?

W: Well, can you see anything that might be related to your current difficulties?

E: Mmm. Well ... I'm not sure.

W: Okay, let me share my reaction. I'm struck by the low scores on affect, sensation, and interpersonal relationships. For example, I wonder if you would benefit from experiencing more feelings in your life. Let's start with that.

E: Feelings? I'm not sure what you mean by that.

W: Well emotions like joy, guilt, happiness, sadness, anxiety, depression, pleasure.

E: Well, I used to get pleasure out of my computer, but the others? I ... er, I'm not sure. I'm puzzled by that. Aren't feelings biological processes that originate in the hypothalamus or is it the thalamus?

W: [ignoring the temptation to discuss the psychophysiology of emotion]: You seem to be finding it difficult to relate to these emotions.

E: Yeah.

W: Well, is this an area we need to explore?

E: [doubtfully]: I suppose so.

---

*See Lazarus (1981) for a full description of the structural profile and how to use it in therapy.

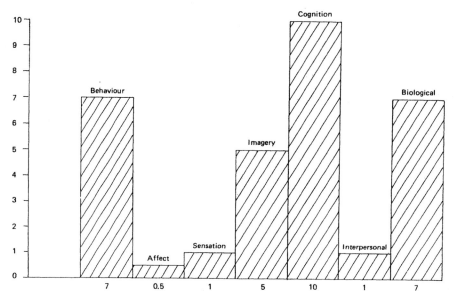

Figure 22.1   Eric's structural profile (session 1).

A similar dialogue occurred on the topic of sensations with Eric specu-
lating on their biological origins rather than on his experience. Following is
the interchange concerning Eric's interpersonal relationships.

W: Now how about your relationship with people?
E: Well, I've never sought people out.
W: Have they sought you out?
E: No.
W: How do you feel about that?
E: What do you mean?
W: [noting the client's puzzled response to another feeling-oriented question]:
           Well you describe your life as being empty of people. What do you think your
           life would be like if there were more people in it?
E: It would distract me from my computer work.
W: So you wouldn't like more people in your life?
E: I wouldn't know what to *do* with them.

The above excerpt shows Eric's dilemma. Feelings are alien experiences
and people are either an unwelcome distraction or a puzzle. He doesn't
know what to *do* with them. I remember experiencing something of a
dilemma myself at this point. How can I help this man entertain experiences that are so alien to him?

I decided to share my dilemma in session 2 when we were talking about
goals. This was an error since Eric could not relate to what I said to him.
However, when I asked him, 'Could these areas be the bugs in your system?'
he reacted with visible (although transitory) alarm. I remember thinking

that I was going to have to use his language to build the bridge between his affectless world and one that held the most promise for him. An investigation into how Eric best learned revealed an overreliance on books, radio and television. These would clearly be of little relevance in our therapeutic work since these media could well reinforce Eric's detachment and intellectualisation. Other learning modes would have to be gradually introduced.

Although I like to set treatment goals early in therapy, I decided to postpone goal-setting for a while and work in a less structured way with Eric for two reasons. First, I did not consider that he would benefit from an early discussion about goals since he could not yet relate to issues about feelings, sensations and relationships. Secondly, I considered that he would initially benefit more from a more open-ended exploration. This would help him to widen his horizons and to loosen up a little.

In session 3 we talked about his thoughts concerning his structural profile and the 'bugs in his system'. He noticed that he tended to drink more at those times he found himself thinking about our sessions. I suggested that he refrain from drinking to experience whatever it was that he might be feeling at those times. I taught him Gendlin's (1978) focusing technique to help him in this regard. This technique is particularly helpful in that it directs clients' attention to their inner sensations and experiences and helps them to articulate what these experiences might be about. In session 4 I helped Eric to attach a feeling label to his experience. He was feeling sad. I helped him to realise that sadness can be a cue that there was something missing from his life, perhaps something other than computers. He nodded imperceptibly in agreement, but wondered what that was. I suggested it was our task to help him find out.

Up to now I would describe my approach to Eric as basically exploratory. I was beginning to 'challenge' him to look at his inner experience, but not in a way that would 'overwhelm' him and possibly scare him away. The two techniques I used in this initial phase were designed to help both of us move into what was for Eric the uncharted waters of his inner world. Neither of us could see at this stage that the next session would be so critical in the therapeutic endeavour.

Middle phase (sessions 5–14)

While reviewing my notes a few days prior to my fifth session with Eric, I noticed that Eric would have his thirty-second birthday on the day of this session. I let my mind wander and experienced a sense of sadness. I pictured Eric on his birthday alone in his flat and guessed that nobody would send him a birthday card. I decided I would buy him a card, which I would give him at the beginning of the session. My decision was prompted by a sense of empathy, but I also reflected on the therapeutic wisdom of doing so. Would he despise me for my open display of caring concern? Would he be affected? What might he experience? Empathy won the day, although I was somewhat apprehensive when I sat down at the beginning of the session. I want to stress that I did not see this purely as a technique. If I did not experience the concern, I would not have given him the card. The following are excerpts from the session.

Session 5 transcript (critical incident)

Windy: Eric, I noticed today was your birthday and I felt that I would like to give you this [handing over the card].
Eric: [puzzled]: What is it?
W: Why don't you open it?
E: [opening the envelope]: Oh! Er ... um ... I don't know ... what to say.
W: You seem agitated.
E: [clearly embarrassed]: Yeah ... well ... that's ... a ... well ... um [bursts into tears].

Eric wept silently for about 5 minutes and was clearly distressed. I felt both touched and concerned lest this was too overwhelming an experience for him at this point.

W: When was the last time you received a birthday card?
E: [distracted]: What? ... er ... well, let me ... see ... er ... I can't remember.
W: When I decided to buy you the card, I felt kind of sad because I guessed that nobody would have sent you one.
E: Pathetic isn't it.
W: What is?
E: Weeping like a baby over a silly card. Oh! I didn't mean ...
W: I know what you mean. How do you feel about weeping with sadness?
E: I feel bloody stupid.

The rest of the session was spent helping Eric to see that he could accept himself for crying and that his sadness was perhaps an indication that some important desires were not being met. However, Eric remained somewhat distracted and I used these strategies to decrease the intensity of his experience (which I hypothesised would have otherwise been overwhelming for him) as well as a method of disputing his irrational belief: 'I am worthless if I cry.'

Towards the end of the session, I wondered aloud whether Eric would find it difficult to come back next session having expressed some strong feelings. He nodded, and I said that I understood that feeling.

Indeed, Eric did not show up for session 6. I was concerned about him, particularly as he did not call to cancel his appointment. I decided to write the following letter:

Dear Eric,
I was sorry that you were not able to attend our session on Wednesday. My hunch is that you feel embarrassed about our last session. If I am right I can understand you

feeling that way. If you recall, I mentioned at our second session that therapy can be difficult at times and there might be occasions when you might not want to come.* However, I feel it is important for us to talk about these experiences in person, so I look forward to seeing you for our next session at the same time next week. Please confirm that this arrangement is convenient.

Yours sincerely,
W. Dryden, PhD

I received a reply from Eric, thanking me for my letter and confirming that he would attend our sixth session. The following is an excerpt from this session.

Session 6 transcript (critical incident)

Eric: You know, when I got home, I found myself with a whisky bottle in my hand before I even knew what was happening. I remembered what you said about not drinking to see what feelings came up. I was overwhelmed with stomach cramps and I began to cry again. Somewhere at the back of my mind I remembered you asking me if I was worthless for crying. I was able to see that I wasn't and for the first time I let go. I cried and cried. I remembered my father saying things when I was a child like: 'Call yourself a boy, stop those tears.' I also remembered my mother getting agitated because I was crying and my father was due home soon.

Windy: Sounds like a lot of hidden feelings came up for you.

E: Yeah. When last Wednesday came, I panicked. You were right, I couldn't face you then. I went to my computer. I realised that I'd been using it as a friend, someone ... something rather ... that I could relate to ... I also remembered what you said about your challenging but not overwhelming principle. I'd had enough challenge for a while and needed to have a rest. Sorry I didn't let you know.
             [And later in the session...]

E: I can see more clearly that I do need to get to know about some of those modalities that were low; you know, affect and the others. That's what I'd like to focus on.

At the end of the sixth session I suggested that Eric think about what kinds of experiences he would like to seek out. He came back with the following list at session 7.

1. Learn to dance.
2. Find myself a girlfriend (about time!).
3. Go walking in the woods.
4. Join 18+.†

Eric devised his own programme and followed it through according to the 'challenging but not overwhelming' principle with good success. On a

---

*I frequently tell my clients that there may be times when they may wish to miss sessions. I do this partly so that I can remind them of the fact if and when the 'going gets rough' for them.
†18+ is a national social club for people between the ages of 18 and 30. A number of the members, however, are older than 30. It has branches throughout the UK.

number of occasions he chose not to go to an event, using his computer as a kind of anxiety-reduction technique.

Mindful of the importance of using emotively oriented techniques to help Eric, I employed a number of these methods to help him focus on avoidance behaviour.

For example, in session 9, Eric reported that he couldn't be bothered to go to 18+ on club night and spent the evening working on his computer. I decided to use a gestalt empty-chair technique to dramatise the situation to enable Eric to identify any possible anxieties.

Session 9 transcript (using a dramatic method to uncover the meaning of Eric's avoidance behaviour)

Windy: Let's see if we can understand whether you were avoiding some important feeling. Now let me explain a drama technique to you. First, can you imagine how you were feeling that night?

Eric: Er ... yeah ... tired.

W: Okay. So one of the players in this play is 'Tired Eric'. Now another one is your computer. (Can you imagine Tired Eric talking to his computer?)

E: [laughs]: Just about.

W: Good. Now, see this empty chair? Imagine your computer on that chair. Got it?

E: Yeah.

W: Now strange as it might seem, I want you as Tired Eric to talk to your computer. And I'll play myself in this. Okay? Right. Okay, Tired Eric, it's time to go out to 18+.

E: [as Tired Eric]: I'm too tired.

W: [to computer]: Is Eric too tired or might he be feeling something else? Eric, change chairs and answer me as your computer.

E: [as computer]: Well, no, he's scared.

W: [to computer]: Scared of what?

E: [as computer]: Well, he's got his eye on a girl at the club but he's scared she might not want to know him.

W: [to computer]: So why don't you tell him to go and face his fears.

E: [as computer]: Er ... because ...

E: [as Tired Eric and changing chairs after being prompted by the therapist]: I know, because he doesn't think I'm strong enough to cope with rejection.

W: [to Tired Eric]: Is that true?

E: [as Tired Eric]: No, but why risk it if it's a possibility?

This dialogue helped Eric and myself see that two important beliefs were holding Eric back. One was 'I'll only do things if they are certain to work out' and the other was 'If I do things and they don't work out, I'm no good'. I then helped Eric to dispute these beliefs using traditional RET disputing methods. He considered a more healthy alternative to both beliefs to be: 'Things won't work out if I don't try. So I'd better increase the chances of getting what I want by going for them. If they don't work out, tough. I'm no less a person.' Eric practised these new beliefs by acting on them. He carried out a number of homework assignments between sessions 9 and 11 which were designed to help him accept himself in the face of failure and to help him work towards goals, the achievement of which could not be guaranteed.

In session 12 it emerged from reviewing these assignments that Eric feared losing control if he experienced strong arousal. His belief here was 'If I get excited, I'll lose control and that would be awful'. In order to test out the prediction that he would lose control if he experienced a lot of arousal, Eric did several things between sessions 12 and 14. He did a number of shame-attacking exercises (Dryden, 1984a). For example, he went into a large department store and shouted out the time. In addition, in session 13, I got him to sprint up and down on the spot and then do a number of expressive meditation exercises designed to raise his arousal level. Finally he went to a dance-therapy workshop and did a lot of vigorous dance exercises. All these experiences helped him to see that he could get highly aroused without losing control.

By session 14, Eric considered that he had made a lot of progress. He was feeling more in touch with his emotions, the range of which had markedly increased. He gained pleasure from walking in the country and enjoyed experiencing a variety of country odours. He had taken up bird watching and had found a girlfriend who also enjoyed these activities. He had made several friends at the 18+ club and was experimenting with a wide range of activities. His enthusiasm for his computer work had returned, but he spent far less of his recreational time at his computer terminal.

End phase (sessions 15–17)

Eric suggested at the beginning of the fifteenth session that he would like to come less frequently and work towards termination. I outlined a number of ways we could terminate our work together. He chose to come twice more at monthly intervals. We spent these final sessions reviewing our work together, and Eric reported that he had maintained the gains he had made in therapy. At the end of session 16, I suggested that Eric might bring to our last scheduled session a written account of what he had achieved in therapy. The following is a verbatim account of what he wrote under the heading, 'What I gained from therapy'.

What I gained from therapy

I have gained a great deal from seeing you, far more than I thought I would. You have opened my eyes to a whole new world of experience that I was only dimly aware of, if at all. I would say first and foremost I feel a more complete human being. Although I still respect my intellect – or the cognitive domain as the American man who invented those sheets calls it – I have learned to experience and gain respect for the other modalities. I have learned that it isn't unmanly to cry and feel sad. I've tried to discuss this with my father, but perhaps predictably he doesn't understand what I'm talking about. I have learned that it's not so bad to try and achieve something and fail. Indeed, if a person doesn't try, he certainly won't achieve. Obvious now, but I didn't see that before.

I have also learned that control has little to do with feeling strongly aroused. To some degree, looking back, I was using my computer to shield me from life, although of course I didn't realise that then. I guess I was using my computer as a substitute friend and yet it was a bit of a one-sided friendship. I now feel much more a part of the social world. 18+ has helped tremendously in that respect. Before I wouldn't have thought I could have so much fun with others. I didn't even think of life as having fun. Strange isn't it! I still have to force myself to go out occasionally when I feel 'tired' but I can now distinguish between genuine tiredness and anxiety.

I've redone those modalities (Figure 22.2) and have enclosed them within. I find the differences interesting. One last thought, I remembered being struck by the name of your therapy before I came to see you – rational-emotive therapy. I was attracted to the word 'rational'. I must confess that I'm now more attracted to the word 'emotive'. I hope you find this instructive.

At the end of the seventeenth session, Eric and I agreed to have two follow-up sessions, the first one being 12 months after our last session. However, this has not yet taken place at the time of writing.

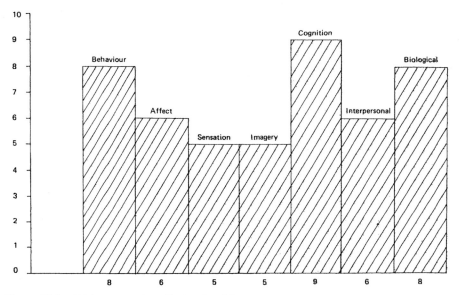

Figure 22.2 Eric's structural profile (session 17).

Therapist's summary

From the point of view of RET, Eric had developed an unsatisfactory lifestyle partly because he had little experience in the affect, sensation and interpersonal modalities but mainly because he held a number of irrational beliefs which led him to avoid experiences in each of these areas. Namely he believed:

1. 'Experiencing emotions and sensations is extremely dangerous and must be avoided at all costs.'
2. 'I must be in control of myself. To lose control would be terrible.'
3. 'I must be certain of achieving something before I try it.'
4. 'I'm no good if I cry or if I fail to achieve important things.'

Adopting a theoretically consistent eclectic view based on my rational-emotive conceptualisations, I decided to emphasise strategies and techniques that were dramatic, affective and expressive in nature. In doing so I was sensitive to avoid overwhelming the client, but to challenge him gradually at first and later increasingly so as therapy progressed and as he began to make significant gains. Thus I decided to use:

1. *Structural profiles* as an assessment tool to help test my hunch about important deficits and to help Eric learn about these deficits.
2. Such techniques as *focusing* to help Eric to identify feelings and articulate what these feelings pointed to.
3. *Gestalt, two-chair dialogue* – to help him identify the meaning behind his avoidance manoeuvres.
4. *Dramatic meditation* and *dance therapy* – to help him learn that strong affective experiences were not dangerous and did not threaten his sense of control.

All these methods were chosen in line with strategies consistent with my RET-inspired formulation and in keeping with my hunches about the importance for Eric of learning to become accustomed to the experiential–affective domain of human functioning.

From the point of view of alliance theory, I was able to develop a well-bonded relationship with Eric. Initially he viewed me as a rather distant 'expert' who would help him iron out the 'bugs' in his system. The birthday card incident confronted him with the fact that I was also a human being who cared about his plight. This touched a deep chord in him and seemed to help him relate to me in a more affective manner. From session 6 our relationship was characterised by mutual respect and trust. I related to Eric in a moderately warm, informal manner without us both losing sight that we had various tasks to achieve.

With respect to the goal domain, I deliberately refrained from setting concrete goals at the outset of therapy. Initially, Eric wanted to pursue goals which, in my opinion, would have not been constructive for him. He wished to strengthen his intellectualised defences and rid himself of the 'bugs' in his system, which he hoped would help him shut out his increasing sense of isolation and dissatisfaction and hence to return to his computer. I did not attempt to deal explicitly with the self-defeating nature of these goals at the outset. I considered that to do this would have been unproductive and might have led to a futile 'intellectual' discussion, which I wanted to avoid. There was also evidence at this initial stage of therapy that Eric would not have understood the importance of goals that emphasised becoming increasingly aware of his feelings and the healing aspects of interpersonal relationships. Instead, I sidestepped the issue of goals by showing Eric the importance of looking at himself as a total individual (by using the structural profile) and how he was living his life against this backdrop. To some degree I think that Eric went along with me because he viewed me as an expert who knew what he was doing and because he was not too insistent about meeting his initial goals. Specific goal setting followed Eric's increasing understanding of the importance that the affective, sensation and interpersonal modalities might play in his life.

As Eric gained this understanding, it was fairly easy to show him that the execution of various tasks could help him achieve his newly discovered goals. The more Eric derived benefit from being able to experience feelings, sensations and the pleasure of relating to other people, the more he was able to see the sense of the evocative techniques that I suggested to him and how they could help him achieve his goals. Interestingly enough, we rarely had to talk *about* the relevance of therapeutic tasks; I believe he and I developed an implicit and shared understanding about these matters.

Following Bordin (1983), I believe that the repair of rifts in the therapeutic alliance can be most therapeutic. That Eric and I were able to sustain our relationship through the birthday card and the missed-session incidents was, I believe, important for a number of reasons. I consider that Eric learned from these two incidents that the expression of strong feelings (i.e. his feelings) could be tolerated by another person and by himself and that no catastrophe would result. I also think that Eric learned it was possible to talk about relationships with another person with whom he was involved and that rifts in these relationships can be repaired when both people show 'good faith'.

Applying the 'challenging but not overwhelming' principle to the case, I would like to make the following points. First, I attempted to provide a therapeutic environment that was increasingly charged with affect to encourage Eric to develop his potential to use the affective, sensory and interpersonal modalities. In this sense, I tried to challenge Eric's use of intellectualisation as a defence against such experiences without overwhelming him in this regard. The birthday card gift could have been an overwhelming experience for Eric, and to some extent I underestimated the effect that it would have on him. However, it was not a damaging experience for him, and indeed it contained important therapeutic ingredients for change (see the section on 'Client Impressions'). Secondly, I explained the 'challenging but not overwhelming' principle outlined earlier, with respect to the execution of therapeutic tasks, and Eric applied it to very good effect in his homework assignments. Indeed, as his own account in the next section shows, Eric has used this principle after therapy ended to maintain and extend his progress.

Client Impressions

Two months after formal therapy had finished, I wrote the following letter to Eric:

> Dear Eric,
> I hope this letter finds you well. I have been asked by Dr J. Norcross of University of Rhode Island, USA, to contribute a case study to a book he is editing entitled *Casebook of Eclectic Psychotherapy*. With your permission I would like to write an account of our therapy and would like to request your permission for this. Your anonymity will of course be preserved.
> If you agree, Dr Norcross also seeks to include the client's impressions of his/her therapy experiences. I would be grateful if you could write your impressions according to the following guidelines:
> 1. What were the most helpful and least helpful aspects of therapy?
> 2. What were your impressions of two critical incidents in therapy. Here I have selected (a) the session where I gave you a birthday card and (b) the session following the time you decided to miss our scheduled appointment (session 6).
> Please feel free to be as candid as you can in your account. I look forward to receiving your reply upon which I will send you a copy of my account.
> > Yours sincerely,
> > W. Dryden, PhD

I received the following reply from Eric which I present as his verbatim account:

> Dear Dr Dryden,
> Thank you for your letter, You have my permission to write about our therapy work. I am pleased to offer my perspective of my therapy experience. I hope that it may be helpful to your colleagues and their clients. I would be interested to see your own account when you have finished it.
>
> **Most helpful and least helpful aspects of my therapy**
>
> As I look back over the period of my therapy I can think of many helpful aspects but only one or two experiences that perhaps weren't very helpful. So my account is somewhat skewed to the positive. The most positive aspect of the therapy was the fact that you helped me discover the importance of feelings and personal relationships in my life. Until seeing you, I had not considered that these had any place in my life. Indeed, I had not really given these matters much thought. Why this should be so is difficult to say, but I suppose it had something to do with my father's attitudes

towards feelings and the fact that my boarding school emphasised the value of hard work rather than the value of relationships between people.

Your suggestion that I refrain from drinking to help me discover what feelings I was hiding from and that focusing technique was particularly helpful in this respect. I also found some of the techniques you suggested that we try out together in our sessions helpful in aiding me to identify my feelings and some of the blocks I set up to stop me being uncomfortable. In particular, those meditation exercises were good and I still do some of them from time to time.

The other helpful aspects of my therapy were those exercises I did outside your office. I enjoyed immensely the dance workshop you suggested I attend. In fact I have joined a regular dance therapy group which I find valuable in helping me to overcome my tendency to what you called 'intellectualisation'. I didn't like that term when you first used it. I still don't like it but I know what you meant by it. I call it 'cutting out'.

The therapy helped me to make much better use of outside resources than I would have done without therapy. Therapy helped me to form some important friendships, in particular my relationship with my girlfriend June, which is still flourishing. Therapy was like a release in this respect.

Looking back I think your patience and understanding was very important (I'll mention your concern for me as a person later). Your easygoing manner was good for me although at the beginning, I'm not sure, but I think I would have preferred seeing an older man, one who was more formal in style and dress. I realise now that these things are unimportant though. I also found some of your explanations helpful. Your own principle of challenging but not overwhelming yourself was valuable, and I still use it as a guideline in my life.

Now some not so helpful aspects, although these are minor. First, at the beginning it might have been more helpful if you could have given me a clearer idea about what therapy was like. I was puzzled for about the first three sessions and was not sure what you expected me to do or say. Finally, it might have been more valuable if we could have spent more time talking about my childhood and my experiences at boarding school. I don't know whether that would have been helpful but I think that it might.

Critical incidents

I can understand why you selected these two incidents. They stood out for me too. I was shocked when you gave me the birthday card – shocked and very embarrassed that I reacted in the way that I did. Your concern for me hit me between the eyes. I wasn't prepared for it and just did not understand at the time why I reacted so strongly. That experience really made me stop and think about my life. It made the meaning of the first profile I did come alive and helped me to see what I had been missing in life. I was, as you suspected, too embarrassed and ashamed to face you the week after. Your letter helped me to come back. You understood what I was feeling and again your concern was an important fact in helping me to return the following week. To be honest, if you had not written, I doubt whether I would have made the first move.

Coming back after the missed session was very important for me. You helped me feel that I wasn't a weak freak and also by not making too much of my missing the session you gave me important breathing space. Your matter-of-fact reaction gave me the impression that it was no big deal and also helped me think that you would not be shocked or startled by whatever I told you about myself. That attitude has remained with me and is also an attitude I can now apply to myself.

Well, I hope that you find these remarks of use. I'm very grateful to you for helping me in the way you did and am pleased to have had this opportunity to repay you in this small way.

Yours sincerely,

Eric

Epilogue

Chapter 23
A Note on How I Used RET to Overcome My Emotional Problems

When I was about four, I developed a stammer which led to a long and persistent period of teasing by my schoolmates in primary and secondary school. As a result, I began to view myself as a bit of a freak which, not surprisingly, hardly helped me to overcome my speech problem. I was taken (and in some instances dragged) to a variety of speech therapists over the ensuing years who uniformly failed to help me one iota with my stammer. I began to withdraw from talking in public, loathed speaking on the telephone and would literally quake with fear if anybody asked me my surname – which at the time was 'Denbin'* because I would give a good impression of a machine gun being fired while trying to pronounce it. I did not have a clear idea of the 'cause' of my anxiety, believing wrongly that the prospect of stammering was the main determinant rather than the 'awfulness' of such a prospect. In my teens, I went to a local elocution teacher who taught me how to speak on the breath and this helped quite a bit, although I was still anxious about speaking in public. It was only when I reached my early twenties that I got my first real concrete help in overcoming my speech anxiety. This came when I saw Michael Bentine on television relating how he overcame his stammering problem. He told himself 'If I stammer, I stammer, too bad', or a similar variant. This seemed eminently sensible to me and I resolved to try this, albeit replacing his 'too bad' with my more evocative 'fuck it!'. I simultaneously came to the conclusion that I had, up to that point, been defining myself as a 'stammerer', which of course, was an overgeneralisation. I undertook to re-define myself as a person who stammered at times, who spoke fluently at other times and who did a thousand and one other things too. With these cognitive techniques, I helped myself to a great

First published in 1990.

*I changed my name from David Denbin to Windy Dryden mainly to avoid feelings of embarrassment concerning my difficulties in pronouncing 'Denbin'. I changed my first name to Windy because it was a nickname given me in my saxophone playing days, and because I liked it. Dryden was the name of our local telephone exchange.

extent, particularly when I backed them up with a fair measure of in vivo exposure. I literally forced myself to speak up in various social situations whilst reminding myself that I could tolerate the discomfort of doing so. All these techniques, I subsequently discovered, are frequently employed in RET. I had, at that time, not heard of psychotherapy let alone RET. Using these techniques, I have, to date, nicely stammered (and more frequently spoken fluently) in various countries without anxiety and can now speak for an hour on local radio without much apprehension and free from anxiety. I achieved this largely as a result of my own efforts (with help from my elocution teacher) and enjoyed the fact that I was the major source of my own improvement.

In the mid-1970s, I trained as a counsellor, being schooled mainly in client-centred and psychoanalytical approaches. I entered therapy, at that time, partly because I thought it was a good idea for a trainee counsellor to be in 'personal therapy', but mainly because I was somewhat depressed. I had three relatively brief periods of psychoanalytical therapy with different practitioners. I found these experiences unhelpful in lifting my mood, was given no guidance on how to help myself and found most of the therapists' interventions puzzling, to say the least. One of my therapists slipped in, as it were, some psychodramatic techniques which helped me to 'see' that my problem basically involved feelings of inadequacy. These were unfortunately traced back to my childhood which distracted me from solving my mood problem. I decided at the end of my third unsuccessful therapy that enough was enough and that I'd better help myself as best I could. I turned to Ellis and Harper's (1975) book *A New Guide To Rational Living* because it stressed the use of self-help methods and because its content reminded me of my own successful efforts at overcoming my speech anxiety. I resolved to stop putting myself down, to accept myself as a fallible human being no matter what, and again pushed myself to do a number of things I wanted to do but was scared of doing because of the perceived threat to my 'fragile ego'. My depression lifted rather quickly and I began to feel more alive. All this without delving into my 'sacred' childhood.

I remembered, at this time, that my clients had, from the beginning of my counselling career, asked for more specific help than I was providing them with through my reflections, clarifications and interpretations. I resolved to get trained in RET, believing then, as I do now, that it is important to be trained in counselling methods before using them with clients. This I did and I noted that (1) the large majority of my clients liked my new, more active–directive counselling approach, and (2) I felt more congruent practising RET. I seemed to have found my theoretical and practical counselling niche.

Since then, I have continued to use RET on myself. I have employed rational–emotive methods to overcome my anxiety about making an important career decision. I decided, as a result, to leave my full-time tenured academic position at Aston University, taking voluntary redundancy. Unfortunately, I overestimated my employability and was unemployed for 2 years during which time I coped with my new status with disappointment but did not make myself depressed. During the 2-year period I applied for and was rejected for 54 jobs or new positions. RET helped me in particular to overcome my anger about being turned down for re-training as a clinical psychologist. On being rejected, I began to believe such self-defeating ideas as 'How dare they refuse ME. Who do they think they are? They should accept such a fine fellow and a scholar as myself and one with such good credentials to boot!'. Noting that I was angry, I first accepted myself for needlessly angering myself and then disputed my irrational ideas. 'Why shouldn't these people have their own [albeit, in my view, misguided] opinions which led them to reject me?' The answer, in both cases, was the same: NO DAMNED REASON. I reminded myself that, whilst I considered them to be wrong, they don't have to be right, and they are obviously right from their perspective. I'm still annoyed about their decisions whenever I think about it – but am not angry.

I have, thus, gained more therapeutic benefit from my own rational–emotive self-help methods than from formal therapy. Consequently I believe that my preferred therapy orientation – RET – reflects both my decided preference for helping myself in my own life and my view that therapists had better directly aid clients to help themselves in their lives. RET nicely succeeds, for me, in both respects.

References

ADLER, A. (1927). *Understanding Human Nature*. New York: Garden City.

ALEXANDER, F. and FRENCH, T.M. (1946). *Psychoanalytic Therapy: Principles and Application*. New York: Ronald Press.

The American Heritage Dictionary of the English Language (1971). New York: American Heritage.

ANCHIN, J.C. and KIESLER, D.J. (Eds) (1982). *Handbook of Interpersonal Psychotherapy*. New York: Pergamon.

ARNKOFF, D.B. (1981). Flexibility in practicing cognitive therapy. In: G. Emery, S.D. Hollon and R.C. Bedrosian (Eds), *New Directions in Cognitive Therapy*. New York: Guilford.

BANDURA, A. (1969). *Principles of Behavior Modification*. New York: Holt, Rinehart & Winston.

BANDURA, A. (1977). *Social Learning Theory*. Englewood Cliffs, NJ: Prentice-Hall.

BARD, J.A. (1973). Rational proselytizing. *Rational Living*, **8**(2), 24–26.

BARD, J. (1980). *Rational-Emotive Therapy in Practice*. Champaign, IL: Research Press.

BECK, A.T. (1964). Thinking and depression: 2, Theory and therapy. *Archives of General Psychiatry*, **10**, 561–571.

BECK, A.T. (1967). *Depression*. New York: Hoeber-Harper.

BECK, A.T. (1973). *The Diagnosis and Management of Depression*. Philadelphia: University of Pennsylvania Press.

BECK, A.T. (1976). *Cognitive Therapy and the Emotional Disorders*. New York: International Universities Press.

BECK, A.T. (1982). Speculations regarding the biology of mental disorders. Unpublished paper, Center for Cognitive Therapy.

BECK, A.T. (1983). Cognitive therapy of depression: New perspectives. In: P. Clayton (Ed.), *Depression*. New York: Raven Press.

BECK, A.T. and EMERY, G. (1979). Cognitive therapy of anxiety and phobic disorders. Unpublished manual, Center for Cognitive Therapy.

BECK, A.T., RUSH, A.J., SHAW, B.F. and EMERY, G. (1979). *Cognitive Therapy of Depression*. New York: Guilford.

BEUTLER, L.E. (1979). Toward specific psychological therapies for specific conditions. *Journal of Consulting and Clinical Psychology*, **47**, 882–897.

BEUTLER, L.E. (1983). *Eclectic Psychotherapy: A Systematic Approach*. New York: Pergamon.

BORDIN, E.S. (1979). The generalizability of the psychoanalytic concept of the working alliance. *Psychotherapy: Theory, Research and Practice*, 16, 252-260.

BORDIN, E.S. (1983). Myths, realities and alternatives to clinical trials. Paper presented at the International Conference on Psychotherapy, Bogota, Columbia.

BOUTIN, G.E. and TOSI, D.J. (1983). Modification of irrational ideas and test anxiety through rational stage directed hypnotherapy (RSDH). *Journal of Clinical Psychology*, 39, 382-391.

BURNS, D.D. (1980). *Feeling Good: The New Mood Therapy*. New York: Morrow.

CARSON, R.C. (1969). *Interaction Concepts of Personality*. London: George Allen & Unwin.

CHESNEY, M.A. and ROSENMAN, R.H. (Eds) (1985). *Anger and Hostility in Cardiovascular and Behavioral Disorders*. Washington: Hemisphere.

CHURCH, V.A. (1974). Rational therapy in divorce practice. *Rational Living*, 9, 34-38.

CLARK, D.M. (1986). A cognitive approach to panic. *Behaviour Research and Therapy*, 24, 461-470.

CLARK, D.M, SALKOVSKIS, P.M. and CHALKLEY, A.J. (1985). Respiratory control as a treatment for panic attacks. *Journal of Behavior Therapy and Experimental Psychiatry*, 16, 23-30.

COLEMAN, R.E. and BECK, A.T. (1981). Cognitive therapy for depression. In: J.F. Clarkin and H.I. Glazin (Eds), *Depression: Behavioral and Directive Intervention Strategies*. New York: Garland.

CRAWFORD, T. (1982). Communication and rational-emotive therapy. Workshop presented in Los Angeles.

DANYSH, J. (1974). *Stop without Quitting*. San Francisco: International Society for General Semantics.

DE FORREST, I. (1954). *The Leaven of Love*. New York: Harper.

DIES, R.R. (1973). Group therapist self-disclosure: An evaluation by clients. *Journal of Counseling Psychology*, 20, 344-348.

DIGIUSEPPE, R. (1984). Thinking what to feel. *British Journal of Cognitive Psychotherapy*, 2(1), 27-33.

DILORETO, A.E. (1971). *Comparative Psychotherapy: An Experimental Analysis*. Chicago: Aldine-Atherton.

DOMBROW, R. (1973). On the use of early childhood material in rational-emotive therapy. *Rational Living*, 8(1), 17-18.

DORN, F.J. (1984). *Counseling as Applied Social Psychology: An Introduction to the Social Influence Model*. Springfield, IL: Thomas.

DRYDEN, W. (1979). Past messages and disputations: The client and significant others. *Rational Living*, 14(1), 26-28.

DRYDEN, W. (1980a). Nightmares and fun. Paper presented at the Third National Conference on Rational-Emotive Therapy, New York.

DRYDEN, W. (1980b). 'Eclectic' approaches in individual counselling: Some pertinent issues. *The Counsellor*, 3, 24-30.

DRYDEN, W. (1983). Audiotape supervision by mail: A rational-emotive approach. *British Journal of Cognitive Psychotherapy*, 1, 57-64.

DRYDEN, W. (1984a). *Rational-Emotive Therapy: Fundamentals and Innovations*. Beckenham, Kent: Croom Helm.

DRYDEN, W. (1984b). Rational-emotive therapy. In: W. Dryden (Ed.), *Individual Therapy in Britain*, pp. 235-263. London: Harper & Row.

DRYDEN, W. (1984c). Therapeutic arenas. In: W. Dryden (Ed.), *Individual Therapy in Britain*. London: Harper & Row.

DRYDEN, W. (1984d). Issues in the eclectic practice of individual therapy. In: W. Dryden (Ed.), *Individual Therapy in Britain*, London: Harper & Row.

DRYDEN, W. (1985a). Marital therapy: The rational-emotive approach. In W. Dryden (Ed.), *Marital Therapy in Britain. Volume 1: Context and Therapeutic Approaches.* London: Harper & Row.

DRYDEN, W. (1985b). Challenging but not overwhelming: A compromise in negotiating homework assignments. *British Journal of Cognitive Psychotherapy*, 3(1), 77-80.

DRYDEN, W. (1987a). Theoretically-consistent eclecticism: Humanizing a computer 'addict.' In: J.C. Norcross (Ed.), *Casebook of Eclectic Psychotherapy*, New York: Brunner/Mazel.

DRYDEN, W. (1987b). *Counselling Individuals: The Rational-Emotive Approach.* London: Taylor & Francis.

DRYDEN, W. and GORDON, J. (1990). *Think Your Way to Happiness.* London: Sheldon Press.

DRYDEN, W. and HUNT, P. (1985). Therapeutic alliances in marital therapy. II. Process issues. In: W. Dryden (Ed.), *Marital Therapy in Britain. Volume 1: Context and Therapeutic Approaches.* London: Harper & Row.

DUCK, S. (1986). *Human Relationships: An Introduction to Social Psychology.* London: Sage.

DUCKRO, P., BEAL, D. and GEORGE, C. (1979). Research on the effects of disconfirmed client role expectations in psychotherapy: A critical review. *Psychological Bulletin*, **86**, 260-275.

DUNLAP, K. (1932). *Habits: Their Making and Unmaking.* New York: Liveright.

ELLIS, A. (1957). *How to Live with a Neurotic: At Home and at Work.* No. Hollywood, CA: Wilshire.

ELLIS, A. (1958a). Rational psychotherapy. *Journal of General Psychology*, **59**, 35-49.

ELLIS, A (1958b). Neurotic interaction between marital partners. *Journal of Counseling Psychology*, **5**, 24-28.

ELLIS, A. (1960). Marriage counseling with demasculinizing wives and demasculinized husbands. *Marriage and Family Living*, **22**, 12-21.

ELLIS, A. (1962). *Reason and Emotion in Psychotherapy.* Secaucus, NJ: Lyle Stuart.

ELLIS, A. (1963). Toward a more precise definition of 'emotional' and 'intellectual' insight. *Psychological Reports*, **13**, 125-126.

ELLIS, A. (1969). A weekend of rational encounter. *Rational Living*, 4(2), 1-8.

ELLIS, A. (1971a). *Growth through Reason.* North Hollywood, CA: Wilshire Books.

ELLIS, A. (speaker) (1971b). *How to stubbornly refuse to be ashamed of anything* (cassette recording). New York: Institute for Rational-Emotive Therapy.

ELLIS, A. (1972a). Helping people get better: Rather than merely feel better. *Rational Living*, 7(2), 2-9.

ELLIS, A. (speaker) (1972b). *Solving emotional problems* (cassette recording). New York: Institute for Rational-Emotive Therapy.

ELLIS, A. (1973). *Humanistic Psychotherapy: The Rational-Emotive Approach.* New York: McGraw-Hill.

ELLIS, A. (1975). The rational-emotive approach to sex therapy. *The Counseling Psychologist*, **5**, 14-21.

ELLIS, A. (1976a). The biological basis of human irrationality. *Journal of Individual Psychology*, **32**, 145-168. (Reprinted by the Institute for Rational-Emotive Therapy, New York.)

ELLIS, A. (speaker) (1976b). *Conquering low frustration tolerance* (cassette recording). New York: Institute for Rational-Emotive Therapy.

ELLIS, A. (1976c). Techniques of handling anger in marriage. *Journal of Marriage and Family Counseling*, **2**, 305-316.

ELLIS, A. (1977a). Fun as psychotherapy. *Rational Living*, **12**(1), 2-6.

ELLIS, A. (speaker) (1977b). *A garland of rational humorous songs* (cassette recording). New York: Institute for Rational-Emotive Therapy.

ELLIS, A. (1977c). Intimacy in psychotherapy. *Rational Living*, **12**(2), 13-19.

ELLIS, A. (1977d). The basic clinical theory of rational-emotive therapy. In: A. Ellis and R. Grieger (Eds.), *Handbook of Rational-Emotive Therapy*, vol. 1. New York: Springer.

ELLIS, A. (1977e). Skills training in counselling and psychotherapy. *Canadian Counsellor*, **12**(1), 30-35.

ELLIS, A. (1977f). Rational-emotive therapy: Research data that supports the clinical and personality hypotheses of RET and other modes of cognitive behavior therapy. *The Counseling Psychologist*, **7**, 2-42.

ELLIS, A. (1977g). Irrational ideas. In: J.L. Wolfe and E. Brand (Eds), *Twenty Years of Rational Therapy*. New York: Institute for Rational Living.

ELLIS, A. (1977h). A rational approach to interpretation. In: A. Ellis and R. Grieger (Eds), *Handbook of Rational-Emotive Therapy*. New York: Springer.

ELLIS, A. (1977i). Review of Beck, A.T. Cognitive therapy and the emotional disorders, New York: International Universities Press, 1976. *Behavior Therapy*, **8**, 295-296.

ELLIS, A. (1978a). Personality characteristics of rational-emotive therapists and other kinds of therapists. *Psychotherapy: Theory, Research and Practice*, **15**, 329-332.

ELLIS, A. (1978b). Toward a theory of personality. In: R.J. Corsini (Ed.), *Readings in Current Personality Theories*. Illinois: F.E. Peacock.

ELLIS, A. (1979a). The theory of rational-emotive therapy. In: A. Ellis and J.M. Whiteley (Eds), *Theoretical and Empirical Foundations of Rational-Emotive Therapy*. Monterey, CA: Brooks/Cole.

ELLIS, A. (1979b). Discomfort anxiety: A new cognitive behavioral construct. Part 1. *Rational Living*, **14**(2), 3-8.

ELLIS, A. (1979c). The practice of rational-emotive therapy. In: A. Ellis and J.M. Whiteley (Eds), *Theoretical and Empirical Foundations of Rational-Emotive Therapy*. Monterey, CA: Brooks/Cole.

ELLIS, A. (1979d). The issue of force and energy in behavioral change. *Journal of Contemporary Psychotherapy*, **10**(2), 83-97.

ELLIS, A. (1979e). Toward a new theory of personality. In: A. Ellis and J.M. Whiteley (Eds), *Theoretical and Empirical Foundations of Rational-Emotive Therapy*. Monterey, CA: Brooks/Cole.

ELLIS, A. (1979f). Rejoinder: Elegant and inelegant RET. In: A. Ellis and J.M. Whiteley (Eds), *Theoretical and Empirical Foundations of Rational-Emotive Therapy*. Monterey, CA: Brooks/Cole.

ELLIS, A. (1979g). Rational-emotive therapy. In: A. Ellis and J.M. Whiteley (Eds), *Theoretical and Empirical Foundations of Rational-Emotive Therapy*. Monterey, CA: Brooks/Cole.

ELLIS, A. (1980a). Discomfort anxiety: A new cognitive behavioral construct. Part 2. *Rational Living*, **15**(1), 25-30.

ELLIS, A. (1980b). Rational-emotive and cognitive behavior therapy: Similarities and differences. *Cognitive Therapy and Research*, **4**, 325-340.

ELLIS, A. (1980c). Psychotherapy and atheistic values: A response to A.T. Bergin's 'Psychotherapy and religious values'. *Journal of Consulting and Clinical Psychology*, **48**, 635-639.

ELLIS, A. (1980d). The value of efficiency in psychotherapy. *Psychotherapy: Theory, Research and Practice*, **17**, 414-419.

ELLIS, A. (1981a). The place of Immanuel Kant in cognitive psychotherapy. *Rational Living*, 16(2), 13-16.

ELLIS, A. (1981b). The use of rational humorous songs in psychotherapy. *Voices*, **16**(4), 29-36.

ELLIS, A. (1982a). Rational-emotive family therapy. In: A.M. Horne and M.M. Ohlsen (Eds), *Family Counseling and Therapy*, Itasca, IL: Peacock.

ELLIS, A. (1982b). Intimacy in rational-emotive therapy. In: M. Fisher and G. Stricker (Eds), *Intimacy*. New York: Plenum.

ELLIS, A. (1982c). The treatment of alcohol and drug abuse. A rational-emotive approach. *Rational Living*, **17**(2), 15-24.

ELLIS, A. (1983a). *The Case against Religiosity*. New York: Institute for Rational-Emotive Therapy.

ELLIS, A. (1983b). How to deal with your most difficult client: You. *Journal of Rational-Emotive Therapy*, 1(1), 3-8.

ELLIS, A. (1983c). The philosophic implications and dangers of some popular behavior therapy techniques. In: M. Rosenbaum, C.M. Franks and Y. Jaffe (Eds), *Perspectives in Behavior Therapy in the Eighties*. New York: Springer.

ELLIS, A. (1983d). Rational-emotive therapy (RET) approaches to overcoming resistance. 1: Common forms of resistance. *British Journal of Cognitive Psychotherapy*, 1(1), 28-38.

ELLIS, A. (1983e). Failures in rational-emotive therapy. In: E.B. Foa and P.M.G. Emmelkamp (Eds), *Failures in Behavior Therapy*. New York: Wiley.

ELLIS, A. (1984a). The essence of RET - 1984. *Journal of Rational-Emotive Therapy*, 2(1), 19-25.

ELLIS, A. (1984b). Rational-emotive therapy. In: R.J. Corsini (Ed.), *Current Psychotherapies*, 3rd edn. Itasca, IL: Peacock.

ELLIS, A. (1984c). *How to use RET to maintain and enhance your therapeutic gains*. New York: Institute for Rational-Emotive Therapy.

ELLIS, A. (1985a). *Overcoming Resistance: Rational-Emotive Therapy with Difficult Clients*. New York: Springer.

ELLIS, A. (1985b). Jealousy: Its etiology and treatment. In: D.C. Goldberg (Ed.), *Contemporary Marriage: Special Issues in Couples Therapy*. Homewood, IL: Dorsey.

ELLIS, A. (1985c). Dilemmas in giving warmth or love to clients: An interview with Windy Dryden. In: W. Dryden (Ed.), *Therapists' Dilemmas*. London: Harper & Row.

ELLIS, A. (1985d). Expanding the ABCs of rational-emotive therapy. In: M. Mahoney and A. Freeman (Eds), *Cognition and Psychotherapy*. New York: Plenum.

ELLIS, A. (1987). A sadly neglected cognitive element in depression. *Cognitive Therapy and Research*, **11**, 121-146.

ELLIS, A. (1988). *How to Stubbornly Refuse to Make Yourself Miserable about Anything - Yes, Anything!* Secaucus, NJ: Lyle Stuart.

ELLIS, A. and ABRAHMS, E. (1978). *Brief Psychotherapy in Medical and Health Practice*. New York: Springer.

ELLIS, A. and BECKER, I. (1982). *A Guide to Personal Happiness*, North Hollywood, CA: Wilshire.

ELLIS, A. and BERNARD, M.E. (Eds) (1983). *Rational-Emotive Approaches to the Problems of Childhood*. New York: Plenum.

ELLIS, A. and BERNARD, M.E. (Eds) (1985) *Clinical Applications of Rational-Emotive Therapy*. New York: Plenum.

ELLIS, A and DRYDEN, W. (1987). *The Practice of Rational-Emotive Therapy*. New York: Springer.

ELLIS, A. and GRIEGER, R. (Eds.). (1977). *Handbook of Rational-Emotive Therapy*, vol. 1. New York: Springer.

ELLIS, A. and HARPER, R.A. (1961a). *A Guide to Rational Living*. Englewood Cliffs, NJ: Prentice-Hall. .

ELLIS, A. and HARPER, R.A. (1961b). *A Guide to Successful Marriage*. North Hollywood, CA: Wilshire Books.

ELLIS, A. and HARPER, R.A. (1975). *A New Guide to Rational Living*. North Hollywood, CA: Wilshire.

ELLIS, A. and WHITELEY, J.M. (Eds). (1979). *Theoretical and Empirical Foundations of Rational-Emotive Therapy*. Monterey, CA: Brooks/Cole.

EMMELKAMP, P.M.G., KUIPERS, A.C.M. and EGGERAAT, J.B. (1978). Cognitive modification versus prolonged exposure in vivo: A comparison with agoraphobics as subjects. *Behavior Research and Therapy*, **16**, 33–41.

ESCHENROEDER, C. (1979). Different therapeutic styles in rational-emotive therapy. *Rational Living*, **14**(1), 3–7.

EYSENCK, H.J. (1970). A mish-mash of theories. *International Journal of Psychiatry*, **9**, 140–146.

FERENCZI, S. (1952-55). *Selected Papers on Psychoanalysis*. New York: Basic Books.

FRANK, J.D. (1970). Psychotherapists need theories. *International Journal of Psychiatry*, **9**, 146–149.

FREEMAN, A. (1981). Dreams and imagery in cognitive therapy. In: G. Emery, S.D. Hollon and R.C. Bedrosian (Eds), *New Directions in Cognitive Therapy*. New York: Guilford.

FREUD, A. (1937). *The Ego and the Mechanisms of Defence*. London: Hogarth.

GARCIA, E.J. (1977). Working on the E in RET. In: J.L. Wolfe and E. Brand (Eds), *Twenty Years of Rational Therapy*, pp. 72-87. New York: Institute for Rational-Emotive Therapy.

GARFIELD, S.L. (1980). *Psychotherapy: An Eclectic Approach*. New York: Wiley.

GARFIELD, S.L. and KURTZ, R. (1977). A study of eclectic views. *Journal of Consulting and Clinical Psychology*, **45**, 78-83.

GENDLIN, E.T. (1978). *Focusing*. New York: Everest House.

GOLDEN, W.L. (1983). Rational-emotive hypnotherapy. *British Journal of Cognitive Psychotherapy*, **1**(2), 47-56.

GOLDEN, W.L. (1985). An integration of Ericksonian and cognitive-behavioral hypnotherapy in the treatment of anxiety disorders. In E.T. Dowd and J.M. Healy (Eds), *Case Studies in Hypnotherapy*. New York: Guilford.

GOLDFRIED, M. and DAVISON, G. (1976). *Clinical Behavior Therapy*, New York: Holt, Rinehart & Winston.

GRIEGER, R. (Ed.) (1986). Rational-emotive couples therapy. *Journal of Rational-Emotive Therapy*, **4**(1), 3–109.

GRIEGER, R. and BOYD, J. (1980). *Rational-Emotive Therapy: A Skills-based Approach*. New York: Van Nostrand Reinhold.

GRIEGER, R. and GRIEGER, I. (Eds) (1982). *Cognition and Emotional Disturbance*. New York: Human Sciences Press.

GUERNEY, B.G. JR. (1977). *Relationship Enhancement: Skill Training Programs for Therapy, Problem-prevention and Enrichment*. San Francisco: Jossey-Bass.

HARPER, R.A. (1981). Limitations of marriage and family therapy. *Rational Living*, **16**(2), 3-6.

HAUCK, P. (1967). Challenge authority: For thy health's sake. *Rational Living*, **2**, 1-3.

HAUCK, P.A. (1971). A RET theory of depression. *Rational Living*, **6**(2), 32-35.

HAUCK, P.A. (1972). *Reason in Pastoral Counseling*. Philadelphia: Westminster.

HAUCK, P.A. (1977). Irrational parenting styles. In: A. Ellis and R. Grieger (Eds), *Handbook of Rational-Emotive Therapy*, volume 1. New York: Springer.

HAUCK, P.A. (1981). *Making Marriage Work*, London: Sheldon Press.

HAUCK, P.A. (1983a). *How to Love and be Loved*. London: Sheldon Press.

HAUCK. P.A. (1983b). Working with parents. In: A. Ellis and M.E. Bernard (Eds), *Rational-Emotive Approaches to the Problems of Childhood*. New York: Plenum.

HEIDEGGER, M. (1949). *Existence and Being*. Chicago: Henry Regnery.

HOEHN-SARIC, R. (1978). Emotional arousal, attitude change and psychotherapy. In: J.D. Frank, R. Hoehn-Saric, S.D. Imber, B.L. Liberman and A.R. Stone (Eds), *Effective Ingredients of Successful Psychotherapy*. New York: Brunner/Mazel.

HORNEY, K. (1950). *Neurosis and Human Growth*. New York: Norton.

HORWILL, F.M. (1983). Thoughts towards a model for conciliation and conflict resolution in the Family Court of Australia. *Australian Psychologist*, **18**(1), 39-53.

JANIS, I.L. (1983). *Short-term Counseling*. New Haven, CT: Yale University Press.

JONES, M.C. (1924). A laboratory study of fear. The case of Peter. *Journal of Genetic Psychology*, **31**, 308-315.

JONES, R.A. (1977). *Self-fulfilling Prophecies: Social, Psychological and Physiological Effects of Expectancies*. Hillsdale, NJ: Laurence Erlbaum Associates.

KASSINOVE, H. and DiGIUSEPPE, R. (1975). Rational role reversal. *Rational Living*, **10**(1), 44-45.

KELLY, G. (1955). *The Psychology of Personal Constructs*, 2 vols. New York: Norton.

KENDALL, P. and HOLLON, S. (Eds) (1980). *Assessment Strategies for Cognitive-Behavioral Interventions*. New York: Academic Press.

KNAUS, W. and WESSLER, R.L. (1976). Rational-emotive problem simulation. *Rational Living*, **11**(2), 8-11.

KORZYBSKI, A. (1933). *Science and Sanity*. San Francisco: International Society of General Semantics.

KOVACS, M. and BECK, A.T. (1978). Maladaptive cognitive structure in depression. *American Journal of Psychiatry*, **135**, 525-533.

KWEE, M.G.T. and LAZARUS, A.A. (1986). Multimodal therapy: The cognitive behavioural tradition and beyond. In: W. Dryden and W.L. Golden (Eds), *Cognitive-Behavioural Approaches to Psychotherapy*. London: Harper & Row.

LAZARUS, A.A. (1976). *Multimodal Behavior Therapy*. New York: Springer.

LAZARUS, A.A. (1978). *In the Mind's Eye*. New York: Rawson.

LAZARUS, A.A. (1981). *The Practice of Multimodal Therapy*. New York: McGraw-Hill.

LAZARUS, A.A. (1984). *In the Mind's Eye*. New York: Guilford.

LAZARUS, A.A. (1985). *Marital Myths*. San Luis Obispo, CA: Impact.

LEDERER, W.J. and JACKSON, D.D. (1968). *The Mirages of Marriage*. New York: Norton.

MACASKILL, N.D. and MACASKILL, A. (1983). Preparing patients for psychotherapy. *British Journal of Clinical and Social Psychiatry*, **2**, 80-84.

McCLELLAN, T.A. and STIEPER, D.R. (1973). A structural approach to group marriage counseling. *Rational Living*, **8**(2), 13-18.

MACKAY, D. (1984). Behavioural psychotherapy. In W. Dryden (Ed.), *Individual Therapy in Britain*. London: Harper & Row.

MACKAY, D. (1985). Marital therapy: The behavioural approach. In: W. Dryden (Ed.), *Marital Therapy in Britain. Volume 1: Context and Therapeutic Approaches*. London: Harper & Row.

MADISON, M. (1983). Defining levels of intervention in dispute resolution. Unpublished Paper, Parramatta Registry, Family Court Australia.

MAHONEY, M. (1977). Personal science: A cognitive learning theory. In: A. Ellis and R. Grieger (Eds), *Handbook of Rational-Emotive Therapy*, vol. 1. New York: Springer.

MAULTSBY, M.C. JR (1975). *Help Yourself to Happiness: Through Rational Self-counseling*. New York: Institute for Rational-Emotive Therapy.

MAULTSBY, M.C. JR, (1984). *Rational Behavior Therapy*. Englewood Cliffs, NJ: Prentice-Hall.

MAULTSBY, M.C. JR and ELLIS, A. (1974). *Techniques for Using Rational-Emotive Imagery*. New York: Institute for Rational-Emotive Therapy.

MEICHENBAUM, D. (1977). *Cognitive-Behavior Modification*. New York: Plenum.

MEICHENBAUM, D. and GILMORE, J.B. (1982). Resistance from a cognitive behavioral perspective. In: P.L. Wachtel (Ed.), *Resistance*. New York: Plenum.

MOORE, R.H. (1983). Inference as 'A' in RET. *British Journal of Cognitive Psychotherapy*, 1(2), 17-23.

MORLEY, E.L. and WATKINS, J.T. (1974). Locus of control and effectiveness of two rational-emotive therapy styles. *Rational Living*, 9(2), 22-24.

NARDI, T.J. (1979). The use of psychodrama in RET. *Rational Living*, 14(1), 35-38.

NATIONAL FAMILY CONCILIATION COUNCIL (1984). Code of practice. *Family Law*, 14 107-108.

NELSON-JONES, R. (1982). *The Theory and Practice of Counselling Psychology*. Eastbourne: Holt, Reinehart & Winston.

NEUMAN, F. (Leader) (1982). *An eight-week treatment group for phobics* (Series of eight cassette recordings). While Plains, NY: F. Neuman.

PARKINSON, L. (1985). Conciliation in separation and divorce. In: W. Dryden (Ed.), *Marital Therapy in Britain. Vol. 2, Special Areas*. London: Harper & Row.

PHADKE, K.M. (1982). Some innovations in RET theory and practice. *Rational Living*, 17(2), 25-30.

PINSOF, W.M. and CATHERALL, D.R. (1986). The integrative psychotherapy alliance: Family, couple and individual scales. *Journal of Marital and Family Therapy*, 12, 137-151.

POPPER, K.R. (1959). *The Logic of Scientific Discovery*. New York: Harper & Row.

POPPER, K.R. (1963). *Conjectures and Refutations*. New York: Harper & Row.

POWELL, J. (1976). *Fully Human, Fully Alive*. Niles, IL: Argus.

PRESTON, G., RALPH, S. and MADISON, M. (1983). The family assessment form. Unpublished paper, Parramatta Registry, Family Court of Australia.

REICHENBACH, H. (1953). *The Rise of Scientific Philosophy*. Berkeley, CA: University of California Press.

RICE, L.N. (1965). Therapists' style of participation and case outcome. *Journal of Consulting Psychology*, 29, 155-160.

RICE, L.N. (1973). Client behavior as a function of therapist style and client resources. *Journal of Counseling Psychology*, 20, 306-311.

RICE, L.N. and GAYLIN, N.L. (1973). Personality processes reflected in client and vocal style and Rorschach processes. *Journal of Consulting and Clinical Psychology*, 40, 133-138.

RICE, L.N. and WAGSTAFF, A.K. (1967). Client voice quality and expressive style as indexes of productive psychotherapy. *Journal of Consulting Psychology*, 31, 557-563.

ROBINSON, M. and PARKINSON, L. (1985). A family systems approach to conciliation and divorce. *Journal of Family Therapy*, 7, 357-377.

ROGERS, C.R. (1957). The necessary and sufficient conditions of therapeutic personality change. *Journal of Consulting Psychology*, 21, 95-103.

RUSSELL, B. (1930). *The Conquest of Happiness*. New York: New American Library.

RUSSELL, B. (1965). *The Basic Writings of Bertrand Russell*. New York: Simon & Schuster.

SACCO, W.P. (1981). Cognitive therapy in-vivo. In: G. Emery, S.D. Hollon and R.C. Bedrosian (Eds), *New Directions in Cognitive Therapy*. New York: Guilford.

SAFRAN, J.D. (1984). Assessing the cognitive–interpersonal circle. *Cognitive Therapy and Research*, **8**, 333–347.

SAGER, C.J. (1976). *Marriage Contracts and Marital Therapy*. New York: Brunner/Mazel.

SAUNDERS, J.B. (Ed.) (1969). *Words and Phrases Legally Defined*, 2nd edn. London: Butterworths.

SAUNDERS, J.B. (1977). *Mozley and Whiteley's Law Dictionary*. London: Butterworths.

SHOSTROM, E.L. (1976). *Actualizing Therapy: Foundations for a Scientific Ethic*. San Diego: Edits.

SNYDER, C.R. and SMITH, T.W. (1982). Symptoms as self-handicapping strategies: The virtues of old wine in a new bottle. In: G. Weary and H.L. Mirels (Eds), *Integration of Clinical and Social Psychology*. New York: Oxford University Press.

STRONG, S.R. and CLAIBORN, C.D. (1982). *Change through Interaction*. New York: Wiley Interscience.

STUART, R.B. (1980). *Helping Couples Change: A Social Learning Approach to Marital Therapy*. New York: Guilford.

SULLIVAN, H.S. (1953). *Conceptions of Modern Psychiatry*. New York: Norton.

SUTTIE, I. (1948). *The Origins of Love and Hate*. London: Kegan Paul.

TEASDALE, J.D. (1985). Psychological treatments for depression: How do they work? *Behaviour Research and Therapy*, **23**, 157–165.

TILLICH, P. (1953). *The Courage to Be*. New York: Oxford University Press.

TILLICH, P. (1977). *The Courage to Be*. New York: Fountain.

TRACEY, T.J. (1984). The stages of influence in counseling and psychotherapy. In: F.J. Dorn (Ed.), *The Social Influence Process in Counseling and Psychotherapy*. Springfield, IL: Charles C. Thomas.

VERTES, R. (1971). The should: A critical analysis. *Rational Living*, **6**(2), 22–25.

WACHTEL, P.L. (1977). *Psychoanalysis and Behavior Therapy: Toward an Integration*. New York: Basic Books.

WALEN, S.R., DiGIUSEPPE, R. and WESSLER, R.L. (1980). *A Practitioner's Guide to Rational-Emotive Therapy*. New York: Oxford.

WATSON, J.B. and RAYNER, R. (1920). Conditioned emotional reactions. *Journal of Experimental Psychology*, **3**, 1–14.

WATZLAWICK, P. (1978). *The Language of Change*. New York: Basic Books.

WEINER, I.B. (1975). *Principles of Psychotherapy*. New York: Wiley.

WEINRACH, S.G. (1980). Unconventional therapist: Albert Ellis. *Personnel and Guidance Journal*, **59**, 152–160.

WERNER, E.E. and SMITH, R.S. (1982). *Vulnerable but Invincible: A Study of Reslient Children*. New York: McGraw-Hill.

WESSLER, R.A. (1978). The neurotic paradox: A rational–emotive view. *Rational Living*, **13**, 9–12.

WESSLER, R.A. (1981). So you are angry: Now what's your problem? *Rational Living*, **16**(1), 29–31.

WESSLER, R.L. (1982a). Alternative conceptions of rational-emotive therapy: Toward a philosophically neutral psychotherapy. Paper presented at the Twelfth European Congress of Behaviour Therapy, Rome, Sept 5.

WESSLER, R.L. (1982b). Varieties of cognitions in the cognitively-oriented psychotherapies. *Rational Living*, **17**, 3–10.

WESSLER, R.L. (1984). Alternative conceptions of rational-emotive therapy: Toward a philosophically neutral psychotherapy. In: M.A. Reda and M.J. Mahoney (Eds), *Cognitive Psychotherapies: Recent Developments in Theory, Research and Practice*. Cambridge, MA: Ballinger.

WESSLER, R.L. and ELLIS, A. (1980). Supervision in rational–emotive therapy. In: A.K. Hess (Ed.), *Psychotherapy Supervision*. New York: Wiley.

WESSLER, R.L. and ELLIS, A. (1983). Supervision in counseling: Rational–emotive therapy. *The Counseling Psychologist*, **11**, 43–49.

WESSLER, R.A. and WESSLER, R.L. (1980). *The Principles and Practice of Rational–Emotive Therapy*. San Francisco, CA: Jossey-Bass.

WEXLER, D.A. (1975). A scale for the measurement of client and therapist expressiveness. *Journal of Clinical Psychology*, **31**, 486–489.

WEXLER, D.A. and BUTLER, J.M. (1976). Therapist modification of client expressiveness. *Journal of Clinical Psychology*, **44**, 261–265.

WHITELEY, R.W. (1981). Depressive patients in therapy. *Midland Journal of Psychotherapy*, **1**, 9–13.

YOUNG, H.S. (1974a). A framework for working with adolescents. *Rational Living*, **9**(1), 3–7.

YOUNG, H.S. (1974b). *A Rational Counseling Primer*. New York: Institute for Rational-Emotive Therapy.

YOUNG, H.S. (1975). Rational thinkers and robots. *Rational Living*, **10**(1), 3–7.

YOUNG, H.S. (1977). Counseling strategies with working class adolescents. In: J.L. Wolfe and E. Brand (Eds), *Twenty Years of Rational Therapy*. New York: Institute for Rational-Emotive Therapy.

YOUNG, H.S. (1980). Teaching rational self-value concepts to tough customers. Paper presented at the Third National Conference on Rational–Emotive Therapy, New York, June 8.

YOUNG, H.S. (1984a). Practising RET with bible-belt Christians. *British Journal of Cognitive Psychotherapy*, **2**(2), 60–76.

YOUNG, H.S. (1984b). Practising RET with lower-class clients. *British Journal of Cognitive Psychotherapy*, **2**(2), 33–59.

YOUNG, H.S. (1984c). Teaching rational self-value concepts to tough customers. *British Journal of Cognitive Psychotherapy*, **2**(2), 77–97.

YOUNG, J.E. and BECK, A.T. (1982). Cognitive therapy: Clinical applications. In: A.J. Rush (Ed.), *Short-term Psychotherapies for Depression*. Chichester: Wiley.

Author Index

315

Subject Index

317